A TRAILS BOOKS GUIDE

THE GREAT WISCONSIN TOURING BOOK

30 SPECTACULAR AUTO TRIPS

Gary G. Knowles

TRAILS BOOKS
Black Earth, Wisconsin

Library of Congress Catalog Card Number: 00-106250
ISBN: 0-915024-84-5

Editor: Stan Stoga
Production: Sarah White
Maps: Mapping Specialists
Cover Design: Kathie Campbell
Cover Photo: Michael Shedlock

Printed in the United States of America.

06 05 04 03 02 01 00   6 5 4 3 2 1

Trails Books, a division of Trails Media Group, Inc.
P.O. Box 317   •   Black Earth, WI 53515
(800) 236-8088   •   e-mail: info@wistrails.com
www.trailsbooks.com

To Dad and Mom,
the late Eugene T. Knowles and Del Knowles (now Fenner),
who introduced me to the joys of back roads travel. And to
my loving family, Mae, Alex, and Carleigh Knowles,
whose patience and companionship
give meaning to every mile.

Superior ❶⁷

Bayfield
Washburn

❷ 13

Ashland ❶

Hurley

Presque Isle

Hayward ❶⁴

Park Falls

Minocqua

Eagle River

Florence

❷

❸

Grantsburg

Spooner

Shell Lake

Rice Lake

Phillips

Rhinelander

Crandon

Washington Island

Balsam Lake

Barron

Ladysmith

Merrill

Antigo

Crivitz

Marinette

Medford

Chippewa Falls ❶⁶

Wausau ❶³

Keshena

Shawano

Oconto

Sturgeon Bay ❹

Hudson

Menomonie

Eau Claire ❽

❶¹

Suamico

Green Bay

Algoma

Prescott

Ellsworth

❾

Durand

Marshfield ❶⁸

Stevens Point

Iola

Waupaca

❺

Kewaunee

Nelson ❶⁵

Whitehall

Alma

Black River Falls

Neillsville

Wisconsin Rapids

❿

Appleton

Neenah

Lake Winnebago

Two Rivers

Manitowoc

Fountain City

❷⁷

Wautoma

Oshkosh

❻

Sparta

Tomah

Friendship

❷⁹

Green Lake

Elkhart Lake

Sheboygan

❼ La Crosse

❷² ❸⁰

Elroy

Mauston

Montello

Marquette

Fond du Lac

❶²

West Bend

Port Washington

Viroqua

Wisconsin Dells ❷⁴

Portage

Beaver Dam

Juneau

Watertown

Milwaukee

Richland Center

Spring Green

Baraboo

Sun Prairie

❶⁹

Prairie du Chien

❷⁰

Dodgeville

❷⁸

Verona

❷⁵

Madison

Waukesha

Jefferson

Racine

❷³

Lancaster

Darlington

Janesville

White-water

❷⁶

Kenosha

Platteville

Monroe

Beloit

Lake Geneva

Contents

Introduction
The Call of the Wiggly Road

The late American Zen master Allan Watts was once asked to reflect on the nature of life and our modern society. He noted that the contemporary Western world (in the 1970s) focused on straight lines, boxes, squares, right angles, and rigidity— "the forms of death," Watts called them.

"The forms of life," he said, "are round, curved, twisted and wiggly. If you really want to live, you've got to lilt a little."

This book is about living. It's about saying yes to the "other road," the one that doesn't necessarily go straight and easy, that has the crazy curves in it, that goes up and over the hill, not around it, that rolls like an amusement park ride, that has switchbacks and hairpin turns, that makes you keep a hand on the wheel and another on the stick. It's the road that makes you glad you've got a good map-reading navigator, the road that makes you wonder if you're still in Wisconsin, the road that you can tell your friends about but they'll never believe you actually drove, the road that is so spectacular that you'll choke up just thinking about it, the road that will bring goose bumps to a rally driver and put a smile on the face of anyone who drives it.

The Great Wisconsin Touring Book is about roads for people who love cars (and motorcycles and SUVs and RVs) and the incomparable feeling people get from running those vehicles as their designers intended. It's about roads that you haven't taken before. It's about discovery, scenery seldom seen, connections to history, exploration, surprises, thrills, exhilaration, and fun.

It's about roads that wiggle for people who love life.

You Ain't Seen Nothin' Yet!

You think you've seen Wisconsin? You say you've been to Door County, the Dells, the North Woods, maybe visited the Apostle Islands, Hurley, and Superior? Maybe you've been to Spring Green, Mineral Point, and New Glarus. It's possible that you've even been down to explore the southwest corner of Wisconsin and seen Prairie du Chien, Cassville, and Potosi.

Guess what. You ain't seen nothin' yet.

Wisconsin, more beautiful, more amazing, more historic, more sublime, more spectacular, and more exhilarating than you ever imagined, is

For driving enthusiasts, this sign means "Exhilaration Ahead." Photo by Gary Knowles.

waiting for you. Get off the main road and see a thousand fascinating Wisconsin faces that most travelers will never enjoy.

I still get goose bumps as I page through the pile of marked-up maps and notes that went into this book. The roads were so much fun to drive, very often surprising, always interesting, and frequently breathtaking. I frequently drove for 5, 6, 8, or 10 hours on winding roads and twisted routes through the Wisconsin hills, wandering its country trails and ending a loop tour you won't find in the tourist books or in any encyclopedia.

It was like discovering a whole new country, another world that existed just over the hill. After living more than 50 years in Wisconsin, I thought I had visited virtually every attraction and site the state had to offer. I thought I had seen just about everything that the guidebooks say to come and see. But I was amazed to find there's so much more.

Wisconsin: The Land of Wiggly Roads. Wisconsin Department of Tourism photo by GK.

bile Association produced great maps, and its wonderful personalized tour plans (called TripTiks) encouraged higher standards in motels and hotels, making it easy to hit the road.

By the mid-1960s the Baby Boomers began to reach driving age and automobile manufacturers started to cater to this huge emerging market. The introduction of "fun cars" like the Ford Mustang in 1964 dropped the green flag on a national cruising mania that continues to this day.

This book is linked in spirit with those first horseless carriage adventurers who rode out to see the country, but its more recent roots are in the "gas glut" of the early 1970s. Fuel was selling for less than 25¢ a gallon, excitement was building in anticipation of the nation's coming Bicentennial, and most Wisconsin communities were just beginning to understand the economic impact of increased tourism. Petroleum dealers (who hoped to sell more gas) teamed up with state tourism promoters to produce and distribute a "loop tour" brochure with annotated routes that made it easy for travelers to get off the beaten path and discover new destinations all over the state.

The popularity of that simple brochure, coupled with the determination of State of Wisconsin Tourism Division Administrator Don Woodruff to more aggressively promote travel to and in Wisconsin in the early 1980s, led to the development and publication of the first *Wisconsin Auto Tours Guide.* I was the Director of the Bureau of Communications and served as the project supervisor and editor.

Our purpose in creating the publication was to build business at Wisconsin tourism attractions, parks, and destination areas and to establish attractive routes using paved, well-maintained state and federal highways. We developed the routes by taking a state highway map, marking the attractions, and connecting them by way of the most interesting and generally direct routes.

The publication was a hit with Wisconsin travelers. It introduced them to dozens of small communities, out-of-the-way attractions, and numerous parks and recreation areas. It went through numerous improvements, additions, and revisions between 1983 and 1997, when the last edition (greatly enhanced by the excellent research and writing of Wisconsin author Don Davenport) rolled off the press.

The Great Wisconsin Touring Book, by contrast, is not driven by the need to visit every attraction in the state. Instead it is focused on unveiling many of the state's most exhilarating drives, twisting back roads, and scenic routes—without neglecting the wealth of Wisconsin's more familiar roadside attractions. Along the way I've listed many of the outstanding reasons to stop: parks, tours, restaurants, scenic waysides, shops, vistas, waterfalls, monuments, and other places of note. I also maintained the criterion that roads must be paved (or in just a few cases where they are not, I suggest paved alternate routes). The goal here is to show

If you have a passion to hit the road and enjoy the drive, there's a whole state full of fun calling you.

Born to Tour—Our National Passion

With all due respect to baseball and football, let's clarify at the outset that America's real passion and national sport is, without a doubt, "driving around." That includes its variations—cruising, Sunday driving, looping the loops, and (more formally) touring. Even before the automobile was very reliable, people felt a need to head out to points unknown and "have a look." When Henry Ford found a way to make it possible for everyone to own a car, touring took off in a big way and continued to grow rapidly through the first half of the 20th century.

After World War II, car culture really bloomed and the two-car family became the rule rather than the exception. Car clubs like the American Automo-

you roads that are fun to drive and fun for passengers too.

Wisconsin—A Land Built for Touring

Wisconsin's varied topography makes it a fabulous place for driving. The sculpting and scraping of the last great glacier, some 10,000 years ago, coupled with the work of its predecessors, left the north and east portions of the state with thousands of sparkling lakes, rolling hills, kettles, moraines, kames, and eskers. Areas of central Wisconsin that were once glacial lakebeds today form the world's most productive cranberry marshes, vast wetlands that are home to migratory birds and wildlife, and great managed forests. In south and west Wisconsin the ancient Driftless Region was never covered by the glacier, and its forested, steep river valleys are rich in history and spectacular beauty.

Of course, great driving requires great roads and again Wisconsin fills the bill. Not only are federal and state roads well maintained, but since the late 19th century a strong dairy lobby has insisted on smooth, paved, and consistently well-maintained county, town and local roads linking every hollow and homestead. The initial purpose was to ensure that milk and produce could quickly find their way to cheese factories and urban markets, but the important side benefit to driving enthusiasts was the creation of one of the finest networks of scenic country roads in the world.

To really put the icing on the cake, these stunning Wisconsin roads lead to interesting historical sites and fascinating stories. Like a great road, a great story should have lots of ups, downs, turns, and twists. Wisconsin has them all—in abundance. These tours will connect you with war heroes, a hall of fame baseball star, an Apollo astronaut, an escape artist, the father of the national parks system, and famous writers. We pass through the town turned to ash by the country's most horrific fire and we pass over much of the battleground of the war that involved three future presidents, one of whom married the other's daughter. Every tour has stories of its own. We'll give you some of the highlights as you go . . . but not everything. An important part of the joy of touring is discovering some things yourself.

How Were the Roads Chosen?

I've had the good fortune to have spent a lot of time exploring the state. When I was a child, my parents, Eugene and Del Knowles, and I frequently hit the road to visit relatives, take Sunday drives, and vacation in the North Woods. I discovered many more great roads while serving the Wisconsin Division of Tourism as Director of the Bureau of Communications for 14 years. In that position I often led groups of VIPs, including travel writers, to see Wisconsin's wondrous nooks and crannies. Since 1993 my communications consulting work has given me the opportunity to travel to many other great places in the state.

All of this wandering was put to good use in 1993 when I joined with my good friend Alex McDonell, a Madison group tour marketer and fellow driving enthusiast, to organize an all-convertible tour to explore the state's great back roads. The Wisconsin Convertible Classic Tour has become an annual four-day event that attracts topless cars from all over the country—and even some drivers from Japan.

In 1995 we added an annual June road tour for sports, GT, and performance cars called the Wisconsin Sports Car and GT Classic. This four-day tour is focused on the state's auto racing history, includes an all-day European style Grand Prix tour, and winds up at Elkhart Lake's Road America, where tour participants get the rare opportunity to do a pace-car-led tour of the famous race circuit. Both tours also commemorate the world's first auto race, which was held in Wisconsin in July 1878. (See article on the following page.)

The commemorative drives of the WCC and the WSCC have taken me on many outstanding roads in every part of the state and have been a great help in finding mile after mile of roads that just call out to be driven.

What Should You Drive?

Much of the country now travels in SUVs, RVs, or some other variation on the "civilized Jeep" theme. These are all fine conveyances for cruising, and the tours in this book will give you good reasons to take them out of town to experience the recreation for which they were built.

Just about all of the roads described in the book are paved (with just a couple of noted exceptions and then alternate routes are given) and were chosen with automobiles or motorcycles in mind, but you could easily enjoy good stretches by bicycle as well. I love motorcycles and owned several great ones before I was married. If you ride

Why Don't We Do It on The Road?—Join a Tour!

A great way to see Wisconsin's backcountry is to join an auto tour. You take your own car and follow mapped routes along a course that has been set up for the whole group. By doing things as a group (not necessarily together, though), you'll often find that you get special access to interesting areas or better prices on meals, admissions, or merchandise that might not be available to individual travelers. Sometimes picnics, receptions, or group functions are planned, so you get the best of both individual travel and group expeditions.

Some car clubs often organize around makes of cars or marques (Corvette, Miata, Ford, Chevy, etc.), and others organize around car types (antiques, street rods, '50s cruisers). You'll find lots of Midwest-based clubs listed in *Old Cars Weekly*, a tabloid published by Krause Publications, (800) 258-0929, 700 E. State St., Iola, WI 54990.

If you're interested in the Wisconsin Convertible Classic (WCC) or the Wisconsin Sports Car and GT Classic (WSCC), you can ask for information by writing to WCC, P.O. Box 44781, Madison, WI 53744; calling the tour line (a three-minute message and voice mail center); sending e-mail to OPENAIR@aol.com; or visiting the Web site at www.wiautotours.com.

Crisp autumn days are made for touring. Wisconsin Department of Tourism photo by GK.

one I'm sure you'll enjoy these runs, but let me remind you that you need to be twice as aware as the rest of the motoring population. I've had too many close calls with inattentive drivers to make them my first choice for touring.

For all-around joy, I don't think you can choose any better vehicle than a good open-air convertible or roadster. There's nothing more exhilarating than cruising a twisty road over hill and dale under a sunny sky, smelling wildflowers, watching clouds and eagles overhead, and feeling the warm breeze rush over you. I own a great old 1961 Buick Electra "duce-and-a-quarter" ragtop and a 1993 Olds Cutlass Supreme convertible and prefer to tour in them, but I have a 1993 Lincoln Continental touring sedan too (with a sunroof!) and have driven it on many of these routes.

When to Go?

Technically, you can tour all year long in Wisconsin. The highway folks do an excellent job of keeping roads passable, but for the most driving fun I recommend doing your major Wisconsin touring between April and mid-November—or a bit later if the snow holds off.

If you catch spring just right, you can see about 100 shades of green as the trees, fields, and hills begin to leaf out. By mid-May to June, the wildflowers and temperatures should be up, making for fine top-down touring all the way through August—and possibly September—from about Wausau to the Illinois border.

During this time, you may get 5 to 10 days of heaven-on-earth weather, sunny days with temperatures in the high 80s, and nights in the high 60s and 70s. This is our hard-earned reward for shoveling snow and scraping windshields. These are the days when you *must* have a convertible for all-day cruising.

Autumn is another great time to go. You'll get a few days with summerlike temperatures, but even on the more common crisp days, you can ramble through mile after mile of nature's most spectacular colors. The sky turns a wonderful shade of blue, the fast-moving weather systems create beautiful cloud formations, and migrating birds fill the

The World's First Auto Race—
Green Bay to Madison

The story goes back to 1873. An outbreak of equine distemper sent most of Wisconsin's horses to the sick bay for weeks. To a state dependent on horsepower to keep the wheels of commerce and agriculture turning, this work stoppage spelled disaster. The state legislature saw the need to stimulate the progress of technology and established a $10,000 prize for a mechanized substitute for horses that could win a race of 200 miles from Green Bay to Madison.

The big purse led to the development of six vehicles, and on July 17, 1878, two of them steamed to the starting line. The "Oshkosh" and the "Green Bay" raced through the Fox Cities toward Madison stirring up clouds of dust, parading before cheering crowds, and startling livestock along the way. Mechanical failure plagued the "Green Bay" and only the "Oshkosh" reached Madison. It took 33 hours and 27 minutes for the winner to cover the 201 miles, an average speed of approximately 6 miles per hour. Alexander Gallinger, builder of the "Oshkosh" claimed the prize.

But the legislature, like all true race fans, wanted "tougher and faster." They said he hadn't achieved all they expected, so they offered him $5,000. Gallinger told them to keep the money and steamed back home. His race car was reported to have been converted into an ice-cutting machine, which some time later sunk to the bottom of Green Bay, where it may still rest today.

skies. Many of these tours have sections of road that go through heavily forested trails and run under a canopy of trees. In autumn a sunny day can light them up and the normally beautiful cruise becomes truly breathtaking.

Go Prepared

You can travel well using just this book, but you'll do even better if you do some advance homework. Be sure to get a free Official Wisconsin Highway Map (ask for the "Official Map" or you could wind up with a map that mostly lists state "attractions" at the expense of standard highway information). Call the Wisconsin Department of Tourism toll free at (800) 432-8747. You can also visit their excellent Web site at *www.travelwisconsin.com* to order a wide variety of free and helpful publications. At the Web site you'll also find an extensive list of links to Wisconsin communities that offer local publications.

I recommend that you get county maps and area brochures and look them over before you leave home to enjoy these tours. There are lots of side trips, attractions, tours, parks, and events that didn't fit here but they may be just what you're looking for.

Another way to get these publications is to visit one of the state's 11 travel information centers located at major highway entrances to Wisconsin. There is also a center in Madison, (608) 266-2161, 201 W. Washington Ave. You'll find that the centers are staffed by knowledgeable, helpful, and courteous travel counselors who often offer special tips and suggestions to enhance your visit.

There are also excellent local and specialty information centers throughout the state. Take time to visit these places to pick up the latest area brochures and event information, get great ideas for area stops, and get a local perspective on fun things to do. A few of my favorites include the Polk County Information Center in St. Croix Falls, the Manitowoc Visitors Center, the Mercer Information Center (with Claire d' Loon just out the door), and the Frank Lloyd Wright Visitors Center in Spring Green.

Additional Tour Notes for Drivers

Here are a few other things to note about the tours in this book in order to enhance your enjoyment of them and the whole driving experience.

Loop Tours: The tours are designed as complete loops but you can do them in pieces as you wish. If you're cruising through an area and have a little time to spare, dash off and enjoy a segment or two! You'll see that these impromptu trips are so much fun that it's hard to break away and get back on the main road—but even a short romp over the back roads can be invigorating. Enjoy as the opportunity presents itself.

Drive Time: Who can say? It depends on your interests and driving style. Most of the tours can be driven in a day, provided you don't stop for too long. If you want to do some additional exploration, take some time for recreation, enjoy some

great restaurants, or visit some of the attractions, I suggest you consider a long weekend—or more!

Road Conditions: Since many of these roads are county or town roads, you should be aware that conditions can change—for better or worse—without notice. In rerunning several segments, I found some with recently laid smooth-as-silk asphalt, a few others with new potholes, and a couple that had been recovered with pea-gravel and asphalt, a surface that kept speeds way down but that eventually will smooth out. Watch those corners where low or no shoulders result in gravel being scattered in the roadway—it makes for some dicey steering.

They ought to erect signs at the state borders that say "Expect Deer *Everywhere* in Wisconsin." Photo by Gary Knowles.

Here a Deer, There a Deer: One of the thrills of getting out in the Wisconsin countryside is seeing the wildlife in its natural habitat. Getting a glimpse of a grazing white-tailed deer makes many of us feel as if we've truly reached the outback. But these creatures (population estimated at about a million) are becoming quite a problem and a deadly road hazard. The Wisconsin Department of Natural Resources estimates that about 45,000 deer are killed each year on state roads—and the number is rising. The real total might be much higher because many collisions are not reported. They cause hundreds of injuries—and sometimes death—for motorists too. As you're driving these great roads, scan the fields for deer, look along the wooded lots, and be especially alert during the dawn and dusk hours. A deer on your grill can spoil your whole day.

Fellow Travelers: Since all the tours in this book involve country roads, be aware that farm implements, RVs, boats, logging trucks, gravel

Some of the finest food you'll ever eat awaits you at small-town cafes. Photo by Gary Knowles.

trucks, and other machinery may be sharing the road. In some rural areas you may encounter horse and buggies, hunters, horseback riders, dog walkers, cats, and cattle crossing the road. You will see lots of people on bicycles. Drive with respect and appropriate caution so that everyone has a great Wisconsin day.

Highway Signs: Most roads are well marked, but be aware that some county or state highways may not be marked at their intersections with town roads or streets. Sometimes street signs are missing or have been switched or reoriented by pranksters. On occasion you may find that signs are painted on boards or the metal markers are rusted. In most instances you won't have a problem but local maps and guidebooks can be handy. And don't be afraid to ask for directions; it's a great way to meet local people.

Back Roads Dining: Wisconsin has a well-earned reputation for great supper clubs and taverns that serve food. Be adventurous and stop at a local cafe or pub if you're in the mood for a burger or bowl of soup. Local cafes are usually great places for breakfasts too.

I've discovered that a good technique is to stop at the post office and ask about good restaurants. If you meet a few local citizens, you'll soon have a good sampling of opinion and maybe two or three good leads. Wherever I ran across an especially good place, I tried to mention it in the tour.

Watch for small-town grocery stores where you'll often find local sausage made according to Old World recipes and bakery shops where fresh breads, cookies, and sweet treats are found. Throughout Wisconsin's backcountry roads in season, you'll find farmers with little produce stands selling apples, cherries, berries, pumpkins, squash, corn, beans, potatoes honey, maple syrup,

and other great products. Enjoy the natural cornucopia that Wisconsin offers.

Getting Lost

If you're using this guide, poking around these back roads tours, you want to see some new places. You are, after all, blessed with a sense of adventure. You want to explore a bit and see where that twisting road leads to. So it stands to reason that you'll get lost.

Lots of things can get you off on an unexpected "explore." Sometimes road names change without warning (I've tried to catch most of those for you) or sometimes you just get caught up in looking at the countryside and, next thing you know, you're somewhere—but you're not sure where it is on the map. Or maybe it's not even on the map.

As I worked on these tours, I'd occasionally head off on a great-looking road that would lead to another and another . . . and pretty soon I'd be turning maps upside down and checking my compass.

And there were plenty of times I didn't know where I was—for a while. Sometimes I would wander around looking at lots of new territory. I got to see many places I didn't know existed. But I was never truly lost. No real explorer ever is. If you wander a bit, you'll find a road that you can identify on the map, and very soon you're back on track. It usually won't take very long to figure out where you are.

One nice thing about getting lost is that you can stop and ask local people for directions. They love it. One nice trait shared by most Wisconsinites is their inability to resist the opportunity to become a walking visitor information service. They long for the chance to help you out. They'll tell you where to find good local food, where to stay, what the community is famous for, where to catch fish, where to play golf. Heck, sometimes you don't even have to say a word. Just pull over, examine your map, look left and right down the road. Soon, someone will come up to your car and ask whether you need help. Then get ready to hear all about the place you didn't even know you were near. It's no accident that the state tourism slogan is "You're Among Friends."

So, go ahead, get lost in Wisconsin. You'll love it.

A Final Word on Touring

I have some mixed feelings about telling you to go out and see these great back roads. I want you to see them but not move there.

Part of the wonder of it all is the vast area of relatively undeveloped, unpopulated, and uncommercialized backcountry that still exists in Wisconsin. It's obvious, however, that more and more people are fleeing the cities in search of country just like this. And the exodus is eating it alive.

It's troubling to drive through the beautiful hills and hollows only to get to the crest of a bluff with a spectacular view and see that someone is leveling much of a small wooded lot to build a dream home. Good for them. Bad for everyone else. It's sad to go to northern Wisconsin and see that the rush to own summer lake property has leached the character out of some wonderful little towns and turned them into little more than the same tasteless franchise strip malls that have cropped up with alarming frequency in the Milwaukee, Minneapolis, or Chicago suburbs.

I don't claim to know the answer to this problem, but I do believe we all can help. Make a promise to yourself that no matter how attractive the backcountry looks, you'll go back home to live. Promise that you won't go out and buy a lot in the country and build on it. If you buy property on a lake, buy something that's been around for years and vow to keep it in good shape. Shop at little country stores and help keep them in business. Insist that state and local governments develop a long-range land use plan that preserves wild areas, rural countryside, and scenic values.

We have just ended the first century of the automobile and live in what must be the best era ever for recreational touring. Cars are more reliable than ever, fuel is still plentiful, and there are still miles of good country out there. Let's enjoy it sensibly and try to preserve this wonderful land for future generations to discover.

Let's keep it wiggly.

Please note: *The tours in this book are designed to be driven in a day, but that includes no time spent at attractions, shopping, or sitting on the beach. On Tour 1, for example, the Madeline Island Ferry trip is an option that can easily take three to four hours. Plan your drives accordingly.*

"Where the heck are we?" "In Wisconsin, among friends." "How do we get back?" "Drive." Wisconsin Department of Tourism photo by GK.

30 SPECTACULAR AUTO TRIPS

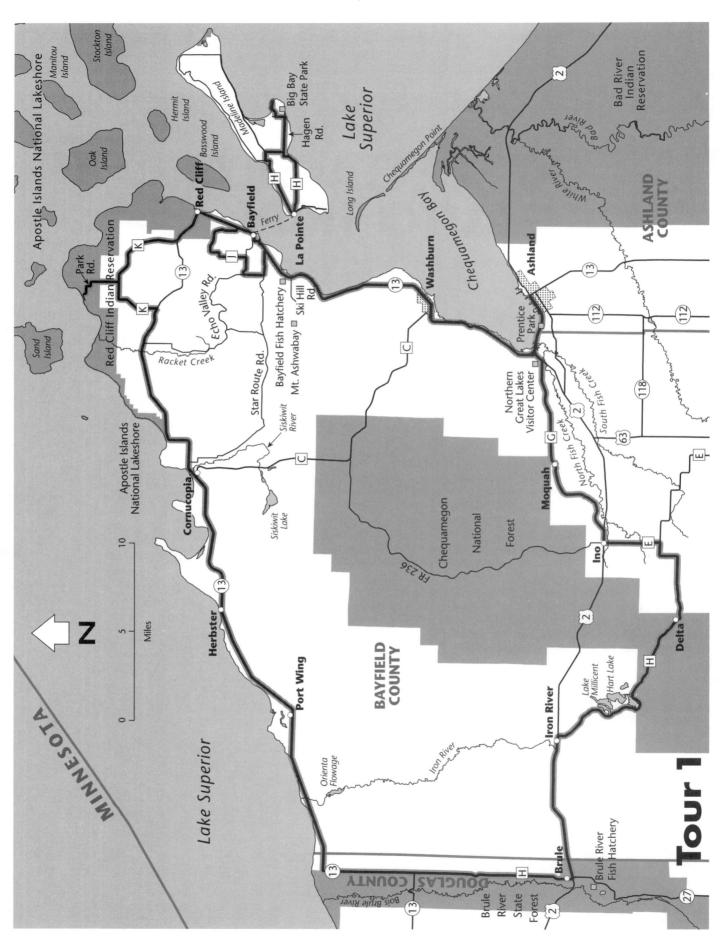

Tour 1

Tour 1
Apostles Country

Ashland—Washburn—Bayfield—Madeline Island—Red Cliff—Cornucopia—Herbster—Port Wing—Brule—Iron River—Moquah—Ashland

Distance: 143 miles (165 miles with the side trip to Madeline Island)

Commercial fishermen deliver fresh, delicious whitefish and trout to Bayfield daily. Photo by Gary Knowles.

Fasten your seatbelts, start your engines, and get ready to redline your thrill meter. Say hello to Ashland, Bayfield, Cornucopia, Lake Superior, and the Apostle Islands. This is where the huge Wisconsin glacier kissed the land and then departed some 10 millennia ago. This sacred region would become the great hunting and fishing grounds of the first people. This is where early French and English explorers established trading posts, where five Presidents have fished, where sailors, lumber barons, and miners made and lost fortunes.

This is also the place auto-loving Wisconsin travelers pretty much kept for themselves right up into the 1980s. Then word started to leak out that something special was up here: fishing villages, rugged lakeshore, Victorian inns, islands to explore, gourmet dining, and people that welcomed you like family. By the start of the new century, Apostles Country had become the place to be. And the best part is that it still is.

This region has the power to charm, beguile, and enchant—a region that will steal your heart and leave you aching when you have to leave. Welcome to a big hunk of heaven.

Start your tour in Ashland, "Lake Superior's Hometown," on historic Chequamegon Bay. You may want to spend some time exploring the downtown, where you can enjoy 19th-century brownstone buildings such as the *Ashland City Hall,* listed on the National Register of Historic Places. The brownstone in these impressive structures was quarried in the Apostle Islands, which also supplied cities all over the country with this remarkable stone.

The history of western Lake Superior can be seen in the *Northern Wisconsin History Center,* (715) 685-9983, 29270 County G, while community history and Victorian-era furnishings are on display at the *Ashland Area Historical Society Museum,*

(715) 682-4911, 509 W. Main St. The *Sigurd Olson Environmental Institute*, (715) 652-1223, at nearby Northland College, carries on the proud legacy of its namesake, a pioneering ecologist; the institute offers literature and exhibits relating to environmental issues. A large rare photo given to Olson by the noted photographer Ansel Adams is also on display here. Entitled *Aspens,* the 40-by-60-inch black-and-white photograph was printed by Adams himself from an exposure he made in New Mexico in 1958.

On the waterfront, two blocks from downtown, is the 1800-foot *Soo Line Ore Dock,* built in 1916, and the full-service *Ashland Marina,* which offers access to the new 6-mile *Shoreline Trail* that follows Lake Superior in the city.

Ashland is justifiably proud of its parks. *Bayview Park* in east Ashland has a good view of the lake and of old *Ashland Lighthouse* on the breakwater. *Maslowski Beach* on the west end of the city features a playground and a nice swimming beach. *Prentice Park* covers one hundred acres, has walking trails, a boardwalk along Fish Creek Slough, a deer yard, lots of wild birds, and an artesian well bubbling cold water that locals say is better than any designer water with fancy names and high prices. Fill your jug and enjoy the local elixir on this drive!

Follow Highway 2/13 in Ashland west along Chequamegon Bay. If you can't wait to get close to Lake Superior, pull off at the scenic overlook equipped with picnic tables and a "vista-dial," which describes various views along the horizon. There are pike, perch, and lake trout in the bay, and you may see migrating Canada geese, swans, ducks, and various shorebirds.

Continue west on Highway 2, just past the point where Highway 13 turns north. Go to the junction with County G and follow G to the *Northern Great Lakes Visitors Center,* (715) 685-9983. Here you can find helpful travel brochures and lake history displays, and see "Up Under the Upper Lake," an excellent show with great music that traces the area's rich history from the time of the glaciers to the present.

Return on G to Highway 2 and go east to the junction with Highway 13. Go north on 13 as it winds about 8 miles through wooded farmland to Washburn. This lakeshore community was named after Cadwallader C. Washburn, Wisconsin's governor from 1872 to 1874 and later the president of the State Historical Society. It has become a favorite with artists. You'll find delightful pottery,

Whitefish Livers, a Local Delicacy!

Once a tasty secret that commercial fishing families kept to themselves, whitefish livers were introduced to Bayfield diners by local restaurateur Vic Gruenke. He prepared the delicately flavored specialty dish with onion and green pepper, but today you'll find other saucy variations on menus all over the Bayfield Peninsula. The livers are generally in good supply from mid-spring through late summer. Favorite places to try them include Gruenke's, the Old Rittenhouse Inn, and Maggie's in Bayfield.

paintings, textile art, carved wood, and photographs in area shops. Antique hunters will want to poke around for artifacts and collectibles that have been preserved from the area's maritime, logging, and mining days. Washburn has many beautiful brownstone buildings, including the library, a domed courthouse, various commercial structures, and the old bank building that now houses the *Washburn Historical Museum and Cultural Center,* (715) 373-5591. In addition to featuring local history, the museum has a fine collection of children's toys. The U.S. Forest Service, which administers several camping areas in the 857,000-acre Chequamegon Forest, has an office in Washburn and is a good source of information on outdoor recreational opportunities in the area.

Continue north on 13. As you motor toward Bayfield you'll pass a barn painted with a mural that recalls the days when iron-ore freighters were a common sight on the bay. Watch for glimpses of the lake as you enjoy the drive. Three miles south of Bayfield at Mt. Ashwabay, watch for Ski Hill Rd. You'll see signs for *Big Top Chautauqua,* (715) 373-5552, a summer old-time tent show that showcases outstanding original musical productions by local professional musicians as well as touring stars. Don't miss the chance to treat the whole family to one of these friendly, foot-stomping extravaganzas.

Drive on and a little farther up the road you'll see the *Bayfield Fish Hatchery,* (715) 779-4021, which has a display of Lake Superior fish. Tours are available.

Continue on 13 to County J and turn left. County J twists, turns, and climbs several hundred feet above lake level. (Golf enthusiasts should take a look at *Apostle Highlands Golf Course*—a highly rated and challenging course that cuts through dense woods and offers breathtaking views of Lake Superior.) This 8.4-mile drive is one of Wisconsin's most spectacular apple and berry country sprints. Your head will spin as you spot one superb panoramic view after another. You'll see the Apostle Islands, Chequamegon Bay, and even Michigan's Upper Peninsula. Bring binoculars and a camera. To add to the fun you'll find it difficult not to stop at two or three of the baker's dozen apple and berry stands along the way. At the *Bayfield Apple Company,* you can see the state's largest raspberry patch and sample fresh fruit. Try some cider, stock up on jam, and, in season, get some fresh-picked fruit to go. If you plan ahead, all this bounty could become part of a shore lunch on Madeline Island.

Follow J back to 13, turn right at the intersection, and head east, then south, into Bayfield.

This picture-postcard town, commercial fishing village, and gateway to the Apostle Islands was named the "Best Little Town in the Midwest" by

Don't miss the 20-minute ferry ride between Bayfield and Madeline Island. Wisconsin Department of Tourism photo by GK.

Chicago Tribune writer Alan Solomon. For information on attractions, lodging, dining, sailing, charter fishing, events, and a ferry schedule to Madeline Island, visit the *Bayfield Chamber of Commerce,* (715) 779-3335, at the corner of Manypenny and Broad Sts.

It's difficult to just breeze through Bayfield. Chances are you'll spend some time hanging out. Wander around town, shop the shops, head to Madeline Island, devour some whitefish livers. Fall in love with the place. It's OK. Everyone does.

Bayfield is named in honor of Admiral Henry W. Bayfield, who served in the British Royal Navy and surveyed Lake Superior for England from 1823 to 1825. The community has seen plenty of traders, loggers, sailors, fishing enthusiasts, apple growers, and land speculators since then. Today the primary business is sharing the tranquility and scenic beauty with travelers.

Stop at the *Apostle Islands National Lakeshore* headquarters, (715) 779-3397, located in a huge brownstone building on Washington St. and Fourth St. to get an introduction to the history of the area, learn about the lighthouses of the Apostles, and explore the variety of recreational opportunities available. On Rittenhouse Ave. you'll find the *Old Rittenhouse Inn,* (715) 779-5111, one of the finest Victorian bed and breakfasts in the country. Dining at the Rittenhouse is open to the public, but call for reservations. A dinner here featuring one of innkeeper and head chef Mary Phillip's special entrees is a memory to treasure.

To see a great '50s-style cafe that was a favorite of the late John F. Kennedy Jr. when he vacationed here, stop in *Gruenke's* at the corner of Rittenhouse Ave. and First St. A few blocks away, on Manypenny Ave., is *Maggie's*, a fun-filled bar-cafe with good food and northern Caribbean decor. If you bought some apples back at the orchard, stop at one of the commercial fishing outlets on Wilson Ave. and buy some smoked whitefish or Lake Superior trout. Get some bread, cheese, and beverages over at the general store. If you're going to Madeline Island, take these goodies out to Big Bay State Park for a four-star lunch.

For a trip to Madeline Island, go to the ferry dock at the foot of Washington Ave. in Bayfield. Check the ferry schedule to allow time to get to the dock. Buy a ticket—you can take your car—and enjoy a 15-to-20-minute crossing to the village of La Pointe, Madeline Island's most populated community (180 residents). From the minute you set foot here, you'll begin to feel the island effect. You'll

The Apostle Islands

In the 1960s, Wisconsin Governor Gaylord Nelson, a noted environmentalist, championed the preservation of the Apostle Islands. President John F. Kennedy toured the area, but it wasn't until 1970 that Congress and President Richard Nixon officially created the Apostle Islands National Lakeshore, which included 20 of the 22 islands and 2,500 acres of the Bayfield peninsula. In 1986 Long Island was added to the others. That leaves Madeline, which is the only island not under National Park Service management. The islands have provided people with safe shelter, trading posts, forts, ceremonial grounds, fishing camps, hunting grounds, a source of lumber, and brownstone building material. Over the years, the Apostles have been carefully preserved so that their rugged beauty can be a source of enjoyment and inspiration for this and future generations.

5

People have enjoyed the tranquility of Madeline Island for hundreds of years. Wisconsin Department of Tourism photo by GK.

realize that you're truly "away from it all." And your link to the world, the ferry, is headed back to Bayfield. Welcome to downtown La Pointe and the island! If you didn't get one of the free island maps on the ferry, stop in any gift shop, restaurant, bike shop, or store to get one.

Madeline Island has been a special place all the way back to the 1400s when the Ojibwa people arrived here from Canada. The island gave them a safe place to live, away from the Fox and Lakota tribes who also lived in the area. In the 17th century, Europeans started moving in, and in 1785 Michel Cadotte married the daughter of Chief White Crane. She was baptized and given the name Madeleine. White Crane then honored her by changing the name of the island to Madeline. The *Madeline Island Historical Museum,* (715) 747-2415, 9 Main St., has a wonderful collection of artifacts, art, and photographs that tell the island's story.

In downtown La Pointe don't miss *Tom's Burned Down Cafe,* a remarkably friendly saloon that looks as if it had been blown in from Key West by some wayward winds. There's good pizza and ice cream at *Grampa Tony's,* excellent whitefish, buffalo wings, and smoked fish and wild rice soup at the *Bell Street Tavern,* and a great cup of latte at *Mission Hill Coffee House.* Also, check out the new *Lotta's Lakeside Café,* (715) 747-2033, (on the site of the old Island Café) for local fish, seasonal vegetables, soups, salads, and dinner specials.

When you exit the ferry at La Pointe, turn right at the first street (south) through town and go for about 0.25 mile to the *Madeline Island Yacht Club Marina*. Take a good look at the dozens of yachts and sailboats anchored there. Many people are surprised to learn that there are more charter and bare-board (rented without crew) sailings in the Apostle Islands than in all of Florida. Nearby is the *Madeline Island Golf Club,* a tough 18 holes designed by the legendary Robert Trent Jones Sr.

From La Pointe, take County H east to Hagen Road and follow the signs to *Big Bay State Park*. Drive carefully because you'll share the road with lots of bikers, motor scooters, and white-tailed deer. Big Bay (permit required) has one of the finest sand beaches in Wisconsin, picnic facilities, camping, and marked nature trails that take you along the rocky lakeshore into the forest and back along the barrier beach.

Leave Big Bay Park on Hagen Road and turn right on Black Shanty Road. Turn left on County H, which will loop back past the airport, heading southwest into La Pointe. Watch the woods and wetlands as you drive slowly back to town: there are lots of deer on the island and they like to see the people roll by! (Most of the rest of the island roads are gravel and there are just a few lake views, so unless you have time to kill and want a dust-covered car, I'd suggest you stay on the pavement.)

Take the ferry back to Bayfield. Exit the ferry parking lot on Washington Ave., turn right (north) on Highway 13, and go 3 miles to the Red Cliff Indian Reservation. Here the *Isle Vista Casino* features Vegas-style gambling that includes slots, video poker, reel slots, and blackjack.

Continue on 13 to County K. Turn right on K and go to its junction with Park Road. You'll see the *Sand Bay Visitor's Center,* (715) 335-6418, for the Apostle Islands National Lakeshore. The center is a good place to get more information about the Apostle Islands. Walk down to the beach and get a look at Sand Island. Most travelers never get up this far. In Little Sand Bay, visit the *Hokenson Brothers Fishery Museum,* a restored facility, including several buildings, that shows what life was like for the area's commercial fishermen in the 1930s and 1940s.

Return on Park Road to County K. Turn right on K and continue to Highway 13. Turn right on 13. Enjoy the open-road sprint over the hills, across Sand Creek, and through the forest. Watch for wildlife. These deep woods are home to deer, black bear, wolves, and elk that have been reintroduced to the area.

Follow 13 to Cornucopia. This is Wisconsin's northernmost community with a post office. Noted for its sandy beaches, good fishing, picturesque harbor, and stunning sunsets, "Corny" also has a delightful "shopping district" of several waterfront fishing shanties converted to gift, antique, and specialty stores. As you drive through town take a jog on County C to view *St. Mary's Russian Orthodox Church.* Built in 1910 to minister to area families, the church was originally served by a Russian-born priest.

Continue south and west on 13 along Lake Superior through Herbster. This is a quiet village with a long sandy beach, a couple of friendly bars, and great fly-fishing on the Cranberry River. Legend has it that the town was named for Billy Herbster, the only man in the Cranberry Lumberjack Camp of the 1890s who could read.

Follow 13 to Port Wing. Want to fish Lake Superior? This is the place. This old logging community not only has the look of a tiny fishing village but also has earned an excellent reputation as a charter fishing spot.

Continue on 13 west, then south to its junction with County H. Follow H south. You'll run through the scenic *Brule River State Forest* along the famous Brule River. For over one hundred years this wilderness river area has been a treasured recreation region. The Brule has been called the "River of Five Presidents" because it was visited by Presidents Grant, Coolidge, Cleveland, Hoover, and Eisenhower.

Continue on H south to Brule and the intersection with Highway 2. The *Brule River Fish Hatchery,* operated by the Wisconsin Department of Natural Resources, is just south of Brule off Highway 27. It raises lake trout and offers free tours, (715) 372-4820.

Turn left (east) on 2. You'll soon come to Iron River, the Blueberry Capital of the World. If you get here in late July you can even pick your own berries in the wild. For ideas and a good cup of coffee, visit the *Java Trout Espresso/Internet Bar & Gift Shop,* (715) 372-5511, on Hwy. 2 at George St.

Continue on 2 to where County H turns right (south). Follow H on a wonderful, twisted dash through glacial lake country. You'll pass near Moon Lake, Half Moon Lake, Perch Lake, Pike Lake, Lake Millicent, Bass Lake, Hart Lake, Twin Bear Lake, Eagle Lake, Hilde Lake, Delta Lake, and others before passing through the little settlement of Delta.

Stay on H to the junction with County E. Follow E north to Highway 2 at Ino.

Quick Trip Option: Head straight north from this intersection on Forest Rd. 236; it's unpaved but provides a delightful self-guided tour of the *Moquah Barrens Wildlife Area* of the Chequamegon National Forest, (715) 373-2667. This "tour" is a nice drive into the woods on 236.

Turn right (east) on 2 and proceed to the junction with County G. Turn left on G. This northeasterly route slips through forestland and hills and past older roads that sprang up along the Burlington Northern railroad. You'll pass through the settlement of Moquah and soon find yourself back at the Northern Great Lakes Visitor Center.

Continue on G to Highway 2; turn left (east) onto 2 and head back into Ashland to complete your tour.

The Apostles Lighthouses

Between 1857 and 1891, guiding lights were built on Sand, Devils, Raspberry, Long, Michigan, and Outer Islands. Though lighthouse tenders have been replaced with automated lamps, their heroic legends and mystique live on in Big Top Chautauqua's "Keeper of the Light" musical show. The Apostle Islands Cruise Service offers guided cruises to the islands, and on Raspberry Island you can tour the lighthouse.

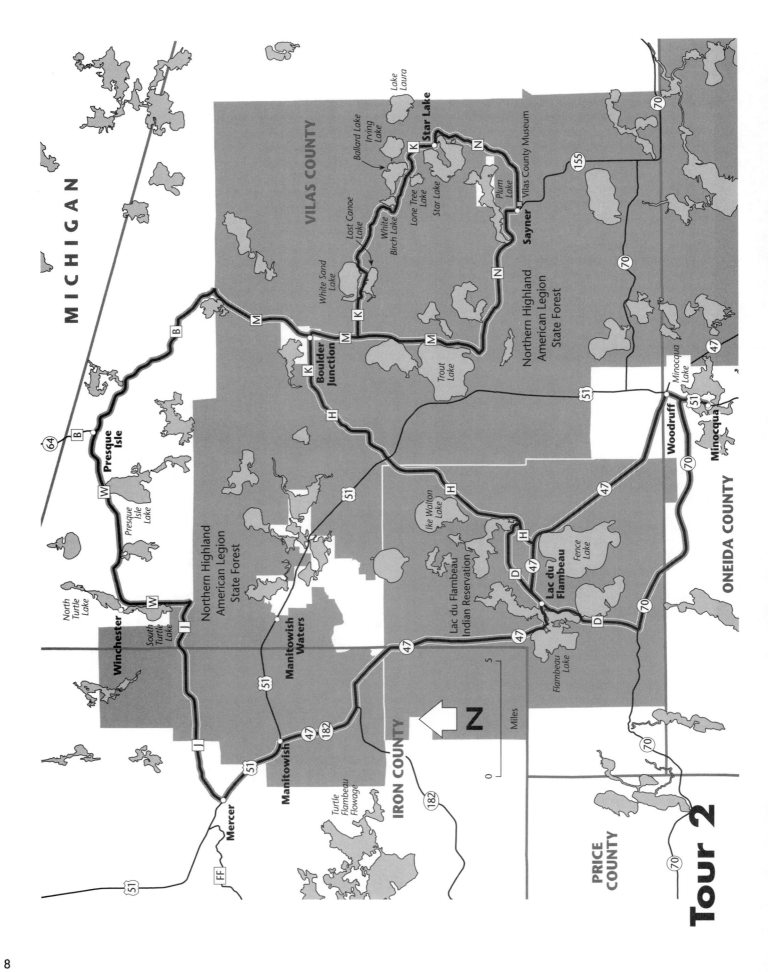

MICHIGAN

VILAS COUNTY

IRON COUNTY

ONEIDA COUNTY

PRICE COUNTY

Northern Highland American Legion State Forest

Northern Highland American Legion State Forest

Lac du Flambeau Indian Reservation

Lake Laura

Star Lake

Ballard Lake
Irving Lake

Lost Canoe Lake

Lone Tree Lake

Star Lake

Plum Lake

Vilas County Museum

Sayner

White Birch Lake

White Sand Lake

Boulder Junction

Trout Lake

Presque Isle

Presque Isle Lake

North Turtle Lake

South Turtle Lake

Winchester

Manitowish Waters

Manitowish

Mercer

Turtle Flambeau Flowage

Ike Walton Lake

Lac du Flambeau

Fence Lake

Flambeau Lake

Woodruff

Minocqua Lake

Minocqua

Star Lake

N

Miles
0   5

Tour 2

Tour 2
North Woods Muskie
and Loon Country

Minocqua—Lac du Flambeau—Boulder Junction—Sayner—Star Lake—Presque Isle—Winchester—Mercer—Manitowish Waters—Woodruff—Minocqua

Distance: 125 miles

This is Ojibwa country, and a good way to experience the rich culture is to take in a powwow. Photo by Gary Knowles.

This spectacular drive starts in the new urban North and weaves through the North Woods forest, past secluded glacial lakes and across vast marshes. These county highways were once Ojibwa trails, fur trade routes, and logging paths. Today they offer nothing less than an awesome asphalt argument that Wisconsin is the finest back-roads driving state in the Union.

For the driving enthusiast, there are plenty of elbows and sweeping turns, especially around the lakes. I'm especially fond of Wisconsin Rustic Road 60, the tight little run on County K between Star Lake and County M. This 11.7-mile sprint is absolutely exhilarating as it sneaks around Star Lake and tunnels through the forest. There are even a few straight sections in between the spaghetti. You might get into high gear, but be careful. A grilled deer can ruin your whole day.

This route is almost as exciting for the history buff. You'll visit a settlement that predates European contact (Lac du Flambeau), see near-ghost-

town communities that once were bustling logging camps (Winchester), and find a backwoods resort where one of the FBI's most notorious criminals made a famous getaway (Manitowish Waters).

It's a great drive in spring (whenever that elusive season hits, anytime from April to May), and just as nice in summer (June to mid-September) but absolutely not to be missed in autumn (late-September through October, most years).

Traffic is generally very light off the main highways and you'll often see eagles overhead, loons on the lakes (especially in the early hours of the day), and lots of deer. With growing frequency, travelers are even spotting black bear in this part of the deep woods. They'll pop out of nowhere, dash across the road and be gone into the underbrush much faster than you'd imagine. If you're lucky enough to see one, you'll probably be left pinching yourself, saying, "Was that really a bear?"

All along the route you'll find tempting state forest trails, county and local parks, waysides, boat

Lac Du Flambeau's NFL Connection

On Super Bowl Sunday, January 25, 1998, in Wisconsin's North Woods, hundreds of people were watching the Super Bowl on a giant TV screen at the Lake of the Torches Casino, cheering for their Packers. Most residents wore Packer green and gold, and there were even a few new Green Bay Packer stockholders among the faithful. But as far back as 1922 these people cheered for an NFL team that really was their team.

Three Lac du Flambeau men were among nine Chippewa or, more correctly, Ojibwa men who were players chosen for the NFL's most unusual team ever: the all-Native American Team—the Oorang Indians.

The team was organized by Walter Lingo, a LaRue, Ohio, businessman who raised and sold Airedale dogs. Lingo, who also had a strong interest in Native Americans, bought an NFL franchise for $100 in 1922. Lingo's motivation was to sell Airedales and he saw the NFL team as a gimmick to attract lots of people to an event where he could showcase and sell his dogs. Lingo's Oorangs not only played football but put on an entertaining halftime show featuring various exhibitions of marksmanship, mock battles, and demonstrations that showed off the dogs' abilities as well.

Lingo hired the famous Olympic athlete and Native American Jim Thorpe to recruit and coach the team. They traveled to various Indian Schools and reservations to find athletes for their roster. The team included Native Americans from several tribes, including Mohawk, Fox-Sauk, Winnebago (Ho-Chunk), Mission, Wyandotte, Cherokee, Seneca, Mohican, and Pomo, but the largest number were Ojibwa (9 of 25). And three of them came from one little reservation town in northern Wisconsin, Lac du Flambeau. They were Ted St. Germaine, George Vetterneck, and Alex Bobidosh.

The team lasted only two years. Although the novelty was a big draw in the first year, crowds started to diminish in the second year and Lingo decided to find other ways to sell his dogs. He returned the franchise to the league and the team was disbanded after the 1923 season. A few players like Thorpe and Jim Guyon went on to other teams and eventually the NFL Hall of Fame. Others went home. Their record was just 3-16, but they will always hold an important place in NFL history as the only all-Native American team.

launches, and dozens of places to pull off the road. Give in. Stop and take a front row seat on the shore of a glistening lake or stretch your legs on a nature trail. Breathe deeply. It's no wonder that so many people are choosing the North Woods for their retirement homes.

Begin in Minocqua on Highway 51. A great starting point is *Bosacki's Boat House*, (715) 356-5292, a restaurant on the shore of Lake Minocqua, one of the finest settings for a lakefront bar/restaurant in the North Woods. Great Bloody Marys. Excellent homemade hot-fudge sundaes. Good American food. Calendar sunsets.

Take 51 north to the junction with Highway 70. Follow 70 west for 2 miles to *Jim Peck's Wildwood Wildlife Park*, (715) 356-5588, a huge "petting zoo" where you'll see trophy-sized muskie

swimming in the ponds, cuddle a raccoon, pet a porcupine, feed corn to the deer, and serve "Bear Beer" to a black bear. (Don't worry; they won't get "liquored up." It's only sweet water!) Just a bit farther west on Highway 70, you'll come to the *Circle M Corral Family Fun Park*, (715) 356-4441, with go-karts, horses, trail rides, a train, bumper boats, water slides, and lots of activities for kids.

Follow 70 west about 7 more miles to the junction with County D. Follow D through the woods to the Lac du Flambeau reservation, the home of the Lac du Flambeau band of Lake Superior Chippewa—the Ojibwa. You may want to stop to see the *George Brown Ojibwe Cultural Center Museum*, (715) 588-3333, downtown. The *Lake of the Torches Resort Casino*, (800) 258-6724, on Lake Pokegama, has deluxe guest rooms, dining facilities, blackjack, and some 650 slot machines. It's one of the finest Native American gaming facilities in the Great Lakes region and one of just a few accessible by float plane.

Quick Trip Option: Go east on Highway 47 to County H, where you turn left and go 0.5 mile to *WaSwagoning Historical Village*, (715) 588-2615. This is one of the nation's finest Native American "living history museums." Take a step back to the 1700s and see how the Ojibwa lived with the seasons. .

Return to County D in Lac du Flambeau. Follow D northeast through the forest to County H. Turn left (north) on H and continue along the lake and wetlands to Highway 51. All along this route are scenic picnic areas, public boat landings, campgrounds, and waysides. Explore as many as you wish. You'll never get too much of this wonderful lake and wilderness country!

Cross 51 and continue to the junction with County K. Turn right and drive into Boulder Junction, "The Musky Capital of the World." It's earned the name as a result of years of being the center of 200 glacial lakes producing more of the huge fighting fish than any other area in the world. Boulder Junction was also voted the "Friendliest Small Town in Wisconsin" in a *Wisconsin Trails* magazine readers poll. Surrounded by 240,000 acres of forests, this is an outdoor lovers' dream town.

Turn right (south) on County M and drive by Trout Lake to the junction with County N. Turn left (east) on N and follow it through Sayner. If you get here before September 30, visit the *Vilas County Historical Museum*, (715) 542-3388, and see the world's first snowmobile, built by Carl Eliason. There's an historical marker here to commemorate his work. The Vilas County Museum

You know you're in the North Woods when you see "Claire de Loon" at the Mercer Chamber of Commerce. Wisconsin Department of Tourism photo by GK.

is one of my favorite underappreciated historical sites—a virtual Bethlehem of winter tourism. The snowmobile is one of those miracles born of cabin fever and Frankensteinian experiments in mechanical husbandry. Who could have guessed that this ugly-duckling offspring of a toboggan and a chainsaw would become the grandfather of a billion-dollar winter tourism industry! There are many other historical artifacts here worth a look.

Stay on N as it turns left and follow it to the junction with County K. Turn left on K. This is the heart of the old lumber country. It has been estimated that one to two billion feet of white pine lumber was cut and shipped from this area between 1895 and 1907.

Follow K to the junction with County M. This fine paved road is officially designated as Wisconsin Rustic Road 60. It winds past Star Lake, Little Star Lake, Lone Tree Lake, Ballard Lake, White Birch Lake, White Sand Lake, and Lost Canoe Lake within the 220,000-acre Northern Highland State Forest.

At the junction with M, turn right (north) and follow M back through Boulder Junction to the junction with County B. Follow B left (north and west) to Presque Isle. Drive into the town to see the walleye-rearing ponds. These are the largest in the state and millions of fingerlings have been produced here for transplanting.

At the junction with County W, turn left (west) on W and proceed into Winchester. Once a bustling logging boomtown, Winchester still has many authentic buildings from that era.

Return to W and drive to the junction with County J. Follow J right (west) to Mercer and Highway 51. Turn left (south) on 51. While in Mercer stop at the friendly Chamber of Commerce office, (715) 476-2389, on the left and have a talk with "Claire de Loon," another fine example of *fauna fiberglassia Wisconsinius,* a species very popular in the state. This loon is 16.5 feet tall and may be the world's biggest.

Follow 51 back to the junction with Highway 47.

Quick Trip Option: If you drive about 5 more miles on Highway 51 past this junction, you'll reach Manitowish Waters and *Little Bohemia Restaurant,* (715) 543-8433, the site of a famous FBI shootout with the outlaw John Dillinger. When he ran from "the heat" of the FBI in Chicago in 1934 he stayed here . . . until the "G-men" caught up with him . . . almost. Dillinger escaped but left some of his personal things—and a few bullet holes—behind. They are still on exhibit today for all to enjoy.

Follow 47 (right) back through the wild woods and wetlands through Lac du Flambeau. About 5 miles out of town you'll find *Fence Lake Lodge,* (715) 588-3255. This beautiful modern log structure overlooks fantastic sunsets on Fence Lake. The restaurant is known for northern gourmet dining and an excellent wine list. In warm weather grab a sandwich on their outdoor deck.

Continue southeast on 47 to Woodruff, where you'll rejoin Highway 51. Turn right on 51 to return to Minocqua.

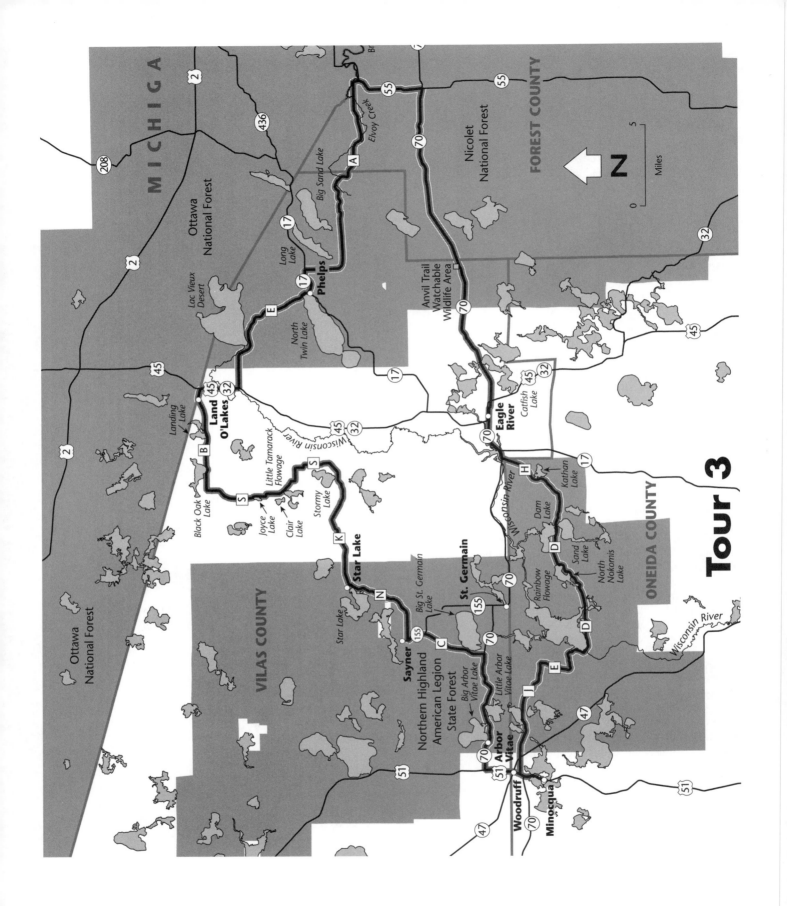

Tour 3

Tour 3
Lumberjack Trails and Wisconsin Headwaters Country

Minocqua—Eagle River—Phelps—Land O' Lakes—Star Lake—Sayner—Arbor Vitae—Woodruff—Minocqua

Distance: 141 miles

Driving enthusiasts and lake lovers should say a special "thank you" to the Native Americans, loggers, and the last glacier before beginning this trip. These incredible trails wind through a forested land speckled with glistening jewels in Oneida, Vilas, and Forest Counties.

After the ice scraped its way north, the first people came and established trails. Loggers later cut roads through the forest, and it's many of these routes, now widened and paved, we'll follow on this tour. They hug the lakeshores, cross marshes and swamps, duck through deep stands of pine and hardwoods, and then pass quickly through towns and villages.

This is where the Wisconsin River gets its start, and this is Wisconsin's prime resort country. Thousands of vacationers trek this way every summer. Nonetheless, most of these routes are just enough out of the way that they're not heavily traveled. People who rent a cottage on one of the lakes generally see only a small part of this country. Most vacationers never have been here before. It's yours to explore, so enjoy!

Along the way you'll do your share of shifting and cornering but plan to pull over at least a few times, rest a while, and soak up some of the serenity of the wilderness. Breathe deeply. Watch a loon. Dip your toe in a lake. It's all part of this Headwaters Country Run.

For years when you made the long drive north up the center of Wisconsin, you crossed the "high-tension line" somewhere around Wausau. You began to smell the pines north of Merrill and could finally, completely, relax when you passed through Tomahawk and Hazelhurst and crossed the bridge across Lake Minocqua. You could almost hear the fish biting by the time you pulled in at Bosacki's Boat House.

Then they went to work on Highway 51. They improved it. Made it a much better drive. They turned two lanes of deer dodging into four fast lanes from the Illinois line right to the Tomahawk area, made it Interstate 39, raised the speed limit, and cut drive time by about an hour. Suddenly True North got a lot closer to the people "down South" (as they say "Up North").

And the little summer tourist-town string of Minocqua-Woodruff-Arbor Vitae added art galleries,

book publishers, fancy shops, stock brokers, coffee bars, franchise food, franchise motels, discount stores, and ugly urban sprawl while metamorphosing into the chic Capital of the New Urban North.

So it's fitting that we begin in Minocqua at *Bosacki's Boat House* on Highway 51. Bosacki's, (715) 356-5292, is one of the finest surviving waterfront supper club-bars of the Old North. You can still rent a boat here, hire a muskie fishing guide, buy some fudge, or sip a spicy Bloody Mary as you watch a sunset streak the sky and lake with fire. Some things will never change. Get a good look at the leading edge of what Up North is becoming and then saddle up for a spirited dash through some of the finest lake country in the world. There's still some Old North out there to enjoy . . . at least for a while.

From Bosacki's, turn north onto 51. You're just a block away from the old downtown shopping district, which has some good bookstores, latte shops, and clothing shops along with T-shirt outlets and souvenir stores. If you want authentic Up North shopping, this is it. As you follow 51 north you'll pass the bigger chain stores, franchises, and strip malls that followed the people who moved up here to escape the city.

Follow 51 until you come to Highway 70. If you're looking for more fun, especially for the kids, you can follow Highway 70 west about 2 miles to *Jim Peck's Wildwood Wildlife Park*, (715) 356-5588, a huge petting zoo where you'll see trophy-sized muskie swimming in the ponds, cuddle a raccoon, pet a porcupine, feed corn to the deer, and serve "Bear Beer" to a black bear. Just a bit farther west on 70 you can take in the *Circle M Corral Family Fun Park,* (715) 356-4441, with go-

Meet 400-Year-Old Hemlocks in the Nicolet Forest

To get to the Nicolet Forest's Franklin Lake Campground, go about 8 miles east of Eagle River on Highway 70 and turn right on Military Rd. (Forest Rd. 2178). Go south 3 miles to Butternut Lake Rd. (Forest Rd. 2181). Turn left and go east 5 miles to the Franklin Lake Campground. Parking for the trail is on the right after you enter the campground. This gently rolling loop trail takes you into a northern hardwood, pine, and hemlock forest with trees over 400 years old. Stop to cool your toes in Butternut Lake or soak in the beautiful lake vista from a bench under huge hemlock trees. A boardwalk crosses a bog with many varieties of marsh plants.

Otter Rapids Hydroelectric Plant and the Chain of Lakes

The first dam and power plant was built just west of Eagle River in 1906, and by 1925 the power line was run to Woodruff, giving the community its first electric power. This was the first of 26 hydro plants on the Wisconsin River, which, in the heyday of hydroelectric power, was known as "The Hardest Working River in the World."

These hydro dams resulted in a waterway that connects 29 lakes with 11,600 acres of surface water and approximately 150 miles of shoreline—creating the largest inland chain of freshwater lakes in the world.

karts, horses, trail rides, a train, bumper boats, water slides, and lots of activities for kids.

Continue north on 51 to County J. Turn right (east) on J and continue across Highway 47. About 2 miles out of town at Madeline Lake is the *Woodruff State Fish Hatchery,* (715) 356-5211. Since 1900 this hatchery has been raising muskellunge fingerlings, northern pike, and walleye to stock Wisconsin lakes. It's a good place to see a variety of Wisconsin's favorite fish in rearing ponds as well as some mounted specimens.

Follow J east as it swings by Carrol Lake, Clear Lake, and Buffalo Lake through the *Northern Highland American Legion State Forest.* Watch for wildlife. There are some 130 species of birds, 27 species of reptiles, and 67 species of fish that call this place home. White-tailed deer are commonly spotted; rare, but very special sightings include black bear, wolves, and bobcats.

Follow J to the junction with County E. Turn right on E and continue to its junction with County D. Turn left (southeast) on D. This is a fine back-road run around Gilmore Lake and then along the west and south shore of the Rainbow Flowage of the Wisconsin River. The road then

twists through wildlife-rich wetlands, past North Nokomis Lake, Paradise Lake, Dam Lake, and Sand Lake.

At the junction with County H, take H east and then north past Arbutus Lake and Kathan Lake to the junction with Highway 70. Just about a mile west on the Wisconsin River is the famous *Otter Rapids Hydroelectric Plant* (see accompanying article).

Turn right (east) on Highway 70 and follow it into Eagle River. Like the Minocqua-Woodruff-Arbor Vitae area, Eagle River has been welcoming North Woods lovers for generations. In the early part of the 20th century, travelers came by train, but before long automobiles began to roll into town. The name "Eagle River" was given to the newly platted community in 1885 by the Milwaukee, Lakeshore and Western Railway people, who stuck with an Ojibwa description of the area as "home of the eagle." Though the birds had been endangered for years, they have made a dramatic comeback in recent years. They're an impressive sight, soaring high over the wild lakes in this area.

Eagle River has managed to retain much of the North Woods mystique that Minocqua traded in when Highway 51 was rerouted as a double lane through the shopping district. Though Eagle River is often bustling, it has the comfortable feel of a northern outpost where you can buy moccasins, fudge, flannel shirts, and big stacks of flapjacks.

If you want to explore the history of the north in more depth, stop at the *Eagle River Historical Museum,* (715) 479-2396, and the *Trees for Tomorrow Camp,* (800) 838-9472, 519 Sheritan St. The museum opened in 1998 to preserve local memories, while the Trees for Tomorrow Camp has a proud history that dates back to the Civilian Conservation Corps of 1936-37. This is where the U.S. Forest Service trained hundreds of people in forest care and management. These workers went on to restore Wisconsin forests that had been logged out in the clear-cut lumber era. Now on the National Register of Historic Places, the Trees for Tomorrow Camp continues to offer a wide variety of classes designed to build a deep appreciation for the recreation and environment of Wisconsin's wilderness.

Another interesting local attraction with a true North Woods flavor is *Carl's Wood Art Museum,* (715) 479-1883. Set in a replica of a trapper's log cabin, the museum holds dozens of woodcarvings, including a 2,000-pound grizzly bear and collections of burls and tree trunks.

Located a short drive north on Highway 45 is the *World Championship Snowmobile Track,* (715) 479-4424, home of the famous annual World Championship Snowmobile Derby.

Rent a pontoon boat at Eagle River and explore hundreds of miles of wilderness shoreline. Wisconsin Department of Tourism photo by GK.

Save room in your trunk for those irresistible backwoods bargains. Photo by Gary Knowles.

Eagle River is in the heart of northern Wisconsin cranberry country, and the *Cranberry Gift House*, (715) 479-8676, on Highway 70 on the west side of town, has a great selection of collectible cranberry glass. A few miles south on Highway 45 in the community of Three Lakes is the *Fruit of the Woods Wine Cellar*, (715) 546-3080, where cranberry wine is a specialty.

Continue east on 70, crossing the channel between Catfish Lake and Voyageur Lake. Enjoy the drive through this segment of the 660,000-acre Nicolet National Forest. For an optional tour, check out the Franklin Lake Campground (see accompanying article).

Continue on 70 for about 9 miles east of Eagle River. Watch for the *Anvil Trail Watchable Wildlife Area*. Bring your binoculars and camera. This hemlock and hardwood forest is home to songbirds, deer, martin, fisher, and even a few black bear. There are 12 miles of walking trail here. If you remember to bring some birdseed, you may be able to get the chickadees at the trail shelter to eat right out of your hand.

Continue on 70 east to the junction with Highway 55. Just another mile farther east on Highway 70 is the *West Allen Creek Watchable Wildlife Area*. If you want to see whole platoons of hooded mergansers, ducks, and migrating geese, this is the place.

Turn left (north) on 55 and continue to Nelma and the junction with County A. Take

A west as it follows Elvoy Creek, passes Robinson Lake, and then wiggles through the wild hills.

At the junction with Highway 17, turn left (west) on 17 and drive into Phelps, located on the great muskie lake North Twin.

In Phelps, turn right and follow County E north and west about 6 miles to West Shore Road. Turn right. In a quarter mile you'll see the parking lot at the headwaters of the Wisconsin River. A walk of about 0.12 mile will take you to the very beginning of this famous river. Take a good look. You'll see the Wisconsin in many shapes and moods as you enjoy the off-the-beaten-track runs in

Fishing? Get A Guide!

Catching a trophy-class fish is a dream shared by most fishing enthusiasts. Some "vacation fishers" wait all year to get out on the water and then hardly get a nibble. They'd be glad just to catch anything legal! Sad to say, most people never will do more than dream about the big one—much less see it get away. If you really want the best of fishing, there is a solution. Hire a guide. It's the best investment any fish hunter can make. In Northern Wisconsin there are dozens of good ones who will teach you fishing techniques that will put fish on your stringer for years to come. They'll show you how to find the kind of fish you want, show you how to catch them, and—if you're lucky—set up a "shore lunch" with bacon, fried potatoes, beans, and the fish you caught. Now there's a gourmet meal! To find a guide just call the tourist information center for the area you'll be visiting. In Eagle River the area guides even have a referral service at (715) 479-8804.

this guide. Born here in the deep-woods serenity of Lac Vieux Desert, it flows some 400 miles through the heart of Wisconsin.

Return to E and continue west to the junction with Highway 32/45. Turn north (right) and drive about 3 miles to Land O' Lakes. Built right on the Wisconsin-Michigan border, this settlement was once the end of the rail line and was named "State Line." The postal authorities said they already had several other "State Line" communities and asked if the local people might consider a name change. Always obliging, the lake property owners chose "Land O' Lakes." Considering that Vilas County has 1,327 lakes covering almost 94,000 acres, they picked a good one.

The impressive log structure, the *Gateway Lodge*, (800) 848-8058, was built in 1937-38. It has a huge stone fireplace and an ambiance that just says "Up North." Visitors have included Bob Hope, Lawrence Welk, Abbott and Costello, and the Eisenhower family. It's reported that NASA astronaut Jim Lovell used the lodge as a favorite personal retreat.

It's always awe-inspiring to be at the beginning, the source, of something great. At Lac Vieux Desert, near Phelps, you'll experience this feeling when you come upon the headwaters of the Wisconsin River. Wisconsin Department of Tourism photo by GK.

Turn left into town and follow County B west. This next stretch of lettered highways, B, S, K, and N, is one of the finest bush runs through northeast Wisconsin. You'll enjoy sweeping curves and discover lakes around the bend. Side roads that lead to the lakes and resorts are marked with white '50s-style signposts. Scattered here and there are friendly taverns where fishing enthusiasts gather to compare notes and only occasionally embellish stories. These routes are favorites any time of year, but you'll really get a foliage color show come autumn. County B winds past Landing Lake, George Lake, and Black Oak Lake,

At the junction with County S, turn left (south) on S, passing Joyce Lake, Clair Lake, the Little Tamarack Flowage, and Stormy Lake.

At the junction with County K, turn right (west) on K to Star Lake and go to the junction with County N. Turn left (south) on N and follow it into Sayner. This popular resort area is a favorite with families and sport-fishing enthusiasts. In the late 18th century this was a center of lumbering activity. The first practical snowmobile was built here in 1924 by Carl Eliason, and you can see it along with Native American artifacts, mounted animals, fish lures, and logging tools at the *Vilas County Historical Museum*, (715) 542-3388, on Highway 155.

In Sayner turn left (south) on Highway 155 and follow it to County C. Take C right (south) as 155 curves back to the east. Follow C past Big St. Germain Lake to the junction with Highway 70. Turn west (right) on 70 and travel past Little Arbor Vitae Lake and Big Arbor Vitae Lake.

At the junction with Highway 51, turn south (left) and pass through Woodruff on your way back to Minocqua. You might want to stop back at Bosacki's Boat House, where you can find out where the fish are biting or strike up a conversation with tourists and tell them about the incredible True North you've just discovered.

Tour 4
Drive Through the Door

Sturgeon Bay—Egg Harbor—Fish Creek—Ephraim—Sister Bay—Ellison Bay—Gills Rock—Northport—Washington Island—Baileys Harbor—Jacksonport—Sturgeon Bay

Distance: 128 miles

Door County, one of Wisconsin's finest and most popular vacation spots, is also a wonderful, underappreciated place to enjoy a drive along the lake and in the country. Sure, people have heard that Door County has more shoreline (250 miles), more state parks (5), and more lighthouses (10) than any other county in the country; but too often they avoid the area. They feel like Yankee philosopher and catcher Yogi Berra, who once said about a New York hot spot, "it's so popular that no one goes there anymore."

The problem is that most people stick to the main highways, 42 and 57, as they rush to the beaches, inns, shops, orchards, fish boils, museums, and parks that make the place so special. They create traffic jams in the little towns and get upset with the crowds that jam the boutiques and gift shops. They waste too much time looking for a place to park, get stressed out, and miss the awesome essence of Door County.

Well this tour is designed to show you sides of Door County that the masses pass by. We'll be taking back roads, visiting out-of-the-way spots, and enjoying the Door County that earned the reputation as Wisconsin's most exquisite destination. Yes, we will get to town, probably see some crowded streets, and maybe get behind a slow-moving vehicle or two. But this route will give you more than your share of the spectacular vistas, the beautiful rural farm country, the rocky beaches, the lighthouses, the fishing boats, and the great little seaside towns.

We're going to send you home with some real Door County tales to tell!

Start this tour in Sturgeon Bay at the junction of Business Highway 42 and Third Avenue

The "boil over" is always a dramatic event at a Door County fish boil. Photo by Gary Knowles.

(County B). This shipbuilding center produces some of the world's finest luxury yachts, commercial ships, and military vessels. The rich history of the settlement dates back to 1835, and the downtown is still bustling with shops and galleries today. The excellent *Door County Maritime Museum,* (920) 743-5958, 120 N. Madison Ave., has 20,000 square feet of space to showcase the area's maritime heritage. Several tugboats and a Coast Guard icebreaker are moored here. The *Door County Museum,* (920) 743-5809, at 4th Ave. and Michigan St., exhibits the flora and fauna of the peninsula, a 1920 fire engine, and a "Streets of Yesteryear" display. The *Miller Art Center,* (920) 746-0707, 107 S. 4th Ave., in the Door County Library, has seven different exhibits per year and a permanent collection that highlights the work of Gerhard C. F. Miller, along with that of other Wisconsin artists.

Follow B north out of the city past Sunset Park. This back-roads route parallels the lakeshore,

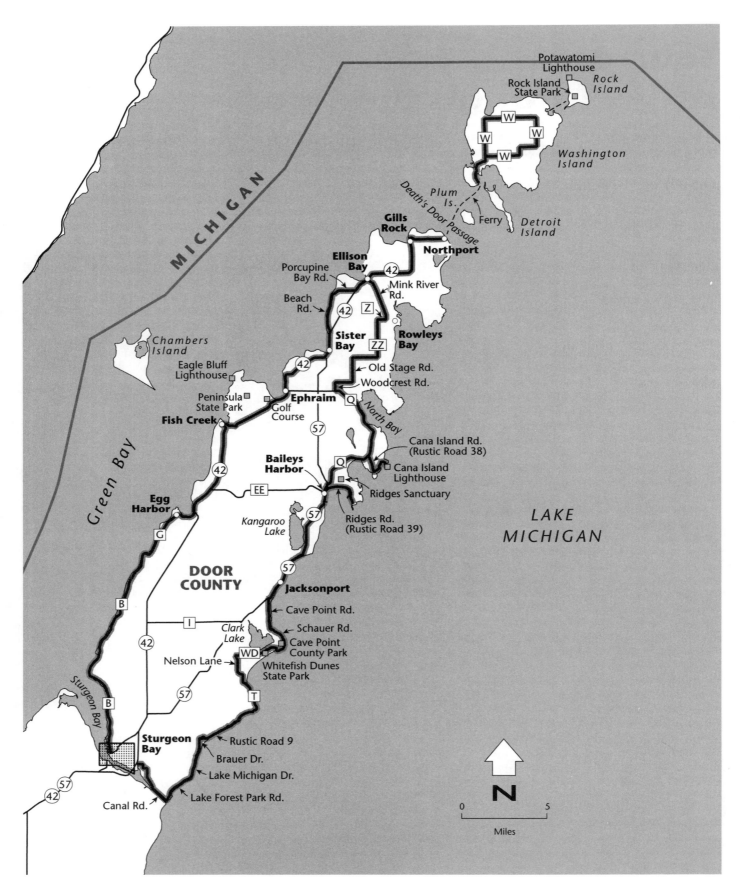

Tour 4

Peninsula State Park juts out into Green Bay, making for some fine views of the surrounding waters. Photo by Gary Knowles.

with resorts and private cottages to your left and farms, woodlots, and orchard-speckled hills to your right. People will tell you that Door County has a split personality. The west shore that you're on now is the peaceful, warmer, more sheltered, more traveled, and commercial side. It's the side favored by tourists. The east shore is the Lake Michigan, wild-open-sea, less developed, and less populated side. Old-timers look at it and recall a less populated Door County, a pre-discovery Door County. Chances are, you'll find good reasons to love both sides.

Continue on B to the junction with County G. Follow G north into Egg Harbor. Why is it called *Egg* Harbor? One legend suggests that Increase Claflin found a nest of duck eggs here as he explored the area. Some say the rocks in the harbor are egg-shaped. I choose to believe the more colorful story set in 1825 that has Commodore Roulette and his men getting into a good-natured, egg-tossing food fight with his underlings, who refused to let his canoe take the lead as they paddled to the shore. Today shopping in Egg Harbor is more popular than egg tossing. Music lovers will want to catch a concert at *Birch Creek Music Center,* (920) 868-3763, just outside town on County E.

At the junction with Highway 42, turn left (north) onto 42. We'll be following much of the Highway 42 route all the way to Gills Rock and Northport, with a few good side routes to get off the beaten path as much as possible

Follow 42 into Fish Creek. Fish Creek is the epicenter of northern Door County, ground zero, the one spot all travelers must include in their passage through the peninsula. This is where Increase Claflin settled in 1835 after some Native Americans drove him out of Sturgeon Bay. His cabin site, with a spectacular view of the bay, is preserved in

Peninsula State Park at Claflin Point. The performing arts have found a happy home near Fish Creek with the *Peninsula Players,* (920) 868-3287, the country's oldest professional summer theater, and *The American Folklore Theater,* (920) 868-9999, producing tales of America's past. If your credit card is healthy, you can give it an intense workout at the galleries and shops here.

Continue on 42 to *Peninsula State Park.* Go to the entrance and turn left into the park, (920) 743-4456. If you don't already have a state park annual sticker, buy one here. You can drive through the park without one if you don't stop, but that's not possible. There are too many tempting scenic pull-offs, lighthouses, and towers to explore. Believe me; buy the sticker. You'll use it on many other tours, too.

The park has roads that go up to Eagle Bluff Lighthouse and shoreline routes with picnic facilities and sandy beaches. There's even a lookout tower to climb (remember to take your binoculars and camera before you go up). From the top of the tower you can see Chambers Island (which has a lake on it with an island in it), and farther across Green Bay you can glimpse Michigan's Upper Peninsula. An exhilarating hiking trail runs along the bluff to the rocky shore. *Peninsula Golf Course,* (920) 854-5791, the only one owned by the state of Wisconsin, is at the park's northern boundary. Built in 1921 and upgraded in the 1970s, it's a well-tended 18 holes with breathtaking views of Ephraim, and it provides a great aerobic walk with lots of elevation changes.

At any of the exits out of the park, turn left (north) on 42 and drive to Ephraim. This pic-

The Door County Fish Boil

If you plan to dine in Door County (and you'd be a fool if you didn't), you must plan to try at least one fish boil. Oh, sure, it sounds pretty bad, but it tastes delicious. It's outstanding entertainment that, according to local tale-spinners, has its roots somewhere back in the Scandinavian settlers' fishing and logging history.

The fish boil requires fresh whitefish, usually cut into big sections. These are boiled with new potatoes and sometimes onions in salted water, outdoors in a huge pot over a wood fire. The natural fish oils rise to the surface of the water, and then the "boil master" raises the heat of the fire by tossing on extra fuel. The superheated contents spill over into the fire, creating a huge hot flame. This not only makes for a dramatic photo opportunity but also yields a scrumptious meal.

Fish boils are served in virtually every community, so watch for signs. Two of the most popular places are *The Viking Grill,* (920) 854-2998, in Ellison Bay, which has been serving traditional fish boils for 34 years, and *The White Gull Inn,* (920) 868-3517, in Fish Creek, which prepares the fish without the onion and serves it in the dining room of this authentic 1896 inn. Cherry pie a la mode is required to complete the feast. After a day of touring through this glorious maritime kingdom, a fish boil is the perfect gourmet exclamation point to make a perfect day.

Whether by yacht, sailboat, or rubber raft, Door County residents are always ready to get out on open water. Wisconsin Department of Tourism photo by GK.

turesque town was settled in 1853 by 40 Norwegian Moravians whose preference for clean lines and white paint in their buildings is still respected today. Art galleries, gift shops, and antiques stores will tempt you at every bend of the road. Wilson's Soda Shop is a required checkpoint for ice cream lovers.

Continue on 42 north to Sister Bay. If you ever longed for a nice little town with a big sandy beach and beautiful harbor on Main Street, you're home. Though it's the largest of the communities north of Sturgeon Bay, Sister Bay retains a friendly, small town feeling. Watch for the goats grazing on the sod roof of *Al Johnson's Swedish Restaurant,* (920) 854-2626. Just up the road is the *Hotel Du Nord,* (920) 854-4221, known for excellent seafood and arguably the finest gourmet restaurant in Door County.

Continue on 42 for about a mile out of Sister Bay and turn left onto Beach Road. This route runs closer to the lake and is more scenic than the highway.

Follow Beach Road to the junction with Porcupine Bay (Hillside) Road. Turn right on Porcupine Bay and continue to the junction with Highway 42. Turn left on 42 and follow it through Ellison Bay into Gills Rock. Many Door County visitors never venture this far up the

peninsula. This is a good place to walk down to the dock, watch fishing boats, or even book a cruise of your own. *Sunset Concert Cruises,* (920) 854-2986, offers three-hour excursions with music, while *The Yankee* and *Island Clippers,* (920) 854-2972, provide narrated cruises to Washington Island. Not to be confused with the museum of the same name in Sturgeon Bay, the *Door County Maritime Museum,* (920) 854-1844, in Gills Rock, has exhibits featuring shipbuilding, commercial fishing, and a real fishing tug.

Continue on 42 to Northport. You can watch the ferry traffic and relax a while or spend some time on Washington Island.

Quick Trip Option: If you want to visit Washington Island, you can take your car on the ferry, (800) 223-2094, which crosses Death's Door (see accompanying article), and circle the island on County W and various local roads. If you decide not to take your car, call ahead and book *Vi's Famous Taxi Service,* (920) 847-2283, to get an unforgettable escorted and personalized tour of the island. Settled by Icelandic people, this is the largest such settlement in the United States. A local tradition is to stop at the tavern or general store and share a shot of bitters with the local residents. Washington Island has quiet beaches, museums, art and craft galleries, a few shops, and a golf course. Visit the Art & Nature Center, (920) 847-2025, which is in the old island school, built in 1904. Some crafts are for sale, and exhibits feature the natural and cultural history of the island. On Little Lake (at the end of Little Lake Rd.) you'll find Jens Jacobsen's home and the Jacobsen Museum, (920) 847-2213. Maritime and other artifacts are displayed. At the

Death's Door

"Ports des Morts" was the name that early French explorers gave to the treacherous body of water that separates the tip of the peninsula from Washington Island. Shifting winds create strong, surging currents here that change rapidly. Sailing ships often cannot make headway against the currents. Many ships and sailors have met their end here, including 24 vessels between 1837 and 1914 and, according to an old legend, a large war party of Native Americans. Before the Sturgeon Bay Ship Canal was completed, this treacherous route was the primary passage into Green Bay from the southeast.

Jackson Harbor Maritime Museum, (920) 847-2522, you'll find commercial fishing artifacts.

To get to Wisconsin's most secluded state park, catch a ferry from Jackson Harbor, on the northeast side of Washington Island, to Rock Island and *Rock Island State Park,* (920) 847-2235. No vehicles are allowed. This island has the Potawatomie Lighthouse, built in 1836—the oldest on Lake Michigan—as well as several extraordinary stone buildings with exhibits.

From Northport, return on 42 to Ellison Bay and turn left onto Mink River Road toward Rowley's Bay. This next series of roads will jog around marshes, through farm country, and past old homesteads. This is the way much of Door County looked before the word got out. Watch for wildlife and enjoy the changing vistas.

At the junction with County Z, take Z west to County ZZ. Follow ZZ as it heads south and then west to the junction with Old Stage Road. Turn left (south) onto Old Stage Road and follow it south and then west to the junction with Woodcrest Road. Turn left onto Woodcrest and go a short distance to County Q.

Turn left (east) on Q and follow it along North Bay. Continue to Cana Island Road (Rustic Road 38) and turn left. For about 2.5 miles along this route, you'll find excellent views of Moonlight Bay and the *Cana Island Lighthouse.* Lighthouse lovers consider this one of the finest on the lake. When it was built in 1851, the lamp was fueled with lard. Of course, they're all automated now. Depending on water level, you may need to wade carefully over a stony causeway to reach it. It's wise to wear beach shoes or old tennis shoes because the rocks can be tough on bare feet.

Return to County Q and turn left (south) to the junction with Highway 57; turn left on 57 and drive a short distance to Ridges Road (Rustic Road 39). Turn left and drive 2.5 miles. Here you'll find a wooded lakeshore leading to the *Old Lighthouse Point Natural Area* and the

Ridges Sanctuary, (920) 839-2802, wildlife area. The Ridges is said to contain every one of 23 varieties of orchid native to Wisconsin as well as many other rare plants and dozens of birds.

Drive back to Highway 57 and turn left (south) to Baileys Harbor. This picturesque harbor was named for Capt. Justin Bailey, who found refuge here from a violent storm in October 1848. Today it's a favorite launching point for sport fishing expeditions.

Continue south on 57, skirting the eastern edge of Kangaroo Lake and then swinging back to the Lake Michigan shoreline.

Continue through Jacksonport to Cave Point Road, where you'll turn left (south). At Schauer Road, turn left and follow it to *Cave Point Park.* You'll want to get out and explore the dramatic shoreline of this county park where huge waves thunder into limestone caverns. This is one of Door County's most memorable parks.

Follow Schauer Road south to County WD and follow the signs to *Whitefish Dunes State Park.* The park has the tallest sand dunes in the state and a long sandy beach. It's another of the parks that are just a bit out of the way for many Door County visitors, so stop and see what many will miss; call (920) 823-2400.

Follow WD (Clark Lake Road) west out of the park to Nelson Lane. Turn left (south) on Nelson Lane to County T. Turn left on T and follow it along the Lake Michigan shore as it becomes Rustic Road 9. This 6.7-mile shoreline drive takes you past an old sawmill, sand beaches, and dunes and provides excellent lake views.

Continue to Brauer Road. Turn left (south) on Brauer Road and continue south on Lake Michigan Drive, which becomes Lake Forest Park Road, then Canal Road. Turn right (west) on Canal Road and continue back into Sturgeon Bay and Highway 42/57.

Door County Bed and Breakfast Inns—A Sampling

The art of the bed and breakfast has been taken to amazing heights in Door County. There are wonderful places tucked into virtually every community. In Sturgeon Bay take a look at the much acclaimed *White Lace Inn,* (920) 743-1105, 16 N. Fifth Ave., an elegant old Victorian bordered by a white picket fence and well-tended gardens; the top-rated *Schofield House,* (888) 463-0204, 908 Michigan St., known for gourmet breakfasts and gracious hospitality; and the romantic *Inn at Cedar Crossing,* (920) 743-4200, located downtown at 336 Louisiana St. In Baileys Harbor, you can nestle in right on the beach at

The Blacksmith Inn, (800) 769-8619, 8152 Highway 57, a 1912 half-timber retreat. In Sister Bay, the *Sweetbriar,* (920) 854-7504, 102 Orchard Drive, is a quiet Cape Cod country home on 16 acres of meadow. The readers of *Wisconsin Trails* magazine named *The White Gull Inn,* (920) 868-3517, 4225 Main St. in Fish Creek, as their "Door County favorite." Get more complete listings in the free, official *Door County Vacation Guide* by calling (800) 52-RELAX or get a free copy of the Wisconsin Bed and Breakfast Association directory by calling Wisconsin Department of Tourism at (800) 432-8747.

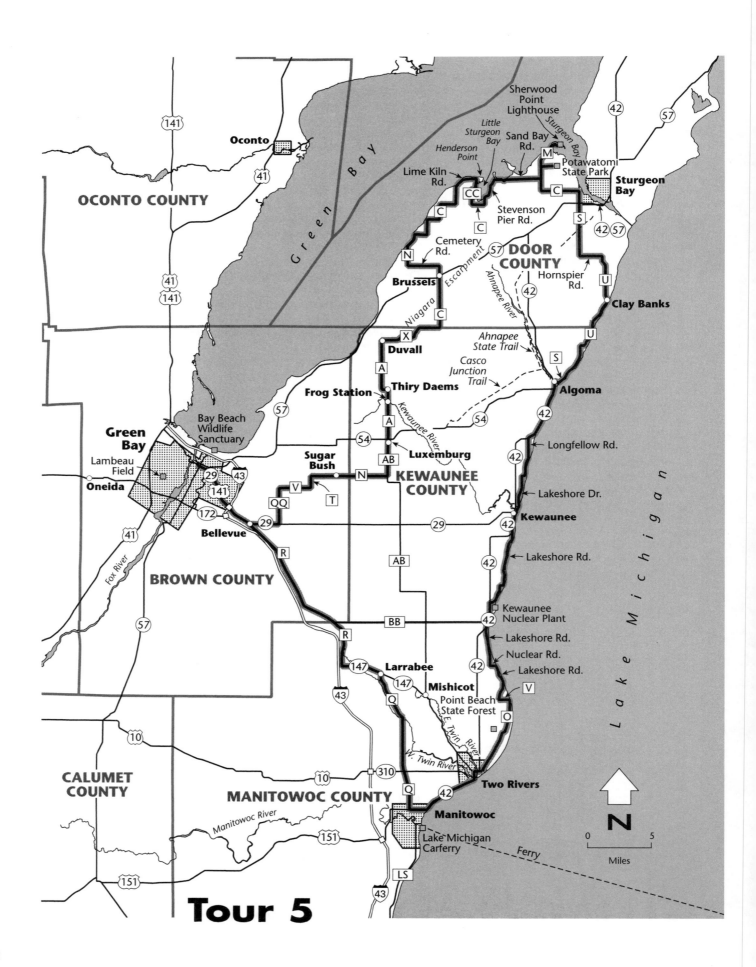

Tour 5

Tour 5
Packers and Ports

Green Bay—Luxemburg—Frog Station—Thiry Daems—Duvall—Brussels—Sturgeon Bay—Clay Banks—Algoma—Kewaunee—Two Rivers—Manitowoc—Larabee—Denmark—Langes Corners—Green Bay

Distance: 162 miles

This drive is full of the kinds of pleasant surprises that make Wisconsin touring so much fun. You'll cruise along beautiful stretches of the Lake Michigan shore that most people miss as they rush up the fast lane to "The Door." You'll discover some of Wisconsin's most picturesque harbors and lighthouses. You'll ramble on old farm country roads through crossroads hamlets and little Norman Rockwell towns where you can still buy Old World sausage, squeaky cheese curds, and homemade pies.

There's also a surprisingly subtle beauty to these gently rolling hills, sun-dappled woodlots, stone silos, and the long blue horizon of the lake. It isn't a bowl-you-over Grand Canyon kind of beauty, but rather the quiet kind. It sneaks up unexpectedly, but convincingly, mile by mile. Drive it and you'll soon realize that you've developed a real affection for the area.

And if you're looking for truly memorable attractions, this is a great tour. The Green Bay Packer Hall of Fame is a model that other sports teams emulate. The USS *Cobia* submarine in Manitowoc is a real WWII fighting machine that sunk tons of enemy ships. The birthplace of the ice cream "sundae" is on this route, as is the famous Natural Ovens bakery—not to mention the last Great Lakes car ferry and a museum that was nearly hit by a piece of outer-space debris. And even more!

Start the trip in downtown Green Bay. This Great Lakes port city grew up just south of Red Banks, the spot where in 1634 explorer Jean Nicolet jumped out of his canoe dressed in red oriental robes, shot pistols in the air, and hoped he'd discovered the "northwest passage" to the Orient. Instead he found the friendly Ho-Chunk (a.k.a. Winnebago) people who treated him to three days of feasting on fish and muskrat. Nicolet was the first European to make contact with the inhabitants of Wisconsin—and experience their hospitality. Today Titletown is the home of the world famous Green Bay Packers and their Hall of Fame (see accompanying article). But what else is there to do in the shadow of Lambeau Field?

Bay Beach Amusement Park, (920) 391-3671, is great for kids, with dozens of inexpensive rides and play areas. *Bay Beach Wildlife Sanctuary,* (920) 391-3671, is a 700-acre urban wildlife refuge with many animals native to Wisconsin. *Great Explorations Children's Museum* in the Port Plaza Mall, (920) 432-GEXP, has hands-on exhibits and interactive programs especially for children. *The Green Bay Botanical Garden,* (920) 490-9457, offers formal flower gardens, plus a children's garden with tree house, maze, and frog pond.

Hazelwood Historic Home Museum, (920) 437-1840, is the restored and authentically furnished, 1837 Greek-revival home of Judge Morgan Martin, who served in the Civil War and was president of Wisconsin's Second Constitutional Convention. *White Pillars* in nearby DePere was built in 1836 as the first bank building in the state and now houses the *DePere Historical Society Museum,* (920) 336-3877. *Heritage Hill Living History Museum,* (800) 721-5150, has 25 historic buildings dating from 1672 through 1905. The *L. H. Barkhausen Waterfowl Preserve,* (920) 434-2824, is a nature center with trails for hiking and cross-country skiing.

The *NEW Zoo,* (920) 448-4466, has 43 acres of natural area with animals from around the world. The *National Railroad Museum,* (920) 437-7623, is a railroad lover's delight, with 77 pieces of rolling stock, including the Dwight D. Eisenhower World War II train, the Union Pacific Big Boy, and the Rock Island Aerotrain. You can even enjoy a ride behind vintage diesel locomotives. Art, science, and history are showcased at the *Neville Public Museum,* (920) 448-4460, on two floors filled with changing exhibits.

Gaming fans will want to visit *Oneida Bingo and Casino,* (800) 238-4263, one of the state's largest casinos with reel slots, video machines,

The Green Bay Packers

Tracing their beginnings back to a brainstorm of Curly Lambeau and George Calhoun in August 1911, the Green Bay Packers are the only publicly owned team in the National Football League, play in the smallest city, and have won the hearts and support of fans around the world—not to mention more world championships (12) than any other NFL team. You can feel the pride of "The Green and Gold" all over Green Bay, and here are some places to enjoy.

The Green Bay Packer Hall of Fame is the epicenter of Packer artifacts and the keeper of the legends, (920) 499-4281. Exhibits, shows, and memorabilia will bring goose bumps to any football fan. *The Packers' Experience,* (920) 494-3401, has more than a dozen interactive football activities. *Lambeau Field,* (888) 442-7225, offers a stadium tour of the hallowed ground as well as press boxes, luxury boxes, and other behind-the-scenes areas.

blackjack tables, and high-stakes bingo. The excellent *Oneida Nation Museum* in Oneida, (920) 869-2768, has the largest exhibit of Oneida history and artifacts in the world. *Titletown Brewing Co.* is in the historic Chicago & North Western Railroad Depot and features specialty beers, a restaurant, and billiards hall.

From downtown Green Bay, take Highway 29 east, then southeast out of town through Bellevue to the junction with County QQ. Turn left on QQ and follow it north to County V.

Turn right (east) on V to County T. Turn left (north) on T to the junction with County N. Turn right on N and continue east through Sugar Bush to County AB. Turn left (north) on AB and go about 2.5 miles to Luxemburg. This community was founded by people who emigrated from Luxembourg in 1883; within a few years German, Czechoslovakian, and Belgian settlers joined them and created their own "little Europe" throughout Kewaunee, Manitowoc, Brown, and Door Counties. At the Kewaunee County Fairgrounds, their descendents and others enjoy the 0.3-mile semi-banked clay oval *Luxemburg Tri-Star Speedway*. Friday night races feature IMCA, IMCA modifieds, wild street stocks, and sport trucks.

Continue north on what is now County A through Frog Station, which earned its name from the loud summer croaking serenades of thousands of frogs that live and breed in the pools of the Kewaunee River.

Continue north on A to Thiry Daems. Another Belgian settlement, this oddly named town pays tribute to a surveyor, Constant Thiry, and a priest, Father Daems, who encouraged family and friends in Belgium to make their homes in New World Wisconsin.

Go north on A to Duvall and the junction with County X. Turn right (east) on X to the junction with County C. Turn left (north) on C. And believe it or not, you'll be in Door County, or at least within the boundary of Door County. Of course many people have the erroneous notion that the "real" Door County starts at Sturgeon Bay. The irony is they rush past this quiet, authentic, and enchanting part of the county only to get stuck in a traffic jam in Fish Creek.

Continue north on C across the *Niagara Escarpment,* a limestone ridge that runs about 900 miles to Niagara Falls. It was created some 400 million years ago when the warm and shallow Silurian Sea covered the area. Marine animals died and their remains were compressed into the sedimentary rock you see as ridges here and all the way to Gills Rock.

Continue on C across Highway 57 through the Belgian town of Brussels to Cemetery Road. Turn left (west) on Cemetery Road and continue to County N. Turn right (north) on N and follow it as it jogs near the Green Bay shore then cuts back east to the junction with County C.

Turn left (north) on C and follow it east to Lime Kiln Road. Turn left (north) on Lime Kiln and follow it to Henderson Point on Little Sturgeon Bay. Once there, return via County CC south back to County C and then turn left (east) to Stevenson Pier Road.

Turn left (north) on Stevenson Pier Road to Sand Bay Road. Turn right onto Sand Bay Road and go east to County M. Turn left (north) on M. You'll soon come to the *Sherwood Lighthouse.* Built in 1853, it was automated in 1983 and was the last manned lighthouse in the United States. It's the only red brick lighthouse in Door County. Today it's a retreat for U.S. Coast Guard personnel.

Return back south on M to Odagard Road. Turn left on Odagard and proceed to *Potawatomi State Park,* (920) 746-2890. This 1,178-acre park has more than two miles of shoreline, great hiking trails, an observation tower, bicycle routes, a boat ramp, and fishing. The granite boulders on the shore were dragged from Canada by the glacier.

Return to County M and take it south to County C. Turn left (east) on C and drive into Sturgeon Bay (Duluth Avenue). (For a guide to the surprisingly varied attractions in Sturgeon Bay, see Tour 4.)

Continue south on C (Duluth Avenue) across Highway 42/57 (where it becomes County S). Stay on S to Hornspier Road. Turn left (east) on Hornspier to County U. Turn right (south) on U, crossing Woodard Creek and Schuyler Creek, through Clay Banks on Lake Michigan, across Bear Creek and Stoney Creek to the junction with County S.

Turn left (south) on S, cross Silver Creek, and then cruise into the port of Algoma on the Ahnapee River. Originally called "Wolf River" when it was settled in 1851, the town changed its name in 1879 to "Algoma," which is a Native American word meaning "park of flowers." In that era the community was a commercial fishing center, and some of that continues today along with charter sport fishing. Photographers will find the harbor and boats hard to resist. The 15.3-mile Ahnapee State Trail for hiking and biking runs between Algoma and Sturgeon Bay, and another trail, Casco Junction, connects Algoma to Casco.

Tour the von Stiehl Winery for a sample of cherry wine. Wisconsin Department of Tourism photo by GK.

The *Crescent Beach and Boardwalk* is Algoma's half-mile award-winning boardwalk along the Lake Michigan shore. A short walk off the boardwalk gets you to Crescent Beach. Local guides offer historic walking tours by prior reservation through the *Algoma Visitor Center*, (920) 487-2041. A great little museum is *Motorcycles of Italy* at Netto Palazzo, which has exotic Italian motorcycles ranging from the Italian-made Harley Davidson Sprint to the hyper-speed Bimota. The *von Stiehl Winery*, (800) 955-5208, is Wisconsin's oldest continually operating winery, with tours and tasting in a Bohemian tasting salon. Von Stiehl is known for its bottles wrapped in white casts, a brainstorm of Dr. Stiehl, who wanted to protect his newly made wines from heat and light.

In Algoma take Highway 42 south about 4.5 miles to the intersection with Longfellow Road. Turn left (south) on Longfellow and follow it along the lakeshore to Rostock. Turn right on First Road, then left on Lakeshore Drive into Kewaunee. The picturesque port city of Kewaunee was originally settled by the Potawatomi in the 14th century. They liked the area, as did explorers and traders, because of the fine natural harbor, abundant wildlife, and great natural resources. The Potawatomi gave Kewaunee its name, which, translators tell us, means "we are lost!"

Local legend has it that it was common for Native Americans to get caught in low-level fogs while fishing on Lake Michigan. They would yell "Kee-waun-ee! Kee-waun-ee!" to those on shore. By listening to the response they would steer their canoes safely back to land through the mists.

Another local legend says that in the 1830s an unknown explorer found what he thought was gold in the Kewaunee River. Expectations were high, but no more gold was found. Before the rush could really get underway, it fizzled.

Lumber eventually proved more valuable than local gold, and in the late 1890s the Kewaunee port became a major shipping facility for rail cars moving across the lake to the markets in the East. Car ferries sailed out of here for almost a century, carrying as many as 300 rail cars per day at their peak.

The *Kewaunee County Jail Museum*, (920) 388-4410, on the courthouse square, retains the original 1876 cell blocks, a life-size carving of Father Marquette, who landed in Kewaunee in 1647, and local historical artifacts. Stop at the *Kewaunee Chamber of Commerce*, (920) 388-4822, for a free guide to a walking tour of Kewaunee's Victorian neighborhood, the *Marquette District*. The tallest grandfather's clock in the world is said to be the one at Svoboda Industries' *Top of the Hill Shop*, (920) 388-2691. The state-of-the-art *C. D. "Buzz" Besadny Fish Facility*, (920) 388-1025, about 3 miles west of town, is a great place to have a picnic, see migrating fish populations (in season), and find additional educational materials.

Leave Kewaunee on Highway 42 south. Just out of the city, turn onto Lakeshore Road, which then becomes Cemetery Road and rejoins 42. This drive meanders along the shore and then swings back west.

Follow 42 south (the Kewaunee Nuclear Plant is just east of here). Just past the junction

During World War II, Manitowoc's shipyards produced 23 submarines that helped the U.S. establish supremacy at sea. Photo by Gary Knowles.

with County BB, which divides Kewaunee and Manitowoc Counties, turn left (south) to follow Lakeshore Road.

Turn left (east) onto Nuclear Road. *The Point Beach Energy Information Center* at 6600 Nuclear Rd. offers interesting state-of-the-art, hands-on exhibits showcasing power generation and discussing nuclear power generation.

Continue east on Nuclear Road and go to Lakeshore Road. Turn right (south) on Lakeshore and go to County V. Turn left (east) on V and go to County O. Turn right (south) on O. You'll soon come to *Point Beach State Forest,* a long and narrow stretch of woods that covers 7 miles of Lake Michigan shorelines (with 6 miles of excellent beaches). The DNR says that occasionally, especially after storms churn up the water, people find pieces of 19th-century shipwrecks deposited on shore. In any case, the sandy shore is a fascinating place just to walk, look, and enjoy the great lake. There is also an *Interpretive Center,* (920) 794-7480, and indoor group camp in the park.

Follow O to 22nd Street in Two Rivers. Turn right on 22nd and go to Highway 42. Turn left (south) on 42 and get into the heart of Two Rivers. The West Twin (Neshoto) and the East Twin (Mishicot) Rivers give this charming community its name. In fact, the early Ojibwa named their settlement "Neshotah," which means "a junction of two rivers," since the Twins join together just before entering Lake Michigan.

As you enter Two Rivers you'll drive by *Neshotah Park,* which has a beautiful beach, two hiking trails, and year-round educational activities; call the *Woodland Dunes Nature Center,* (920) 793-4007, in the park for more information. The rivers and lake are still the pride of the community. *Two Rivers Fishing Charters,* (800) 533-3382, bring visitors from throughout the Midwest to catch the big ones. Even if you're not fishing, it can be fun to watch the bustle of activity at various marinas, including *Twin Cities,* (920) 793-2715, and *Seagull,* (920) 793-3321. Clean and wide sand beaches are favorites for swimming, wind surfing, beach-combing, and sunbathing.

The city's maritime history, including shipwreck items, is preserved at the *Rogers Street Fishing Village and Coast Guard Museum,* (920) 793-5905, while the *Two Rivers History Museum,* (920) 793-1103, has ethnic, social, civic, and religious items on display.

In 1881 Ed Berners created the first ice cream sundaes and sold them, only on Sunday, of course. Today you can choose from 18 different sundaes on any day at the *Historic Washington House,* (888) 857-3529. This former hotel serves as a museum with historic photos, local brewery memorabilia, and area artifacts. Two Rivers is also the home of the new *Hamilton Wood Type and Printing Museum,* (800) 228-6416 or (920) 794-6272. Wood type was manufactured from 1880 into the 1980s—and is now made as a fund-raising project. This unique museum is another example of Wisconsin's outstanding specialty museums.

Leave Two Rivers and head south on 42 into Manitowoc. Stay on 42 as it swings west, away from the lake, and go to County Q (18th Street). From here you can explore Manitowoc's attractions, many of them reflecting the city's rich maritime heritage. Manitowoc was once a center of cross-lake commerce and played a crucial role in World War II submarine building. Today, with the *Burger Boat Company,* (920) 684-1600, building "yachts for kings" and the city serving as the western port of entry for the Lake Michigan car ferry, Manitowoc continues to reign as "Wisconsin's Maritime Capitol."

This port has long been recognized for its

beauty and the people for their friendly manner, so it's no surprise that the Native Americans who settled here called it "Munedoo-owk," which translates as "home of the good spirit." French trappers arrived here in about 1673, and in 1795 the Northwest Fur Company established a trading post. The tide of immigration brought Bohemians, French, Germans, Irish, Norwegians, and Poles to homestead near the lake.

The *Visitor and Convention Bureau,* (800) 627-4896, offers guests a free Anchor Pass Card, good for discounts on admissions, meals, lodging, merchandise, and even a free cup of coffee. The center, at the intersection of Highway 151 and I-43 (exit 149), will give you the pass and help you plan to see the area's many attractions. Here are some of your options.

Explore over a century of Great Lakes lore at the *Wisconsin Maritime Museum,* (920) 684-0218), the largest maritime museum on the Great Lakes. Stroll through a shipping port, marvel at model ships, and then climb aboard the WWII submarine USS *Cobia.*

Nearby is the *Manitowoc Marina,* (920) 682-5117, a state-of-the art, full-service, 250-slip marina and yacht club. The *Badger,* the workhorse of the *Lake Michigan Carferry,* (888) 947-3377, can hold 180 vehicles and 620 passengers. It is the last great car ferry on the Great Lakes and from mid-May to the end of October offers daily crossings (about four hours) to and from Ludington, Michigan. The *Riverwalk* is a paved walkway that leads to the *Manitowoc Breakwater Lighthouse.*

Just west of Manitowoc you'll find *Pinecrest Historical Village,* (920) 684-5110, with 25 authentic historic buildings from the 1850s to the 1900s. Visit the new *Manitowoc County Heritage Center,* (920) 684-4445, 1901 Michigan Ave., in a renovated building that once was home to a county teachers college. It has exhibits on local history and a research library.

Manitowoc's downtown is on the National Register of Historic Districts and is a shopper's paradise. Treat your sweet tooth with a visit to *Beerntsen's Confectionary,* (920) 684-9616. Here you can sit in antique black-walnut soda-shop booths and indulge your need for exquisite ice cream or homemade chocolate treats. Antique and gift shops abound, and one, *Timeless Treasures,* (920) 682-6566, was tapped by Hollywood to provide vintage clothing used in the making of the movie *Titanic.* Down the street is *Cooks' Corner Factory Outlet,* (920) 684-5521, the largest kitchen supply and gadget store in the nation. The *Capitol Civic Centre,* (920) 683-2184, a restored vintage vaudeville house, offers entertainment year-round.

The *Rahr-West Art Museum,* (920) 683-4501, housed in an exquisite 1890s Victorian mansion, features major American art, including work by Wisconsin's own Georgia O'Keefe, 19th-century furnishings—and a replica of a piece of Sputnik,

the first satellite to orbit the earth. This one-of-a-kind display is here because when Sputnik dropped out of orbit and split into pieces, a smoldering hunk of it landed in the street in front of the museum. The original was sent back to its Russian home and a copy given to the museum.

Of interest to car lovers is *Zunker's Antique Car Museum,* (920) 684-4005, with 40 antique autos and related auto memorabilia on display.

Since 1934 garden lovers have raved about the six acres of magnificent floral exhibits at *West of the Lake Gardens,* (920) 684-6110, along the Lake Michigan shore.

Manitowoc is also the home of *Lincoln Park Zoo,* (920) 683-4685, a free, newly redesigned natural zoo featuring animals of the North Woods in a wooded park setting.

Manitowoc offers some very special tours. Few can resist the aroma of fresh baked bread and the taste tests at *Natural Ovens,* (800) 558-3535, a 32,000-square-foot bakery with a custom-built brick hearth oven that produces 20,000 loaves daily—all without preservatives or sugars

Next door is the free *Farm & Food Museum,* where you can get up-close and personal with llamas, goats, Belgian horses, lambs, and other animals and see antique tractors and a wheat-harvesting museum.

Golfers often use Manitowoc as a base to play an incredible variety of courses (see article). For horse lovers there's riding on 200 acres of trails at the *Hillcrest Dude Ranch,* (920) 682-0158.

A short drive to the north will bring you to *Mishicot Village,* (920) 755-2291, with the Norman Rockwell Centre, Frances Hook Museum, and shops in its historic old school.

At the junction of 42 and County Q, take Q north past the Manitowoc Airport, following the West Twin River past Kingsbridge to Larabee and the junction with Highway 147.

Turn left (west) on 147 to the junction with County R. Turn right (north) on R. This is a scenic sprint across the gently rolling hills of the Devil's River Valley, past the towns of Denmark and Langes Corners.

Continue on R to Highway 29 just outside Green Bay.

Great Lakeshore Golf

Not all your great drives in this area will be in your car. Golfers know that this diverse area is also famous for its golf courses. Many people use Manitowoc as a base for golf expeditions. Check with hotels for package specials. Outstanding area courses include: *Alaskan,* Kewaunee, (920) 388-3940; *Autumn Ridge,* Valders, (920) 758-3333; *Badger Creek,* New Holstein, (920) 898-5760; *Idlewild,* Sturgeon Bay, (920) 743-3334; *Fox Hills,* Mishicot, (800) 552-1836; *Meadow Links,* Manitowoc, (920) 682-6842; *Brown County,* Oneida, (920) 497-1731; *Wander Springs,* Greenleaf, (920) 864-4653; and just to the south, the famous Pete Dye-designed Kohler courses *Whistling Straits* (named host course for the 2004 PGA Championship), *Irish,* and *Blackwolf Run,* (800) 618-5535. For a free guide to more than 400 Wisconsin golf courses call the Wisconsin Department of Tourism at (800) 432-8747.

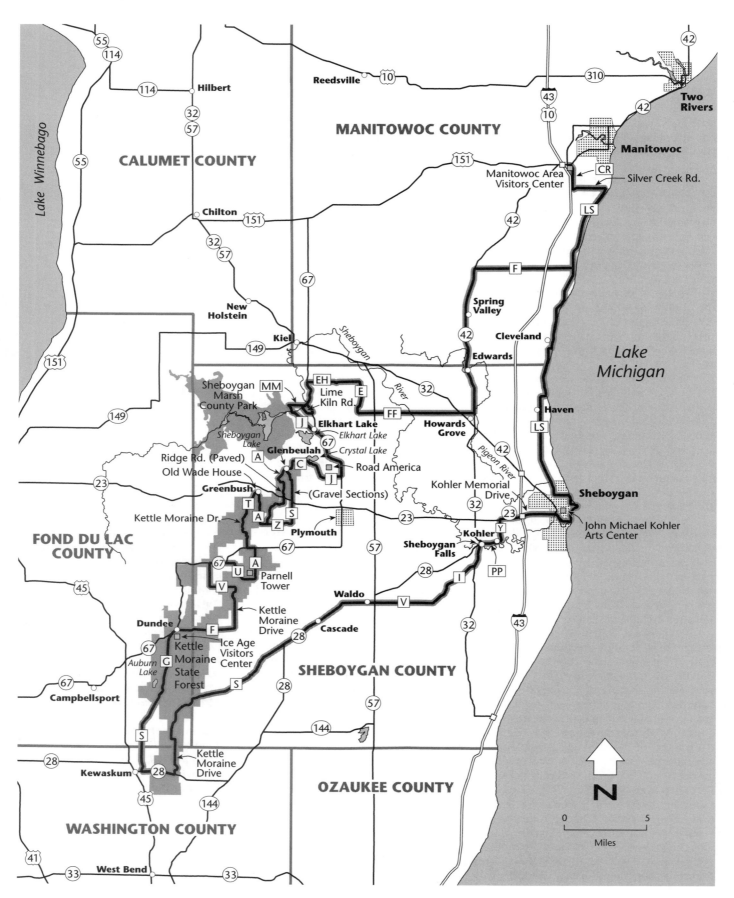

Tour 6

Tour 6
Kettles, Links, and Waves

Manitowoc—Haven—Sheboygan—Kohler—Sheboygan Falls—Waldo—Cascade—Kewaskum—
Dundee—Greenbush—Glenbulah—Elkhart Lake—Howards Grove—Edwards—Spring Valley—
Manitowoc

Distance: 134 miles

If you could put two of America's finest golf courses, its greatest international road-racing circuit, the sputnik landing site, one of the world's most famous glacial landform areas, a killer submarine, and a top-rated resort on one tour—and lace it together with miles of outstanding scenic driving roads, you'd be on this tour.

Toss in classic resort communities, a stagecoach inn, a few double brats, and friendly people just for good measure. It makes for tough choices all along the route: do I stop and enjoy a museum or just cruise and enjoy the road? Should I eat a brat with "the works" or go for the seven-course gourmet meal? If I stop to see sputnik in Manitowoc, will I have time for the "Great Wall of China" at Kohler? Decisions, decisions.

The best part is that no matter which you choose, you're in for some fine touring.

Start in the *Manitowoc Area Visitors Center*, (800) 627-4896, located just east of I-43 at Exit 149 and just south of Highway 151. Stop in and collect area brochures, maps, and information. Ask for an Anchor Pass savings card to save on Manitowoc area attractions and accommodations. (For a full list of Manitowoc attractions see Tour 5.)

From the visitors center turn right on County CR. The *Natural Ovens* bakery, (800) 558-3535, offers free tours and delicious samples. Next door, the *Farm & Food Museum* has lots of animals to see, some to pet, and antique farm equipment.

Follow CR to the junction with Silver Creek Road. Turn left (east) on Silver Creek Road and cross Silver Creek to the junction with County LS. Turn right (south) on LS. This is a delightful winding route that parallels the shore of Lake Michigan, crosses Calvin Creek, Pine Creek, Point Creek, Fischer Creek, and Centerville Creek before passing through the community of Cleveland, crossing Meeme Creek, hugging the shore, and dodging west across Sevenmile Creek.

At the junction with County FF, turn left (east) to Haven. There, you'll find *Whistling Straits*, (800) 618-5535, N8501 County LS, one of the finest golf courses in the world. It is reminiscent of courses in the birthplace of the game of golf, the British Isles. It was commissioned by area industrialist and golf lover Herb Kohler and designed by noted architect Pete Dye. Set in the sand dunes along 2 miles of Lake Michigan shore, the Straits course changes elevation from lake level to 80-foot bluffs and berms. True to the best tradition of golf, it's a walking course with caddies required. Dye said, "I should say this with some degree of modesty. But in my lifetime I've never seen anything like this. Anyplace. Period."

Whistling Straits, despite its young age, is ranked as one of the top golf courses in the U.S. and will host the PGA championship in 2004. Photo courtesy of the Kohler Company.

In keeping with traditional golf, caddies (look for their white suits) carry players' bags on this walking course, and no golf carts are used. Even non-golfers will enjoy a visit to the massive stone clubhouse with exposed hewn-timber cathedral ceilings. A gourmet restaurant is open to the public, as is the pro shop and upper-level Irish pub. Be sure to wander out to the front of the clubhouse to get a look at the spectacular course.

In 2004 Whistling Straits hosts the PGA Championship Tournament, one of the most prestigious of all golf events.

In the summer of 2000 the latest and perhaps final Dye course at Kohler was unveiled. Named, appropriately enough, Irish, the new layout is built across the berms from the Straits course. It features four creeks and promises lots of the drama Dye and Kohler have served up so well in their other courses. Call (800) 618-5535 for more information about both Whistling Straits courses or the two other Dye-Kohler courses at Blackwolf Run in Kohler (also see p.32).

Return to County LS, turn left (south), and go about 5 miles into Sheboygan where LS becomes 15th Street. Sheboygan is known worldwide as the "Bratwurst Capital of the World" (see article), and more recently (1997) *Reader's Digest* named it is the "Number One City in America to Raise a Family." This community has been popular for a long time. It traces its heritage back to the Chippewa and Lakota, who followed earlier Paleo-Indians to the beautiful and abundant shores of Lake Michigan. The very name "Sheboygan" is said to be a Native American word relating to water. Jean Nicolet explored here in 1635, Joliet and Marquette in 1643, and a trading post was built on the shore by 1795. It was officially "settled" in 1814 when William Farnsworth, a pioneer, married Queen Marinette of the Menominee nation and built a successful trading business. By 1842 there were 200 people in Sheboygan County, but by 1846 immigration had swelled the number to 4,637 and to 8,836 by 1850. Most immigrants came from Germany, the Netherlands, and Ireland, and industry and agriculture flourished as a result. The residents of Sheboygan County are proud of their heritage, and you'll find it well preserved in museums, festivals, and a naturally warm welcome wherever you visit here.

Follow 15th Street to North Avenue. Turn left (east) onto North Avenue and follow it until it ends. Turn right on North Third Street and take it to Park Street. Turn left on Park and follow it to Lincoln Avenue where you'll turn left and follow Broughton Drive. You'll pass the Sheboygan Lighthouse, Northside Beach at Ontario Ave., the wreck of the *Lottie Cooper,* and the *Harbor Center Marina,* (920) 455-6665, 821 Broughton Dr. To get the most from the Sheboygan lakefront, take a stroll on the *Lakefront Promenade,* (920) 457-9495), which starts out at the marina. Enjoy the soothing rhythm of the waves on a paved all-purpose trail all the way to the North Point Overlook near Lincoln Ave.

The *Lottie Cooper,* (920) 458-2974, is a schooner that capsized and sunk in gale force winds in 1894 just off the Sheboygan Harbor. Her remains were discovered during surveying work on the harbor floor prior to construction of the marina. They were recovered, re-assembled, and are now displayed at Deland Park at Wisconsin Ave. and Broughton Dr.

A good way to see the area is on the *Harbor Centre Trolley,* (920) 459-3281, the Midwest's only battery-operated trolley car reproduction. It operates from late May through early September.

The *Riverfront Boardwalk,* (920) 457-9495, runs from the *Rotary Riverview Park* harbor overlook to the Eighth St. Bridge and is Sheboygan's answer to Fisherman's Wharf. It passes a row of weathered shanties originally built for use by commercial fishermen. Some maintain that purpose, but others have become restaurants, art galleries, and retail shops.

"A national treasure" is the phrase used by a Wisconsin Arts Board evaluation panel in its review of the *John Michael Kohler Arts Center,* (920) 458-6144, 608 New York Ave. It is one of the finest contemporary art centers in the Midwest. Named after the founder of the Kohler Company and located in his 1882 home, the center focuses on temporary exhibitions of contemporary work.

The *Sheboygan County Museum,* (920) 458-1103, 3110 Erie Ave., is housed in the 1850s home of Judge Taylor. It features several interesting rooms, each devoted to a theme. Also on the grounds is the *Weinhold Family Homestead.* Built in 1864 and furnished with pioneer items, it is one of the last remaining log cabins in the county. Recently added is an 1867 cheese factory.

Above & Beyond Children's Museum, (920) 458-4263, 902 N. Eighth St., has 12 hands-on interactive exhibits for children of all ages.

Just south of Sheboygan you'll find beautiful sand dunes, a fascinating landscape, and abundant wildlife at *Kohler-Andrae State Park,* (920) 451-4080, 1520 Old Park Rd. A state park sticker is required.

Indian Mound City Park, (920) 459-3444, 5000 S. Ninth St., an effigy burial grounds, has a self-walking tour and exhibits of unique mounds built by nomadic Native Americans between 500 and 1000 A.D. A boardwalk nature trail showcases wetlands and northern hardwood foliage.

Follow Broughton Drive as it swings west and becomes Pennsylvania Avenue. Continue to North Eighth Street, turn right and go to Erie Avenue (Highway 23). Turn left (west) on 23, where it becomes Kohler Memorial Drive, passing under I-43. Go to the County Y exit, follow it south, and proceed into the village of Kohler. The Kohler Company, established in 1873, and the village of Kohler, born in 1912, became one of the nation's earliest planned com-

Brats or Bratwurst

Brats (for the benefit of those of you who haven't spent more than five minutes in these parts) are pork sausages made according to Old World recipes and are a staple of life in Sheboygan County. Sheboygan calls itself the Bratwurst Capital of the World and there apparently is no dispute about that.

The spicy, flavorful sausages are best prepared over a charcoal fire and are turned frequently for some 20-25 minutes to prevent the hot fat from bursting out of the casing. A popular and delicious cooking variation calls for presoaking and par-boiling them in beer, mustard, and onions before grilling *(frying,* in Sheboyganese) and then returning them to the warm beer mixture after they've "fried." Purists turn up their nose at this method; however, it is preferred by many.

There is near-universal agreement that brats should be eaten two at a time (a "double") on a hard roll with lots of raw onions and brown (never yellow!) mustard. However, many like catsup, sauerkraut, tomato, pickles, and (recently) jalapeno peppers on them. Try them as you like, chances are you'll become a brat fan. As you travel through the small towns, look for little meat markets (butcher shops) where time-honored local recipes are a specialty.

The Walderhaus is reminiscent of the Kohler family's ancestral home in Bavaria. Photo by Gary Knowles.

munities—symbolized by a garden at the factory gate—and one of a very few to survive successfully into the 21st century. The village, with about 2,200 residents, has grown into the Midwest's premier resort destination. The whole Kohler recreational complex has two hotels, four 18-hole golf courses, 10 restaurants and cafes, a health and racquet facility with salon and day spa, a wilderness preserve, and shopping opportunities galore. A popular misconception has it that you must work at Kohler to own a home here. Not true. In fact, the majority of residents in the village are not Kohler Company employees. The restaurants, golf courses, salon, day spa, and Kohler Design Center are open to the public and enjoyed by the local community as well as visitors. The Sports Core health and racquet club and River Wildlife wilderness preserve and lodge are the only private facilities. However, both are available for use by American Club guests.

The American Club, (920) 457-8000, on Highland Dr., is the Midwest's only AAA-rated Five Diamond resort hotel. It offers a level of service and luxury that place it among the best in the world. The 236-room hotel is a stately red brick structure that was built in 1918 to house the many immigrants, "single men of modest means," who came to work at the Kohler Company. It was a place that enriched their lives and celebrated the "American spirit." In 1978, the building was placed on the National Register of Historic Places. Carefully refurbished and reopened in 1981 as a luxurious resort hotel, it continues to honor its heritage today, welcoming guests with an Old World elegance and style. Each room features some of the Kohler Company's top quality bath furnishings and some upper-level suites have bath "environments" that equal and surpass the comfort of the finest spas.

This community of 2,200 people has restaurants that are all very good, some extraordinary. Favorites? For northern Italian try *Cucina,* (920) 452-3888, in the Shops at Woodlake. *The Blackwolf*

Run Clubhouse Restaurant, (920) 457-4446, has excellent steak, fowl, and seafood in a beautiful mountain log clubhouse. *River Wildlife* offers unforgettable hearty hunters' fare, while the *Immigrant Room,* (800) 344-2838, is a top-rated gourmet spot.

Blackwolf Run, (800) 618-5535, 1111 W. Riverside Dr., is a set of two 18-hole Scottish-style golf courses conceived and designed by Pete Dye and Herbert Kohler and rated among the finest in the world (see accompanying article).

The *Kohler Design Center,* (920) 457-3699, on Highland Dr., presents one of Wisconsin's most unusual and interesting exhibits. The world of gracious living is on display here in the premiere showroom for the nation's leading plumbing products manufacturer. Walk through some two dozen designer baths, along with product displays for Baker and McGuire furniture and Ann Sacks Tile & Stone in a dramatic 36,000-square-foot, three-level space. Visit the ceramic art gallery showing the company's long-term commitment to the arts and historic displays related to Kohler Village and the Kohler Company.

Kohler Company Factory Tours, (920) 457-3699, are some of the most interesting you'll find anywhere. They're open to visitors 14 and older Monday through Friday (except holidays) at 8:30 a.m. Reservations are required 24 hours

Wisconsin Ethnic Settlement Trail (W.E.S.T.)

The Statue of Liberty may stand in New York, but no state in the Union has opened its arms and heart to immigrants with more pride than Wisconsin. When the Ho-Chunk people met the first European, Jean Nicolet, in 1634, they threw a huge feast and set a standard that lives on to this day. Within two years of becoming a state, in 1850, about one out of three people in Wisconsin were immigrants.

The Wisconsin Ethnic Settlement Trail (W.E.S.T.) is an official state heritage project designed to preserve and interpret the settlement and living legacy of Wisconsin's immigrants. It includes an area from Marinette and Gills Rock in the north to Kenosha in the south and then swings inland some 40 miles to Fond du Lac, Appleton, and Green Bay. As you travel in these areas you'll enjoy the foods, culture, celebrations, and architecture that early settlers brought with them from Iceland, Belgium, Germany, Poland, Ireland, Africa, Sweden, Luxembourg, England, France, Italy, Greece, Mexico, Wales, Slovakia, Norway, and dozens of other countries. There are many projects, memorials, museums, and events that make up the W.E.S.T. effort.

For a helpful, free statewide *Heritage Guide* call the Wisconsin Department of Tourism at (800) 432-8747. To obtain a free *Visitor's Guide to Wisconsin's Ethnic Settlement Trail (W.E.S.T.),* call (414) 961-2110, or write Wisconsin's Ethnic Settlement Trail, 5900 N. Port Washington Rd., Suite 146, Milwaukee, 53217.

Pete Dye and Herbert V. Kohler Jr.

Except for the last glacier, nothing has had anywhere near as big an impact on Wisconsin golf as the combination of Herbert V. Kohler Jr. and Pete Dye. That mile-high sheet of ice scratched and gouged its way across Wisconsin, leaving great lakes, sandy beaches, rivers, and a verdant countryside behind. Ten thousand years later, Herb Kohler took a look at his internationally famous company and the planned community that shares his name. He decided that it needed something more—something like a world-class resort and golf course. Schooled in dramatic arts, Kohler knew instinctively that a great golf course is really good theater played out over a spectacular landscape. He chose Pete Dye, a maestro who had built a reputation as a "total immersion, hands-on style designer" noted for creativity, innovation, and a natural talent for building golf courses loaded with "the wow factor." In 1985 construction began; the 18-hole course opened in June of 1988 and was named "Best New Public Course in the USA in 1988" by *Golf Digest Magazine*.

Not content, Kohler and Dye pushed ahead, adding nine more holes in 1989 and another nine in 1990. At that time the entire 36 holes were reorganized into the River Course and the Meadow Valleys course. "The 200-acre site selected for the course is one of the finest natural settings for golf I have ever seen," Dye said. To Kohler, respect for the land was important; he said that Dye designed "Blackwolf Run to suit the natural environment instead of changing the land to accommodate the course."

No other course in Wisconsin offers such an extraordinary combination of spectacular beauty and ungodly trouble. Just the way golfers like it! Laid out across the glacial terrain of the Sheboygan River and meticulously tended, the work is a "dye-abolical" golf masterpiece. Every hole requires careful thought and each shot requires proper execution. Stray off the lush fairway carpet and you'll chop, punch, and wail your way through a living museum of leafy, viny, spiny plants and shrubs that Darwin himself would avoid. Not to mention the yawning bunkers, Sahara-sized sand traps, and greens with more undulations than Little Egypt.

By 1993, in its first year of eligibility, the River Course had been named to the *Golf Digest* list of "America's 100 Greatest Golf Courses." In 1996 *Condé Nast Traveler* ranked it among the top four golf resorts in the world. In 1995, 1996, and 1997 the course hosted the Andersen Consulting World Championship of Golf, bringing in players such as Paul Azinger, Corey Pavin, Ernie Els, Greg Norman, David Frost, and Nick Price for match play. In 1998 the most exciting and well-attended (124,500 spectators) U.S. Women's Open Championship in history built a new golf legend here. Se Ri Pak (a professional) and Jenny Chuasiriporn (an amateur) played a total of 92 holes of championship golf (another record) before Pak finally claimed the title of 53rd U.S. Women's Open Champion.

And not to be forgotten are the Whistling Straits and Irish courses mentioned earlier. These are two of the world's most daring and innovative golf courses created in the last 20 years.

It will be a long time, maybe the next ice age, before anything or anyone comes close to matching the positive mark Pete Dye and Herb Kohler have carved into the Wisconsin golf landscape.

in advance. Wear comfortable shoes for the two-and-one-half-hour tour.

Walderhaus, 1100 W. Riverside Dr., a replica of the Kohler ancestral home, means "house in the woods" and reflects the spirit and architecture of the Bregenzerwald region of Austria. It was designed by the Austrian sculptor and architect Kaspar Albrecht. The building features intricate carvings, woodcuts, reliefs, iron and pewter work all executed by Albrecht. Interesting furnishings include glass globes with candles, a tile stove, and wrought iron radiator covers.

Artspace: A Gallery of the John Michael Kohler Arts Center, (920) 452-8602, located in the Shops at Woodlake, presents a wide variety of contemporary art, including paintings, prints, photographs, sculpture, and craft-related forms by contemporary American artists. Artspace also includes a sales gallery devoted to the finest in contemporary American crafts, porcelain, earthenware, jewelry, glass, painted silk, wood, and furniture created by more than 200 artists.

Follow County Y (Highland Avenue) south to County PP. Turn right (west) and drive into Sheboygan Falls. In the middle of town, turn left (south) on Highway 32. Continue about 1 mile to the intersection with County I. Turn right (southwest) on I and continue to County V. Turn right (west) on V and cross Highway 57 as you go to Waldo, where V joins Highway 28. Follow 28 west and south to Cascade. Along the way, you'll cross a gently rolling, glacial landscape dotted with woodlots and dairy farms. Cascade was born to harness waterpower off the north fork of the Milwaukee River. Legend has it that it was rather rowdy in these parts back then, so they called it "Nineveh" after the infamous biblical city. Sometime later the town fathers decided to upgrade their image and changed the name to "Cascade."

Follow 28 southwest and just past Chambers Creek. At the junction with County S follow S southwest as 28 curves to the south. County S is a pleasant run through some wetlands, woodlots, and glaciated hills. You will pass Beechwood Lake and then cross into the Kettle Moraine State Forest.

Stay on S into Fond du Lac County, through New Fane, to the junction with Kettle Moraine Drive. Turn left (east) on Kettle Moraine Drive and follow it south to Highway 28. Turn right (west) on 28 and continue into Kewaskum. *Kewaskum* is a Potawatomi word that means "to return along the same track." Most believe this refers to the sharp turn the river makes here. The village has some interesting antique and craft shops.

When 28 rejoins County S, turn right (north) on S, which soon becomes County G. This is an exhilarating drive through some of the finest glacial hills and dales in the world. This twisting, rolling terrain runs through the 27,500-acre *Kettle Moraine State Forest,* (262) 626-2116, near Buttermilk Lake, Auburn Lake, and across the Zillmer Trail, an 11-mile trek through glacial wilderness.

At the junction with Highway 67, turn right. *The Henry S. Ruess Ice Age Visitor's Center,* (920) 533-8322, has fascinating geo-historical interpretations of the surrounding glaciated landscape with explanations of the features you'll see throughout the Kettle Moraine area. Stop and learn about eskers, kames, drumlins, kettles, and moraines. Try to find out what an "errant" is. Now we'll do a little glacial twist and shout, so enjoy the ride.

Follow 67 to Dundee and the junction with County F. Turn right (east) on F and drive about 3 miles to the junction with Kettle Moraine Scenic Drive (County V). Turn left (north) on V and follow it to the junction with Highway 67. The road twists around this glaciated area and over the Parnell Esker.

Turn right on 67 and go to the junction with County U. Turn right (south) on U and follow it as it turns east and joins with County A. As U turns eastward, stay on A to the junction with Highway 67. (If you're feeling particularly energetic, stop where A and U diverge, and climb the Parnell Observation Tower!)

Turn left (west) on 67 and then turn right (north) back onto the Kettle Moraine Scenic Drive, where after 2.5 miles you'll join County T, which takes you into Greenbush. Along the way, you'll pass the Greenbush Kettle and enjoy the exhilaratingly twisty drive. Greenbush, a Yankee town, was built in the 1850s as a stagecoach stop on the road from Fond du Lac to Sheboygan. The *Wade House,* (920) 526-3271, a state historic site, preserves that era and, along with the 100-vehicle *Wesley Jung Carriage Museum,* offers a great glimpse of life in frontier days. Local legend has it that Abe Lincoln once stopped here, but there seems to be no proof.

In Greenbush, turn right on Old Plank Road and drive to the junction with County A. Turn right (south) on A and go to the junction with County Z. Turn left (east) on Z, *where you'll have to make a choice—gravel or pavement.*

The Gravel Option
Continue on Z for about 2 miles to the junc-

About 10,000 years ago, the Wisconsin glacier retreated, creating kettles, moraines, and eskers and leaving huge boulders in its wake. Photo by Gary Knowles.

tion with County S. Turn left (north) on S; as you cross Highway 23 you'll be on Rustic Road 63, which leads into Glenbeulah. Here you'll see one of the finest Kettle Moraine Forest switchback roads, with about a mile and a half of gravel. After a half mile or so of roller-coaster swells, you'll swing down though a series of S curves that follow the tops of glacial hills and curve around the sides of beautiful kettles into the River Heights section of Glenbeulah (where your author lived his first 18 years). You'll cross the Mullett River and enter the village's quiet downtown.

The Pavement Option
If you opt for the safer (but tamer) ride, turn left (north) from County Z onto Ridge Road and follow it across Highway 23 about 4.5 miles to the junction with County A. Turn right on A and head into Glenbeulah. The village was named Glenbeulah (beautiful land) after the mother of Edward Appleton, who platted the community in 1856. A hundred years later it was regarded as having "the nicest name of any small town in Wisconsin." A quiet millpond stands where the old mill and factory once turned out brooms.

Follow A east and then north out of Glenbeulah about 1 mile to the junction with County C. Turn right (east) on C and follow it to the junction with County J. Stay on C and J to the point where J turns left (east) and follow it up the hill to Highway 67. Along the way, you'll pass the *Crystal Lake Golf Course,* (920) 892-4834, wind around Crystal Lake, and skirt the south edge of *Road America* auto racetrack, (800) 365-7223, (see accompanying article).

Turn left (north) on 67 and continue past the main entrance to Road America into the town of Elkhart Lake (see article). At the stop sign, turn left (west) on Rhine Street and, at the town square, bear right (northwest) on County J.

Continue northwest on J to *Sheboygan Marsh County Park*. This is a 13,000-acre wildlife area with excellent fishing, hunting, camping, and a bar/restaurant, (920) 876-2535. (If you go on J for about 3 miles from Elkhart Lake, then turn left on Sexton Rd., then onto Holstein Rd., you can visit *Henschel's Museum of Indian History*, (920) 876-3193, a wonderful private museum devoted to preserving Native American artifacts found on the site—some of which date to 8,000 B.C.).

About 1 mile past the park, turn right on County MM and drive about 0.5 mile to Lime Kiln Road. Turn right on Lime Kiln and follow it as it swings east to Highway 67. Turn left (north) on 67, a saucy 2 miles of rock n' roll highway to County EH.

Turn right and follow EH about 3 miles to County E. Turn right on E and head south to the junction with County FF. Turn left (east) on FF and go to Highway 42 at Howards Grove. Along the way, you'll cross Highway 57, pass near the Schuet Creek State Fish Hatchery area, cross the Sheboygan River, Fisher Creek, and Highway 32.

Turn left (north) onto 42 and follow it across Pigeon River, past Edwards into Manitowoc County, through Spring Valley, to the junction with Highway F. Turn right (east) on F and follow it about 5.25 miles to County LS. Turn left (north) on LS, taking it back along the Lake Michigan shore about 5 miles to Silver Creek Road. Turn left on Silver Creek Road to County CR.

Turn right (north) on CR and follow it back to the Manitowoc Area Visitors Center. Stop in and tell the friendly greeters what you saw.

Elkhart Lake, Road America, and Auto Racing

In the mid 1940s, following the return of World War II soldiers from Europe, and amid the growing prosperity of the United States, the sport of auto racing began to catch the interest of the American public. Along with the New York resort community of Watkin's Glen, Wisconsin's Elkhart Lake became a center of sports car racing activity. In 1950, '51, and '52, street races running through the town of Elkhart Lake, around the resorts, and through the surrounding countryside captured the imagination of car enthusiasts, sports writers, and local businesspeople. A group of local investors formed Road America Corporation to build a race track on terrain that, according to Everett Nametz, chamber of commerce leader, business owner, and visionary who served as secretary for the company, "was so different from all other racing circuits that after the course was built it would continue to hold the esteem of racing fans and respect of competition drivers down through the years." Nametz championed the development of road racing in Elkhart Lake and with the opening of the 44-mile, 14-corner track in 1955 wrote: "Road America is the first major league Road Racing plant in good old USA, built completely on privately owned land, completely Cyclone fenced, and built with one purpose in mind—designed, engineered and built to be the finest and safest Road Racing Circuit in all the world."

In the near half-century since then, that dream has become reality. Some of the greatest drivers in auto racing history have competed here, including Bruce McLaren, Denny Hulme, A.J.Foyt, Al Unser Jr., Mario Andretti, Emerson Fittipaldi, Christian Fittipaldi, Swede Savage, Danny Sullivan, Phil Hill, Sam Posey, David Hobbs, and a virtual *Who's Who* list of champions. They rate this track as one of the most challenging and exciting racing venues in the world, (800)-365-RACE.

The track also is used heavily in the non-snow season from about April to November for a variety of driver's school events, club outings, commercial shooting, tire testing, auto introductions, and other testing. The race season now includes major motorcycle events such as the AMA Super Cycle Classic, traditional amateur sports car racing, vintage auto races, open wheel auto racing, and the CART–Indy-style professional racing series.

In Elkhart Lake stop at the *Village Green*, (920) 876-3288, to hear excellent live blues. You'll find traditional racing ambiance at the popular crew hang-out, *Siebken's Tavern*, (920) 876-2600. The walls are filled with team decals, logos, memorabilia, and Germanic wisdom while the bar is bustling with racing team support staff, media, company reps, photographers, sponsors, resorters (also the name of high school team), a few drivers without rides, drivers with broken cars or those who've finished racing, hangers-on, and various "volunteers." Few people know that an even more famous, tiny, and cozy racing bar frequented by big name drivers and other celebrities like Paul Newman (who, with wife Joanne Woodward and Robert Wagner, shot the racing movie *Winning* in the Elkhart Lake area) is tucked behind Siebken's main dining room. Stop at the reception desk and ask for it. They'll show you.

In summer, during the June sprints and vintage races, the streets of the village become a showcase displaying sports, exotic, and classic cars. People stroll the streets sipping cocktails and rub shoulders with drivers and crew. Lake St. past Siebken's was the first short straight of the old street course. As you walk among the sleek new machines and classics, you can feel some of the same excitement of 50 years ago rise like magic from the concrete. They haven't added the street to the National Register of Historic Places yet, but they should.

Tour 7
Run Through the Garden of Eden

La Crosse—La Crescent (Minn.)—Winona (Minn.)—Arcadia—Ettrick—Galesville—Mindoro—
West Salem—La Crosse

Distance: 127 miles

"There is no more beautiful country in the world than that which is to be seen in this vicinity," wrote artist George Catlin about the upper reaches of the Mississippi River. Towering bluffs rise some 600 feet over the forested river valley below. Closed-end valleys, called *coulees*, run through the hills, with rivers laced through them daring artists and photographers to capture even a bit of the enormous beauty they exude. Look in any direction and there's another incredible vista to take in.

Those who love performance cars, sports cars, grand-touring cars, roadsters, or any kind of motorcycle will think this is heaven. The roads here follow the contour of the

The view from Granddad Bluff is one of the finest on the Great River Road. Wisconsin Department of Tourism photo by GK.

earth, sweeping around hills, climbing steep grades, switching back along the sides of bluffs, running down to the valley, or hugging the upper bank of the river.

There are some parts of Wisconsin that are so visually stunning, spotted with interesting historic sites, and so exhilarating to drive that they keep us coming back again and again. This tour—and most others along the Great River Road—are like that.

Enjoy. Then come back for more.

Begin in La Crosse. Native Americans made this spectacular area their home for hundreds of years before Father Louis Hennepin arrived in 1680. The name was said to have come from French fur traders who saw the Ho-Chunk people playing a ball-and-stick game on the prairie. They thought it resembled a French lawn tennis game called *la crosse,* which got it's name because the long stick that was used looked like a bishop's crozier. By the 1820s steamboats were making their way upriver

to Fort Snelling, and in 1842 a permanent fur trading post was established by Nathan Myrick, who did a brisk business with the Ho-Chunk. By 1879 lumber and milling had become major industries and more than 1600 steamboats docked in the city—more than any other community north of St. Louis. As a frontier city and gateway to the west, La Crosse flourished. It's said that the local opera house often welcomed Buffalo Bill (William F. Cody), Sitting Bull, Annie Oakley, and Wild Bill Hickok to its stage. As the lumber business eventually diminished with the cutting of the northlands, the brewery business grew. With a fine supply of excellent water and lots of people passing through the city, six brewers thrived in La Crosse. The city today has a population of about 51,000 with some 150,000 people living in the metro area. Forty-two parks include many right on the water. The University of Wisconsin-La Crosse keeps this a lively, young city. The campus has served as the summer training grounds for the New Orleans

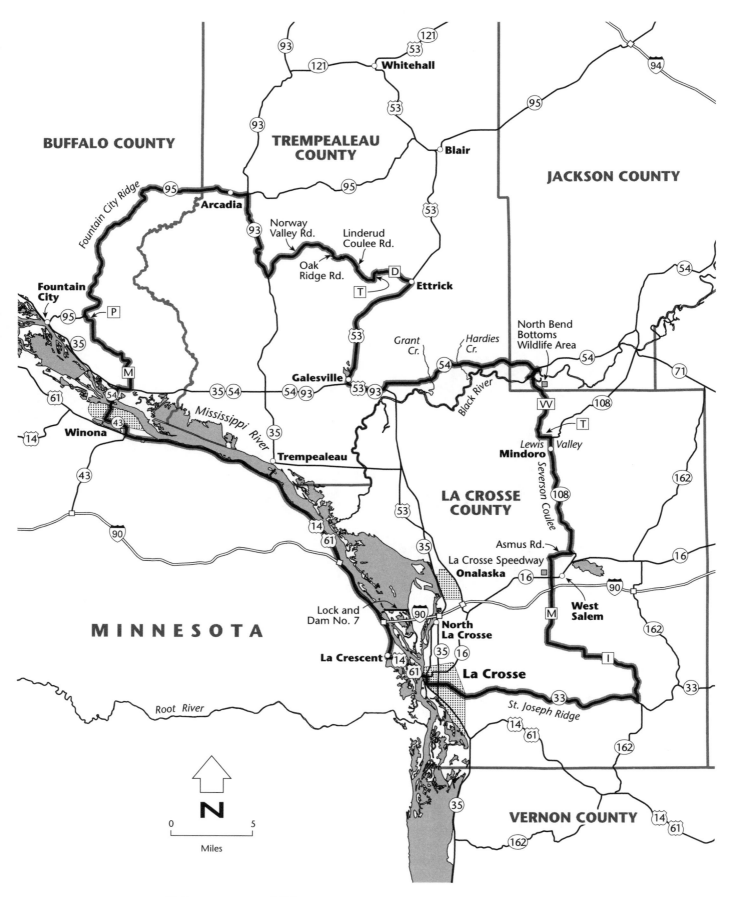

Tour 7

Saints of the National Football League. Here are some not-to-be-missed attractions in this great river town.

Granddad Bluff is perhaps the most famous La Crosse city park, watching over the city from 600 feet up a cliff. Follow Main St. east, which becomes Bliss Rd. as you ascend the bluff. At the top, turn right on Granddad Bluff Rd. This is one of the finest views of the Upper Mississippi Valley. From here you can see for about 25 miles into Minnesota, Iowa, and Wisconsin. Readers of *Wisconsin Trails* magazine voted this "the most scenic view in the state."

Riverside Park, (608) 782-1980), at the western end of State St. at the Mississippi River, is probably the second favorite park in La Crosse. It's an excellent place to sit and watch river traffic and other park goers (a delightful way to spend an afternoon!). It has the very helpful *La Crosse Convention and Visitor's Bureau Information Center,* (877) LOVE-LAC, 410 Veterans Memorial Dr., and the *Riverside Museum.* The exhibits chronicle the history of La Crosse, concentrating on the Mississippi River and its importance to the area. See interesting prehistoric artifacts, riverboat photos, large collections of birds and freshwater clams, a video of the area, and artifacts of the steamboat *The War Eagle* on display. Open daily 10–5, Memorial Day through Labor Day.

The riverboat *Julia Bell Swain*, (800) 815-1005, 200 Main St., boards at Riverside Park. This authentic steamboat is a rarity. It's one of just six left on the river and it maintains the legacy of those that traveled these waters for a century. Lunch and dinner cruises, as well as two-day all-inclusive trips, are available.

The Island Girl Cruiseliner, (608) 784-0556, 621 Park Plaza Dr., is another classy way to tour the Mississippi River. The two-hour cruises on this ship offer a climate-controlled area and an open deck to enjoy river life and spot eagles and barges passing by. The *La Crosse Queen* paddle wheeler, (608) 784-8523, is a replica of earlier paddle wheelers and offers daily cruises from the north end of Riverside Park.

The *Hixon House and La Crosse County Historical Society,* (608) 782-1980, 429 Seventh St., is one of the finest and most interesting house museums in Wisconsin. The home of a lumber baron in 1860s La Crosse, Hixon House has an Italianate design that reflects the Victorian style. Don't miss the Turkish Nook. Open Memorial Day through Labor Day, 1–5 p.m. daily.

The *Swarthout Museum* in the Public Library, 112 S. Ninth St. at Main St., features changing exhibits reflecting the rich history of the area from prehistoric to modern times, (608) 782-1980.

The *Museum of Modern Technology,* (608) 785-2340, offers a fresh look at modern science and its application in our lives. New displays are offered every month. Located on the corner of Sixth St. and King St. in historic downtown La Crosse, the museum is open year-round and features a children's room, library, and gift shop.

The *Mississippi Valley Archeology Center*, (608) 785-8463, on the University of Wisconsin-La Crosse Campus (1725 State St.) is a fascinating museum with changing exhibits about the history of the valley.

The *La Crosse Doll Museum*, (608) 785-0020, 1213 Caledonia St., houses over 6,500 dolls dating from the pre-Columbian era to the present. There is also an 82-foot-long Barbie activity case. Hours: 10–5 Monday–Saturday, 11–4:30 Sunday. Admission is $3.50 for adults, $1 for kids under 12. The *Children's Museum of La Crosse*, (608) 784-2652, 207 Fifth Ave. S., is a hands-on place where the young and the young-at-heart can explore, create, learn, and exercise their imaginations.

The *Riverside Amusement Park*, (608) 781-PLAY, just off I-90 at Exit 3, offers mini-golf, go-karts, and lots of family fun. Then there's *Myrick Park Zoo*, (608) 789-7190, near the UW-La Crosse campus, which has a children's zoo, playground, and kiddie rides. *Kid's Coulee* at the park has a big variety of playground structures that children will love.

The *Pumphouse Regional Center for the Arts*, (608) 785-1434, 119 King St., features work by local and touring artists and hosts performances.

If food is what you're looking for, you're in the right town. Phone ahead and Rudy will whip up some chili dogs and deep-fried cheese curds for you at the retro-style *Rudy's Drive-In*, (608) 782-2200, at the corner of 10th and La Crosse Sts. Stay in your car. In season, he'll send a roller-skating carhop out to deliver the goodies! For barbecued pork or beef ribs all you need to know is *Piggy's*, (608) 784-4877, overlooking the Mississippi on South Front St. It has a great piano bar too.

Freighthouse Restaurant, (608) 784-6211, 107 Vine St., is a top choice for prime rib, seafood, steaks, and overall friendly ambiance. *Traditions Restaurant*, (608) 783-0200, in a former bank building on Main St. in Onalaska, serves distinguished American Regional cuisine with a French twist. With a great wine list, it's very highly rated and very busy but well worth a visit.

Some favorite places to stay include the *Radisson*, (608) 784-6680, 200 Harbor View Plaza, and the *Courtyard Marriott*, (608) 782-1000, 500 Front St., both offering excellent riverfront views, and the *Holiday Inn Hotel & Suites,* (608) 784-4444, 200 Pearl St. All are conveniently located downtown.

Start at the junction of Highway 33 and Highway 14/61 (Fourth Street) in La Crosse and head north on 14/61 to Cass Street. Turn left (west) on Cass, crossing the Mississippi River on Highway 14/61/16. You might want to make a brief stop at *Pettibone Park*, a city park with public beaches located on Barron Island, west across the Cass Street Bridge.

Continue into La Crescent, Minnesota. This area is famous for orchards, and the Apple Blossom Scenic Drive winds through 1,400 acres of orchards. It's a scenic detour that's worth the time.

Follow Highway 14/61 north about 2.5 miles to the intersection with I-90. Just to the north is the *Lock and Dam No. 7.* Here you can watch 400-foot barges, boats, and other river craft "lock through" as they pass up and down the river.

Continue on 14/61 north along a spectacular drive with panoramic vistas of the islands and river life on the Mississippi River.

Stay on 14/61 to Highway 43. Turn right (east) and go into downtown Winona.

Yes, actress Winona Ryder was born in Winona on October 29, 1971. Winona is a Native American name meaning "first born" or "eldest" daughter. The city was founded by a steamboat captain in 1851, and its island location in the Mississippi made it a prosperous transportation hub. It was one of the world's richest cities by 1900. This legacy remains in the form of historic buildings and in its citizens' continuing love affair with the river.

For a magnificent view of the river valley, head up the bluffs to *Garvin Heights City Park.* This

Archaeology on the Highway

On this tour, and all the others, we'll pass through a land that has yet to tell all the stories of the people who have called it home. From the first humans, the Paleo-Indians who came in at the retreat of the glaciers, to the traders of the 17th century and immigrants of the 19th century, people left behind tools, toys, utensils, and the debris of living that archaeologists examine to get a better look at what life was like in those days.

One of the interesting unintended consequences of building highways is the occasional unearthing of information about our past. Road work has unearthed wooly mammoth remains near Kenosha, dug around effigy mounds in central Wisconsin, discovered one-thousand-year-old Native American structures near Waunakee, found ceramic vessels in northwest Wisconsin, unearthed spear points in Price County, and found early U.S. coins at a European farmstead near Superior.

Fortunately, Wisconsin highway builders now take this into account before they build. As engineers study a road construction project, they call in archaeologists to study the area for possible sites that need to be preserved or carefully excavated.

As far back as 1906 there was federal legislation that protected our cultural heritage, and the 1966 National Historic Preservation Act required that agencies using federal funds give consideration to archaeological sites in project development. In 1987 Wisconsin strengthened its laws that protect cemeteries and burial sites.

As you travel and explore the communities and back roads of Wisconsin, stop at the small community museums and historical sites. Many have artifacts that were discovered over the years by people who built the highways. For more information contact the State Historical Society of Wisconsin, Museum Archaeology Program, 816 State St., Madison, 53706, (608) 264-6560.

scenic drive will reward you with a view from 575 feet above the river. You can see 20 to 30 miles up and down the valley.

The *Winona Commercial Historic District* has more than 100 sites on the National Register, the largest grouping of Victorian commercial buildings in Minnesota. Most are Italianate or Queen Ann-style dating from 1857 to 1916. Free downtown walking tour brochures are available at the *Convention and Visitors Bureau,* (507) 452-2272.

The *Merchants National Bank,* (507) 457-1100, is a Prairie School-style building designed by Purcell, Elmslie & Feich and completed in 1912. It features an extraordinary terra cotta ornament and two great stained glass windows. The *Winona National and Savings Bank building,* (507) 454-4320, was designed by George Maher in the Egyptian Revival style, while the interior enjoys a Prairie School look with stained glass and bronze work by the famed Tiffany Studios of New York. There is a small museum on the second floor. One architectural writer has said that "there is nothing else quite like it in Minnesota, or the country for that matter."

The *Julius C. Wilkie Steamboat Center,* (507) 454-1254, displays an actual-size replica of a steamboat and an exhibition area on the first deck with artifacts of river history.

Stained glass is the pride of Winona and particularly two firms. *Cathedral Crafts Inc. Studios of Fine Glass,* (507) 454-4079, and *Conway Universal Studios of Fine Glass,* (507) 452-9209, are well known for their excellent work. Both offer tours to groups.

The *Polish Cultural Institute of Winona,* (507) 454-3431, preserves the rich Polish history of Winona and houses Kashubian artifacts, family heirlooms, religious articles, and folk art.

The *Winona Armory Museum,* (507) 454-2723, is housed in a 1915 brick armory and is one of the largest historical society museums in Minnesota. Displays of artifacts of Winona and Winona County history include a stained-glass window exhibit. An award-winning children's exhibit features a replica limestone cave, tepee, and steamboat pilot house, complete with bell.

Follow 43 across the Mississippi River, where it becomes Highway 54 in Wisconsin. (This is the Wisconsin portion of the Great River Road.) Turn right on 54 and travel about 1 mile to County M. Turn left and follow M. Along the way, you'll drive up a bluff and along beautiful Buffalo Ridge.

Continue on M to County P. Turn left and continue to the intersection with Highway 95. Turn right on 95 and continue into Arcadia. Early in this section you'll experience a fantastic drive along Fountain City Ridge. Arcadia was settled in the 1850s by Polish and German immigrants looking for areas to farm. Visit *Memorial Park,* which features a unique tribute to veterans of all wars and armed conflicts. Stroll along *Soldiers Walk*, with memorials to the fighting men and women who fought for the freedom we enjoy today. The walk is laid out as a timeline depicting the history of Arcadia since 1856. Each one-meter block represents one year in history.

Continue through Arcadia on 95. At the intersection of Highway 93, turn right (south) on 93, cruising along what is called Skyline Drive. As you climb the hills you will be treated to some breathtaking scenery. Scenic overlooks give you a fantastic view of the valleys, coulees, and family farms nestled in the rolling terrain. You can see why the locals (and even a beer company) called this "God's Country."

Continue about 5 miles to the intersection with Norway Valley Road. Turn left (east) on Norway Valley and follow it 4.8 miles to the intersection with Oak Ridge Road. Turn right and go about 0.3 mile to the junction with Linderud Coulee Road. Turn left on Linderud Coulee and wind through the hills to County T.

Turn left on T and go 0.5 mile to County D. Turn right on D and go into the town of Ettrick and the intersection with Highway 53. This little town was named after the Ettrick Forest in the Scottish Highlands. Trout-fishing enthusiasts will want to check out the excellent fishing on the north and south branches of Beaver Creek.

Turn right (south) on 53 and continue about 8 miles to Galesville. Back in 1869 a local minister, looking out on this beautiful green valley, started doing a little figuring. Interpreting a variety of biblical verses with some enthusiastic license, he deduced that Galesville, tucked between Lake Marinuka and High Cliff, was indeed sitting just about dead center on the Garden of Eden. (Some local merchants still sell the pamphlet.) Looking at the area even today, you can rather easily forgive his enthusiasm. If the season is right you might even find some local apples for sale! Care for a taste?

Be sure you have a full tank of gas because we're going to run through the coulees of God's Country and gas stops may be limited! Get ready for some Coulee Country Cruisin'!

Follow 53 as it joins Highway 54/93 and turns to the east. About 2.25 miles out of Galesville, follow Highway 54 east through Butman Corners, across Grant Creek and Hardies Creek, and into Jackson County. At County VV, turn right (south), crossing the Black River and the *North Bend Bottoms Wildlife Area*, continuing into La Crosse County, and intersecting with County T in the Lewis Valley.

Wisconsin has dozens of excellent auto racetracks, such as the La Crosse Speedway near West Salem. Wisconsin Department of Tourism photo by Chuck Deery.

Turn left on T about 0.8 mile to the intersection with Highway 108. Turn right (south) on 108 and drive into Mindoro. When this 25-foot-wide road was hewn by hand through the huge 74-foot rock face in the 19th century, it was the second largest hand-cut rock passage in the country. A marker here tells the story.

Follow 108 along the Severson Coulee to the junction with Asmus Road. Turn right (west) on Asmus and continue about 1.5 mile to the junction with County M at the Larson Coulee. Turn left (south) on M and pass the La Crosse Speedway near West Salem. West Salem is most famous as the home of noted Pulitzer Prize-winning author Hamlin Garland, who was born here in 1860, and wrote about the hardships of life on the Wisconsin frontier. His home, (608) 786-1675, is on the National Register of Historic Places and is open for tours.

A few other things to see in town include the *Palmer-Gullickson Octagon House*, (608) 786-1675, once owned by Dr. Mary Lottridge, the second woman doctor in the United States. The structure was built in 1856, and many of the original furnishings remain on display. The *Westview Inn* in the downtown area has earned a reputation for good food, reasonable prices, and friendly service. The *La Crosse Fairgrounds Speedway*, (608) 786-1525, features exciting racing every Saturday from April to September.

Continue south on M, cross I-90, and stay on M as it turns southeast to the intersection with County I. Turn left (east) on I and follow it up and over numerous ridges to the intersection with Highway 33. Turn right on 33 and enjoy the scenic run on St. Joseph Ridge back into La Crosse where we started.

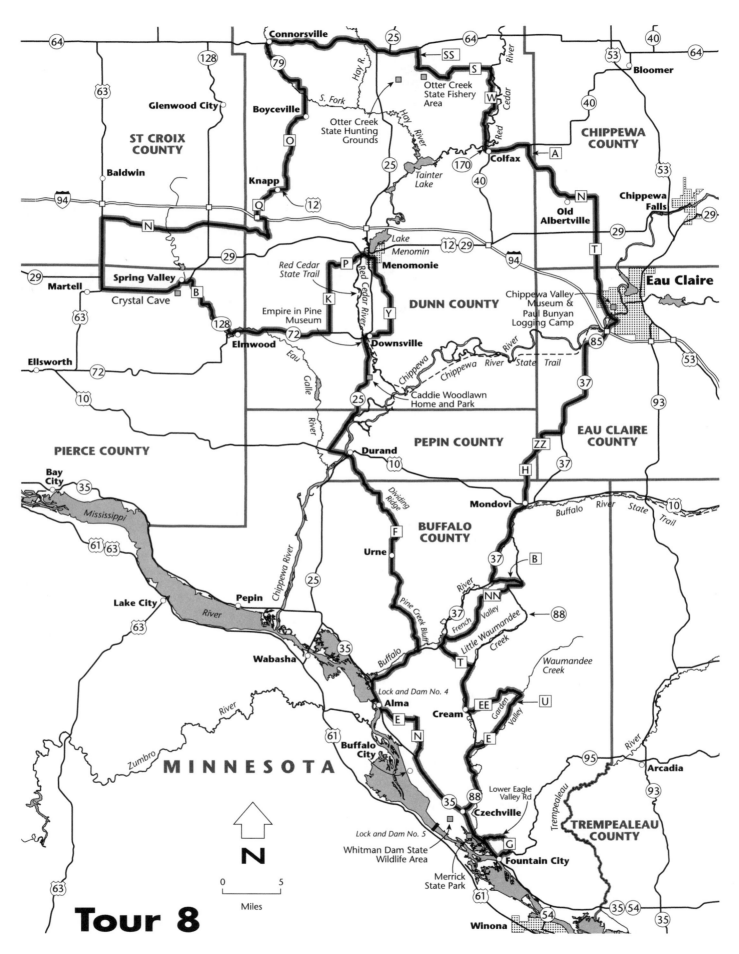

Tour 8

Tour 8
Clear Water and Green Valleys

Eau Claire—Mondovi—Cream—Czechville—Fountain City—Buffalo City—Alma—Urne—Durand—Downsville—Menomonie—Elmwood—Spring Valley—Knapp—Boyceville—Connersville—Colfax—Eau Claire

Distance: 244 miles

I almost didn't include this tour in this book. It's one of my favorites. Some of Wisconsin's most extraordinary scenery and lost beauty are here in Eau Claire, Buffalo, Pepin, and Dunn Counties, hidden between the Chippewa, Buffalo, Red Cedar, and Mississippi Rivers. It's not really on the way to anywhere. It's not even really between stops. If you get over here, it's either intentional—to take a look at it—or you're totally lost.

You see, there's really no reason to just drive here unless you're looking for something—like steep hills, soaring bluffs, and deep valleys laced with mad rushing rivers.

This is a country you come to when you have the time. And if you take the time to see it, you'll likely be torn, as I am, between telling everyone what they're missing—and telling no one.

So I choose to tell you.

Drive carefully and have a fantastic trip. Be nice to the people you meet. Don't even think of moving here. Let's hope it stays this way for a long, long time.

We'll start the tour at the junction of Highway 37/85 and I-94 just southwest of Eau Claire.

Before heading into the countryside, definitely plan on spending some time in Eau Claire. French explorers and fur traders, who knew this place as the point where the copper-tinted Chippewa River turned into "clear water," gave it its name. The city has its roots planted deep in the state's logging and milling history, beginning right after the United States signed a treaty with the Ojibwa in 1837 that gave access to the great white pine forests of Northern Wisconsin. By 1873 there were a dozen mills operating in Eau Claire. One huge mill in Chippewa Falls was said to turn out 400,000 board feet of lumber in a 12-hour day. People came here to seek their fortunes, including many immigrants from Northern and Western Europe looking to make a good life in a new land. Though early loggers believed the forests were unending, it took only some 40 years to harvest more than 46 billion board feet of lumber and reduce the land to a vast rock and stump garden.

Breweries, agriculture, and manufacturing provided jobs, but no one industry dominated after the lumber industry was gone. Today Eau Claire boasts a wide variety of businesses and is home to a fine University of Wisconsin campus. Tourism has become an important element of the local economy and there is much to enjoy here.

Carson Park is a great place to stop, because it's a big (134 acres), beautiful park with great vistas and a real steam-powered railroad, and it's home to the Chippewa Valley Museum. But for baseball fans it's extra special because it's where "Hammerin' Hank"—Henry Aaron—started on the road to the big leagues (see article). Today it's the home of the Eau Claire Cavaliers minor league team. For an event filled with baseball lore and stories, try the "It's a Hit!" tour of the ballpark, (715) 836-0091. The *Chippewa Valley Museum*, (715) 834-7871, is one of Wisconsin's finest award-winning county history museums, with Ojibwa life exhibits, rural heritage displays, doll houses, a turn-of-the-century ice cream parlor, a log cabin, and a one-room school.

The *Paul Bunyan Logging Camp*, (715) 835-6200, a lasting tribute to the pioneers of the lumbering era, is also located in Carson Park. Built in the early 1930s, it authentically represents an 1890s logging camp, including a bunkhouse, cook's shanty, dingle (an all-purpose pantry), wanigan (a camp store), filer's shack, blacksmith shop, horse and ox barn, artifact displays, children's area, gift shop, and heavy logging equipment.

The *Chippewa Valley Railroad Association*, (715) 835-7500, a volunteer, non-profit organization, provides train rides through Carson Park over 0.5 mile of 16-inch narrow-gauge track with authentic coal-fired steam and diesel locomotives, and a variety of passenger coaches. The railroad is complete with depot, passenger waiting area, round house and turntable, and switchyard.

'Hammerin' Hank' Aaron

Back on June 14, 1952, the Eau Claire Bears Class C minor league team introduced a new player in a game against St. Cloud, Minnesota. With fast hands and great vision, he started producing immediately by getting two run-scoring singles in his debut at Eau Claire's Carson Park. He went on to hit .336 with nine home runs and was named "Rookie of the Year" in the Northern League in 1952. Henry "Hammerin' Hank" Aaron thrilled Wisconsin fans for years by hitting "taters" over the fences at County Stadium as a Milwaukee Brave. He returned to end his career with the Milwaukee Brewers in 1976, rewriting the record books with a career total of 755 home runs. Thirty years after his start here with the Bears, Hammerin' Hank was inducted into the Baseball Hall of Fame. A statue at the front gate of the ball diamond features a young Aaron, bat in hand ready to make his mark. Today baseball fans consider it good luck to touch the bronze bat.

Many great scenic routes go unidentified, so it's hard to resist the invitation when a sign like this appears. Wisconsin Department of Tourism photo by GK.

The *Schegelmilch McDaniel House*, (715) 834-7871, was built in 1870 and is open to rent, but there are no regular tours. It contains many antiques and artifacts.

An elegant dinner theater, the *Fanny Hill Dinner Theater and Restaurant*, (800) 292-8026, 3 miles southwest of Eau Claire at 3919 Crescent Ave. (County EE), has been entertaining groups for over 20 years with matinee and evening shows. Decorations both inside and out change with the season. The restaurant here is one of the finest in the Chippewa Valley. For additional art and culture, check out the University of Wisconsin-Eau Claire campus and the *Foster Art Gallery*, (715) 836-4833, one of the best university galleries in the Midwest, with two major shows each year and many smaller exhibits. *The Cabin*, the oldest coffeehouse in the state, offers contemporary folk, jazz, blues, and comedy performances.

If it's food you crave, try *Mike's Smokehouse*, (715) 834-8153, 2235 N. Clairemont Ave. The Texas-style barbecue beef, ham, pork, ribs, chicken, and fish are delicious—all slowly cooked over a hickory pit. The atmosphere is Texas casual bunkhouse. A Chippewa Valley favorite, especially for breakfasts, are *Heckels Restaurants*, (715) 834-2076, a wholesome Midwestern family restaurant chain. You'll find one in Eau Claire at 1106 W. Clairemont Ave., just north of our starting point.

At the junction of Highway 37/85 and I-94 take 37/85 south. Stay south on 37 as 85 swings west. We'll be driving some extraordinary roads through the wooded hills and beautiful farm country in the wild Chippewa Valley. There are sensational views at every turn, so enjoy the ride!

Stay on 37 past County ZZ east to the junction with ZZ west (about 9.2 miles). Turn right (west) onto ZZ and go to the junction with County H. Follow H (bear left) south along Brownlee Creek and past Mirror Lake into Mondovi.

They say Harvey Farrington settled here about 1855 and for a while it was known as "Farringtons." Later it was called "Pan Cake Valley" but it was left

to Elihu B. Gifford, the only person in the valley who subscribed to a newspaper, to give the community its name. Gifford read an account of Napoleon's exploits in the *New York Ledger*. A victory in Sardinia at a place called Mondovi fascinated Gifford, who decided to keep a bit of the Napoleonic legend alive in the wilds of Wisconsin.

Today Mondovi is better known as "The Horse Capital" of Wisconsin. It's the legacy of a legendary draft horse, Old Greeley, a Percheron whose proud descendents are known for their strength and stamina. As you drive through this area you'll see lots of horses in the fields and at farms.

Bicycle riders—or hikers—may want to explore the beautiful *Buffalo River State Trail*, (608) 266-2181, that extends some 36 miles to Fairchild in Trempealeau County.

In downtown Mondovi, pick up Highway 37 and follow it along the Buffalo River to County B. Turn left (east) on B and go to Highway 88. Turn right (south) on 88 and go about 1 mile to County NN. Turn right (southwest) on NN. Enjoy the beautiful scenery, especially French Valley and Hutchinson Creek.

Continue to Highway 37, turn left (southwest), and go about 1 mile to the junction with County N. Turn left (southeast) on N and proceed to the junction with County T. Turn left (southeast) on T and continue to Highway 88.

Turn right on 88 and go to the junction with County EE. Along the way, you'll run south along Little Waumandee Creek and through the town of Cream. They say that Cream was quite the thriving spot during the prohibition era. The name notwithstanding, Cream bistros served some pretty potent liquid that had nothing to do with the dairy business. Today one tavern remains, fully legal and delighted to welcome visitors.

Turn left (northeast) on EE and continue to County U, running up through the hills and then down into the Garden Valley, crossing Waumandee Creek. *Waumandee* is an Indian word said to mean "clear and sparkling water." This area is said to have the most fertile soil in the country and you'll see many prosperous farms nestled in the valleys or estates built up into the ridges.

Turn right (southwest) on U, passing through Garden Valley and Waumandee Valley, and continue to Highway 88. Turn left (south) on 88 and drive through Czechville before meeting Highway 35, the Great River Road. Turn left (south) on 35.

For a short side trip, turn right on Highway 35 and go to Prairie Moon Rd. There you'll find the delightful folk art display called *Prairie Moon Sculpture Garden*. A farmer, fiddler, and self-taught artist named Herman Rusch created this roadside celebration of the imagination that contains a 267-foot arched fence and 40 sculptures, including a "Hindu Temple." Restored in 1994 by the Kohler Foundation, there is now a museum as well, which is open Sundays in the warmer seasons.

Go south on 35 about 2.3 miles to *Merrick State Park,* (608) 687-4936, one of the finest "undiscovered" parks in the Wisconsin State Park system. Watch for herons, egrets, muskrat, mink, and otter in the marshes and eagles overhead. There are beautiful river vistas, hiking, nature trails, riverside camping, and excellent fishing in this 297-acre gem.

Continue south on 35 to Fountain City. With 550-foot bluffs, among the highest on the Mississippi, called "hard heads," standing over it, you can see why Fountain City is known as "the most picturesque river town along the Great River Road." It was settled about 1839 by Thomas Holmes, who planned to set up a trading post and service the steamboat trade. As the town grew, Holmes's landing added all the amenities of civilization, even including capped springs, which are the local "fountains."

In 1995 one of the beautiful bluffs shed a 55-ton boulder, which bounded quickly down the slope and crashed through the side of a house. The resident inside was narrowly missed, unhurt but somewhat shaken. Showing much of the same ingenuity as the founders of Fountain City, the owners of the house opened it to the public as a tourist site. Today you can visit the famous *Rock in the House,* (608) 687-6106.

Antique collectors will enjoy the shops here and won't want to miss *Elmer's Auto and Toy Museum,* (608) 687-7221, with over 500 pedal cars, thousands of toys dating to the 1800s, 100 antique and classic cars, dolls, bikes, and motorcycles. The *Fountain City Historical Museum,* (608) 687-3221, is on Main St. and has quite a collection of arrowheads and artifacts. The *Leo Smith III Folk Art Collection,* (608) 687-6698, 121 S. Main St., is the largest collection of his carvings in the country.

Continue on 35 south to Highway 95 and head into the hills. Turn left (east) on 95 and go to County G. Turn left on G and go to Lower Eagle Valley Road (about 2 miles). Turn left on Lower Eagle Valley and continue back to Highway 35.

Turn right (north) on 35 (the Great River Road) to Buffalo City. Along the way, *Goose Lake Memorial Park* is a good place to see Canada geese or have a picnic. Buffalo City is a delightful little detour off the highway. Check out *Foelsch Riverside Nature Park,* 10 wooded acres on the Mississippi River with walking trails. The *Mississippian Restaurant and Lounge,* (608) 248-2464, is known for fine food, breakfast specials, and a great boat dock.

Follow 35 north to the junction with County N. Turn right (northeast) on N, heading up into the bluffs to the junction with County E. Turn left (west) on E toward Alma. As you get near Alma you'll arrive at an intersection with a stop sign. To the right is a road to *Buena Vista Park.* For a view considered by many to be the finest on the Great River Road, turn right and get a look at the Mississippi from 500 feet over Alma. This is a good place to picnic and don't forget your camera and binoculars!

Continue on E, turn right, and go down the steep hill into Alma. Like many of the river towns along the St. Croix and Mississippi Rivers, Alma is built on land that was once inhabited by Native Americans—Lakota and Ojibwa in this case. After they signed treaties allowing settlers in the area, steamboat traffic and, later, lumbering brought additional settlers in the mid-1800s. Alma was favored by Swiss immigrants and many of their descendents remain in the area. In addition to the steamboat trade and lumber-related businesses, beer and cigar production employed early residents.

You'll notice that the tall bluffs create a rather long and narrow town. The settlers used an Indian trail along the river to create two streets that run along the foot of the bluffs. Main (or First) St., which is also Highway 35, and Second (or Upper) St. are connected by short streets, some of which allow auto traffic; others are designed for people and bikes only.

Alma has done a great job of preserving the historic buildings in the community. Much of the city is on the National Register of Historic Places and many of the houses are over one hundred years old. To find out more about Alma, visit the *Alma Museum,* (608) 685-3352, located in the Buffalo County Courthouse on Second St. It is open to visitors on weekends during the summer.

There are many interesting shops and antique stores here, among them *River Road Antiques,* (608) 248-2004, and the *Buffalo Trading Company,* (608) 685-4555, which are favorites with travelers.

An annual wildlife happening begins in mid-October and runs to the end of November when the migrating tundra swans return. These magnificent birds rest and feed here during their migration to the East Coast. *Reick's Lake Park* is a great viewing spot. To get current information, call the Swan Watch line at (608) 685-4249. Bald eagles are often seen roosting and fishing along the Mississippi River during the winter.

For a real "spirit of the river" festival, come for *Mark Twain Days* during the Labor Day weekend. You can help Tom Sawyer paint a picket fence, get into a frog-jumping contest, taste catfish on a stick, watch a parade, or even cruise the river.

For a sense of river town life, get down to *Lock and Dam No. 4* where boats and barges pass through as they move up and down the river. If you

Buena Vista Park towers some 500 feet over historic Alma and is one view you won't want to miss on the Great River Road. Photo by Gary Knowles.

get real lucky you may catch the *Delta Queen* or *Mississippi Queen* riverboats passing through. Listen for the wistful sound of their calliopes playing a traditional riverboat farewell as they depart.

Continue north on Highway 35 through Alma to the junction with Highway 37 at the Buffalo River. Turn right (northeast) on 37 to the junction with County F. You'll follow the river back upstream past the community of Tell.

Turn left (north) on F and continue to Urne, following Pine Creek along Pine Crest Bluff and along Little Bear Creek. This area was once inhabited by bison. Recent archeological digs in Buffalo County have unearthed bones of the extinct "bison occidentalist" that wandered through these hills some five to ten millennia ago.

Continue driving north on F through a spectacular section of Wisconsin seldom seen—or appreciated—except by the friendly folks who live here—and the few others of us who wander by.

Twist, turn, climb, and descend along F, cross into Pepin County, and cruise into the city of Durand, where you'll meet Highway 10. Durand was platted in 1856 by Miles Prindle, who had seen Chippewa, its predecessor community, get four feet of snow in winter and then watched a spring flood on the Chippewa River nearly wash the little settlement away. Prindle named the new community Durand, his mother's maiden name. Today this Pepin County seat has several art galleries, gift shops, restaurants, and the *Old Courthouse Museum and Jail,* (715) 672-8673. It was built in 1874 and is the last wooden courthouse building left in Wisconsin. The *Durand Public*

Library, (715) 672-8730, was built in 1906 with a donation from Andrew Carnegie.

Turn left on 10, which is soon joined by Highway 25. Take Highway 10/25 west across the Chippewa River, cross Thompson Lake, and stay on 25 as it swings north and east. Stop in at the *Eau Galle Cheese and Gift Store,* (715) 283-4211, which has a wide variety of delicious Wisconsin cheeses (some to sample!), jams, preserves, candy, and an incredible collection of Christmas Village ceramic buildings, collectible statues, and other interesting arts and crafts.

Enjoy the scenic *Chippewa River* wayside, then continue a few miles to the historic *Caddie Woodlawn Park,* (715) 235-9087. You can walk through the real home of Caroline "Caddie" Woodhouse, who lived on the banks of the Red Cedar River in the 1860s and whose Dunn County pioneer stories were recorded and published in the 1930s as *Caddie Woodlawn* (a 1935 Newberry Award winner) and *Magical Melons.* There is a picnic area here, rest rooms, a shelter, fresh water, and, somewhere out in those fields behind the house, the unmarked grave of one of Caroline's little sisters who succumbed to illness.

Drive north on 25 to the junction with County C and turn into Downsville.

This tiny town has a surprising number of great things to see. The *Empire in the Pine Lumber Museum* (715) 235-9087, on First St., features a replica of an early Dunn County logging camp. There are displays depicting operations of the Knapp, Stout & Company, once the largest white pinery in the world, muzzle-loading bunk beds (you climb in feet first), a lumber camp kitchen, blacksmith shop, bateau, Caddie Woodlawn artifacts, Civil War weapons, household accessories of the era, a one-cell village jail, and an 1865 post office that served this area until the advent of rural delivery. Open from Memorial Day through September, Tuesday–Saturday, 12–4 p.m.; and Sunday, 1–5 p.m.

One of the finest restaurants, inns, and small conference centers in northwest Wisconsin is *The Creamery*, (715) 664-8354, a family-owned and operated inn. Housed in the old Downsville Cooperative Creamery building, it was remodeled by the Thomas family and opened in 1985. Since then, the Creamery has won acclaim for its extraordinary dining, lodging, and warm hospitality. There are 20 rooms and an executive conference center overlooking the beautiful Red Cedar Valley.

Continue through Downsville, north on C, to County Y. Turn left on Y and follow it into the city of Menomonie to 13th Avenue. Turn left and go to Highway 25. Turn right and drive to the junction with Highway 29.

The history of Menomonie is tied to the lumber industry. In 1822, Harding Perkins built a lumber mill at the confluence of Wilson Creek and the Red Cedar River. Floodwaters blew out the dam and mill. Eight years later, lumbering operations were re-established on the site. This was the first permanent settlement at Menomonie, thus making it older than Madison, (1837), St. Paul (1838), Hudson (1841), and Eau Claire (1845).

In 1853 a corporation known as Knapp, Stout & Company was formed. Two decades later, the company employed 1,200 workers, commanded 115,000 acres of pine forest, and had become the world's biggest lumber company, milling more than five million feet of lumber. The present city of Menomonie grew up here on the shores of beautiful Lake Menomin.

Wilson Place Mansion, (800) 368-7384, is a fine museum constructed as a Colonial-style home in 1859 by Captain William Wilson, founder of the city of Menomonie and the Knapp, Stout & Company. The mansion has an 1890s Queen Anne wing remodeled by Senator James Stout, who married Wilson's daughter. In 1921, the structure was remodeled to resemble a Mediterranean villa when George Wilson, a grandson, acquired the home. The present collection spans the years 1846 to 1974 and the interior is primarily Victorian.

The *Russell J. Rassbach Heritage Museum*, (715) 232-8685, 1820 Wakanda Rd., owned by the Dunn County Historical Society, has turn-of-the-century rooms and furnishings, an auditorium, genealogy center, innovation room, and gift shop.

The *Mabel Tainter Memorial*, (715) 235-0001, a Victorian opera house gem, was presented to the city of Menomonie by lumber baron Andrew Tainter and his wife, Bertha, in memory of their daughter, Mabel, who died in 1886 at the age of 19. This beautifully restored building is listed on the National Register of Historic Places, a charter member of the League of Historic American Theatres,

and a designated Wisconsin historical marker site. The 331-seat theater is surrounded by sparkling Victorian architecture with intricate hand-stenciled walls, superbly crafted woodwork, shining brass fixtures, marble staircase, ornate fireplaces, leaded-glass windows, and a rare Steere and Turner Tracker pipe organ.

The theater hosts professional performing arts events featuring nationally recognized artists as well as outstanding local theatrical and musical talent. Don't miss the authentic 19th-century public Reading Room, with a collection of local and Wisconsin historical photos, articles, historic American theater books, a selection of current newspapers and periodicals, and a quiet area for reading and study. The gift shop features Victorian souvenirs, dolls, dollhouse furniture, toys, and music tapes. The theater is open daily. Guided tours are offered Monday through Sunday (unless theater is in use).

The University of Wisconsin-Stout, with some 7,000 students from 30 states and 35 foreign countries, adds elements of culture and vitality to this community. It was founded as a private institution in 1891 by Senator James Stout. The school is known for its prominence in industrial, vocational, and home economics education.

You'll find lots of shopping opportunities in downtown Menomonie, along with coffee houses, galleries, gift shops, and specialty shops. The city is also the trailhead for the 14.5 mile *Red Cedar State Trail,* (715) 232-1242, enjoyed by 42,000 bicyclists and hikers annually.

The *Bolo Country Inn and Restaurant,* (800) 553-BOLO, is a unique 25-room bed and breakfast that is also well known for fine dining. *Jakes Supper Club,* (715) 235-2465, "where prime rib is king," is also a top choice for steak, Friday fish frys, and a buffet. It's located on Tainter Lake just north of Menomonie off Highway 25 on County D.

At the junction of Highway 25 and Highway 29, turn left (west) on 29 and go a short distance to County P. Turn left on P and follow it to County K. Turn left (south) on K and go to Highway 72. Turn right (west) on 72 and drive into Elmwood.

Elmwood is one of two Wisconsin communities that calls itself "The UFO Capital of Wisconsin." (The other is Belleville, south of Madison.) A few years ago there were strange lights in the sky cruising the coulees for quite a few nights and no explanation of what they might be. A guy from out of town came forward with the idea of building a flying saucer landing strip at the top of one of the hills. When I traveled through the area

The World's Greatest Garage Sale

In spring people in a dozen Mississippi Valley towns on both the Minnesota and Wisconsin sides of the river clean out their attics, basements, and garages to host a garage sailor's dream: 85 miles of antiques, trash, treasure, and collectibles. Get lucky and you may find Mark Twain's riverboat hat (yes, he captained a steamboat up this way), Laura Ingalls Wilder's summer bonnet (a native of Pepin, she wrote *Little House in the Big Woods* and *Little House on the Prairie*), or a steamboat pilot's wheel. There's always something unusual and plenty of surprises along the way. The dates of the sale vary, so call for the current information, (888) 999-2619.

Mile after mile, these splendid roads reveal one breathtaking vista after another. Photo by Gary Knowles.

to check this route, I asked where the UFO landing area was built. A gas station attendant said, "Oh that? There isn't any. The guy collected money to build it and then disappeared." I asked if he might have been abducted by a UFO. "Hell no. I think he's in Mexico. If you find him let me know. We're looking for him." The Elmwood folks still hold UFO days every year with a picnic and parade, but no one has seen the UFO lights again.

Follow 72 to Highway 128. Turn right (north) on 128 to County B. Turn left on B and wind through the hills into Spring Valley and the junction with Highway 29. Take 29 left (west) out of Spring Valley. *Crystal Cave*, (800) 236-CAVE, is about a mile out of Spring Valley and is a magnificent three-level cave with some 30 chambers to explore.

Continue west on 29 to the junction with Highway 63. Here you'll find the *Red Barn Antique Store*, (715) 778-5522, packed with treasure, a great ice cream shop, a friendly restaurant, and gas station.

Turn right (north) on 63 and go about 6 miles to County N. Turn right (east) on N and enjoy a pleasant run across the Eau Galle River to County Q. Turn left (north) on Q, cross I-94, and go to the junction with Highway 12. Turn right (east) on 12, passing through Knapp, and continue to County O. Turn left (north) on O and go to Highway 170. Turn right (east) and head into Boyceville.

Be sure to check out *Andy Pafko Park*. Baseball fans will remember Andy Pafko as a player with the Milwaukee Braves (1953–59) and, before then, with the Chicago Cubs, and as the player on card

number one in the 1952 Topps Baseball card set. That card is very rare. In 1998 one in virtually perfect condition sold for $83,870. Pafko, who was known for his tenacity and "give it everything" style of play, lives in Eau Claire. The Associated Press reported that when he heard of the sale he said that Topps had given him boxes of the cards. "I just gave the cards to the kids in the neighborhood and they put them in their bicycle spokes. And there went the money—click, click, click."

Stop in Boyceville and check the antique stores. Maybe some of those kids didn't put the cards in their spokes!

In Boyceville go to Highway 79. Turn left (north) and continue on 79 as it runs along the Hay River to Highway 64 at Connersville. Turn right on 64 and cross Beaver Creek, the Hay River, and Highway 25 at Blairmoore River before meeting County SS.

Turn right (south) on SS and go to the junction with County S. Turn left on S and continue to the junction with County W. Turn right (south) on W and continue to Highway 170 at Colfax. Go to Highway 40, turn left (east), and continue on 40 to County A.

Turn right (south) on A and go to the junction with County N. Follow N south and east to the junction with County T. Turn right (south) on T to the junction with Highway 12. Follow 12 (North Clairemont Avenue in Eau Claire) south and east across the Chippewa River to Highway 85.

Turn right on 85 and go to our starting point at I-94 and Highway 37/85.

Tour 9
Run the Wild River Valley

**Prescott—Afton (Minn.)—Stillwater (Minn.)—Marine on St. Croix (Minn.)—Taylors Falls (Minn.)—
St. Croix Falls—Dresser—Osceola—Somerset—Hudson—River Falls—Prescott**

Distance: 113 miles

This exciting loop through part of the St. Croix River territory may be the best undiscovered wild river drive in the region. If you enjoy driving through deep forests, cruising on long sweeping curves, and running at a nice pace on a highway stretched out over roller-coaster hills, you'll enjoy this tour.

It has dramatic river vistas, two handfuls of towns with interesting architecture, historic sites that go back to the opening of the territory, and such gorgeous scenery that you'll never grow tired of gawking at it.

You'll see potholes carved 13,000 years ago and a hidden waterfall. You'll see a rare lift bridge and the town where Minnesota was born.

It's a bit different from most of our other tours that try to stay off main highways in order to sample the backcountry. On this tour we're on state or federal highways most of the way, but that's because they are the best routes to use to really see this spectacular river valley.

Start this tour in Prescott. The town of Prescott stands as a witness to the wedding of the wild St. Croix River and the great Mississippi. From *Mercord Park* just off Highway 35, you can see the blue waters of the St. Croix River rushing in ripples and waves to join the big muddy Mississippi. It's a nice park and well worth a look. For another good view, higher up, from the junction of Highway 35 and 10 downtown, take 35 south about 6 blocks and follow the sign (turn right) into *Freedom Park*.

Prescott was settled by 1840 and called at various times "Mouth" because it was the mouth of the St. Croix, "Elizabeth," after the first girl born there, and finally "Prescott," in honor of Philander Prescott, a trapper and fur trader who built a trading post on the site after buying it in cooperation with some officers from Fort Snelling. The village was officially created in 1851. Prescott prospered thanks to river shipping, steamboat transportation, and milling. Immigrants arrived via the steamboats and settled in Minnesota and Wisconsin.

Today the community is a favorite with antique fanciers, fishing enthusiasts, hunters, and people looking for a beautiful spot to get away from the fast pace of the city. One fine Prescott

The Mississippi River meets the St. Croix in Prescott, one of the many spectacular views along the way. Wisconsin Department of Tourism photo by GK.

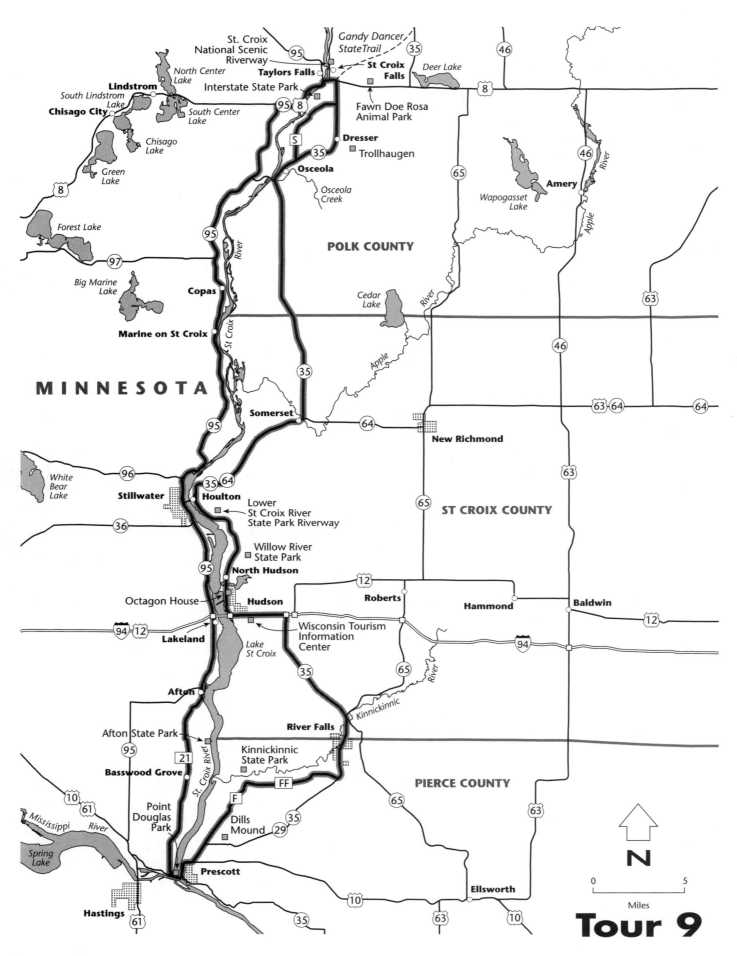

St. Croix
National Scenic
Riverway

Gandy Dancer,
State Trail

95 · 35

46

Taylors Falls

St Croix
Falls

Deer Lake

8

North Center Lake

North Center Lake

Lindstrom

Interstate State Park

95 · 8

Fawn Doe Rosa
Animal Park

South Lindstrom Lake

Chisago City

South Center Lake

S

Dresser

65

46

River

35

Trollhaugen

Chisago Lake

Osceola

Osceola Creek

Amery

Wapogasset Lake

Green Lake

8

95

River

POLK COUNTY

Apple River

63

Forest Lake

97

Copas

Big Marine Lake

35

Cedar Lake

Apple River

46

63 · 64

64

MINNESOTA

Marine on St Croix

St Croix River

Somerset

64

New Richmond

63

95

96

35 · 64

White Bear Lake

Stillwater

Houlton

Lower
St Croix River
State Park Riverway

ST CROIX COUNTY

65

36

Willow River
State Park

12

95

North Hudson

Roberts

Hammond

Baldwin

Octagon House

Hudson

Wisconsin Tourism
Information
Center

65

94

12

94 · 12

Lakeland

Lake St Croix

35

Afton

65

Kinnickinnic River

Afton State Park

River Falls

95

21

Kinnickinnic
State Park

FF

St Croix River

PIERCE COUNTY

Basswood Grove

F

65

63

10 · 61

Point
Douglas
Park

Dills
Mound

35

29

Mississippi River

Spring Lake

Prescott

Ellsworth

N

0   5
Miles

Hastings

61

10

63

10

Tour 9

bed and breakfast, *The Arbor Inn*, (888) 262-1090, is done up in English cottage style with a stone foundation and covered with grapevines. Furnished in antiques and set high above the rivers, it features one of the finest full gourmet breakfasts of any inn in Wisconsin. Don't pass up the strawberry-stuffed French toast.

To see displays of area history and get information about the Pierce County area, stop at the *Welcome and Heritage Center*, (715) 262-3284, 237 Broad St. N. It houses the *Prescott Area Chamber of Commerce* and *Prescott Area Historical Society*.

From Prescott, if you were to follow Highway 35 south, Wisconsin's Great River Road, you would see some of the greatest river scenery in the country. About the only trip that can compare is the one we'll be taking into wild river county and the St. Croix Valley.

From downtown Prescott at the junction of Highway 35 and Highway 10, take 10 west into Minnesota. About a mile out of town in Minnesota's Washington County you'll see *Point Douglas Park* where you can pull over to get another good view of the rivers.

Continue on 10 to the junction with Highway 21. Turn right on 21 and follow it to the right (north) into Afton. This route will take you through wooded hills and valleys, past Lake St. Croix, and over bluffs until you get to Afton. This friendly little community has the quiet charm and pace of an earlier time. Like many of the communities on the river, it was first established in the era of exploration by French fur traders. Next came the New Englanders who platted the village in 1855 and influenced its simple, straightforward architecture. As you pass through the area, look for a few of the virgin pines that have survived to this day. In season you'll see wild flowers, migrating Canada geese, white tail deer, and lots of songbirds.

Shoppers may want to stop in town to check out a nice variety of shops, marinas, galleries, pastry stores, and restaurants. Many village businesses are in 19th-century houses or buildings, which adds a pleasant ambiance to your shopping experience. The *Afton Historical Society Museum*, (651) 436-3500, has displays and artifacts, and *Afton State Park* just south of town is known for its fine hiking trails.

Continue on 21 north to join Highway 95 north, following the St. Croix River Valley through the communities of Mary's Point and Lake St. Croix Beach to Lakeland. This town was once called "Shanghai Coulee" because of the huge free-range Shanghai chickens that ruled a ravine nearby. Logging, fishing, and tourism have all played a part in the history of Lakeland. At one time a St. Paul newspaper gave away tiny lake lots here as a subscription premium.

Continue on 95 through Bayport to Stillwater. Stillwater, generally regarded as "the birthplace of Minnesota," is a town that was built on lumber and the logging industry. It started after an 1837 treaty with the Lakota opened the St. Croix Valley to settlement by pioneers and the vast white pine forests of Wisconsin and Minnesota territory became available for logging. The St. Croix River served as the main transportation system for a logging operation that made Stillwater a thriving boomtown until the forests were finally clear-cut by the early 1900s.

The homes and commercial buildings that once served the lumber barons and their workers have been preserved as beautiful landmarks, bed and breakfast inns, commercial business quarters, and historical centers. A Stillwater group concerned with historical preservation has published a walking tour brochure for visitors that explains the wide variety of architecture in Stillwater. You can get a good overview of Stillwater by taking the 45-minute *Trolley Tour*, (651) 430-0352.

Several museums focusing on local history, logging, and the river are also active and open to the public, especially during the summer and fall tourism seasons. If you have time for just one, see *The Depot Museum*, (651) 430-3000, with an excellent collection of artifacts and photos. Others include the historic courthouse, (651) 430-6233; *Minnesota Historical Society*, (651) 296-6126; *Rivertown Restoration*, (651) 430-9599; *The Warden's House Museum*, (651) 439-5956; and the *Washington County Courthouse*, (651) 439-3220. Stillwater today is a favorite escape for Twin Cities area residents. The city has a great selection of "painted ladies"—restored Victorian homes—that delight bed and breakfast fans.

Shopping is a big sport here. With 400,000 new and used books for sale, Stillwater's bookstores have earned a reputation as excellent places to look for rare and out-of-print titles. On summer weekends wall-to-wall visitors also enjoy a variety of restaurants, coffee shops, antique stores, and boutiques. On the waterfront, *Lowell Park* follows the river's edge and is a good place to stretch you legs or sit in the gazebo. If you have time for a boat ride, you can try the *St. Croix Boat and Packet Company*, (651) 430-1234. On the north side of town is Battle Hollow, which marks the site of an 1837 battle between the Dakota and Ojibwa nations. The old territorial prison is here. This was a home to the Younger brothers who rode with Jesse James.

You may want to reserve a spot on the *Minnesota Zephyr*, (800) 992-6100, an elegant dining train right out of the 1940s. The adventure takes a little over three hours and travels along the river, streams, and woodland bluffs of the beautiful St. Croix River Valley.

Before you leave town, drive to the riverfront and cross the Stillwater Bridge to Highway 35 near Houlton, Wisconsin. The bridge is one of two lift bridges of its kind still in operation (the other is in Duluth) and in 1990 was put on the National Register of Historic Places. When this bridge is lifted to accommodate river traffic, the cars back up into Stillwater and into Wisconsin, causing mini-Los Angeles-style traffic snarls. The subject of much controversy, it will likely be replaced in the near future, so check it out now before it's gone.

Follow 95 (the St. Croix Trail) north out of Stillwater. Give in to the temptation to stop at a few of the scenic pull-offs and waysides. They all seem to offer interesting vistas that make your river trip all the more memorable.

Continue on 95 to Marine on St. Croix. You'll want to stop for a while in this little community nestled in the bluffs. They say that Garrison Keillor, the creator of public radio's *Prairie Home Companion,* described this community as "closer to the mythical Lake Wobegone than any other Minnesota town." There's a little waterfall rippling through downtown, a gazebo, a collection of clothing shops, outfitters, chic restaurants, sidewalk cafes, and an irresistible ice cream shop, *The Village Scoop,* (651) 433-3030. *The Stone House Museum* is a one-room town hall. The town has been a Hollywood favorite, with scenes for *The Cure, Beautiful Girls,* and *Grumpier Old Men* having been shot here.

Follow 95 north out of Marine on St. Croix, through Copas, to *Interstate State Park.* This 293-acre park, (651) 465-5711, was established in 1895 in a joint venture with Wisconsin's Interstate State Park just across the river, creating the nation's first interstate park. In 1968 the U.S. Congress designated the St. Croix as a Wild and Scenic River. The park is excellent for hiking and offers some wonderful views of the St. Croix.

During the summer, the park naturalist provides tours of the glacial potholes, a landmark of the park, along with programs about the natural history of the area. At least 10 different lava flows are exposed here, along with two distinct glacial deposits, and traces of old stream valleys and faults. The glacial potholes here are the greatest concentration of such phenomena in the world, and the "bottomless pit" pothole at 60 feet deep is the world's deepest explored pothole. (Note that a vehicle permit from either Wisconsin or Minnesota Interstate Park is good for admission to both parks, Monday–Friday, holidays excluded.)

Continue north on Highway 8/95 to Taylors Falls. The town is another interesting river community that traces its history back to the days of the logging camps. It's been a headquarters for steamboat transportation and sightseeing on the river since 1838. Today you can choose from five

daily tours (Memorial Day through Labor Day) that will take you through the dramatic *Dalles of the St. Croix.* If you do only one river tour on this trip, do this one. For almost a century, *Taylors Falls Boat Tours,* (800) 447-4958, has provided access to the wild river to area visitors. The narrated tour will give you a water-level perspective. Watch for the diving fools as your tour shoots through the steep Interstate Park bluffs. These divers enjoy thrilling passengers as they leap off the cliffs into the swirling river. Every year some of them wind up injured and have to be flown by helicopter to hospitals with broken bones, damaged kidneys, or worse.

Downtown Taylors Falls is another interesting collection of outfitters, boutiques, old-time soda fountains, antique stores, and gift shops. For a great latte try *Coffee Talk,* (651) 465-6700, and for a 1950s poodle-skirted thrill, cruise into the *Drive In,* (800) 996-4448, for a burger and old-style root beer. For bed-and-breakfast fans, *The Old Jail,* (651) 465-3112, really was a jail but now it's a far, far friendlier place, and the food is wonderful too! *The Springs Inn* has Jacuzzi suites and a friendly bar, (800) 851-4243. By the way, if you're looking for the falls in Taylors Falls, it's still here, just hidden beneath the water that the dam backed up when it was built in 1906!

Cross the St. Croix River Bridge on Highway 8 and continue into St. Croix Falls, Wisconsin. Like many of the communities along the river, St. Croix Falls grew up as the white pine came crashing down. Logging and milling were primary industries here a century ago, but what fuels much of the economy today are tourism dollars. Spend some time here.

A smart first stop is the *Polk County Information Center,* (800) 222-7655, on Highway 35 at its intersection with Highway 8. This visitor center has enthusiastic staff, all the area brochures, and up-to-the-minute information about events all along the river.

The National Park Service's *National Scenic Riverway Headquarters and Visitor Center,* (715) 483-3284, has interesting exhibits relating the history of the river and some good brochures. *Lions Park* downtown has nice river views, a playground, and docks. The *State Fish Hatchery* raises brown and brook trout for area streams and tours are available weekdays. If you'd like to see deer, bear, and mountain lions up close and personal, *Fawn Doe Rosa,* (715) 483-3772, a wildlife park just east of town on Highway 8, will be a memorable stop.

Stop downtown to shop for fine art at *Luhrs/Bjornson Art Works,* (715) 483-9612, or for unusual gifts at *Once in a Blue Moon,* (715) 483-3513; or check out the famous *Majestic Falls Avenda Day Retreat Spa,* (715) 483-3175, fre-

quented by Hollywood stars and Nashville recording artists. And now that you're back in Wisconsin, it's safe to buy cheese again! *Lake Country Cheese*, (715) 483-3169, east on Highway 8, is an excellent shop and they'll let you sample some.

Gaming enthusiasts may want to take a 20-minute jaunt to the east on Highway 8 to Turtle Lake and *The St. Croix Casino*, (800) 846-8946. This 97,000-square-foot facility has 1,000 reel slots, video poker, and video keno machines as well as blackjack 24 hours a day.

The *Gandy Dancer State Trail* runs for 98 miles along the old Soo Line railroad grade from St. Croix Falls to Superior, and about 48 miles of it is "paved" with crushed limestone. This portion also serves as the northern end of the *Ice Age Trail*.

Quiet and comfortable St. Croix bed and breakfast inns include *Wissahickon Farms Country Inn,* (715) 483-3986, and *The Amberwood Bed and Breakfast*, (715) 483-9355.

At the junction of 8 and Highway 35 in St. Croix Falls, turn right (south) on 35. You'll soon come upon Wisconsin's *Interstate State Park*, (715) 483-3284, the first park in Wisconsin's park system. This is another great stop where you can see the effects of ancient geological forces. Hike the Pothole Trail to see some incredible holes worn in the rock by glacial action. *The Ice Age Interpretive Center* has exhibits and displays about the Ice Age. There are excellent picnic and swimming areas.

Continue south on 35 through the woods and rolling hills to Dresser. This town welcomed its first train in 1887 and became well known for mining "trap rock," which is known as "the hardest rock in North America." The *Trollhaugen Ski Area,* which includes a convention center and restaurants, (800) 826-7166, is located here.

Quick Trip Option: **After turning south on 35 in St. Croix Falls, go about 1.5 miles to the junction with County S. Turn right (west) on S and go about 6 miles to where S rejoins 35.** This is a delightfully scenic drive through the woods that is close to the St. Croix River.

Continue south on 35 to Osceola. If you didn't get to see the falls at Taylors Falls or St. Croix Falls, we'll tip you off to a beautiful hidden falls right here in downtown Osceola. *Cascade Falls* is one that you could easily miss if you just cruise through town quickly. At the corner of First St. and Cascade St., stairs lead down to one of the best waterfalls in Wisconsin. Follow the path for an invigorating walk and a great view.

Then visit one of Wisconsin's greatest outdoor coffee shops, the Secret Garden at the *Coffee Connection,* (715) 755-3833. Here, sitting right over

The St. Croix River Valley— A Billion Years in the Making!

If the timeline of the history of the St. Croix Valley stretched a mile, the day or two we spend driving this magnificent tour would be about a tenth the size of the period at the end of this sentence. Yet if you measure how good it can feel to get out in your car and drive the route, this tour is near the top.

Consider that a little more than a billion years ago the North American continent began to rip apart at the seams, at least from where Lake Superior is today down to Iowa. As the crack grew, molten lava came flowing out and later hardened into that dark gray rock you see all long this tour. That rock is basalt and it's what makes up those cliffs at the Interstate Parks. More recently, just 500 million years ago, the area was covered by a sea. Over millions of years the sand and sea silt was squashed into sandstone and shale. You can see these rocks in the parks as well as throughout the valley. In some cases the tides and waves of the sea worked basalt rocks loose. These fell into the ocean and were covered by silt and sand, hardening to become what geologists call "conglomerate." Then, quite recently, only a million years ago, came waves of glaciers. Ice fields miles thick inched their way across the area, retreated, and reappeared. Just 10,000 to 13,000 years ago, as the last glacier melted, the mother of all torrents of water rushed south through the basalt, sandstone, and conglomerate, sculpting what we call the St. Croix Valley and the Dalles of the St. Croix. Humans moved in about 6,000 years ago. The first European explorer in the area, Daniel Greysolon Sieur Duluth, arrived in 1680. The first trading post was built in the late 1700s. In 1837 treaties with Native Americans opened the land to settlement. The logging industry cleared out the white pines by the early 20th century. Tourists have been coming for about 150 years. And Congress officially recognized the St. Croix as a Wild and Scenic River in 1968.

Welcome to the St. Croix. Let's enjoy it, respect it, and leave it in good condition for a while . . . say maybe another million years?

the falls, you can enjoy desserts, a cup of Java, and all the negative ionization the falls kicks out. Contemplate life here a century ago when the falls powered the mill and passengers queued up below for steamboat excursions on the St. Croix River. There are interesting gift and antique shops to explore all over downtown.

For a fun trip, stop at the beautiful Osceola depot (built in 1916) to get a ticket for the scenic *Osceola and St. Croix Valley Railway,* a nonprofit organization featuring vintage railroad equipment. Ride steam- or diesel-powered trains that follow scenic routes through the valley, (800) 711-2591.

Continue on 35 south to Somerset. Check out the Apple River, the "Tubing Capital of the World." Rent an inner tube here and spend a lazy day floating on the river. There are a number of tube and raft outfitters in town who rent tubes and provide return transportation.

Stay on 35 headed south as it winds back

Young divers at Interstate Park wait for riverboats to pass by, then leap off the steep cliffs into the St. Croix—as spectators gasp in disbelief. Photo by Gary Knowles.

through farm country and woodlands to Houlton. If you didn't get a chance to cross the Stillwater Bridge earlier, here's another opportunity to make a quick tour.

Follow 35 south to Hudson. This community was first called Willow River, then Buena Vista because of the picturesque view. In 1852 the first mayor, A. D. Gray, decided that the town should be named Hudson because he thought it resembled that New York river valley. In 1914 and 1915 it was known as a center for boxing, attracting up to 15,000 fans on Saturday nights. Until 1951 there was a toll bridge across the river to Minnesota, so property taxes hovered near zero. With the development of I-94 and speedy access to the expand-

ing Twin Cities metro area, Hudson has seen a growth spurt of its own. However, there is still charm and excitement here. Visit the business district near the waterfront and enjoy the shops. Stop at the beautiful *Octagon House*, (715) 386-2654. Built in 1855 it's now a museum with interesting furnishings including a grand piano that was twice submerged in the Mississippi. *The Phipps Center for the Arts,* (715) 386-8409, hosts theatrical productions and art exhibits. *Willow River State Park*, (715) 386-5931, on the north side of town, has 2,800 wooded acres, a trout stream, a waterfall, and prairie remnants. *St. Croix Meadows Greyhound Park,* (715) 386-6800, presents exciting racing action daily.

There are several fine bed and breakfast inns in Hudson, and two of our favorites are the elegant and gracious *Baker Brewster Victorian Inn,* (715) 381-2895, and a ranch home with an outstanding art collection, the *Stageline Inn Bed & Breakfast,* (715) 386-5203.

Follow 35 south through Hudson to River Falls. The Kansas City Chiefs professional football team uses the facilities of the University of Wisconsin-River Falls as a summer training headquarters in July and August, so watch for the big guys at the ice cream shop who order nine scoops of ice cream in their sundae!

Why do the Chiefs choose River Falls? A former coach said it was the ideal weather conditions, outstanding practice facilities, and support of the local community that make River Falls the perfect place to begin a run to the Super Bowl.

If you're a trout angler, you're home. The Kinnickinnic River, known locally as "the Kinni," is a Class I trout stream that emerges in the center of St. Croix County and then heads 20 miles southwest before merging with the St. Croix River. At its midpoint sits the only city on the river, River Falls. Some big fish have been caught right in the middle of town!

From River Falls take Highway 29/35 south to the junction with County FF. Turn right (west) on FF. This is an enjoyable run that parallels the Kinnickinnic River Valley.

Continue on FF to the junction with County F. *Kinnickinnic State Park* is just to the north (right turn on F). The Kinnickinnic River forms a large sandy delta as it flows into the St. Croix River. This park offers some fine hiking, river scenery, trails meandering through tall grass prairies and upland forests, a large swim area, and boat-in camping.

Turn left (south) on F and follow it to the junction with Highway 29/35. Turn right (southwest) on 29/35 and go to Highway 10. Follow 10 back into Prescott where this tour began.

Tour 10
Cranberries and Wildlife

Wisconsin Rapids—Stevens Point—Marshfield—Arpin—Vesper—Rudolph—Monroe Center—
Necedah—Mather—Warrens—Dexterville—Nekoosa—Port Edwards—Wisconsin Rapids

Distance: 219 miles

Every year millions of vacationers, hunters, and fishing enthusiasts travel out of Illinois and southeast Wisconsin headed north on I-39 to see the great forests, waters, wildlife, and Native American land of the North Woods. This new four-lane expansion of old Highway 51 gets them there fast—after four, five, or six hours of 70-mile-per-hour cruising.

On the way, they pass by much of what they're looking for and miss some outstanding drives, beautiful rivers, vast wetlands, unique wildlife preserves, historic sites, and interesting communities.

Here, hidden in central Wisconsin, is an extraordinary driving tour in a land most people miss. It's a double-loop, figure-eight tour with Wisconsin Rapids at the center, so you could just loop north (about 100 miles) or south (about 118 miles) if your time is limited. Whatever you do, don't miss it! It's a run through the central back roads you won't forget.

Start in Wisconsin Rapids at the junction of Highway 13/73 and Highway 34. Wisconsin Rapids grew up as a logging community. Huge rafts of white pine were floated down the Wisconsin River and the first sawmill was built here in 1831. By 1837 the first paper mill followed and started an industry that still is one of the keys to the area economy. In the wetlands that surround the area the world's most productive cranberry marshes have flourished. Early in its history it consisted of two towns, Grand Rapids and Centralia. In 1938 the U.S. Postal Service was mixing up mail for Grand Rapids, Michigan, with that for Grand Rapids, Wisconsin, so the name was officially changed to Wisconsin Rapids.

Today the river and waters are still central to the economy, but rather than bringing white pine they're attracting visitors seeking scenic and recreational treasures.

"The Rapids" is a fine place to use as your tour headquarters. You'll find comfortable accommodations and fine dining at reasonable prices.

One of the area's many attractions is the *Alexander House,* (715) 887-3442, a center for art exhibits and archives. It is located along the beautiful Wisconsin River at 1131 Wisconsin River Dr. in Port Edwards.

Wood County is the most productive cranberry-growing region in the world. Photo by Gary Knowles.

The *Rapids Municipal Zoo,* (715) 421-8240, 1911 Gaynor Ave., is open May 1 through October 15. There are playground and picnic facilities and the stars of the show: animals native to Wisconsin!

The *South Wood County Historical Museum,* (715) 423-1580, 540 Third St. S., features central Wisconsin history and special exhibits and displays. Be sure to see the cranberry and logging exhibits to get a good understanding of these important parts of the Rapids history.

You can tour *Consolidated Papers Wisconsin Rapids and Converting Divisions* at 10 a.m. on Wednesdays, Thursdays, and Saturdays year-round. You may also tour Consolidated's recycling operations. Tours are by appointment for groups of six or more. Children must be accompanied by adults. Call (715) 422-3789 for more information.

The *Cranberry Highway Tour* was first developed in 1999 and is updated annually to offer an informative, fun, and educational tour of Wood

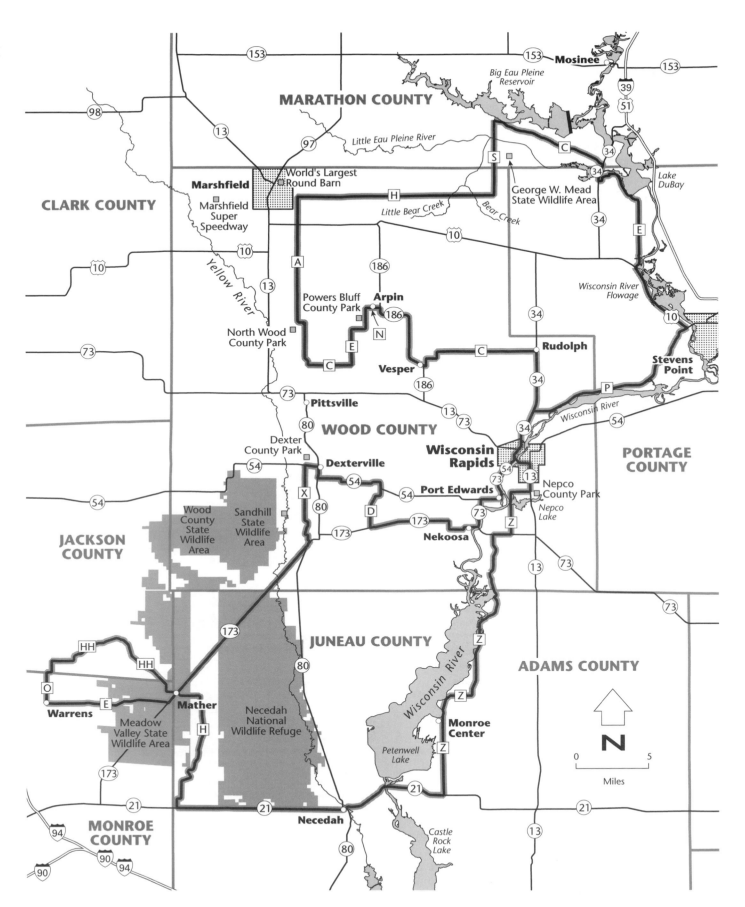

Tour 10

County's cranberry marshes and other cranberry-related businesses. In autumn, you can take a tour of the marshes as the harvest is in progress. One grower will even let you gather a crate of your own, for a fee. Call (800) 544-4484 for a free current route map and tour information. (See accompanying article.)

Bicycling is popular in the area, and the newest route is called the *Cranberry Trail,* which highlights the cranberry region. Call (800) 554-4484 to request the local trail maps.

The *Rainbow Casino,* (715) 886-4560, 949 County G, outside Nekoosa, has excellent buffets and lots of gaming and bingo excitement. In 1998, a man won $7.4 million here with one pull of a slot machine. It's the largest slot jackpot ever paid in Wisconsin.

Wisconsin golfers have long favored Wisconsin Rapids as a golf getaway. Hotel-golf packages are available. Check with the *Wisconsin Rapids Area Convention and Visitors Bureau* for current offers, (800) 544-4484. (See accompanying article.)

The *Hotel Mead,* (800) 843-6323, 451 E. Grand Ave., is an excellent choice (and surprising discovery) for those who want a full-service hotel with great restaurants and all the best amenities. Be sure to try the house breakfast specialty, Chef Crueger's cranberry French toast. There are many other fine places to stay, including the *Best Western Rapids Motor Inn,* (715) 423-3211, 911 Huntington Ave.; *The AmericInn,* (800) 634-3444, 3010 Eighth St. S.; *Super 8,* (800) 800-8000, 3410 Eighth St. S.; and the *Econo Lodge,* (800) 755-1488, 3300 Eighth St. S.

For excellent northern Italian dishes in a friendly, casual restaurant, try the *Cafe Mulino,* (715) 422-7000, in the Mead Inn.

To get an idea of what burgers and shakes used to taste like, you won't find a better drive-in (where you can dine inside too) than *Hershlebs,* (715) 423-1760, 640 16th St. N.

Go northeast on Highway 34 to the junction with County P. Turn right on P and follow it about 13.2 miles to the junction with Highway 10 just west of Stevens Point. In this stretch, you'll cruise alongside the historic Wisconsin River, see barns built generations ago, go from Wood to Portage County, and cross Mill Creek and Rocky Run Creek.

Stevens Point is just over the bridge to the right. This is the city the Native Americans knew as Hemlock Island because of the large stand of hemlocks that grew here. George Stevens built a trader's shack here in 1838 and within a few years the loggers were calling it "The Gateway to the Pineries." By 1850, it was named Stevens Point. Today the city has a diverse economic base, with major employers including Sentry Insurance, the University of Wisconsin-Stevens Point, and Consolidated Papers.

The area enjoys productive farmland, known as the Golden Sands for the wealth of the crops,

including potatoes and vegetables that grow here. If you're looking for city diversions, there are plenty—and they are diverse.

In town, you'll find the *Main Street Historic District,* which includes some 60 important historic buildings on a downtown walking tour, (715) 344-2556. *The Riverfront Arts Center,* (715) 343-6251, 600 Main St., has art exhibits and workshops. The *Stevens Point Brewery,* (715) 344-9310, 2617 Water St., is one of the few remaining little breweries in Wisconsin still in operation. Tours are available.

The *Beth Israel Synagogue and Portage County Historical Society,* (715) 344-4423, 1475 Water St., has a display of Jewish heritage and artifacts from the area. *Central Wisconsin Children's Museum* at *CenterPoint MarketPlace,* (715) 344-2003, is an interactive play space for children from pre-school to 12 years. From spring to late fall, the *Farmer's Market* can be found downtown in the public square.

The University of Wisconsin–Stevens Point campus, (715) 346-4242, 2100 Main St., has a number of fine attractions that appeal to a wide variety of guests. The *Carlsten Art Gallery* in the Fine Arts

Cranberry Country

When it comes to cranberries, Wisconsin is the king. With some 15,000 acres of cranberries under cultivation, the state produces about 40 percent of all cranberries consumed in the United States. The annual crop is worth about $334 million to the economy and the industry employs over 7,000 people.

The cranberry is one of just three fruits native to North America (the others are the blueberry and the Concord grape), and more of these bright-red berries are grown and harvested in central Wisconsin than in than any other place in the world. The cranberry vine is grown in peat swamps or marshes where the soil has an acidic nature and there is an abundant supply of water and sand. Water is used for irrigation, frost protection, winter flooding for weather protection, and harvesting. Sand is used to rejuvenate vines, encourage new rooting, and provide upright growth.

The vines are annual plants and some of the marshes have been tended and have produced fruit for over a century.

Cranberries are Wisconsin's number-one fruit crop. Travelers can see the beautiful red berries and join in harvest celebrations that traditionally begin in late September and run through most of October, with the peak time in mid-October. But another good time to visit the marshes is in midsummer as the little white "crane-head"-shaped blossoms appear.

A delightful side effect of all the wetlands tended by cranberry growers is the great wildlife and migratory bird populations they support. Keep your eyes open for these beautiful and sometimes rare inhabitants of the area.

Wood County, especially around Wisconsin Rapids, is the most productive growing region in the world for cranberries. You'll see plenty of marshes (not "bogs" in this part of the state) and cranberry-related facilities—especially in the south loop of this tour.

Please remember to park only in designated areas and always use caution. Marshes and dikes are wetlands and you can easily slip off a dike and into a marsh.

Center, (715) 346-4797, shows contemporary art by students and faculty. The *Museum of Natural History*, (715) 346-2858, has exhibits that trace earth's history back to the dinosaurs, while the *Planetarium* at the Science Building, (715) 346-2208, exhibits the wonders of the universe.

Schmeeckle Reserve, (715) 346-4992, at North Point Dr., is a 200-acre research and teaching reserve open for biking, hiking, and jogging. *The Wisconsin Conservation Hall of Fame*, (715) 346-4992, also on North Point Dr., honors the state's rich legacy of leadership in stewardship and preservation of our natural resources.

Finally, the *Green Circle Trail* is a 24-mile linked trail along the Wisconsin and Plover Rivers for walkers, runners, bikers, and in season, cross-country skiers. For a free guide call (715) 344-2556.

At the intersection of County P and Highway 10, go northwest on 10, which is soon joined by County E. When County E splits off to the right after about 4 miles, follow it and continue to the junction with Highway 34. On this stretch you'll drive along the Wisconsin River shoreline and then north to Lake DuBay.

Turn right (north) on 34 and drive to the junction with County C, driving into Marathon County across the Little Eau Pleine Flowage.

Turn left (northwest) on C and go about 8.2 miles to County S. Here you'll cruise through a nicely wooded expanse, including the *George W. Mead Wildlife Area*, which teems with migratory birds, deer, songbirds, and raccoon.

Turn left (south) on S and drive about 5.3 miles to the junction with County H. You'll be cutting back across the Little Eau Pleine River and encountering more wildlife as you drive into Wood County.

Note: The Yellowstone Trail, a coast-to-coast route developed by early auto adventurers in 1912, follows some of the country trails we've been traveling on this tour. In 2000, a group of Wisconsin historians and community leaders produced a free brochure showing some of the old trail routes. You can get a free copy by calling (800) 236-4636.

Turn right on H, crossing Bear Creek, Little Bear Creek, and South Creek and meeting County A just southeast of Marshfield.

Wisconsin's Hidden Golf Hub

Golf enthusiasts have their favorites, and this area is one of them. Prices are very reasonable and the quality of golf courses is excellent. Wisconsin Rapids has quietly become a hub for golfing getaways.

The *Lake Arrowhead Golf Course*, (715) 325-2929, near Nekoosa (to the south on Highway 13), has 36 championship holes and is ranked as one of the best golfing values in the United States by *Golf Digest* magazine. *The Ridges*, (715) 424-3204, is an excellent woods-and-river 18 in Wisconsin Rapids. Stevens Point has the highly ranked Robert Trent Jones II–designed *SentryWorld*, (715) 345-1600, and, along the Wisconsin River, the beautiful *Wisconsin River Golf Club*, (715) 344-9152. Up the highway, Marshfield offers the excellent *Marshfield Country Club*, (715) 384-4409, and the always-challenging *Riveredge*, (715) 676-3900).

But before you proceed, spend some time in Marshfield. The Wisconsin Central Railroad built a line extending west from Stevens Point and it's said by some that the stop here was named after Marshfield, Massachusetts. Others claim that the name came from John J. Marsh, who owned much of the town, and still others point to the wetlands and farm fields in the area as the inspiration.

Regardless, it's a gem of a community that has been tabbed "Wisconsin's Best Small City." Today it enjoys a national reputation for its excellent medical facilities: *St. Joseph's Hospital* and the *Marshfield Clinic*. More than 550 Marshfield Clinic physicians serve some 4,000 patients each day at the main campus and 38 regional medical centers. St. Joseph's admits nearly 19,000 patients a year, and the state's largest medical laboratory will conduct over one million tests per year for physicians, hospitals, and patients in five surrounding states. Group tours of the medical complex can be arranged by calling or stopping by the *Visitors and Promotion Bureau*, (800) 422-4541, 700 S. Central Ave.

The community hosts a wide variety of events throughout the year, including a Mothers Day Art Fair, Dairyfest, Zoofest, the Central Wisconsin State Fair, and a Fall Fest as well as other occasional celebrations. In 2000 the Marshfield Chamber of Commerce held the first annual search for "the world's cutest cow." The winner was Heidi, a Holstein owned by Jenny Junghen of Darien.

Be sure to visit *Fair Park* and get a photo of the *World's Largest Round Barn*, (715) 387-1261, listed on the National Register of Historic Places.

The Upham Mansion, (715) 387-3322, 212 W. Third St., was built by Wisconsin Governor William Henry Upham in 1880. This represents mid-Victorian architecture at its finest. The furnishings of the mansion are vintage Victorian, many of them left by the Upham family. There are photos, Native American artifacts, and period furnishings. The mansion is listed in the National Register of Historic Places and also serves as the center for the *North Wood County Historical Society's* featured monthly exhibits.

Foxfire Gardens, (715) 387-3050, just out of Marshfield at M220 Sugarbush Lane, is an extraordinary Japanese- and Western-style natural garden area that welcomes visitors to a beautiful seven-acre oasis of peace, harmony, and tranquility. Not far away you'll find amazing metal swamp creatures in a place called *Jurustic Park*, (800) 422-4541. These fanciful dinosaurs are art pieces welded from machine scraps, pipes, and cast-off hunks of metal and are a delight for all ages.

The *Marshfield Public Library*, (715) 387-8495, 211 E. Second St., houses the famous Stierle Bird Exhibit. One of the finest taxidermic collections in the country, it has 380 birds of 140 species in addition to 1,890 eggs.

Shoppers will want to visit *Figi's Cheese and Gifts* retail outlet at 1302 N. Central Ave. Antique hunters have kept this area a well-guarded secret for years, and a stop at some of the area shops will show you why. A wide variety of antiques, furniture, glassware, collectibles, and paper items at reasonable prices is truly a source the "pros" would rather not share! Call or stop and ask the Visitor and Promotion Bureau for a current listing.

New Visions Gallery, (715) 387-5562, 1000 N. Oak Ave., is Marshfield's special place for the visual arts. The nonprofit community museum is located in the lobby of Marshfield Clinic. New Visions organizes changing exhibitions every four to six weeks, including a variety of art forms, national traveling exhibitions, significant works on loan from private and public collections, and quality regional art. New Visions also maintains a permanent collection of contemporary original prints, Japanese prints, fine-art posters, Haitian paintings, Australian Aboriginal art, West African sculpture and masks. An art reference library is available for browsing and there is an excellent gift shop.

The *Wildwood Park and Zoo,* (715) 384-4642, off Highway 13 on Roddis Ave., is recognized as one of Wisconsin's finest municipal zoos. Built in 1924, it covers 60 acres and has more than 200 animals from North America and around the world. Favorites are the wolves, mountain lions, prairie dogs, bald eagle, and grizzly bears. Canada geese, ducks, muskrat, rabbits, and squirrels have free run of the property. A new drive-by part of the park features buffalo, elk, Barbary sheep, turkeys, white-tailed deer, and timber wolves.

The area welcomes outdoor sports enthusiasts, and golfers will enjoy the area links. The *Marshfield Super Speedway* hosts late-model and pure super-stock races every Saturday from mid-April to mid-September, (715) 384-8325.

Good lodging is easy to find at a wide variety of motels in Marshfield. In addition, the *Evergreen Inn Bed and Breakfast* offers a gracious and elegant way to enjoy your visit, (715) 389-8087.

The *Marshfield Visitors and Promotion Bureau,* (800) 422-4541, in the Chamber of Commerce office, 700 S. Central Ave., will provide area brochures and a warm welcome.

From H turn left (south) on A, crossing Mill Creek and Beaver Creek and, about 9 miles from Marshfield, passing the entrance to *North Wood County Park,* (715) 421-8422. This well-tended park has 172 acres with camping facilities and two small lakes. There's a spectacular 225-foot suspension bridge that crosses the Yellow River and two step dams.

Continue on A to County C. Turn left (east) on C and go about 3.5 miles to County E. Turn left (north) on E and follow it as it jogs east and north to Bluff Drive. If you turn left on Bluff Dr. you can visit beautiful *Powers Bluff County Park,* (715) 421-8422, the 13th highest spot in Wisconsin. This 160-acre park is a snow lover's delight, with winter skiing and one of the state's best tubing runs. In summer the park is an excellent hiking area. Try the *Potawatomi Nature Trail* for a great outing. For generations

before European settlement, the area was a ceremonial gathering spot for Ojibwa, Ho-Chunk, and Potawatomi people.

Follow E north to County N at Arpin. Turn right on N and go through town to the junction with Highway 186. Turn right (south) on 186 crossing Hemlock Creek and continuing into the town of Vesper, where you'll meet County C. A local story has it that Vesper was originally called "Hardscrabble," an apt name to describe the tough life in these parts. However, when the first post office was set up, a Mr. Cameron, who served as first postmaster, asked the postal authorities to come up with a "better" name and "Vesper" it was, and is. There is no report whether the conditions improved after the renaming.

In the Stevens Point area, descendants of early Polish settlers preserve their culture in festivals held throughout the year. Wisconsin Department of Tourism photo by GK.

Turn left (north) on C and follow it north and then east about 8.5 miles into the town of Rudolph, where you'll meet Highway 34. The *Dairy State Cheese Factory,* (715) 435-3144, makes fresh cheese and you can watch the process through a window. If your timing is right, you can get some squeaky fresh cheese curds here. The store sells dozens of delicious specialty cheeses, including cranberry jack made in season with local fruit. The store also have delicious ice cream! And the *Rudolph Grotto* has outdoor religious art, including caves, bridges, and flower gardens.

Turn right (south) on 34 and cruise back into Wisconsin Rapids to the junction with Highway 13. Take 13 south through the city, crossing the Wisconsin River on the Riverview Expressway (Highway 13/54). Stop at the *Wisconsin Rapids Area Visitor Information Center,* (800) 554-4484, 1120 Lincoln St.. The friendly staff has lots of information and publications about area attractions and "Cranberry Highway" maps to help you plan your area touring.

Follow Highway 13 south to County Z. Turn right (west) on Z. If you turn left on Z and go a few blocks, you can visit *Nepco County Park,* (715) 421-8422, on Nepco Lake. This 125-acre park has a great beach and picnic area, and the lake is known for good fishing too.

Follow Z west, then south, as it jogs past cranberry marshes. (There's a pull-off here where you can get a good view of the marshes and vines. Be careful . . . and stay off the dikes. There is a lot of water out there and the grass gets pretty slip-

Land Of the Giants! 700-Pound Pumpkins!

They spend most of their lives lounging in fields, growing to about the size of a Lazyboy, and getting so heavy it takes five strong men to lift one. They drink lots of water and soak up the rays. Then on the first Saturday in October, they gather for the weigh-in, go on display, amuse the kids (and adults too), and get in on the big competition. What are these gargantuans?

They're giant pumpkins, the "fruit" of the pumpkin vine, and they roll into Nekoosa, Wisconsin, for the *Annual Pumpkin Fest and Official Central Wisconsin Pumpkin Weigh-in* the first Saturday in October. All of them will be patted, hugged, and photographed as they take center stage on their big day.

The Nekoosa festival is a part of the worldwide competition organized by The Great Pumpkin Commonwealth, an organization of growers dedicated to growing them big and setting records. The Nekoosa competition is one of the best in the nation and it has become one of the most popular pumpkin festivals in the Midwest.

"We get people from all over Wisconsin and even Minnesota and Illinois bringing their pumpkins, squash, and watermelons here to be registered," said John Weidman, President of the Central Wisconsin Pumpkin Growers. "In 1999, we had more than 80 Giant Pumpkins with the top 10 averaging well over 700 pounds each. It's fun and friendly competition—an event that's great for the whole family." For more information on the festival, area lodging, biking, golf, and a free map and guide to the area, phone (800) 554-4484. Sometimes, if you ask, they'll even send free giant pumpkin seeds and a set of instructions, so you can grow your own!

pery. An unplanned dip in the marsh can spoil your whole day!)

Continue on Z as it joins Highway 73 for a short run to the west, then leaves it. This is a delightful drive through rolling woods and plenty of water. You'll travel through marsh and woodlands along the wild Petenwell Flowage. This area offers excellent fishing and water recreation. Watch for deer and wild turkey all along this stretch of road.

Follow Z south through Monroe Center to the junction with Highway 21. Turn right (west) on 21, cross the Wisconsin River, and drive into Juneau County and the city of Necedah. *Necedah* is a Ho-Chunk word that is said to mean "land of yellow waters." It refers to the general area where water colored by soils and minerals drains into the Wisconsin River. The area was a favorite with many Native American people, including Potawatomi, Ho-Chunk, Fox, Sauk, and Ojibwa.

Four miles west of town is the *Necedah National Wildlife Refuge*, (608) 565-2551, a 43,656-acre area north of Highway 21 that was established by President Franklin D. Roosevelt in 1939 as a refuge and breeding ground for migratory birds and other wildlife. It's managed by the U.S. Department of the Interior and is an excellent place to hike, observe wildlife, and enjoy nature. There are more than 200 species of birds that have been observed here, and gray wolves, bald eagles, and the Karner blue butterfly are some of the creatures that have also been spotted.

Visit the headquarters by driving north off of Highway 21 on Headquarters Rd., where you'll find lots of information about animals and plants in the refuge, as well as pamphlets detailing trails and viewing stations in the park.

Stay on 21 and go to County H. Turn right (north) on H and go to Highway 173 at Mather,

motoring through the Meadow Valley State Wildlife Area near Eagle Nest Flowage, crossing Silver Creek, and then turning west.

Turn left (southwest) on 173 and go about 1 mile to County E/EW. Bear right (west) on E/EW and drive into Warrens. Along the way, you'll go through wetlands, cross Dead Creek, and pass cranberry marshes. The village of Warrens has earned recognition worldwide for its annual *Cranberry Festival*, (608) 378-4200, held late in September each year. Tens of thousands of people come to celebrate the harvest, sample the product, and tour the cranberry marshes. A farmers market and flea market top off the big festival.

In Warrens, turn right (north) on County O and go into Jackson County to County HH. Turn right on HH and go to Highway 173 at Mather. Turn left (northeast). You'll see numerous cranberry marshes, pass quickly through Monroe and Juneau Counties, cross Beaver Creek, and numerous others before entering Wood County and the *Wood County State Wildlife Area.*

Go to County X and turn left (north) on X. You'll drive along the eastern edge of the *Sandhill State Wildlife Area.* Logging roads, service roads, dikes, and other unmarked trails provide opportunities to "get off the beaten path." The area will charm you with its abundant solitude, marshes, ducks, woods and ferns, bison herds, deer, beaver, and a host of other native flora and fauna. Auto trails and observation towers let you see nature first-hand in the 9,500-acre tract. Watch for the magnificent sandhill cranes throughout this area. No wildlife lover should pass without stopping to take a look.

Continue north on X to Highway 54. Just north of 54, *Dexter County Park* has 1,000 acres of land with abundant wildlife and great fishing. There is a hiking trail and a handicapped fishing access area.

Turn right (east) on 54 and pass through Dexterville to the intersection with County D. This area is the heart of the world's most productive cranberry region.

Turn right (south) on D, passing through Cranmoor Township and past marshes to the junction with Highway 173. Turn left (northeast) on 173 and follow it into Nekoosa and the junction with Highway 73. Turn left (north) on 73 and go to the junction with Highway 54. Follow 73/54 through Port Edwards along the Wisconsin River back to downtown Wisconsin Rapids.

Tour 11
Waterfalls and Solitude, Whitewater and Fire

Suamico—Little Suamico—Oconto—Peshtigo—Marinette—Wausaukee—Amberg—Pembine—Niagara—Iron Mountain (Mich.)—Spread Eagle—Florence—Dunbar—Crivitz—Suamico

Distance: 256 miles

Tucked away in northeast Wisconsin are dozens of fascinating little communities, excellent fishing waters, and great getaway routes. Because it's not between other major destinations, this remote but thoroughly enjoyable part of the state is not heavily traveled or all that well known. But take this tour and you'll see some of the finest waterfall country in Wisconsin—and you'll probably like it all the better because you'll have it almost to yourself. Solitude is an abundant natural resource here.

Don't miss two stops: the first is Marinette, a truly friendly and picturesque little port; and the second is the Peshtigo Fire Museum—a place that tells a story so gripping that you will carry it with you for life.

The roads that connect these and other communities are generally quiet and well maintained, but be sure to stay alert for wildlife because there's plenty to see and some of it may try to cross the road in front of you.

Now have fun, enjoy those back roads, and don't miss a chance to take a dip in a secluded lake or a serene waterfall pool!

Begin just north of Green Bay in Suamico on Highway 41/141 at the junction with County B. The Menominee nation once had a large settlement at Suamico and its name is derived from their words meaning roughly "place of the yellow beaver."

Take B east to County J. Turn left (north) on J and continue to the junction with County S at Little Suamico. Turn right on S, crossing Kirchner Creek and passing through Oak Orchard in the *Green Bay Shores State Wildlife Area* as you follow the little-traveled west shore of Green Bay. Watch for wildlife here and all along the road as you enjoy the sights.

Stay on S and head into the city of Oconto. Here, you'll cross the Oconto River, which is said to have been noted on a 1695 map published by Cornelli in Venice, Italy. The name is probably Menominee and refers to the "plentiful fishes" that were found at the mouth of the river.

Some 5,000 years ago, this area was inhabited by Paleo-Indians, now known as the Copper Cul-

ture People. They lived along the banks of the Oconto River and buried their dead here. You can visit the *Copper Culture Mounds State Park*, (920) 492-5836, on the west side of town, just off Highway 22; and you can see artifacts from that era, the oldest forged instruments in North America. At the *Beyer Historic Home and Museum Annex,* 917 Park Ave., Oconto, (920) 834-6206, you can catch a glimpse of the lives of well-to-do 19th-century Wisconsinites, along with artifacts of pioneer families and early settlers. Two electric cars are of special interest. Open June 1 to Labor Day.

Downtown Oconto offers even more history. Twenty historic structures, including three blocks of residences on West Main St., have been placed on the National Register of Historic Places. A self-guided tour booklet of the city is available at the *Oconto Visitor Center*, (920) 834-2255, located in

The Peshtigo Fire—America's Deadliest

OK . . . a show of hands. Who knows about the Chicago Fire? OK. Almost everyone. Right, the cow got blamed and it was October 8, 1871. Now, who can tell us about the Peshtigo Fire? As I expected . . . very few. The Peshtigo Fire took place *on the very day* that Chicago burned. No one was killed in the Chicago Fire. Some 800 people perished in Peshtigo. The fire came through with the sound and speed of a tornado. "Like bolts from hell," balls of fire fell on the prosperous little milling town. For 20 horrific minutes the roar of the fire drowned out most every sound, except the screams of the victims. Families tried to escape but were covered with burning showers of ash. Dozens tried to flee to the river but the fire burned the bridge out from under them. Those that made it to the river were knocked off logs by cows and horses gone wild. Faced with what seemed certain, horrible death, one father slashed the throats of his children and wife—then killed himself. A whole town was reduced to ashes. Blackened bodies lined the streets. Those who survived were faced with a cinder field the next day. The whole incredible story was told in painful detail by the *Peshtigo Times* and is reprinted in a pamphlet available free from the *Peshtigo Chamber of Commerce,* P.O. Box 36, Peshtigo, 54157, (715) 582-0327. In addition to the Peshtigo Fire Museum, you can visit the cemetery where a mass grave holds the remains of those who were burned beyond recognition. Help to tell the story of the fire that ranks as the worst and most deadly in American history. Oh, yes. One further irony: most of the lumber that built—and rebuilt Chicago—came from the forests of northern Wisconsin.

189
70
2 **141**
Menominee River
95

M I C H I G A N

N
0   10
Miles

70 Florence
2 **141**
Spread Eagle
Lake Antoine
N Iron Mountain
FLORENCE COUNTY
2

139
101
N
Niagara
141 **8**

8
O
FOREST COUNTY
Dunbar
Goodman
8
8
Long Slide Falls
Pembine

8 **32**
MARINETTE COUNTY
141

32
Benson Lake Rd.
Parkway Rd.
Goodman County Park
Amberg

McClintock County Park
Wausaukee R.

52
Parkway Rd.
180
Wausaukee
35

Twin Bridges Park
141
Lake Noquebay

64
Veterans Memorial Park
W
Crivitz
Menominee River
41
Chambers Island

64
64
Peshtigo River
180
57

MENOMINEE COUNTY
32
64
Menominee
Marinette
41
BB Shore Dr.

Wolf River
141
W
Peshtigo
B **BB**
Y

OCONTO COUNTY
Copper Culture State Park
41
Y
42

22
22
Oconto
Green Bay

Shawano
29
22
J
41

Shawano Lake
32
S
DOOR COUNTY

SHAWANO COUNTY
41 **141**
57
42

47
Little Suamico
J

156
55
29
Suamico
Green Bay Shores State Wildlife Area
KEWAUNEE COUNTY

156
29 Green Bay
B
57
BROWN COUNTY
Lake Michigan

OUTAGAMIE COUNTY
32
43
54
54
163
42

Tour 11

the Z-Cheese Shop, 110 Brazeau Ave. (Highway 41).

Turn right on County Y in Oconto, traveling through the *Oconto Marsh-Rush Point Wildlife Area,* running close to the shore of Green Bay, crossing Thomas Slough, and then heading north, away from the bay.

Take Y to its junction with Highway 41. Turn right on 41 and head into Peshtigo. The *Peshtigo Fire Museum,* 400 Oconto Ave., (715) 582-3244, tells the story of the horrible tornado of fire that burned this town to the ground in 1871. (See accompanying article.)

Take 41 north to its junction in Peshtigo with County B. Turn right on B and follow the Peshtigo River. Turn right on County BB. This wilderness trail follows the Peshtigo River in a southeasterly direction to its mouth on Green Bay and then circles back east and north along the western Green Bay shore to Marinette.

Follow BB (Shore Drive) into Marinette. This interesting Wisconsin port city often gets overlooked and overshadowed these days because it's not situated on a major route. It wasn't always that way. In the logging era it was called "the White Pine Capital of the World," and sawmills lined the banks of the Menominee River.

You can trace some of the area's proud history at the *Marinette County Historical Museum,* (715) 732-0831, on Stephenson Island, just off Highway 41 as you cross into Michigan. There's a wonderful diorama depicting life in a logging camp, a restored log cabin, Native American artifacts, and "lumber hookers"—Great Lakes schooners that carried lumber to the big cities "down below."

If you're looking for great charter fishing for trout or salmon, call the *Marinette Chamber of Commerce,* (715) 735-6681, and you'll be put in touch with some outstanding charter services. The chamber also publishes a guide that will direct you to several good waterfalls in the area that this tour doesn't visit.

Stay on Shore Drive in Marinette all the way to Main Street. Turn left on Main and continue to Hall Avenue. Turn left on Hall and continue to Roosevelt Road (County T). Turn right on Roosevelt and cross Highway 64 where Roosevelt becomes Highway 180.

Dave's Falls is named for a lumberjack who lost his life breaking up a logjam there. Wisconsin Department of Tourism photo by Jim Bach.

Drive north out of Marinette on 180 about 32 miles until it meets Highway 141. This beautiful drive wiggles northward through wetlands, resort and recreation areas with picnic and boat-launching facilities along the Menominee River to McAllister, and then cuts west past Bear Point to Wausaukee.

Wausaukee is a Menominee word that means "river in the hills." The town was started in 1863 by John S. Monroe, who bought 160 acres of land and built a mill to supply the railroads with lumber for bridges and culverts. His first building was a log cabin home that was also used to board the mill workers. Eventually, as the town grew and more people moved in, his log cabin grew into an inn and was the only public eating establishment north of Green Bay. Today farming and tourism are the major pillars of the local economy.

Turn right (north) on 141 and go through Wausaukee, crossing the Wausaukee River, passing Lost Lake, and reaching *Dave's Falls Park.* Here you can walk to Dave's Falls. Dave was a young lumberjack who lost his life breaking up a logjam on the Pike River back in the lumberjack days. The trout fishing is good here. Call the *Marinette County Tourism Office,* (800) 236-6681, for more information.

Drive a little farther north on 141 to Amberg. The *Amberg Museum,* (715) 759-5672, exhibits will give you a glimpse of the days when logging, granite mining, and early farming made up the area's economy.

Stay on 141 north past Beecher Lake, through Beecher and Pembine. The name Pembine is

Wet and wild, the Peshtigo River is one of Wisconsin's finest for whitewater rafting. Wisconsin Department of Tourism photo by GK.

derived from *pemen,* the Menominee word for cranberries. About five miles north of Pembine you can turn east on Morgan Park Rd. and follow the signs to *Morgan Park.* It's about a 0.25-mile hike to Long Slide Falls on the Pembonwon River, which takes a spectacular 50-foot plunge through the rocks. This is a wonderful place to just sit and enjoy some magnificent sights. If you're adventurous you can take the little path (unmarked) upstream about 0.5 mile to Smalley Falls.

Follow 141 into Niagara, then into Michigan, where you'll meet Highway 2 before heading into the town of Iron Mountain. The town traces its fame to the Menominee Iron Ore Range. In 1879, the Chapin Mine, widely regarded as among the greatest iron mines in the world, was started. This mine was huge! It was 6,100 feet wide and up to 150 feet deep. Cut out from under a cedar swamp, it was also one of the wettest. To deal with the problem, a new pump, the Cornish Pump, was designed by the Allis-Chalmers Company. It could handle 3,400 gallons per minute, or five million gallons each 24 hours. Today the mine is a National Historic Site, National Historic Mechanical Engineering Landmark, and a Michigan Historic Civil Engineering Landmark. In the years between 1880 and 1932, the mine produced 27,506,868 tons of iron ore before closing on August 1, 1932.

Stay on Highway 2/141 past Lake Antoine and Moon Lake, winding west back into Wisconsin and Florence County. Unlike other parts of Wisconsin that were visited by explorers and fur traders in the 17th and 18th centuries, the Flo-

rence County area saw its first non-Native American in 1840, when a U.S. Army officer, Captain Thomas Jefferson Cram, explored the region. The Menominee and Ojibwa people, of course, had been here for years, hunting and fishing along the wild rivers. In the 1870s iron ore was discovered and the mining industry flourished. The Vulcan Mine in Florence was started in 1879 and was productive until 1920.

The area was logged off in the period from 1868 to just after the turn of the century. The first to go was the white pine, which easily floated; then when that was gone the loggers took the denser hardwoods.

Today the area is again a green, wild, wonderful place. Watch for eagles, ospreys, bear, deer, fisher, and even timber wolves. There are 265 lakes, 165 miles of rivers, and a population of less than 5,000 good people on some 495 square miles. It is one of two Wisconsin counties (the other one is Menominee) without an incorporated town or village. There are no traffic lights in Florence County.

It has, however, two of the three rivers designated as Wisconsin Wild Rivers: the Pine and the Popple (the Pestigo is the third). In addition, there is excellent canoeing on the Brule River. All of these rivers have portions that flow within the 660,000-acre Nicolet National Forest. Additional information is available from the *Wild Rivers Interpretive Center,* HC 1 Box 83, Florence, 54121, or by calling (888) 889-0049.

Stay on 2/141 north through Spread Eagle. Just south of Spread Eagle is a rare ecological wilderness area called the *Spread Eagle Barrens.* This rather derogatory designation was given to it by early surveyors, who saw the area as a brushy and scrubby "waste area," not completely understanding its importance in the environment. In fact it is a biologically rich and diverse area with lots of plants that are endangered or very scarce. It serves as an excellent wild area for many varieties of songbirds. Note that access is best by hiking in or by four-wheel-drive vehicle. Get more information and a map at the Wild Rivers Interpretive Center.

Continue on 2/141 to Florence, past Fisher Lake, and then to the junction with Highway N. (If you continue a bit farther on 2/141 to its junction with Highway 70/101 just west of Florence, you'll find the Wild Rivers Interpretive Center. It has interesting exhibits, including a rare albino white-tailed deer, and offers information to help put the importance of wild places in perspective.)

Turn left (south) on County N and go south, then east, driving across numerous creeks and through some great wild country, crossing the Pine and the Popple Rivers, and following the Menominee River.

Stay on N through Aurora, then back to Marinette County, to the junction with County O. Turn right (south) on O and continue as it turns right (west) and then left (south) to the intersection with Highway 8. Turn right (west) on 8 through Dunbar and continue about 7 miles to Parkway Road about 2 miles east of Goodman.

Turn left (south) on Parkway Road and continue across Camp F Creek, Harvey Creek, and Avery Creek to Benson Lake Road. Turn right on Benson Lake Road and then left into *Goodman Park.* To see picturesque *Strong Falls,* situated on the Peshtigo River, take a short hike through the park.

Follow the road through the park to Parkway Road. Turn right (south) on Parkway and continue to *McClintock Park.* Park here and walk to see the series of rapids called McClintock Falls. You can see some great views and get great photos from the bridges here.

Return to Parkway Road and continue south. (This is Wisconsin Rustic Road 32.) At the junction with County C, Parkway jogs east (left) with C briefly before turning back right (south). While in this densely wooded area, check out the possibilities for whitewater rafting. The accompanying article has the names of several outfitters who will gladly get you real wet while you ride the wildest water in Wisconsin.

Fishing enthusiasts should also stop and wet a line. The Peshtigo River is a great fly-fishing favorite, but all along this tour you'll find lakes, rivers, and creeks that look like they might be productive. And they are. The High Falls Flowage and the Caldron Flowage are an angler's paradise.

Continue on Parkway Road, passing Old Veterans Campground and Twin Bridge Park before reaching *Veterans Memorial Park.* Set on the Thunder River, the park features steep slopes leading to a wooden bridge and falls. You'll find camping and picnicking areas in the park.

Return to Parkway Road and follow the drive around to the south and east and to the junction with County W. Turn left (east) on W and continue east into Crivitz. The *Crivitz Museum,* (715) 854-3278, on South St. in this friendly little town, has been in operation for about a decade, and it's well worth a stop. Get a look at the history of the area as it passes from logging to railroads to the early resorts.

Follow W east out of Crivitz, then south, eventually crossing the Peshtigo River. Continue to the junction with Highway 41 at the Oconto County line. Turn right (south) onto 41 and go to Highway 22 on the west edge of Oconto.

Turn right (west) on 22 and go to the junction with County J. Turn left on J, proceeding into Brown County and the intersection with County B east of Suamico.

Turn right on B to return to Suamico, our starting point.

Ride Wisconsin's Wildest Rivers!

The Pike, the Peshtigo, the Menominee. These are more than just pretty rivers. They'll give you the ride of your life if you let them! In the Athelstane area there are a number of outfitters ready to put you in the water upstream and then pick you up after you've enjoyed Mother Nature's washing machine. Choose your watercraft and go it alone, pair up, or have a real group session. The outfitters rent rafts, kayaks, canoes, and "funyaks" (inflatable rubber kayaks) and provide some instructions and shuttle service at the end. Not all outfitters have every type, so call ahead to reserve your choice of conveyance. The season runs from early April to late October, with the wildest water usually running in spring and the incredible fall colors starting in mid- to late September. Among the best are *Kosir's Rapid Rafts & Campgrounds,* W14073 County C, Athelstane, 54104, (715) 757-3431; *Mt. Jed's Camping and Canoing,* W13364 County C, Athelstane, 54104, (715) 757-2406; *Thornton's Whitewater Rafting Resort & Campground,* W12882 Parkway Rd., Athelstane, 54104, (715) 757-3311; and *Wildman Whitewater Ranch,* N12080 Allison La., Athelstane, 54104, (888) 813-8524.

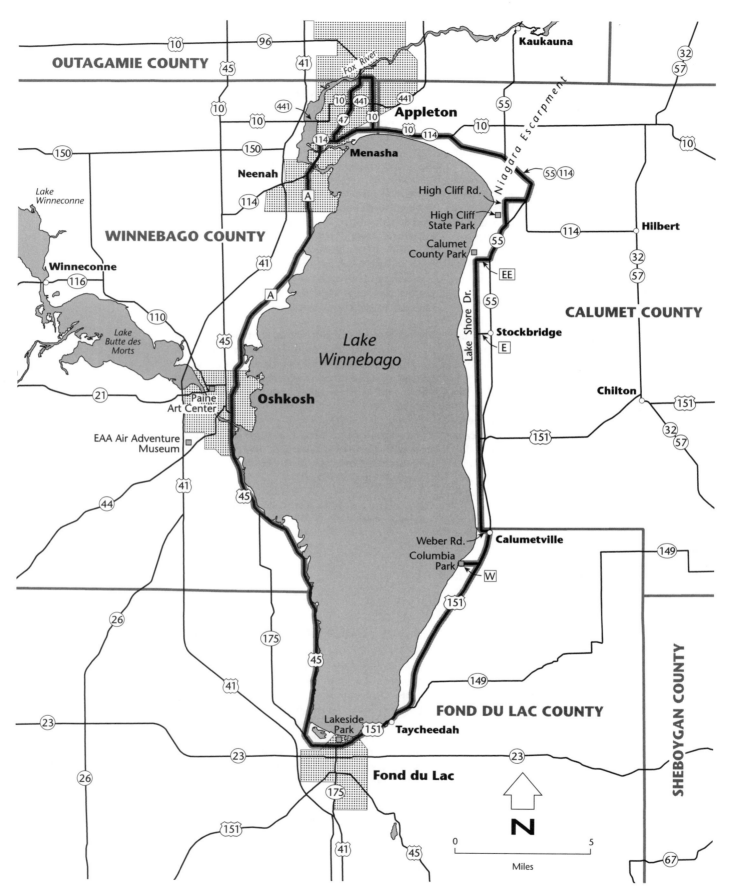

OUTAGAMIE COUNTY

Kaukauna

Fox River

Appleton

Menasha

Neenah

Lake
Winneconne

WINNEBAGO COUNTY

Winneconne

Lake Butte des Morts

High Cliff Rd.

High Cliff State Park

Calumet County Park

Niagara Escarpment

Hilbert

CALUMET COUNTY

Lake Shore Dr.

Stockbridge

Chilton

Lake
Winnebago

Paine Art Center

Oshkosh

EAA Air Adventure Museum

Weber Rd.

Columbia Park

Calumetville

SHEBOYGAN COUNTY

Lakeside Park

Taycheedah

FOND DU LAC COUNTY

Fond du Lac

N

0   5
Miles

Tour 12

64

Tour 12
Winnebago-land

Fond du Lac—Calumetville—Stockbridge—Kaukauna—Appleton— Menasha—

Neenah—Oshkosh—Fond du Lac

Distance: 69 miles

The Lookout Lighthouse Tower at Lakeside Park in Fond du Lac is a popular starting point for road rallies.
Photo by Gary Knowles.

The concept of driving around Lake Winnebago has always appealed to me. It was a favorite spot for Native Americans and served as the first route for European explorers. It promises some interesting roads and lake views on the east shore and historic cities on the west.

If you like lakes, you'll love Wisconsin. The state has 15,057 of them, each a different size, including some still unnamed. But get out the map and Wisconsin's biggest lake, Winnebago, all 215 square miles (138,000 acres) of it, in east-central Wisconsin, jumps right out at you.

Ranking among the largest freshwater lakes in the world, Lake Winnebago has 88 miles of shoreline and is quite shallow, with a maximum depth of about 21 feet. Fishing enthusiasts know it's a great place to catch pan fish and walleyed pike, but it's even more famous as home to the world's largest population of lake sturgeon, a fish whose gnarly looks make the Creature from the Black Lagoon seem cuddly by comparison!

In winter Winnebago is an ice fishing paradise dotted with colorful ice shanties. In summer the waters are speckled with all manner of watercraft, powered by motor, sail, or paddle. In any season, exploring Winnebago promises to be an adventure for all your senses.

A great way to experience "Winnebago-land" is to drive around the lake. Plan on at least a half day if you're just cruising, grabbing a fast lunch, and making a couple of quick "shoot a picture and run" camera stops. But to really appreciate the area, plan a full day and stop at a few of the special places listed below.

Start in Fond du Lac (preferably in the morning) at *Lakeside Park*. Follow Highway 151 north and east through Fond du Lac. (We'll feature the city's attractions at the end of the tour.) We suggest leaving in this direction and at this time to ensure that the sun will be lighting the eastern side of the lakeshore that you'll be explor-

Hearthstone in Appleton was the first residence in the U.S. to enjoy hydroelectric-powered illumination. Wisconsin Department of Tourism photo.

Continue on Lake Shore Road for about 10 miles to County E. Turn right (east) and drive into the little town of Stockbridge. This community was established in 1833 by Reverend Eleazer Williams, a "mixed blood" St. Regis Missionary minister, and 230 Stockbridge and Oneida Indians who came from Kaukauna. They had settled there in 1821 after being pressured out of New York by white settlers eager to control the land. Their settlement at Kaukauna was under a treaty with the Menominee who controlled the mouth of the Lower Fox River. Rev. Williams encouraged them to make the move to escape the "evil ways" of the white settlers. It may also have been the case that their "semi-Christian ways" irritated the other Native Americans in the area. By 1837 the American Presbyterian Church stopped supporting this mission, and Williams left in dismay. Later, as the growing pressure to gain access to native land resulted in treaties and the desire to move tribes west, the Stockbridge people were "given" U.S. citizenship and moved to Shawano. Some remained in the area and others returned later.

ing, and by the time you reach the opposite side of Winnebago, it will be in the west sky illuminating the western shore.

After about 10 miles, turn left from 151 onto County W and enter *Columbia Park,* (800) 937-9123. Here you can enjoy almost 2,000 acres, two boat launches, a playground, a pavilion, and an 80-foot observation tower. This park offers a fine welcome and a great view of Lake Winnebago.

Return to 151 and continue north. You'll see many more signs for Winnebago beaches, but save your time because most of these are deceptive. Until Calumet County Park (about 20 miles farther north) and High Cliff State Park (about 45 miles farther), you'll find the others are just semiprivate drives with rather limited or no public access to the waterfront.

Follow 151 about 3 miles to Calumetville, turn left on Weber Road and go about a mile to Lake Shore Road. Turn right on Lake Shore. This is a beautiful lake country drive that's a pleasant and pastoral alternative to the hurried pace of traffic on Highway 151 and Highway 55.

The influence of later European settlers is still evident. Stop at *Hemauer's General Store* (established in 1911), (920) 439-1175, and buy some tasty Old World sausage made according to traditional German recipes. Pick up some locally made cheeses and something to drink. Take these delicious treats just up the road and enjoy a picnic lunch at Calumet or High Cliff Park.

Return to Lake Shore Road and go north to County EE. Turn left (west) and drive to *Calumet County Park.* This is a hidden lakeshore treasure with picnic areas, grills, 71 campsites (including 49 electric sites), handicapped accessible bathhouse, nature study areas, a concession stand, Laundromat, and two golf

courses within a few minutes drive. The upper ledge of the park is on the exposed Niagara Escarpment, a limestone ridge that runs from Niagara Falls through Wisconsin to parts of Iowa and Illinois. There is a six-boat launching facility and great lake access. Call (920) 439-1008.

Take EE east to Highway 55. Turn left (north) on 55, go about 5 miles to High Cliff Road, turn left, and enter *High Cliff State Park,* (920) 989-1106). As long as humans have roamed these hills, this has been one of the favorite places to appreciate the moody beauty of Lake Winnebago. Native Americans, including the Ho-Chunk (formerly called Winnebago) of this area, greeted explorer Jean Nicolet as he landed up north at Red Banks in 1634. At least a dozen effigy mounds built at the beginning of the last millennium (1000 A.D.) are preserved here. A statue of the famous Ho-Chunk chief Red Bird stands high on a cliff overlooking this sacred ground that he loved.

A century ago, steam-powered excursion boats would bring day-trippers from Green Bay via the Fox River to the area for picnics and outings. Until the late 1940s there was a thriving quarry and kiln business operating here and later an amusement park. In 1956 the state bought it and opened the area as High Cliff State Park a year later. Today the Department of Natural Resources tends 112 campsites, a group camping area, a beach, hiking trails, and a marina. There are two golf courses nearby. The limestone evens holds some fossils, so check out the rocks along the way as you explore the park.

Return to 55, turn left (north), and go to Highway 114. Turn left (west).

Quick Trip Option: If you're doing a quick trip around the lake, follow 114 through Menasha to Neenah. Follow County A, which runs through the city and then takes you into Oshkosh. Then take Highway 45 south from Oshkosh and follow it along Lake Winnebago back to Fond du Lac.

If you have time to explore the Fox Cities, a historic and rapidly growing area, there are lots of good reasons to veer a bit away from the lake and explore the dozens of attractions. Contact the various visitors information offices given in the rest of this tour for a complete list. You'll need weeks if you want to do them all, but pick any two or three of these for a super getaway. For more information, call the *Fox Cities Convention and Visitors Bureau,* (800) 2DO-MORE.

In the general area, be sure to visit the *Charles A. Grignon Mansion,* (920) 766-3122, 1313 Augustine St., in Kaukauna (take Highway 55 north off Highway114). The site is a preserved homestead

The Fox and Wisconsin Rivers Heritage Corridor

The Fox and Wisconsin Rivers form a historic waterway that connects Lake Michigan with the Mississippi and thus the Port of New Orleans and the Gulf of Mexico. It was a trading route for Native Americans long before European contact. It consists of the Lower Fox, the Upper Fox, and the Lower Wisconsin Rivers. Lake Winnebago connects the Lower and Upper Fox, and the historic Portage Canal joins the Upper Fox and the Wisconsin Rivers. The 250 miles of rivers served as the passage through which Marquette and Joliet journeyed in 1673 as they explored the land we now call "Wisconsin." From its source near Portage to its mouth in Green Bay, the Fox is one of just a few major rivers in America to flow north. From Lake Winnebago to Green Bay, the Lower Fox River falls 160 feet in 37 miles. A system of 17 locks was built more than 140 years ago to allow for easier navigation between Lake Winnebago and Green Bay. The industrialized Lower Fox connecting Green Bay, Appleton, Oshkosh, and Fond du Lac as well as other smaller cities is known for having the world's largest concentration of paper mills. Today the locks are used primarily for recreational boating.

The Upper Fox connects through lakes and marshes. It is a prime waterfowl area with over 100 miles of navigable waters. The major cities on the Upper Fox are Portage and Berlin.

The Lower Wisconsin flows from the hydro plant at Prairie du Sac some 93 miles to feed the Mississippi. Along the way the river flows unrestricted past huge bluffs where eagles soar, the works of Frank Lloyd Wright at Spring Green, the "World Capital of Morel Mushrooms" at Muscoda, the hotel where the idea for the *Gideon Bible* took root at Boscobel, and one of Wisconsin's most spectacular state parks, Wyalusing, near Prairie du Chien.

depicting life in the 1840s. *Simon's Specialty Cheese,* (920) 788-6311, at the junction of Highway 41 and County N (north of Highway114) at Little Chute, is one of Wisconsin's finest cheese stores. Can it really be Wisconsin if you don't eat cheese? Stop in for some fresh squeaky curds or tasty smoked string cheese!

To visit Appleton, take Highway 114 west to Highway 10. Turn right (north) on 10 at Oneida Street and continue on Oneida into Appleton after 10 turns left (west). There are lots of Appleton attractions to chose from, so enjoy!

The *Fox Cities Children's Museum,* (920) 734-3226, 100 W. College Ave., is a clever way to tickle the senses and jump-start the brains of children of any age who've been riding too long. It also houses the Amelia Bubholz Doll Collection, a display of more than 1,000 costumed dolls. *Hearthstone Historic House Museum,* (920) 730-8204, 625 W. Prospect Ave., is a beautiful home that was the first residence in the world to run on electricity supplied by a hydroelectric dam.

Winnebago by Water, Winnebago by Air!

To fully appreciate Lake Winnebago you should get out on it in a boat or get up over it by air. Here are three fun ways to see more than just lakeshore.

By water: *Pioneer Princess Excursion Yacht Cruise,* 1000 Pioneer Dr. (at the Pioneer Inn) in Oshkosh, offers a variety of cruises, some with dinner or entertainment, on Winnebago and the historic Fox River (weather permitting). Call (800) 683-1980.

By air: *Fond du Lac Skyport Scenic Rides,* at Highway 151 and Highway 23, offers half-hour plane rides for up to three persons, 8 a.m. to dusk. Call (920) 922-6000 for reservations.

By air: *Experimental Aircraft Association Air Adventure Museum's Pioneer Airport,* 3000 Poberezny Dr. in Oshkosh, offers flights on weekends in good weather, in a historic 1929 Ford Tri-Motor airplane or in a vintage open cockpit biplane. Call (920) 426-4800.

No trip to the city would be complete without the Houdini tour. Visit the *Outagamie County Museum* and *Houdini Historical Center,* (920) 735-9370, 330 E. College Ave. This was Houdini's hometown and there's a historic walking tour route map available, as well as a wonderful display about the illusionist's feats, fame, and fate. The county museum also features interesting exhibits on papermaking.

Vande Walle's Candies, 400 Mall Dr., Appleton, (920) 738-7799, is a real candy and cookie factory! Willie Wonka, eat your heart out! For a taste of something a bit different, try the *Appleton Brewing Company,* (920) 735-0507, 1004 S. Old Oneida St., a microbrewery that makes a tasty root beer and other specialty brews each season.

From Appleton, take Highway 47 south to Highway 114 in Menasha. Turn right (west) on 114 and drive to the *Tayco Street Bridge Tower Museum,* (920) 967-5156, at Tayco St. and Main St. in Menasha. It's a good way to see what the life of a bridge tender was like.

Follow 114 south into Neenah, then turn left onto County A. In Neenah, take in the *Bergstrom-Mahler Museum,* (920) 751-4658, 165 N. Park Ave.; this structure shows you what a Winnebago mansion is like and has an outstanding collection of glass paperweights and German glass. The *Octagon House,* 336 Main St., was built in 1856 and houses the *Neenah Historical Society,* (920) 729-0244, and the *Paper Industry Hall of Fame.* The *Doty Cabin* in Doty Park, (920) 751-4614, 701 Lincoln St. (on the Fox-Winnebago waterway in Neenah), re-creates life at the time of Wisconsin's second governor, James Duane Doty.

Continue on A as it parallels the lakeshore

and take it into downtown Oshkosh. On the drive, you'll get only occasional brief views of the lake because the shore is heavily developed.

Oshkosh was first settled in 1836 by Webster Stanley, a ferry boat operator. By 1839 the community grew to 100 people and adopted the name "Oskosh" after the Menominee chief by that name. (The spelling changed later to by the addition of the *h* after the first *s.*) The first sawmill was started in 1847 and soon others were built along the Fox River. When Chicago burned in 1871 (the Peshtigo Fire happened that same day!), the subsequent rebuilding craze and demand for lumber turned Oshkosh into a boomtown and earned it the nickname "Sawdust City." By 1873 there were 24 sawmills, 15 shingle mills, and 7 sash and door companies operating here. Today you can still enjoy some of the grandeur of those days by visiting the museums in the mansions and homes that the barons of the age built, and see the art and artifacts they left for us to enjoy.

There are many attractions to take you a bit "off course" in this city too. So, it would be worthwhile to check with the *Oshkosh Convention and Visitors Bureau,* (877) 303-9200, for ideas on what to see and do. Here are some possibilities.

Menominee Park and Zoo, (920) 236-5080, at Hazel Ave. and Merritt St. (on Lake Winnebago) is Oshkosh's showcase park with a petting zoo, boat launches, biking trails, floral gardens, amusement rides, and a statue of Chief Oskosh, the Menominee chief for whom the city is named. The *Oshkosh Public Museum,* (920) 424-4730, 1331 Algoma Blvd., is housed in a lumber baron's 1907 Tudor-style mansion with interiors designed by Tiffany Studios. Don't miss the 1895 Apostles Clock. This is a great place to get a sense of the history of the people and commerce that thrived in the area.

The *Paine Art Center,* (920) 235-6903, 1410 Algoma Blvd., is an exquisite gem of a 1920s Tudor Revival mansion filled with American and French art. It has six fabulous gardens, gallery spaces, 19th-century American and French art, and special programs. The *Grand Opera House,* (920) 424-2355, 100 High Ave., is a restored 1883 Victorian opera house and performance center. The *Morgan House,* (920) 232-0260, 234 Church St., is a Queen-Anne-style house from 1884 that houses the *Winnebago Historical Society.*

Military Veterans Museum in the Park Plaza Complex, (920) 426-8615, displays military memorabilia that is "dedicated to peace." The *EAA Air Adventure Museum,* (920) 426-4818, 3000 Poberezny Dr., south of Oshkosh, is world famous for its rare aircraft displays (over 100) and dedication to the thrill of flying. Whatever else you do, don't miss this winner of the coveted Midwest Travel Writer's GEMmy Award.

The *Priebe Art Gallery,* (920) 424-2235, 926

Woodland Ave., in the Communication Arts Center at the University of Wisconsin-Oshkosh, has frequently changing exhibits and offers a good opportunity to see avante garde art as well as fine mainstream work. *Prime Outlets* offers shopping at 55 outlet stores just off Highway 41 at the Highway 344 exit, across from the EAA Adventure Museum. (See the accompanying article for a few more Oshkosh adventures.)

In downtown Oshkosh take Highway 45 south, traveling along the western shore of Lake Winnebago for about 21 miles to Fond du Lac. Back in 1835 the territorial governor, explorer, wheeler-dealer, politician, judge, and land speculator James Duane Doty platted out the community of Fond du Lac. The name translates as "foot of the lake" and is carried over from its early Ho-Chunk days. By 1847, with a population of 519 people, it officially became a village, and by 1852 it became a city with over 2,000 residents. Today the population is about 40,000.

Back in the city where this tour started, there's even more fun waiting. Your first move should be to call or visit the *Fond du Lac Visitor Information Center*, (800) 937-9123, 19 W. Scott St., where you can check out the *Talking Houses Tour*, in which 24 historic homes are included in a self-drive tour, and 14 of them will talk to you over your car radio! The *Galloway House and Village*, (920) 922-6390, 336 Old Pioneer Rd., is an out-standing 30-room mid-Victorian-era mansion and a turn-of-the-century village with photographer's shop, country store, print shop, church, and more.

Try your luck on the "Miracle Mile." That's the name given to South Main St. by the *Chicago Tribune* after two major lottery winners bought tickets at stores here. Then in 1993 the largest lottery jackpot to that date, $111 million, was won by a Fond du Lac couple. Another $160 million in winnings have rolled out of here since.

The 1856 Octagon House, (920) 922-1608, 276 Linden St., is a restored 12-room Civil War-era home that was built as a fort and now houses a ghost and nine underground passageways. The house was a link in the Underground Railway. *St. Paul's Cathedral*, (920) 921-3363, 51 W. Division St., is a must-see for anyone who appreciates great woodcarving. There are German and American masterpieces in an English Gothic setting. *Kristmas Kringle Shoppe Limited.*, (800) 721-2525, 1330 S. Main St., has the largest collection of Italian-glass Christmas ornaments in the United States and lots of other Christmas items.

Lakeside Park, on Lake Winnebago at the end of North Main St., is the 400-acre park where our tour started. Now you can climb the *Lookout Lighthouse Tower*, see the white-tailed deer exhibit, ride the bumper boats and aqua bikes, or rent a canoe. Or, just sit on the shore and marvel at one of Wisconsin's biggest and finest natural wonders: Lake Winnebago.

The EAA Fly-In Convention

In an age when thrills are a dime a dozen and "big thrills" tend to be mostly "big hype," the EAA flies and delivers. A celebration to mark the joy of "breaking the surly bonds of earth" takes place in Oshkosh in late July each year at the Experimental Aircraft Association Fly-In Convention. Everyone who loves to fly, watch, or dream about any kind of aircraft is welcome to join the EAA and come to the event. When the first fly-in took place in 1953 there were a handful of enthusiasts, but today the EAA counts over 180,000 members and draws some 12,000 aircraft and nearly a million people to the week-long event. A "Fly-Market" offers everything from pieces of vintage aircraft to whole build-it-in-your-basement kits to autographed books by real air aces from around the world. Civilian as well as military aircraft come from all over the world. Pilots, aircraft manufacturers—and even some astronauts—come in flying machines that range from old vintage biplanes and experimental ultra-lights to the U-2, the Concorde, the Stealth, and jets someone built in their basement. A daily air show is always exciting, and the best ones to see are the weekend shows that feature special fly-bys with vintage warbirds or new experimental planes. So far no alien spacecraft have been sighted, but when they arrive you can bet they'll be welcome here. Call (920) 426-4800 for more information.

Future Convention Dates

2001: July 25–31	2005: July 27–August 2
2002: July 24–30	2006: July 26–August 1
2003: July 23–29	2007: July 25–31
2004: July 28–August 3	2008: July 23–29

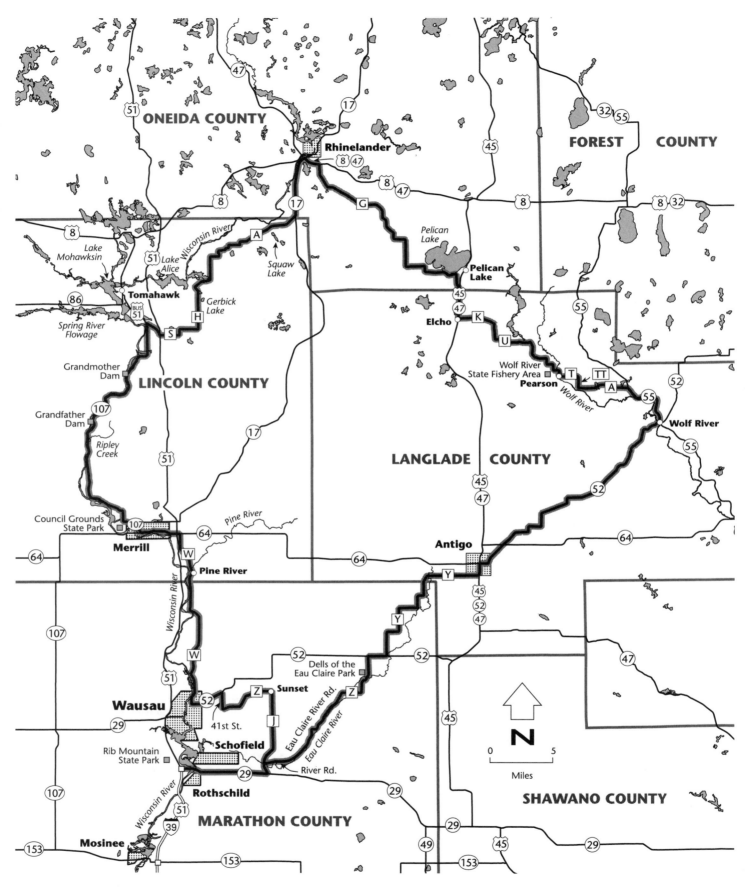

Tour 13

Tour 13
Bull Falls, Hodag Howls, Wolf Tracks

Wausau—Sunset—Pine River—Merrill—Tomahawk—Rhinelander—Elcho—Pearson—Wolf River—Antigo—Wausau

Distance: 193 miles

Okay. Everybody heading north on Highway 51 (I-39), we're going to do a bit of a detour. Instead of driving hell bent for Minocqua, We'll take a turn, head off into the underbrush, and find some great little places you've missed all these years. We'll go backcountry cruising, see some dense forest, run with the wild rivers, and discover one of Wisconsin's neatest unexpected waterfalls.

If you're looking for souvenirs, plan to lay in some Hodag potholders, Mepps fishing lures, and a few hundred pounds of potatoes.

We'll find miles of beautiful driving roads, a few gearbox testers, and plenty of "burn-the-carbon-out" stretches too. So slow down when you see that Highway 29 sign and get ready to enjoy some parts of Wisconsin that only a few local residents ever knew existed.

Begin at the junction of Highway 51 and Highway 29 in Rothschild, just south of Wausau. This northern Wisconsin city traces its beginnings back to the days of the early explorers. As they came upon this part of the Wisconsin River, they heard a roaring sound, so they named the area "Big Bull Falls." Later the name was changed to an Ojibwa word meaning "far away"—Wausau. The city became an important lumber town and today the area paper mills still play a significant role in the area economy.

Wausau attractions include the *Leigh Yawkey Woodson Art Museum*, (715) 845-7010, 700 N. 12th St. The museum is known worldwide for its art collection that includes nature, historic and contemporary paintings, sculptures, and drawings that use birds as the main theme. The annual Birds in Art exhibition in September and October attracts international artists and visitors. Be sure to see the gardens and outdoor sculpture galleries.

The *Marathon County Historical Museum*, (715) 848-6143, 403 McIndoe St., was once the home of Cyrus Yawkey, a wealthy, prominent citizen of early Wausau. The 1900-era house is a carefully

The Dells of the Eau Claire Park is one of the many sites on this tour that leave little doubt you're in the North Woods. Here, you'll see abundant rapids and waterfalls, as well as spectacular woodland scenery that's enchanting all year round. Wisconsin Department of Tourism photo.

They say the Hodag likes to feast on bulldogs, but today it's more fond of tourist dollars. Wisconsin Department of Tourism photo by Ronda Allen.

restored Victorian classic with an authentically furnished music room, dining room, and parlor. You will get a good feeling for what living the good life was like a century ago. The rooms of the second and third floors have been remodeled to house rotating and visiting exhibits and the library of the Historical Society.

The I. S. Horgen Antique Farm Machinery Museum, (715) 261-1550, 1201 Stewart Ave., in Marathon Park, showcases an outstanding and well-organized collection of antique farm equipment, vintage dairy equipment, large wagons, carriages, and common household items.

The Center for the Visual Arts, (715) 842-4545, 427 Fourth St., features specially themed exhibits during the year and offers classes in all art media to all age groups. It is housed in a registered Landmark building and offers a space for exhibitions for local and regional artists in all media.

The Grand Theater (Opera House), (715) 842-0988, 415 Fourth St., is a wonderfully restored 1927 classical-revival theater with marvelous colonnades, marble statues, and solid Bedford limestone. It has been given a thorough but unobtrusive modernization with a fully computerized lighting and sound system and extensive stage rigging. The theater hosts both touring and local productions and concerts.

Rib Mountain State Park, (715) 359-4522, off Highway 51, Exit 188, covers over 860 acres and, at 1,940 feet, is the third highest spot in Wisconsin. Climb the observation tower for spectacular views. There are well-maintained hiking and nature trails lined with wildflowers and woodland plants.

Blessed with the fast-moving Wisconsin River, Wausau has harnessed this resource that powered the lumber mills to become the site of world-class

whitewater kayak and canoe competitions. The unique Wausau course combines a natural riverbed and vertical drop with dam-controlled water flow. It offers a consistent, controllable level of difficulty in any weather. Because it runs through the downtown, it's one of the finest competitive courses for spectators anywhere in the world. Wausau's whitewater program has been named a Center of Excellence by the United States Canoe and Kayak Team, making it a top U.S. training site.

Lodging is no problem in Wausau. You'll find comfortable rooms all around the town.

Go east on 29 and follow the divided highway 7.1 miles to County J. Turn left (north) on J, driving through the suburban Wausau area, passing the crossroads settlement of Callon, the Eau Claire River, Little Sandy Creek, and Big Sandy Creek, to Sunset (6.9 miles) and the intersection with County Z.

Turn left (west) on Z and go about 7 miles to 41st Street. Along the way you'll cross Prahl Creek and see farms that have fields covered with shades; these are ginseng farms. Wisconsin is the world leader in growing ginseng, which is used primarily in Asian countries as a folk medicine. In fact, most of Wisconsin's crop is sold in Asia.

Turn right (north) on 41st Street (County X) and go 1.3 miles to the intersection with Highway 52. Turn left on 52 and go west 2.7 miles to County W.

Turn right (north) on W, go through Granite Heights and along the Wisconsin River, cross Little Trappe Creek, pass the hamlet of Pine

The Gold Star is one of many moving commemorative markers at the Highground, a site just outside of Neillsville
that honors the memory of all U.S. veterans, their families, friends, and loved ones.

Wisconsin has never received the kind of national reputation for fall foliage that New England has enjoyed, but you can see the truth for yourself around every spectacular curve in the road.

The Cana Island Lighthouse near Baileys Harbor in Door County is a spectacular reward for those willing to take a short back road drive.

Along Washington Island's back roads are reminders that nature will make art of civilization's discarded creations.

Some of Wisconsin's early immigrants were lead miners whose simple stone homes survive as Pendarvis in Mineral Point.

Bayfield's colorful commercial fishing boats bring delicious Lake Superior whitefish and trout to local markets and create a scene irresistible to artists and photographers.

Bring your binoculars and sit quietly, or take a little hike, and you'll be rewarded with extraordinary bird sightings (like this great blue heron).

The Amish are hard-working people whose style of farming recalls a less hurried period of our history.

Driving Wisconsin's back roads is like visiting the "world's greatest barn museum," with displays of all sorts of barn styles, shapes, and colors.

Potato River Falls, in Rusk County, is one of the most beautiful but least visited of Wisconsin's Iron Range waterfalls.
One suspects that a more exciting name, like Fighting Bear Falls, would draw more adventurous tourists to visit.

One of the great joys of traveling Wisconsin's back roads is being able to buy food products directly from farmers
and to see the land on which the bounty was grown, harvested, and produced.

Hail, hail, Wisconsin dairy cow! We love your cheese and ice cream but driving enthusiasts thank you all the more for being the reason behind the state's extraordinary network of excellent country roads.

Old World Wisconsin, near Eagle, is an award-winning living history museum that invites you to step back in time to witness the daily life of many of Wisconsin's early ethnic settlers.

Today the most visible feature of the Ojibwa lifestyle may be Northwoods-themed establishments like the Lake of the Torches Resort Casino in Lac du Flambeau. Profits from the gaming enterprise have helped support and preserve many Native American schools and museums, such as WaSwagoning, which interprets the proud history and season-oriented lifestyle of the Ojibwa people.

Experience a northern Wisconsin autumn morning on a clear glacial lake, breathe crisp, fresh air under deep blue skies surrounded by blazing foliage, and you'll never want to miss another.

Breathtaking scenery draws many travelers to the Wisconsin stretch of the Great River Road (Highway 35), but this "Greatest Undiscovered Drive" is just the prelude to some amazing pretzel-bent roads, mind-boggling switchbacks, and exhilarating roller-coaster runs that climb through bluffs and river valleys.

River, cross the Pine River, and in 15 miles reach the junction with Highway 64. Turn left (west) on 64 and drive 3.2 miles into Merrill; go to Grand Avenue (Highway 107).

Merrill is a good enough name for this friendly community with such interesting downtown buildings. The name honors a general manager of the Chicago, Milwaukee, St. Paul, and Pacific Railroad—probably a nice enough guy—but before it was Merrill, Merrill was "Jenny."

Jenny was the loggers' name for a popular daughter of a Potawatomi chief. When she died in pregnancy her father asked that she be honored, and in respect the men took to calling the community "Jenny Falls" and later just "Jenny." In 1881 the Wisconsin State Legislature, more impressed with the prominent Mr. Merrill, officially changed the name to honor the rail baron.

In 1895 a local mill was said to be capable of turning out 25 million feet of lumber and 20 million shingles. The year 1892 marked the peak of the lumbering boom. There were eight mills turning out some 150 million board feet of lumber and 86 million shingles. But soon the last pine would crash to the ground and the lumber era with it.

Today Merrill is known as "The City of Parks." *The Lincoln County Courthouse* stands high above the horizon and its clock tower is the official logo of the city. In the courthouse are interesting murals picturing the logging history of Lincoln County. The building is listed on the National Register of Historic Places.

Other attractions in Merrill include the *Merrill Historical Museum,* (715) 536-5652, 804 E. Third St. Housed in the home of Merrill's first mayor, Thomas B. Scott, the museum has a rare, square Steinway piano and an Edison phonograph. Another section recalls the mercantile history of the town; the Pinery Logging Museum in the same facility traces the history of "Jenny Bull Falls" with original artifacts recovered from the banks of the Wisconsin River.

If you happen to get to Merrill in time for breakfast, one of the best cafes in the north is the *Pine Ridge Café,* (715) 536-3010, on Highway 64 just west of Highway 51. The pancakes and hash browns are delicious and served in logging camp portions.

The community also has some good antique shops like the *River Street Antique Company,* (715) 536-7246, 1500 River St., with two historic buildings full of treasure.

Bear right on 107 and follow it out of Merrill about 1.5 miles. On this scenic route, you'll pass the road to *Council Grounds State Park,* (715) 536-8773, the legendary site of many Native American encampments.

Go north on 107 for about 13.5 miles to the junction with County S. As you follow the Wisconsin River, you'll pass lots of places to pull over, shoot a picture, launch a canoe, or just smell the

pines. You'll drive over Nine Mile Hill, along the Posey Rapids, across Ripley Creek, past Grandfather Dam, and Grandmother Dam.

Quick Trip Option: **At S, turn left onto Business Highway 51 and go 3 miles into Tomahawk.** This town seems to have it all in the right proportions: just enough city, just enough North Woods. Plenty of waterfront lodging, good food, and lots of recreational opportunities make Tomahawk an attractive destination. Attractions here include tours of *The Harley-Davidson Plant,* (715) 453-2191, 426 E. Somo Ave., and the local history museum, the *Tomahawk Area Historical Center,* (715) 453-3628, 18 Washington St. A stop at the *Tomahawk Chamber of Commerce,* (800) 569-2160, 208 N. Fourth St., will put you eyeball to (glass) eyeball with a mounted 700-pound black bear with a 22-inch skull, probably the largest ever shot with a bow or gun in Wisconsin. You'll find lots of helpful area information about local resorts and activities too!

Turn right (east) on S and go for 5 miles to County H. Turn left (north) on H, passing

The Horrible Hodag!

What is a Hodag? A relative of the Sasquatch? A crazed cross of a bear and a pig? Some people once reported that it was the fiercest, strangest, most frightening monster ever to set razor-sharp claws on the earth. The Rhinelander Chamber of Commerce reports that the Hodag made its first appearance near this North Woods Wisconsin city in 1896.

Gene Shepard, a Rhinelander pioneer, timber cruiser, and creative storyteller, said he snapped its picture just before the beast sprang at him from behind a white pine log. Shepard described it as a hairy animal seven feet long and 30 inches tall with an ugly glare—and there it was, clear as life, in his photograph, copies of which still can be seen. The Hodag sported a dozen white horns and had wicked-looking tusks that hung from viselike jaws. The claws on its short, muscular fore and hind legs were long and needle sharp.

A party of brave lumberjacks led by Shepard reported that they "captured" the monster in a cave by putting him to sleep with a chloroform-soaked sponge tied to the end of a 30-foot bamboo pole. He said the Hodag had a favorite food: white bulldogs, which it would hunt at night.

Shepard eventually was forced to admit that the Hodag was a hoax. Its hairy body was made of wood and ox hides. Its armor of horns once belonged to various bulls. Those vicious claws were bent steel rods.

But the people of Rhinelander had developed a fondness for the critter. Today you'll see pictures of it hanging on banners from lampposts, on signs on top of taverns, and even on potholders. The Hodag is the symbol of the city and its slogan is "The Home of the Hodag." Rhinelander's biggest recreation area on Boom Lake is Hodag Park. The school athletic team is called the "Hodags."

If you want to know more, read the book *Long Live the Hodag! The Life and Legacy of Eugene Simeon Shepard: 1854-1923,* by Kurt D. Kortenhof. Copies can be purchased by contacting Hodag Press, 5552 Jennie Webber Lake Rd., Rhinelander, 54501.

Gerbick and Bass Lakes, then jogging east and north past Lake Alice 6.3 miles to the junction with County A. Proceed straight ahead on A, following it past Lake Clara and Squaw Lake about 9 miles to Highway 17.

Turn left (north) on 17 and go 4.9 miles to the intersection with Highway 8/47 just southwest of Rhinelander.

This town earned its fame as a lumber center in the 1800s. This wasn't at all surprising: it was in the middle of an area boasting 700 million feet of pine and 300 million feet of hemlock and other timber. Three railroads made the city a terminal and supply point for the logging camps spread all over the North Woods as far as the Michigan border. Logging hit its peak in the lumberjack town during the 1890s. Growing urban areas had a voracious appetite for lumber, and as the cities grew, the forest was reduced to a stump field. And even then the demand for Wisconsin pine seemed insatiable. The forest seemingly evaporated—vanished—at the rate of millions of feet a year. By the early 1910s the industry was virtually at an end. The last drive for a downstream mill on the Pelican River occurred in April 1923.

And, of course, Rhinelander is home to the legend of the Hodag (see article).

The Rhinelander Logging Museum complex, (715) 369-5004, contains a rural schoolhouse, the Civilian Conservation Corps Museum, and restored Soo Line Depot. Located in Pioneer Park, on Business Highway 8 (Oneida Ave.), it has fascinating exhibits that take you back into the logger era. It is the most complete display of its kind in the North Woods and certainly one of the best bargains (admission is free with donation) in the state. You'll see a collection of logging artifacts: peavies, pike poles, cant hooks, and cross-cut saws, as well as a superb collection of photographs that give a good look at the hard life of a logger. There's an 1879 narrow-gauge railroad engine, Soo Line President Jack Mylrea's private car, one of the few steam-powered snow snakes in existence (used to haul sleds of logs over iced highways), a turntable, and a road icer. Even the gift shop is a special place, with North Woods crafts (I love the Hodag hot pads!) made by senior citizens who work at the museum, pictures and books about the North Country, Hodags, T-shirts, and souvenir postcards. The walls are covered with pictures of early logging days and Rhinelander's main street in 1892.

Football fans will recognize the name Heisman, but most don't know that the man for whom the award is named, John Heisman, is buried here in the Donaldson plot at the Rhinelander Cemetery. Heisman was instrumental in getting the New York Downtown Athletic Club's Outstanding Football Player of the Year Award off the ground in 1934, and the first award was made in 1935. Heisman died in October of 1936 and his wife, Edith (Cole) Heisman, a Rhinelander native, had his remains buried here in anticipation of moving back to the community. She returned to Rhinelander and was 95 when she passed away in 1963. Though Heisman never lived here, he and Edith had visited a number of times. There is a Heisman bust at the Rhinelander Airport.

Turn right on Highway 8/47 and drive 1.2 miles to County G. Turn right on G and go 18.6 miles to the junction with Highway 45/47. You'll cruise through immense wetlands left by the retreating glacier, crossing Cuenin Creek, Bergman Creek, and Enterprise Creek before passing near Pelican Lake.

Turn right on Highway 45/47 and go 2.3 miles into Langlade County to County K in Elcho. Langlade County is famous for its pristine wilderness environment, great fishing waters, and relaxed living. There are 123,000 acres of county forestland, some 843 lakes, and 387 miles of trout waters. The Wolf River is a trout-fishing enthusiast's dream stream. It flows quietly in the northern part of the county and picks up speed and whitewater as it drops toward the south. Beautiful any time of year, in autumn the colors are extraordinary. Whitewater rafting, canoeing, and kayaking are popular on the Wolf, which has 17 named rapids (Class II and III) in Langlade County. For more tourist information about the county, call (888) 526-4523.

Turn left (east) on K and go 2.9 miles to County U. Turn right (south) on U and drive 8.1 miles to County T. Turn left (east) on T through Pearson and go 2.4 miles to County TT. At Pearson, you'll cross the Wolf River, which gets its name from a bad bit of translation by early settlers. The Native Americans had called it "Muk-wan-wish-ta-guon," which translates as "the Bear's Head River." To the early settlers who listened to the animals howling every night, "wolf" seemed just fine.

Turn right (south) on TT and go to County A. You'll pass through the Wolf River State Fishery Area.

Turn left (east) on A and go for about 4 miles to Highway 55. Turn right (south) on 55, following the Wolf River for 4.7 miles to the town of Wolf River at the junction with Highway 52.

Turn right on 52 and go for about 22 miles to Antigo. This is a fabulously twisted run for about 5 miles, then it winds along another 17 miles through forest and potato country. This is the Antigo Flats area, where the official Wisconsin state soil, Antigo Silt Loam, yields some of the finest potatoes in the world. Buy some to take home.

Follow 52 through Antigo, where it joins Highway 45/47, and go to the junction with County Y (Forrest Street) on the south side of

Autumn on a North Woods glacial lake is a gift to be savored. Wisconsin Department of Tourism photo by Don Johanning.

the city. Antigo is the American home of Mepps fishing lures, the world's number-one lure. They are made by *Sheldon's Inc.,* (715) 623-2382, 626 Center St. (on the north side of town, just off of Highway 45/47). Stop by for a visit and take a free, 30-minute guided tour. Watch as the lures are hand made and get a look at the fabulous collection of trophy mounts.

The *Langlade County Courthouse* is listed on the National Register of Historic Places. The *Langlade County Historical Museum,* (715) 627-4464, on Sixth Ave., has area historical exhibits, Native American and lumbering artifacts, and early agricultural implements. The *Deleglise Cabin* was the first home in the community and was moved to the museum grounds in 1914.

Turn right (west) on Y and go for 17 miles to the *Dells of the Eau Claire Park.* Along the way, you'll drive through the farm county, woods, and wetlands of the Eau Claire River Valley. The Dells of the Eau Claire is a beautiful park that just pops up out here amid the farms. A series of picturesque rapids and waterfalls is formed as the Eau Claire River rushes through a rugged gorge. The river drops 65 feet in 1.5 miles through high cliffs and exposed rocks. Visit in the spring to see the most water or in the fall to see beautiful foliage.

Continue on Y another 1.3 miles to County Z. Turn right (west) on Z and go 1.5 miles to Eau Claire River Road. Turn left on Eau Claire River Road and follow it 3.6 miles to County N. Turn right on N and go about 0.5 mile to River Road.

Turn left on River Road and follow it for 5.3 miles to County J. Turn left on J and go for .8 mile to Highway 29. Turn right on 29 and go about 7 miles back to I-39 where we started.

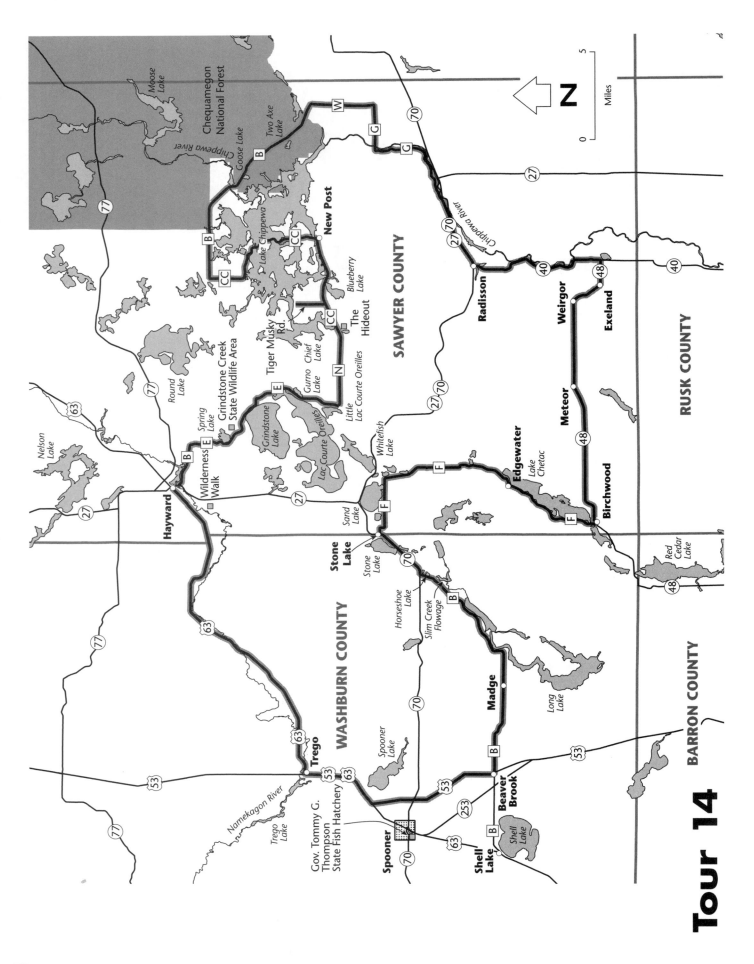

Tour 14

Tour 14
Big Muskie Run in Birkie-land

Hayward—Radisson—Exeland—Weirgor—Meteor—Birchwood—Stone Lake—Madge—Spooner—Trego—Hayward

Distance: 135 miles

Wisconsin's love of fiberglass creatures reaches a peak at the National Freshwater Fishing Hall of Fame in Hayward. Photo by Gary Knowles.

Beautiful and wild northwest Wisconsin is the land of the fighting muskie, the spectacular Chippewa Flowage, glacier-sculpted lakes, and historic rushing rivers. If you're looking for a backwoods getaway where you can slip away from the high-tension zone down south, this is it.

The Chippewa Flowage and the Hayward Lakes area are known for their friendly, comfortable, and fun resorts and memory-making sunsets.

For driving enthusiasts, it's also a land of sweeping curves, rolling hills, inviting straightaways, and lots of "driver's roads" off the main highway. This invigorating sprint will give your car a chance to exercise most of its muscles and send you home with a smile on your face!

Begin in Hayward at the junction of Highway 27 and County B. Hayward was named after the man who built the first sawmill back in the early logging days. The community has earned an international reputation based on a big fish (a four-

story-tall fiberglass muskie!) and four big events: the American Birkebeiner cross-country ski race (held in February), the Musky Festival (50 years old in 2000!), the Lumberjack Championships (in July), and the Chequamegon Fat Tire Festival (an off-road bicycle event in September). Now the golf courses in the area are beginning to get recognition (see accompanying article).

The National Freshwater Fishing Hall of Fame, (715) 634-4440, on County B, just off Highway 27, has the undisputed world's largest muskie—it's a 143-foot-long, four-and-a-half-story building that houses part of the museum's collection of 400 mounted fish, 5,000 legendary lures, antique fishing gear, early outboard motors, tributes to 70 Hall of Fame anglers, and lots of photos. The critter will make you want to get out and catch one! And—yes—people have been married in the muskie's mouth. It can hold about 20 average-size fishing enthusiasts.

Hayward-area historical artifacts, especially

those relating to the timber industry, are well preserved at the *Sawyer County Historical Museum,* (715) 634-8053, on County B. At the top of the *Hayward Library,* (715) 634-2161, on Main St., is a fine memorial to Native Americans carved from a 175-year-old oak by Peter Toth.

If you want to literally "put the pedal to the metal" or give up the whole game of golf except for putting, get over to the *Hayward Amusement Park,* (715) 634-3510, on Highway 27 south, which has both go-karts and mini-golf.

Want to get wet? Try the *Raging Rapids Water Slide,* (715) 634-6952, on Highway 63. The skills of the logging era are kept alive and well at the *Scheers Lumberjack Show,* (715) 634-2893, with demonstrations of log rolling, climbing, axe dexterity, and speed sawing. Three miles south of Hayward on Highway 27 is *Wilderness Walk,* (715) 634-2893, a 35-acre animal park and petting zoo.

Go east on B out of Hayward to County E. If you continue east on County B for about 2 more miles, you'll come to the Lac Court Oreilles *LCO Casino,* (800) 526-5634, which offers slots, blackjack, video poker, and a fine restaurant, as well as a 56-unit lodge.

Turn right (south) on E past Spring Lake through the Grindstone Creek State Wildlife Area, past Christner Lake and Grindstone Lake.

Stay on E to the junction with County N. Along the way, you'll cross Squaw Creek and go past Gurno Lake, Lac Courte Oreilles, and Little Lac Courte Oreilles.

Turn left (east) on N to the junction with County CC. Here, you'll see *The Hideout,* where Chicago's infamous Al Capone came to spend time away from the "heat" of the city. His North Woods retreat, (715) 945-2746, has guided tours May to October and displays of Roaring '20s gangland activity.

Bear left (northeast) on CC, passing south of Chief Lake. If you turn left at Tiger Musky Rd., just ahead, you'll find the *Tiger Musky Resort,* (715) 945-2555, one of the most popular in this area. It's operated by Moose and Millie Speros. Moose was appointed Wisconsin director of tourism in 1991 and then named the first secretary of the new Department of Tourism by Governor Tommy Thompson. Stop and ask Moose where the fish are biting. He'll

know! And Millie will give you a warm Wisconsin welcome too.

Continue on CC and go to County B. You'll pass north of Blueberry Lake and south of James Slough, then head north at New Post, eventually crossing Lake Chippewa.

Turn right (east) on B. If you want the best view of the Chippewa Flowage, stop for a ride on the *Chippewa Queen,* (715) 462-3874, at Treeland Resort just down the road at Treeland Lane (to the right after you cross Musky Bay).

Continue on B east and south to the junction with County W. You'll go through the Chequamegon National Forest, past Goose Lake and Two Axe Lake.

Turn right (south) on W and go to the junction with County G. Turn right on G and cross the Chippewa River, following its west bank to the junction with Highway 27/70. Follow 27/70 west and go to the junction with Highway 40 in Radisson. This little logging town was one of the later ones to be established, starting in 1902 as the lumber era was moving from harvesting white pine to cutting the denser hardwoods. Mr. Orrick Whited, who built much of the town, chose the name to honor Pierre Esprit Radisson who, with Sieur des Grosseilliers, explored this area in 1659.

Turn left (south) on 40 and cruise to the intersection with Highway 48. You'll follow the Chippewa River as it twists and winds through this wilderness area and then past Jacques Lake.

Turn right (west) on Highway 48, passing through Exeland, Weirgor, and Meteor, to County F. Turn right (north) on F.

Quick Trip Option: If you continue on Highway 48, you can visit the North Woods community of Birchwood, the "Bluegill Capital of Wisconsin," which has a 14.5-foot bluegill in the park to welcome you.

Continue north through Edgewater, then west on F, until its junction with Highway 70. You'll swing past inviting resorts on the west shore of Big Chetac Lake, which covers 1,920 acres and is excellent for walleye, bass, and pan fish. At Stone Lake, you'll enter Washburn County, which is laced with miles of rivers, dotted with more than 900 lakes, and covered with thousands of acres of forests.

Turn left (southwest) on 70 and go about 2.5 miles to where 70 and County B diverge. Stay on B south as 70 turns west. You'll pass Horseshoe Lake and Slim Creek Flowage before driving along the west shore of Long Lake.

Golf in the Wilderness

For half a century this region of the state has been best known for its fishing, but lately the talk has turned to golf. In 1997 the people in Hayward declared their city the "Golf Capital of Wisconsin." After the fishing enthusiasts picked themselves up off the floor, they looked at the map and—sure enough—there were lots of golf courses out there: five 18-hole courses and three 9-holers within easy reach and even more if you travel a little farther. If you get the urge to slay sod, try the very enjoyable classic *Hayward Golf and Tennis Club,* (715) 634-2760, the old woodsy *Telemark Golf Club,* (715) 798-3104, and the new wooded beauties *Teal Wing,* (715) 462-9051, near Hayward, and *Lakewoods Forest Ridges,* (715) 794-2561, near Cable. *Hayward International,* (715) 634-6727, is a new, challenging 18-hole layout just south of Hayward. And don't ignore the 9-holers. One of the most testy little courses in the north is *Tahkodah Hills Golf Club,* (715) 798-3760, near Cable.

Stay on B as it swings west through Madge and meets Highway 53.

Quick Trip Option: For an interesting side trip, stay on County B for about 4 miles to Shell Lake, then turn right (north) on Highway 63 and go about 0.5 to the *Museum of Woodcarving,* (715) 468-7100. This museum is known world-wide for its one hundred life-size figures of Christ and other biblical personages, as well as more than 400 miniatures. The carvings are by Joseph T. Barta, who spent 30 years turning wood into art. His masterpiece is the life-size *Last Supper.*

For a thrilling treetop adventure and a great view of North Woods glacial lakes, catch a ride on a floatplane. Photo by Gary Knowles.

Turn right (north) on 53, passing east of Spooner and joining Highway 63. Spooner is well worth a short detour. You can visit the world's largest muskie hatchery, the *Governor Tommy G. Thompson State Fish Hatchery,* (715) 635-4147, just west of Spooner on Highway 70. More than two million walleye, 100,000 muskies, and a whole bunch of northern pike are hatched here each year. Of course, they're hungry . . . so they eat. They're fed two million sucker eggs annually. You can tour this amazing facility year around.

Railroad lovers will want to stop at the *Wisconsin Great Northern Railroad Excursion Train,* (715) 635-3200, at Front St. The steam train runs several times each day from June to October. For more rail fun, try the *Railroad Memories Museum,* (715) 635-3325, on Front St., to see historic photos, videos, model trains, and railroad artifacts. If you feel the need for racing competition, *Bulik's Amusement Center,* (715) 635-7111, offers

go-karts. There's also miniature golf and water-slides.

Continue north on Highway 53/63 to Trego. Here the Namekagon River spreads out into Trego Lake. The Namekagon rushes for 50 miles through Washburn County and is part of the *St. Croix National Scenic Riverway.* Canoeists, trout fishing enthusiasts, and even tube riders enjoy the virtually undeveloped waterway where osprey, deer, bald eagles, beaver, muskrat, mink, and lots of other wildlife thrive. Want to try it? There are outfitters in Trego who will equip and shuttle you as needed. The *Namekagon Visitor Center,* (715) 635-8346, in Trego, can give you more helpful information about the ecology and recreation opportunities in the area.

In Trego, continue on 63 east, following the Namekagon River north and east back to Hayward.

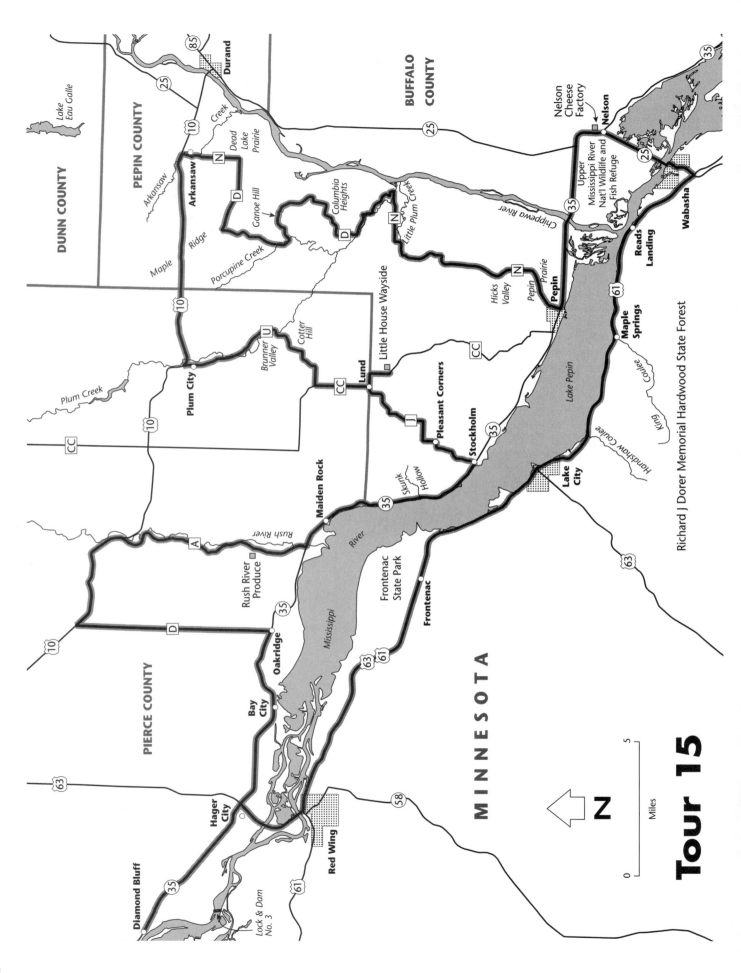

DUNN COUNTY

PEPIN COUNTY

Lake Eau Galle

Durand

85

25

Arkansaw Creek

Dead Lake Prairie

Arkansaw

N

D

Ganoe Hill

10

Maple Ridge

Porcupine Creek

Columbia Heights

Little Plum Creek

D

N

BUFFALO COUNTY

25

35

Chippewa River

Nelson Cheese Factory

Nelson

25

Upper Mississippi River Nat'l Wildlife and Fish Refuge

Wabasha

Reads Landing

10

Plum Creek

Cotter Hill

U

Brunner Valley

Plum City

CC

Lund

Little House Wayside

N

Pepin Prairie

Hicks Valley

Pepin

CC

61

Maple Springs

10

CC

Pleasant Corners

Stockholm

35

Lake Pepin

King Coulee

Handshaw Coulee

Richard J Dorer Memorial Hardwood State Forest

Maiden Rock

Rush River

A

Skunk Hollow

River

Lake City

63

PIERCE COUNTY

Rush River Produce

35

D

Oakridge

Mississippi

Frontenac State Park

Frontenac

61

63

10

63

Bay City

Hager City

Red Wing

58

61

MINNESOTA

N

Diamond Bluff

35

61

Lock & Dam No. 3

Miles

0   5

Tour 15

Tour 15
The Green Hills' Yang, the Freeways' Yin

Nelson—Pepin—Arkansaw—Plum City—Stockholm—Maiden Rock—Oakridge—Bay City—Hagar City—Red Wing (Minn.)—Lake City (Minn.)—Maple Springs (Minn.)—Reads Landing (Minn.)—Wabasha (Minn.)—Nelson

Distance: 123 miles

Yeeeee-haa! Say it with me now.
YEEEEE-HAA!

Good. Practice that. You'll need it. Yes, even you Texans, roller coaster fanatics, and rally drivers.

There are some routes that are so exhilarating, so sensational, and so purely joyful for drivers (and passengers) that you'd drive them even if there were no gas stations, no food, no shops, no attractions—nothing but roads and scenery—between the start and end of the route.

Big portions of this route—and several others in western Wisconsin—come very close to fitting that bill.

The fact that this route has the great shops, good eating, and enough gas makes it all the more inviting. So . . . check it out.

Be ready to lose contact with ordinary driving: you're about to see—and enjoy—the green hills' yang and the freeways' yin.

Get ready to say it: *YEEEEE-HAA!*

Begin in Nelson on Highway 35, the Great River Road.

Ask most people who have traveled the upper Great River Road what they remember about Nelson, and most will tell you it's a nice little town on the Tiffany Bottoms and it has a cheese factory that sells ice cream cones. That would be the *Nelson Cheese Factory*, (715) 673-4725, where you can also sometimes buy *today's* fresh cheese curds. (But ask when they were made! Don't buy *any* that were made "fresh yesterday and kept in the cooler overnight." Get *today's* fresh, squeaky curds. If they don't have them, get an ice cream cone.)

Fishing in these parts is legendary. Walleye are popular but they say the northern pike here grow almost muskie size.

As you cruise by Nelson keep an eye on the tops of those tall bluffs. They're a favorite spot for hang gliders, and it's fun to watch them soar and glide.

Follow 35 north, then west through the *Mississippi River National Wildlife Refuge* and across the Chippewa River to Pepin. Watch for heron, Canada geese, deer, and egrets as you run through this wildlife area.

Pepin is not far from the rural birthplace and early home of Laura Ingalls Wilder and from beauti-

This wayside park and replica cabin commemorate Laura Ingalls Wilder, who was born near here in 1867 in "the Big Woods." Wisconsin Department of Tourism photo courtesy of the Pepin Chamber of Commerce.

ful Lake Pepin. The village park here has been named in honor of this world-famous writer, and the *Pepin Historical Museum*, (715) 442-3011, 306 Third St., has so many exhibits about her that it is sometimes called the Laura Ingalls Wilder Museum. It's a must-see for anyone who has ever read the books or watched the TV program.

The *Pepin Railroad Depot Museum*, (715) 442-3011, on Highway 35, is also a fine stop with many artifacts from the area's history, including a photo of riverboat captains that has Samuel Clemens (Mark Twain) in it.

Pepin has a scenic marina and waterfront area just a few blocks off the highway. The shimmering "lake," which is a natural widening of the river, is often flecked with white sails. If you can spend a night here, try to get down to the water to watch the sun set.

Shoppers will find antique stores, artisan jewelers, a rock shop, gift shops, and friendly restaurants. Favorites include *The Pickle Factory*, (715) 442-4400, for great burgers, pasta, and salads, and *The Harbor View*, (715) 442-3893, which is always busy (no reservations accepted) and has been rated among Wisconsin's top 10 eating places!

Lodging options range from motels to fine bed and breakfast inns. *The Sea Wing Inn*, (715) 442-2315, is a great Victorian with a double whirlpool room, while the *Pepin Motel*, (715) 442-3411, has 16 comfortable units.

In Pepin turn right on County N. Here the fun level picks up a few notches as you drive north and east across Hicks, Little Plum, and Plum Creek Valleys.

Continue on N to its junction with County D. Follow D left. The road twists and turns northward as it tracks along Plum Creek and then heads up to the top of Columbia Heights Ridge before diving back down Ganoe Hill to the Porcupine Valley. Had enough? I didn't think so. So climb over "the Hog Back" to Big Coulee and then breathe again as you cruise across the prairie.

Continue on D until it rejoins County N. Turn left (north) on N and follow it through Dead Lake Prairie to the town of Arkansaw and the junction with Highway 10. This little settlement built overlooking a gorge in the river was named Arkansaw because some of the early settlers saw a resemblance to towns on the Arkansaw River.

Easy Creek, (715) 285-5736, is one of those great little bar-eateries that you'll want to go home and tell your friends about. Known for its chicken, seafood, and various pesto dishes, you'll want to drop in on a Thursday night when bands such as

Lauraland

When you visit the little wayside park and replica cabin that commemorate the life of Laura Ingalls Wilder, think about this region as it was in 1867, the year Laura was born, before the loggers cleared the abundant forestland and the rutted wagon trail to town became paved.

Laura's book about her early years, *The Little Cabin in the Big Woods*, and her other stories of pioneer life on the new American frontier were the basis for the popular TV series *Little House on the Prairie*. They have become required reading as basic English texts all over the world. In fact, they are so popular in Japan that a replica of this cabin has been built in a prefecture near Tokyo. Japanese travelers visiting the Twin Cities area consider a visit to Pepin, the Pepin Historical Society, and this wayside an absolute requirement for a great trip. Laura died in Mansfield, Missouri, February 10, 1957.

Every September Pepin hosts *Laura Ingalls Wilder Days*, (715) 442-3011, which feature historical reenactments, a parade, pancake breakfast, a craft sale, and the Laura look-alike contest for 8- to 10-year-old girls (pre-registration required).

A brochure published by the Laura Ingalls Wilder Memorial Society (Box 269, Pepin, 54759) quotes a letter written by Laura in 1942 to schoolchildren in Chicago: "The Little House Books are stories of long ago. The way we live and your schools are much different now; so many changes have made living and learning easier. But the real things haven't changed. It is still best to be honest and truthful; to make the most of what we have; to be happy with the simple pleasures and to be cheerful and have courage when things go wrong."

"Girls With Trucks" play their brand of Wisconsin hill country swing music. Friday and Saturday features other regional musical talent playing everything from jazz to country.

Turn left (west) on 10 across Maple Ridge and go about 8 miles to the junction with County U in Plum City. Plum City takes its name from the wild plum trees that grow along the banks of the Plum River.

Turn left (south) on U and go to the junction with County CC, crossing Plum Creek, Brunner Valley, and Cotter Hill. As you travel these back roads watch for some of the great old round barns. Why build a round barn? One explanation has it that evil spirits like to lurk in corners so they won't stay in a round structure. Another explanation says that round barns do better in strong winds. A more reasonable, practical explanation might be that they require less material per finished square foot of space. Whatever, they never won over the farmer enough to prevail, and the old rectangular barn seems to have survived the fad.

Turn left (south) on CC and follow it to the *Laura Ingalls Wilder Little House*. This little three-acre park and replica cabin commemorate Laura Ingalls Wilder, who was born near here in what she later memorialized as the Little Cabin in the Big Woods (see accompanying article). Look around the surrounding countryside and you may spot a round barn.

Return on CC about 1.9 miles back to the junction with County J. Turn left on J and drive into the town of Stockholm. This little community was founded in the 1850s by Swedish immigrants and is the oldest Swedish settlement in western Wisconsin. It has an easy, natural charm and friendliness that can be hard to resist. In summer nearly every home and business is decked out with flowers and gardens.

Your first stop may be at the big gray *Amish Country Store*, (715) 442-2015, where you'll find the museum quality furniture, quilts, and crafts to be virtually irresistible. Across the street is *Stockholm Antiques*, (715) 442-2113, which is stocked full of treasure.

You'll find beautiful Mississippi pearl jewelry at *Pottery and Mercantile*, (715) 442-9012, and ceramics and gifts at *Spirit of the River*, (715) 442-2900. *Pepin Toys*, (715) 442-5007, has great classic wooden toys.

Rest and sit in the garden at the *Bogus Creek Cafe and Bakery*, (715) 442-5017, or grab a good lunch at *The Star Café* (715) 442-2023.

Turn right (northwest) on Highway 35 in Stockholm. Follow 35 north into the community of Maiden Rock. As you cruise along the Mississippi, watch for the famous bluff that gives the community its name. The story has it that a

Native American woman, Winona, a chief's daughter, leaped off the 400-foot bluff rather than marry a man she didn't love.

In Maiden Rock, *The Harrisburg Inn*, (715) 448-4500, is a popular bed and breakfast inn known for lake views, excellent breakfasts in a sunny dining room, and pleasant conversation on the screened porch. This is a comfortable headquarters for area shopping and touring.

Continue on 35 north from Maiden Rock and go to County A. Turn right. Head up into the hills on this beautiful river run. Watch for signs on 420th St. leading to *Rush River Produce*, (715) 594-3648, on 200th Ave., where you can pick raspberries and currants in July and blueberries in July and August.

Continue north on A, a wiggly 9-mile drive up the Rush River to Highway 10. Turn left (west) on 10 and go to the junction with County D. Turn left (south) on D and drive about 7 miles back to Highway 35 at Oakridge.

Turn right (northwest) on 35 and drive to Bay City. This little settlement is a favorite with fishing enthusiasts, antique shoppers, and eagle spotters. *The Lavender Rose Restaurant*, (715) 792-2464, serves delicious and creative regional cuisine and is ranked with the best in the area.

Continue north on 35 to the intersection with Highway 63 near Hagar City. (The drive on Highway 35 to Diamond Bluff, about 6 miles farther northwest, is a nice option if you want to see more river country scenery in Wisconsin.)

Turn left on 63, crossing the Mississippi River into Minnesota, and drive to the city of Red Wing and Highway 61. This frontier town is built up in the bluffs overlooking the Mississippi River. It's a popular stop because it's loaded with 19th-century architecture, lots of antique and gift shops, art galleries, and friendly Minnesotans.

Start you exploration at *Levee Park* and the *Milwaukee Depot*, just below the St. James Hotel. Levee Park holds the *Sea Wing Memorial*. *The Red Wing Visitor and Convention Bureau* is now housed in the restored depot. Call (800) 498-3444 for information on any aspect of Red Wing and ask for a free walking guide, "Footsteps through Historic Red Wing."

For the committed hiker, try the *Barn Bluff* walk. Henry David Thoreau of *Walden* fame climbed Red Wing's dramatic Barn Bluff in 1861 and wrote glowingly of the grandeur and beauty of the region. Routes begin at the end of East Fifth St. Take the one to the right for the most scenic trail. (*Watch your step as the trail sometimes experiences erosion problems*.) If you want another adventure, watch eagles soar over the Mississippi at *Colvill Park*, east of downtown on Highway 61.

Rent a houseboat, camp on a sandbar, and explore the Mississippi. Wisconsin Department of Tourism photo.

Red Wing is one of the most famous brands of pottery in the world. A collection of its early specimens is on display in the Red Wing salesroom, (800) 228-0174, 1995 W. Main St. Check out the renovated former Red Wing factory, which now houses the *Historic Pottery Place Mall*. You can see the remains of the kilns and historic displays as well as unique specialty and antique shops and factory outlets. The modern-day *Red Wing Stoneware Company* is 4 miles west of downtown, along Highway 61. Viewing windows let visitors watch the process, (651) 388-4610.

Cruise the big river and put on your riverboat gambler's hat at *Treasure Island Resort and Casino*, (800) 222-7077. It has more than 1,600 slot machines, 50 blackjack tables, high stakes bingo, and pull tabs, as well as four restaurants and a 250-room tropical theme hotel.

Watch the river traffic at *Lock and Dam No. 3* a few miles north of the city. Drive past Treasure Island Resort and Casino and the Northern States Power nuclear power plant. The viewing platform is open during the day as soon as the snow is gone, April through October. For information, call (651) 388-5794.

Pottery isn't the only thing Red Wing is known for. At the *Riverfront Center* take in the *Red Wing Shoe Museum*. See how the famous Red Wing shoes are made, view scenes of the factory from a 1925 film, and read interesting testimonials extolling this famous footwear.

The *Sheldon Theatre*, (800) 899-5759, has been called Red Wing's "jewel box." This historic performing arts theater was opened in 1904 on the corner of Third St. and East Ave. The country's first municipal theater now serves as a cultural center.

Red Wing Antique Emporium, (888) 407-0371, is a box full of treasures that you'll have to poke around in. Be sure to visit the lower basement level to see one of the many springs that feed Red Wing's "hidden Jordan River," 420-430 W. Third S.

The *Goodhue Country Historical Museum*, (651) 388-6024, 1166 Oak St., has interesting exhibits covering local history from A to Z and is regarded as one of the finest museums in Minnesota.

A great place to watch the river and the river traffic is *Bay Point Park and Boathouse Village*. (Take Levee St. from Levee Park to Bay Point Park.) The lighted walking path is kept open throughout the year. Come anytime, the Mississippi has moods that change frequently and with the seasons. Here you'll find *Boathouse Village*, one of the only remaining "gin pole" boathouses in the country. Individual floating boat storage houses ride up and down on poles, adjusting to the river's level.

Red Wing is well known for its hotels and bed and breakfast inns. Among the best are *The Candlelight Inn*, (800) 254-9194, built in 1877 and listed on the National Register of Historic Places; *The Golden Lantern Inn*, (888) 288-3315, done in Tudor Revival style; the *Hearthwood*, (651) 437-1133, set on a 10.7-acre river valley estate; and the famous landmark downtown, the elegant 60-room *St. James Hotel*, (651) 388-2846, with two restaurants, two lounges, and nine shops.

From Red Wing head southeast on Highway 61/63 about 10 miles to *Frontenac State Park*, known for spectacular scenery from sky-scraping bluff tops to the waves lapping at the shores of Lake Pepin. Migratory birds seem to consider this area a checkpoint on their route, as do bird watchers. Call (651) 345-3401.

Continue on 61/63 to Lake City, situated on the west bank of Lake Pepin. Enjoy the breathtaking views of the Mississippi River as you enter the city.

Lake City has a number of good shopping, lodging, and dining options. *Home Traditions*, (651) 345-2017, has everything from decoys to wooden rocking chairs. *Treats and Treasures*, (651) 345-2882, has fudge, collectibles, and unique gifts, while *Bushel & Peck*, (651) 345-4516, sells delicious apples, strawberries, and pumpkins.

If you're looking for good food, try *Waterman's Restaurant*, (651) 345-5353, which offers lake view dining. *The Gallery*, (651) 345-9991, is great for Sunday buffet, and the *Chickadee Cottage*, (888) 321-5177, is known for delicious homemade specialties.

Want to stay a while? *The Victorian*, a bed and breakfast, (888) 345-2167, has great lake views, and the *Red Gables Inn*, (888) 345-2605, captures the essence of the Victorian era in a romantic setting. More contemporary amenities are available at the *Americinn* (651) 345-5611.

Stay on 61 and continue southeast through Maple Springs and Reads Landing. In the logging era Reads Landing was the western-most logging center for the Wisconsin lumber industry. At one time 27 hotels (and 21 saloons!) served the hundreds of loggers who piloted the rafts of logs—some up to three acres in size—down the river. During the height of the era through the early 1900s, some 2,000 of these log rafts would float down the Mississippi each year. To learn more of the area history, visit the *Wabasha County Museum*, (651) 345-3097, housed in a historic brick schoolhouse at Reads Landing.

Continue south on 61 to the junction with Highway 60. Turn left on 60 and proceed into Wabasha. This is the oldest town in Minnesota, established in the 1830s and today best known as the location where the two *Grumpy Old Men* movies were filmed. In fact, they hold a Grumpy Old Men Festival here on the iced-over bay each February.

Wabasha has one of the largest concentrations of wintering bald eagles in the lower 48 states. Eagles congregate here in winter because the rapidly moving river currents keep the water from freezing. The big birds dine on the abundant non-game fish called "gizzard shad"—and sometimes even on road kill. For more information about various eagle-related programs, contact the *National Eagle Center* at (651) 565-4989.

The *Eagle Valley Café*, (651) 565-2040, is known for its breakfasts, Friday fish frys, and Sunday chicken specials.

Wabasha has preserved the past by finding new uses for old buildings. The *City Hall Chambers* now hold the *Heritage* gift shop, the old library has become *Old City Hall Antiques*, the *Fire Hall* is a collection of artisan and pottery shops, and the old jail is now (what else?) *The Cooler*, a homemade ice cream shop where, they say, "you'll enjoy doing some time." Doll collectors will want to visit *The Girls*, (651) 565-4026, to see the extensive line of dolls and related gifts.

Slippery's Bar and Grill, (651) 565-4748, is the original location for some scenes in *Grumpy Old Men*. Sorry, but there's no bait, just lots of good food, at *Chucks Bait Shop*. For a good cup of coffee and friendly talk, visit the *Eagle's Nest Coffee Shop*, (651) 565-2077.

Where to stay? The *Eagles on the River* bed and breakfast, (800) 684-6813, has quite a view and is rather secluded, while *Bridgewaters Bed and Breakfast*, (651) 565-4208, is a quiet, comfortable inn with a fireplace.

An unusual, privately operated museum is the *Arrowhead Bluffs Museum*, (651) 565-3829, 2 miles west of Wabasha on Highway 60. It has a huge gun collection featuring one of every Winchester made from 1866 to 1982, as well as Native American and pioneer artifacts and mounted animals.

From Wabasha, cross the Highway 25 bridge into Wisconsin and return to Nelson.

Tour 16
The Neatest Little River Drive You've Never Seen

Chippewa Falls—Jim Falls—Cornell—Holcombe—Ladysmith—Bruce—Chippewa Falls

Distance: 122 miles

Maybe it won't rank up there with Newton getting bonked by an apple, but here's a weird little pseudo-scientific revelation that hit me as I was cruising along the Chippewa River and pumped with driver's endorphins deep in the exhilaration zone: This land is a living thing that needs to attract humans to scratch around on it, plant it, plow it, and sometimes just rub its back.

Early on it lured the hunter-gatherers who got rid of those pesky mammoths. Then it captured the loggers, who shaved off the big white pine and hardwoods. More recently it attracted the tourists to come in and mix up the water a bit, poke around on the shore, and catch a few of those annoying 50-pound muskie. And now it needs a good rubdown.

There I was running my tires over its back, giving it a Goodyear massage along the twisting trail of Highway178 that snakes along with every change of direction beside this delightfully slithering Chippewa River.

Maybe I'm wrong. But hey, drivers, come on up, test the theory. Just like the Native Americans, loggers, and resorters before you, you'll get what you need. And the land will be happy!

Begin at the intersection of Highways 124 and 178 (Grand Avenue) in Chippewa Falls. The name of the city is a variation of the word *Ojibwa*, the Native Americans who had inhabited northern Wisconsin for generations. The first non-Native American settlers came here in 1837 and by 1853 a village had sprung up. The city grew up with sawdust in its veins, after the big trees were gone, when railroads and shoe factories provided employment. Today the community is proud to be known for its role in the development of the supercomputer and for the fine beer made by the Leinenkugel Brewery. You'll find much of this history preserved at the area's *History Center,* (715) 723-4399, 123 Allen St.

The Chippewa Falls Museum of Industry and Technology, (715) 720-9206, 21 E. Grand Ave., interprets the area's manufacturing history from the 1840s through the computer age. *The Cook-Rutledge Mansion,* (715) 723-7181, 505 W. Grand Ave., is a must-see for antique lovers and fans of High Victorian-Italianate architecture. The home is considered one of the most beautiful and elegant in northern Wisconsin and is listed on the National Register of Historic Places.

Take a tour of the *Jacob Leinenkugel Brewing Company,* (715) 723-5557, 1 Jefferson Ave. The founder, whose name still graces the company, opened his brewery in 1867 to help quench the thirst of all those immigrants coming to town to cut trees. Today Leinenkugel's beer has achieved a kind of cult status and beer lovers seek out its specialty brews. Many travelers say the visit to the suds factory is a highlight of their trip to the North Woods. Stop in and watch how their specialty beers are handcrafted in small 160-barrel batches. At the end of your tour enjoy a couple of samples of Leinenkugel's and browse through the extensive gift shop.

The Heyde Center for the Arts, (715) 723-2097, 3 High St., is a new art center that was once a school but now is used for art exhibits, shows, theatre, music, and dance.

Gardeners will especially like the rose garden and lily garden at the corner of Jefferson and Bridgewater Aves. The gardens are spectacular with more than 500 roses—teas, floribunda, grandiflora, miniatures, and climbers.

Northeast of Chippewa Falls, on County O, is *Lake Wissota State Park,* (715) 382-4574, a 1,062-acre expanse with a 6,300-acre lake. It's a beautiful, relatively undiscovered northern getaway with excellent camping; hiking; horse trails; walleye, muskie, and bass fishing; and swimming.

The Old Abe Trail, (888) 723-0024, is a paved 19.5-mile route that connects Lake Wissota State Park with Brunet Island State Park in Cornell. The trail, an abandoned railroad grade, has been developed for use by bicyclists, snowmobilers, hikers,

Old Abe came from the Jim Falls area and is revered as a symbol of courage and fierce determination throughout Wisconsin. Photo by Gary Knowles.

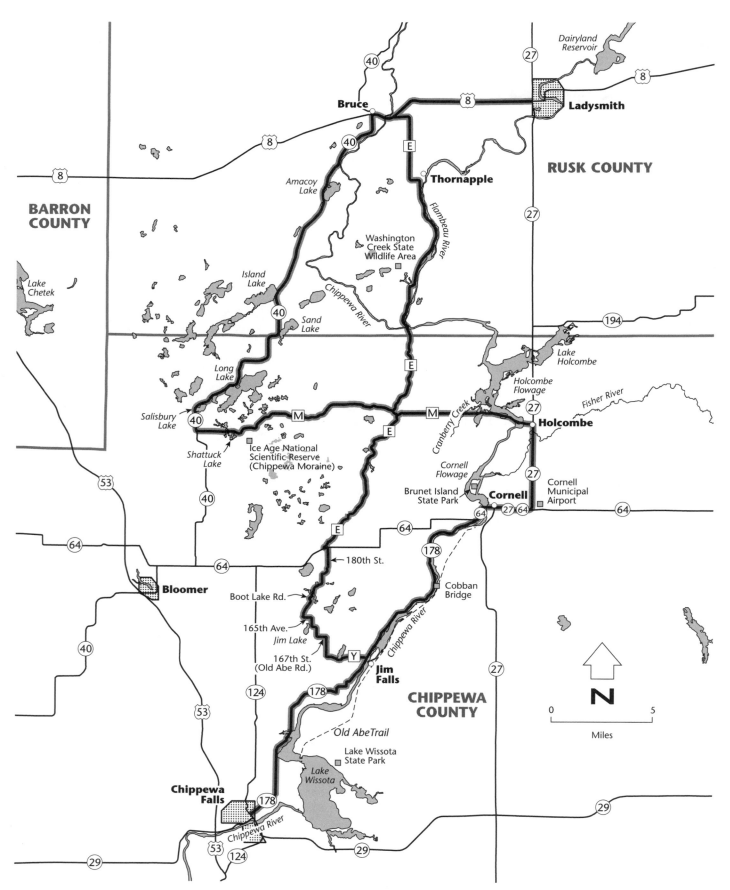

Tour 16

horseback riders, and in-line skaters. Passes are required for all persons 16 years or older for biking, in-line skating, and horseback riding.

Drive north on 178 out of Chippewa Falls and go about 12 miles to Jim Falls. This drive passes through Chippewa Falls residential areas, the suburbs, the new suburbs, and eventually into the lake country. Certainly the folks around here know this beautiful stretch of road, but they sure haven't told the rest of the world about it. As you get a few miles out of town you'll begin to see what a great run of about 20 miles has been waiting for you on the west bank of the Chippewa River. Along the way, watch for the historical marker for "Old Abe, the War Eagle" that tells of how an eagle from this area went into battle and inspired Wisconsin soldiers in the Civil War. (See article.)

Jim Falls is the site of an early 1800s trading post. The first hydroelectric plant was built here in 1923 and has since been replaced. You can cross the river here and see the statue that memorializes Old Abe. The Falls Dairy offers tours. For Jim Falls information call (800) 866-6264.

Continue north on 178 for about 5.3 miles to Cobban Bridge. The road hugs the shore of the Chippewa River, then reaches this historic and picturesque bridge, one of the last of its kind in the nation. Built in 1908, this Pennsylvania truss bridge was first used about 15 miles downriver before the Wissota Dam flooded the original site. In 1918 it was brought upriver on the ice by sled to replace a ferry. It's a one-car-at-a- time antique structure, but don't pass up the thrill of driving over it. Just check first to be sure there's no car coming from the other direction, drive up the incline, and cruise right down the middle. When you get across, turn around and return to 178.

Follow 178 north about five miles to the junction with Highway 64. Stay on 64 and cross the Chippewa River into Cornell.

This community saw its first settler, Jean Brunet, move his family upstream from Chippewa Falls in the early 1800s. Later Ezra Cornell claimed the nearby heavily timbered land and then went on to fund Cornell University with the fortune he amassed. And the town now shares his name. Cornell was the world's last huge pulpwood stacker, and there are lots of interesting artifacts attesting to this bygone era at the *Cornell Museum and Visitors Center*, (715) 239-3713, in the mill yard on Bridge St.

Brunet Island State Park, (715) 239-6888, is just north of Cornell at the confluence of the Fisher and Chippewa Rivers. This 1,030-acre park lies on an island in the Chippewa River and is a great place to camp, fish, swim, and hike.

Go east out of Cornell on 64 to the junction with Highway 27. Follow 27 as it swings north at the Cornell Airport, following it

across Buck Creek and Fisher River about 4.1 miles to Holcombe.

This community serves as the friendly gateway to the Lake Holcombe area. The lake has more than 120 miles of shoreline and 3,900 acres of water fed by the Chippewa, Flambeau, and Jump Rivers. Fishing enthusiasts may not want to travel any farther. This lake is known for having lots of muskie, pike, walleye, bass, crappie, bluegill, catfish, and even river sturgeon.

In Holcombe, turn left on County M. You'll spot the *Big Minnow Bar*, (715) 595-6362, a family bar with good burgers, pizza, and lots of video games.

Follow M west across Lake Holcombe and drive for about 2 miles. Here you'll come across one of the finest of the many resorts in the area: *Paradise Shores Resort*, (715) 595-4227, on Lake Holcombe. This year-round retreat has 43 guest rooms overlooking the lake and several suites with fireplaces. The amenities include an indoor pool, spa, game room, and fitness room. What makes this property even more special is *Smokin' Joe's*, (715) 595-4701, a superb "southern grill" restaurant fea-

Old Abe, the War Eagle

Many fighting units in the Civil War had their own mascots. The animals included some dogs, horses, and even a goat. But none had the fame and glory of Old Abe, an eagle from Wisconsin. Abe was captured from a nest on the Flambeau River by Ojibwa Indians who traded him to a farmer for some corn. The farmer sold him at Jim Falls to some recruits in the 8th Wisconsin Infantry Regiment. To honor President Lincoln they named the eagle "Old Abe." His presence and demeanor earned the unit the nickname "The Eagle Regiment."

They say that Old Abe was carried into more than a dozen battles and skirmishes with the soldiers. He was tied to a staff with a cord around a leg so that he could fly a bit. Stories tell of Old Abe flying and screeching over Confederate lines during battle, frightening the rebels and boosting the morale and fighting spirit of the Union men.

After the war, Old Abe was given his own honored place in the state capitol building, went on a national tour, and was brought out to lord over every gathering of Wisconsin's Civil War veterans. They say that photos of Old Abe were so popular that they brought in over $16,000, and at one time P. T. Barnum offered $25,000 for the bird in hopes of exhibiting him with Jumbo the elephant. But in 1881 the capitol burned and though Abe was pulled out of the building, he died from complications of smoke inhalation.

His body was preserved, mounted, and for years sat on a roost high over the State Assembly chambers. Then a second capitol fire occurred in 1904 and Abe was lost. Replicas were created and one still stands in the Assembly chambers while another is on display at the Veterans Museum in Madison. The Eau Claire Memorial High School sports teams use the nickname "the Old Abes," his image is the eagle on the Racine-based Case Company logo, and he served as the inspiration for the U.S. Army's 101st Airborne Division's "Screaming Eagles," which saw extensive action in World War II, Vietnam, and the Persian Gulf.

turing some of the finest creative cooking in the North. House specialties include the Cajun ribs, chicken, and trout.

From Paradise Shores continue on M across County CC and Cranberry Creek, then go another 3.6 miles to the junction with County E. Just a bit farther west, follow E as it turns right (north). This is Wisconsin Rustic Road 6, which follows the Old Flambeau Trail that was a favorite Ojibwa route adopted by traders, trappers, and early immigrants as they moved into the North. The glaciers gouged out this land, and the beautiful rolling hills are part of the *Ice Age National Scientific Reserve.* Enjoy the ride through wooded rolling hills and wetlands, crossing the Chippewa River at the confluence with the Flambeau River.

Continue north on E along the banks of the Flambeau, passing through the *Washington Creek Wildlife Area* to Thornapple. Follow E west and north to the junction with Highway 8. Turn right (east) on 8 and drive about 7 miles into Ladysmith. You can see a little red schoolhouse and the old Glen Flora wooden jail, along with hundreds of other items (but nothing from the town's namesake, Lady Smith), at the *Rusk County Historical Museum,* (800) 535-RUSK, on the Ladysmith Fairgrounds. (See the accompanying article if you're wondering about Lady Smith and the name of the town.)

Ladysmith has a fine selection of restaurants offering good food. If the shopping urge is bothering you, you can spend some time here to satisfy it.

Backtrack west on 8 and drive into Bruce and the intersection with Highway 40. Turn left (south) on 40 and go to the junction with County M. You'll follow the Chippewa River, then pass west of Amacoy Lake, cross Maple Creek, Potato Creek, and Island Lake. You'll skirt the west shore of Sand Lake, wind down to Long Lake, past little Larabee Lake, and finally Salisbury Lake.

Turn left (east) on M, climbing over the Chippewa Moraine of the Ice Age National Scientific Reserve. The *Chippewa Moraine Ice Age Interpretive Center,* (715) 967-2800, overlooks Shattuck Lake and has exhibits, displays, and films that interpret the impact of the

How Ladysmith Got Its Name

This community should be honored in the Nice Try Hall of Fame. The name of the town was originally Corbett, then Flambeau Falls. But local economic developers decided that they'd be glad to give up their name for a new factory. The owner of a woodenware business, a Mr. Smith, liked the idea of moving here, but his wife just wouldn't hear of it. And if she didn't want to come, well, Mr. Smith would have it tough at home. So to lure her in, the town fathers thought they might show how much they cared for her happiness. Perhaps an appeal to her vanity might work. They dumped the name Flambeau Falls and promptly changed the signs to read "Welcome to Ladysmith." Well it worked, sort of. Mr. Smith brought the factory to town and jobs were created. But Lady Smith wasn't convinced. She never set foot here.

Take a thrilling drive over the Chippewa River on the Cobban Bridge, built in 1908. Photo by Gary Knowles.

glaciers. You'll then pass many little lakes that are the slowly disappearing tracks of the ice mass that left here some 10,000 years ago.

Stay on M to the junction with County E and follow M/E a short distance. Turn right (south) on E (Rustic Road 6), following it as it skirts around lakes, rolls through wooded glacial kettles and moraines, and crosses the North Fork of Bob Creek.

Now we'll wander on a crooked, narrow trail that weaves between pretty little lakes and cuts through the forest. Ready for a bit of "soft adventure"? Great. (If you get off course or lost, don't worry. Just keep heading south and east and eventually you'll be somewhere!)

At the junction of E and Highway 64 cross (south) onto 180th Street and follow it 1.5 miles to 171st Street. Bear left on 171st and go about 0.5 mile to Boot Lake Road. Turn left (south) on Boot Lake Road and go two miles to 165th Avenue.

Turn left (east) on 165th Avenue, which quickly jogs right (south) as 167th Street (Old Abe Road). Here you'll pass Jim Lake and Old Abe's Bar. (At this point, you might want to stop at Old Abe's Bar and ask where the heck you are.)

Continue south on Old Abe Road and go to County Y. Turn left on Y and go about 2.7 miles to Highway 178. Turn right (south) on 178 and follow it about 10 miles back to Chippewa Falls.

Tour 17
Superior Waterfalls and the Iron Range Run

Superior—Poplar—Lake Nebagamon—Drummond—Cable—Clam Lake—Mellen—Gurney—Saxon—Upson—Montreal—Hurley—Odanah—Ashland—Superior

Distance: 278 miles

Since the dawn of civilization, waterfalls have mesmerized everyone who stopped to have a look. Big ones thunder and make the ground tremble. Some smash water on the rocks and cast a misty veil. Others are little more than babbling brooks with big aspirations. No matter. It's the same magic that lives in the glowing embers of a campfire or the rhythmic beating of waves on the shore. Sit close to a waterfall, breathe deeply, and let the falling water work its magic on you.

Some people believe that the rushing water releases negative ions into the air, creating a pure, natural feeling of relaxation and quiet elation. Some of us feel that same high when we accelerate a lively automobile through a series of turns on a pretzel-curved road or when we drive for miles on great back roads packed with scenic beauty.

On this tour you'll have plenty of opportunities to test all these theories. Wisconsin's Lake Superior territory has more than its share of all of these treasures connected by some exciting, historic, and scenic routes—not all well known, but easily accessible to those willing to veer a bit from the road more traveled. (Note: This is a long tour, best done in several days or in pieces as time permits.)

We'll begin in downtown Superior. The city is the westernmost port of the world's greatest lake, Superior. There's plenty to see and do here, as well as in adjoining Duluth, Minnesota. Here's a sample of what's on the Wisconsin side.

Fairlawn Mansion and Museum, (715) 394-5712, 906 E. 2nd St., is a 42-room mansion that was home to Superior's second mayor, lumber baron Martin Pattison. Later we'll visit the magnificent state park he donated to Wisconsin. The extraordinary house is a superb exhibit, recalling the early days of Great Lakes Victorian elegance, maritime commerce, and Native American lore. It includes an exceptional collection of photographs of Native Americans.

On Barker's Island, check out *Vista Fleet Harbor Cruises,* (715) 394-6846, which offers narrated tours of the world's largest inland port and the unusual Duluth Aerial Lift Bridge. See grain elevators, freshwater ships ("lakers"), and ocean-going ships ("salties"). Tours depart from Barker's

The SS *Meteor* is the last of the whaleback freighters whose snubbed bow earned them the nickname "pig-boats." Wisconsin Department of Tourism photo by GK.

Island. Don't pass up an opportunity to see this great harbor.

Also on Barker's Island is the SS Meteor *Maritime Museum,* (715) 394-5712. Launched in Superior in 1896, the SS *Meteor* is the world's only remaining whaleback freighter. The rounded "snout" on these ships led to their nickname "pig-boats." The ship was a forerunner of the huge lakers that cruise in and out of the Superior harbor today. Nearby is the *Seaman's Memorial,* dedicated to the sailors of the *Edmund Fitzgerald,* which sailed from Superior on November 9, 1975, bound for Cleveland. Many of her 29 men lived in the area and all were lost when the ship went down in a fierce storm at the east end of the lake the next day.

If you've ever dreamed of reeling in a "big one" in deep water, you'll want to contact the *Lake Superior Charter Captains Association.* The group can provide the equipment and guide service to help you catch that dream fish! Choose from half- and full-day charters for parties up to six. They're experts on fishing know-how for walleye, lake trout, king and coho salmon. For a list of captains, contact the *Superior and Douglas County Visitors Bureau,* (800) 942-5313, 205 Belknap St.

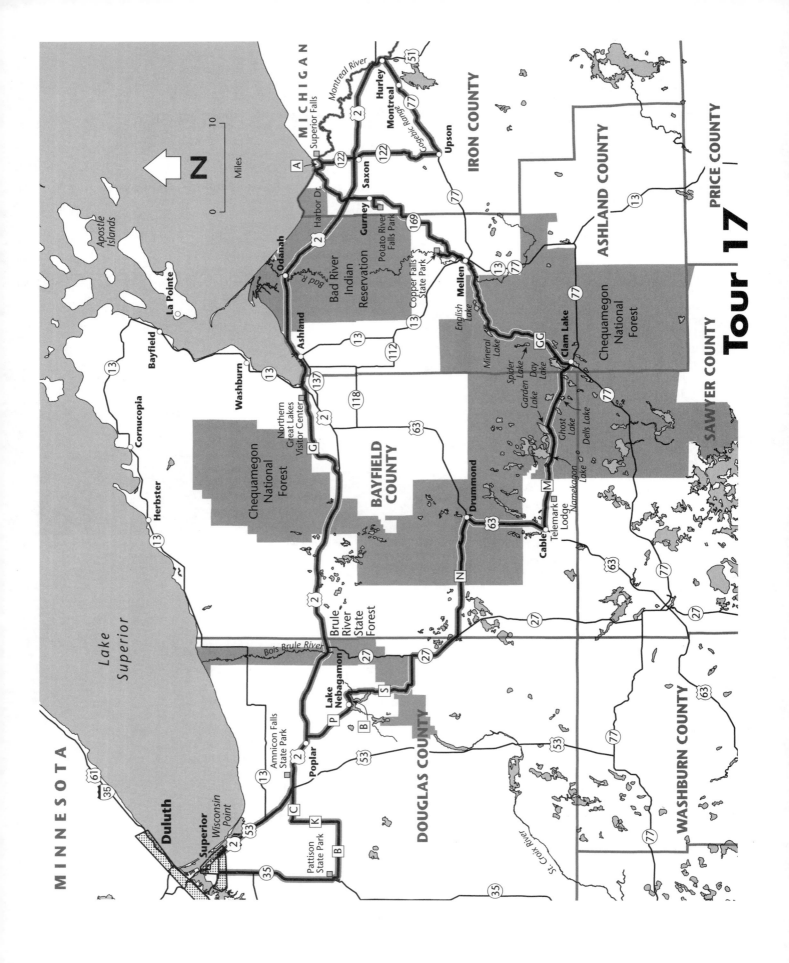

MINNESOTA

Lake
Superior

Apostle
Islands

La Pointe

Duluth

Superior

Wisconsin Point

35
61

53
35

2

Pattison State Park
B

C
K

Poplar
2

Amnicon Falls
State Park
13

53

53

Lake
Nebagamon
P
B
S

27

27

27

27

Bois Brule River

Brule River
State Forest
2

2

Cornucopia

Herbster
13

Bayfield
13

Washburn
13

Ashland
2
137
G

Odanah
2

Bad R.

Harbor Dr.
2

Superior Falls
A

122
122

Saxon

Gurney
169

Montreal River

Hurley
51
2
77
Montreal
Gogebic Range

Upson

IRON COUNTY

77

Northern
Great Lakes
Visitor Center

118

63

BAYFIELD
COUNTY

Chequamegon
National Forest

112

13

13

Bad River
Indian
Reservation

Potato River
Falls Park

Copper Falls
State Park

English
Lake

Mellen
13
77

77

ASHLAND COUNTY

13

PRICE COUNTY

77

Drummond
63
N

M
Telemark
Lodge
Cable

Namekagon

Ghost
Lake
Dells Lake

Day
Lake
Garden
Lake

Spider
Lake

Mineral
Lake

Clam Lake
GG
GG

77

Chequamegon
National Forest

SAWYER COUNTY

Tour 17

63

77

27

27

St. Croix River

WASHBURN COUNTY

63

77

DOUGLAS COUNTY

N

10
Miles
0

MICHIGAN

90

The Old Firehouse and Police Museum, (715) 392-2773, 23rd Ave. East and Fourth St., is a turn-of-the-century fire station that has been restored and is open to the public. It features antique equipment, including a 1906 steam pumper.

Wisconsin Point, located on the city of Superior's eastern edge, on Moccasin Mike Rd., offers a fine panorama of Lake Superior, a picturesque lighthouse, and an inviting sandy beach. Rock collectors can hunt for semiprecious, red-brown Lake Superior agates and driftwood for souvenirs. Also in the city limits is the *Superior Municipal Forest*, a 4,500-acre recreational area featuring 28 kilometers of hiking and cross-country ski trails. Golfers will want to swing by Superior's highly regarded *Nemadji Golf Course*, (715) 394-0266, which boasts 36 holes and plays to a par 71 and 72 at 6,337 yards and 6,683 yards. Auto racing enthusiasts will enjoy stock car racing every Friday night at the *Head of the Lakes Fairgrounds* in Superior, (715) 394-7848.

The Wisconsin Travel Information Center, (715) 392-1662, located at Rest Stop 23 on Highway 2/53, will help you plan your visit to Superior and give you up-to-the-minute brochures, guides, and information about any area in the state. It's well worth a stop to collect county maps and community brochures before you go. The staff also can tell you if there are any major road construction projects in progress.

From downtown Superior, take Tower Avenue south (it starts as Business Highway 53, then becomes Highway 35) for 13 miles to *Pattison State Park,* (715) 399-3111. The major attractions here are *Big Manitou Falls* and *Little Manitou Falls*. These are two of Wisconsin's finest waterfalls, but because of their slightly remote location, they are not seen or appreciated as much as they ought to be. Big Manitou, a spectacular drop of 165 feet, is regarded as the fourth tallest waterfall east of the Rockies. Little Manitou, falling 30 feet, has a wild, calendar-quality beauty all its own. This area has been sacred ground to humans for over 9,000 years, since the retreat of the Wisconsin glacier. "Archaic Culture" Native Americans hunted and foraged here, and the Ojibwa (Chippewa) have called this country home since 500 A.D. The 1,373-acre park's treasures were spared from power companies' development in 1918 by Martin Pattison, the lumber magnate, developer, and mayor of Superior who owned the land. Plans called for the destruction of Big Manitou Falls to make way for a power dam, but just days before his death, Pattison donated the land he loved to the people of Wisconsin to preserve as a state park. Thanks to improvements by President Franklin D. Roosevelt's Civilian Conservation Corps in the 1930s and the stewardship of Wisconsin Department of Natural Resources, we enjoy the falls today as nature sculpted them over the millennia.

From Pattison Park, turn right (north) on 35 to the intersection with County B. Turn right (east) on B to County K. Turn left (north) on K to County C. Turn right (east) on C to the junction with Highway 2/53.

Continue on Highway 2 east to the junction with County U. Turn left (north) on U to *Amnicon Falls State Park*. The Amnicon River plunges 180 feet as it races over the Douglas Fault to Lake Superior. Along the way it drops over three falls, each over 30 feet high. This dramatic landscape is the creation of billions of years of volcanic and glacial activity. Pick up a detailed explanatory booklet at the park office. Bring a picnic lunch, enjoy the falls, and walk over the historic, 55-foot Horton "bow-string" bridge—one of only six in the world. Good campsites are also available. Call (715) 399-8073 for winter reservations, (715) 398-3000 for summer reservations.

Follow County U left (south) out of the park entrance, back to the junction with Highway 2. Turn left (east) on 2 and continue to Poplar. This quiet little community was the home of World War II flying ace Richard Ira Bong, the "Ace of Aces." A memorial here commemorates his incredible record of 200 missions, 500 combat hours, and 40 air battle victories in his P-38 Lightning, for which he received the Medal of Honor. His gunnery instructor at Luke AFB in Arizona was Captain Barry Goldwater, who later became a U.S. senator. Bong's Medal of Honor was presented to him by General Douglas MacArthur. The flyer was killed when his P-80 jet crashed on takeoff August 6, 1945—the same day the *Enola Gay* dropped the first atomic bomb on Hiroshima. Both the Richard I. Bong Bridge on Highway 2 and the Richard I. Bong Airport in Superior honor his memory.

Continue on 2 to the intersection with County P. Turn right (south) on P to its junction with County B. Turn left (east) on B and go through the community of Lake Nebagamon to the junction with County S.

Turn right (south) on S, traveling through the *Brule River State Forest* and crossing the West Fork of the Bois Brule River, the "River of Five Presidents" (see Tour 1).

Lake Superior

Stretching 383 miles to Sault St. Marie on the east and 160 statute miles north to south, "Gitchi Gumi" (Hiawatha's "big water") covers 31,820 square miles—a surface area about the size of South Carolina. "Upper Lake," as the French knew it, has 2,800 miles of rugged, mostly wooded shoreline. Superior has an average depth of over 500 feet and a maximum depth of 1,333 feet. The water stays cold most of the year—an average temperature of 40 degrees F. When ships would go down in this frigid water, the drowned victims would often sink to the bottom and stay there because the cold water does not support the organism that usually causes a body to "bloat," and decay does not occur. Thus the line in Gordon Lightfoot's song about the ill-fated *Edmund Fitzgerald*: "Superior, it's said, never gives up her dead."

On the sunnier side, there are some beaches and bays where the water does get warm enough for swimming. One of the finest is Big Bay Beach at Big Bay Park on Madeline Island where July and August offer good opportunities to take a plunge. With three quadrillion gallons of water, Superior is so big it could fill all the other Great Lakes and have enough water left over for three more Lake Eries.

Early spring and late autumn are ideal times to enjoy the tranquility of Amnicon Falls State Park. Wisconsin Department of Tourism photo by GK.

At the junction of S and Highway 27, turn right (south) on 27 and follow it to the junction with County N. Turn left (east) on N and follow it across the Continental Divide and to Highway 63 at Drummond. The *Drummond Museum*, (715) 739-6260, in the library building has an interesting collection of artifacts, mounted animals, newspapers, photos, and maps of the area dating back to the logging era.

Turn right (south) on 63 and proceed to the junction with County M at Cable. The *Chequamegon Fat Tire Festival*, one of the nation's premiere mountain bike races, takes place here each year. The *Cable Natural History Museum*, (715) 798-3890, has interesting nature displays and mounted wildlife.

Turn left on M and go past Telemark Lodge, where the *American Birkebiener* cross-country ski race takes place each year, then passing near Lake Namekagon.

Golfers may want to take a break for 18 challenging holes at *Forest Ridges Golf Course* at *Lakewoods Resort*, (800) 255-5937. This course was designed by Joel Goldstrand and is a fine example of the new northern courses that bring woods, water, and picturesque scenery into play. You can even rent a cart equipped with a Global Positioning Satellite system to tell you exact distances from your ball to the green. Lakewoods is one of northern Wisconsin's finest full-service resorts, featuring cottages, condos, and lodge units with marina, indoor and outdoor pools, and excellent food.

Lake Namekagon marks the western end of the Gogebic Iron Range, which from the 1880s to the 1960s yielded some 70 million tons of iron ore for steel that helped build the United States. It extends some 80 miles northeast to Lake Gogebic in Michigan's Upper Peninsula. Combined with the glacial lakes and great forests, it makes for some interesting topography for driving enthusiasts!

Continue on M to the junction with County GG just outside Clam Lake, passing Garden Lake, Ghost Lake, Dell's Lake, White Bass Lake, and Day Lake on the way. In 1995 a herd of 25 elk was released near here in an attempt to reintroduce elk into the area. The combination of wetlands, dense forest, and availability of aspen (a favorite winter food) were favorable to the herd's survival. As of October 1999 the herd was reported doing well and had grown to some 60 animals.

Turn left (northeast) on GG and follow it into Mellen. Enjoy the twists, turns, hills, and scenic vistas as you head through the *Chequamegon National Forest* toward Mellen. You'll swing through some wonderful lake country. Cruise past the east side of Day Lake, near East Twin; cross Spider Creek, McCarthy Creek, and Camp Six Creek; then pass Mineral Lake, Potter Lake, and English Lake. Look for the signs for the scenic overlook just outside Mellen.

The Mellen Historical Society, (715) 274-2330, is located in the wonderfully restored Victorian *Mellen City Hall*, which is listed on the National Register of Historic Places.

In Mellen take Highway 13 left (north) to Highway 169, then turn right on 169 and turn onto the park road to *Copper Falls State Park*, (715) 274-5123. Visit this park once and you'll be back often. Here the Bad River drops 40 feet at Copper Falls. Tyler Forks of the Bad River shimmers in delightful cascades, then leaps over Brownstone Falls (30 feet), and joins the waters of Copper Falls on a roiling ride through the 60- to 100-foot walls of Devil's Gorge. All are within easy walking distance of the parking area. Hike the 2.5-mile trail to see the backwoods beauty Red Granite Falls. The park was established in 1929 and has 56 campsites, a picnic area, log shelter, concession stand, and children's recreation area. If you have time for just one waterfall trek, make it the one to Copper Falls. Recently, as the result of miners' blasts that rerouted the river 90 years ago, Copper Falls has started to crumble, cave in, and lose height. Park officials predict further changes in the coming years, so plan to see it soon. Brownstone Falls is unaffected and continues to offer impressive views.

Leave Copper Falls State Park and return to 169. Turn left (northeast), heading through the forest across the Scott Taylor River, Gehrman Creek, Camp Four Creek, Feldcher Creek, and Tyler Forks, then crossing into Iron County.

Turn left (west) onto Potato River Falls Road (just outside Gurney) and continue for about 1.5 miles to *Potato River Falls Town Park*. This is one of the North Woods' most beautiful undiscovered wilderness treasures. Surrounded by undeveloped forestlands, the river's swirling waters drop 90 feet through three huge cataracts creating long white lacy streamers. With a slightly more inspired name, Potato River Falls might have been a honeymoon village. Enjoy the town park with its rustic picnic facilities and basic camping area. Newly installed boardwalk trails make access to new vistas of the falls better than ever. Once word gets around, traffic will definitely pick up at this North Country treasure. Call the *Hurley Chamber of Commerce* for more information, (715) 561-4334.

Return on Potato River Falls Road to 169. Turn left (north) and go through Gurney to Highway 2. Turn right (east) on 2 and proceed about 4.5 miles to Highway 122. Turn right (south) on 122 and head to Saxon. This town was called Dogwood until 1892. Mail sacks were loaded on the train here and thus "sacks-on" was the popular local name that stuck.

Continue on 122 for about 10 miles past Saxon to Upson. This route, blazed in 1856, runs through the hills of the Gogebic Iron Range and a dense hardwood forest. For a little-known treat, check out *Upson Falls.* Just north of Upson, watch

for Town Park Rd.; turn right on it and then left across the bridge to Upson Town Park. Tucked out of the way in the park, the falls, with an 18-foot drop, are well worth the time to stop and enjoy them. Photographers should be sure to take a camera and hike a bit on the rocky path to find some wonderful views. Return to 122.

On 122, go to the junction with Highway 77 at Upson. Turn left (northeast) on 77 and follow it to Montreal. You'll cruise through the mining towns of Iron Belt and Pence (noted for having the highest per capita concentration of log buildings in Wisconsin). Designed in 1921, Montreal's white frame houses are set on well-landscaped streets in the only planned mining company town in Wisconsin. It's on the National Register of Historic Places.

In Montreal turn right onto Kokogan Street, then turn right on Gile Falls Street and go to the *Gile Falls Overlook.* There's a bridge over the top of this falls and it offers another interesting photo opportunity. That huge pile of rock across from the falls is waste tailing from the iron mine,

The Chequamegon and Nicolet National Forests—and the CCC

This tour and several others take you driving through some fascinating forests, including the Chequamegon and Nicolet National Forests. The Nicolet is spread out over 661,377 acres in Florence, Forest, Langlade, Oconto, Oneida, and Vilas Counties; the Chequamegon covers 858,416 acres in Ashland, Bayfield, Sawyer, Price, Taylor, and Vilas Counties.

These national forests were established by presidential proclamations in 1933, about three decades after the great native forests of the Upper Great Lakes were nearly completely clear-cut back in the logging days.

Of course, the "first people" were here living on the land, using the resources some 10,000 years before. The Paleo-Indians were followed by the Archaic Indians and most recently by the Woodland Indians. The Europeans—missionaries and fur traders—first arrived in what is now Wisconsin in the 1600s. Next came the lumbermen who established the timber industry. Early loggers used rivers as their highways to carry pine logs to sawmills. When the old-growth pinery was cleared, they built railroads to haul the heavier hardwood logs to mills. After the forests were gone, the cutover land was sold to immigrants who hoped to build farms and homesteads. But the crops would not grow. The soil was more conducive to growing trees. To add to the devastation, wildfires blew across acres of stump-filled fields. Many farms were simply abandoned.

By 1928, the federal government, authorized by the Weeks Law of 1911, began buying abandoned and tax delinquent land in the North Woods, hoping to establish a national forest. In 1929, a Forest Service office was set up in Park Falls to oversee land acquisitions, and in March 1933,

shortly before he left office, President Herbert Hoover issued a proclamation establishing the Nicolet National Forest.

Shortly thereafter, in November 1933, President Franklin Roosevelt signed into being the Chequamegon National Forest as a separate unit carved from Nicolet's western acreage.

Nicolet National Forest bears the name of Jean Nicolet, the French explorer and fur trader who came to the Great Lakes region in the 1600s. The Chequamegon National Forest is named after an Ojibwa word meaning "place of shallow water," and refers to Lake Superior's Chequamegon Bay, east of the Bayfield Peninsula, north of Ashland.

When the Great Depression gripped the United States, the Civilian Conservation Corps was created and these national forests provided jobs by the thousands. The Trees for Tomorrow Camp at Eagle River and many of the logging museums around the state tell the CCC story. During the 10 years the CCC was active, Corpsmen planted thousands of acres of jack pine and red pine, built fire lanes, and constructed recreational facilities throughout these northern forests.

Cruise through these reforested lands, look up at the eagles, watch loons on these sparkling lakes, and keep an eye on the side of the road for deer. If you're lucky, you may see a bear, wolf, or—especially in the Clam Lake area—an elk that is part of the growing herd started in 1995. Stroll down the stone stairs in a park, relax in a rock shelter building, or walk along a hiking path near a falls. There's hardly a northern park or forest that is not better or more enjoyable because of the work the CCC crews did more than 60 years ago.

The cascading waters of Tyler's Falls are just one of the delights to be found during a hike in Copper Falls State Park. Wisconsin Department of Tourism photo by GK.

which went a mile beneath the surface. The deepest iron ore mine in the world, it provided jobs for local residents until it closed in the 1960s.

Return to Highway 77 and turn right (east) toward Hurley. Just before town, on Ringle Rd., is the *Cary Mine Building*, on the Penokee Iron Range , an art deco structure that once housed a working iron mine. From 1886 to 1964, the Cary Mine produced high-grade iron ore that went into steel production. When it closed, it marked the end of an 80-year-old industry and the end of a way of life for the people who worked in it.

Continue on 77 into Hurley to the intersection with Highway 51. This community is the county seat of Iron County and was once the center of iron ore mining on the great Gogebic Range. The historic *Iron County Courthouse* is a unique turreted structure with a four-faced working clock. The courthouse was originally built for the town of Vaughn in 1893. Today it is listed on the National Register of Historic Places and home to the *Iron County Historical Museum,* (715) 561-2244. It has an interesting collection of Penokee Iron Range artifacts and displays. You may also get to see rag rug weaving demonstrations. For additional area historical information, pick up a copy of the free *Iron County Historic Touring Guide,* (715) 561-2922.

At 51 turn left (north) and drive through Hurley. Check out the *Wisconsin Tourist Information Center,* (715) 561-5310, on the north edge of town. The people here are very helpful and will give you brochures, maps, and publications that can make your drive more enjoyable.

Follow 51 to Highway 2, turn left (west) and go 11 miles to Saxon.

Quick Trip Option (about 13 miles total): *Superior Falls*, one of the finest waterfalls in Iron County, is at the end of this detour, but it does include a stretch of gravel road. So keep that in mind if you're in a Porsche Boxster. Take Highway 122 right (north) down the big hill toward Lake Superior. Wisconsin ends after 4.2 miles at the Montreal River. Cross the bridge into Michigan and continue about 0.5 mile east, then turn left at the second road, a gravel road that ends at a parking lot at the Superior Falls Hydro Plant. Here the Montreal River takes a 90-foot dive into a spectacular gorge and then surges out to join Lake Superior. If you plan to shoot photos, you'll want to be here between 10 a.m. and about 1 p.m. because the gorge is pretty steep and dark. There are a couple of hiking trails here that offer views of the lake and falls.

Return to Highway 122 and go south to the intersection with County A. Turn right (west) on A and go to Saxon Harbor, and then follow Harbor Drive, the gravel road, west and south. This rustic gravel road "tunnels" through the dense hardwood forest canopy, passing near the graves of the Chippewa Chief Oronto and his daughters. Stay on Harbor Drive about 4 miles to Highway 2 west.

Follow 2 west to Odanah. The Bad River band of Lake Superior Chippewa operate the friendly *Bad River Casino* and bingo hall here, (715) 682-7121.

Continue on 2 to Ashland. (See Tour 1 for information on Ashland.)

Continue west on 2 just past the point where Highway 13 turns north, and continue to the junction with County G. Follow G to the *Northern Great Lakes Visitors Center*. Here, you can find helpful travel brochures and displays of lake history and see "Up Under the Upper Lake," an excellent show with great music that traces the area's rich history from the time of the glaciers to the present. Call (715) 685-9983 for more information.

Continue on G west to Highway 2. Turn right on 2 and follow the road back through the Chequamegon National Forest and the Brule River State Forest about 48 miles to Superior.

Tour 18
On Higher Ground

Neillsville—Willard—Eau Claire—Brackett—Strum—Hale—Osseo—Pigeon Falls—Hixton—Alma Center—Humbird—Neillsville

Distance: 147 miles

This drive is all about savoring the good life. You can do the tour anytime, but for best effect try it on a warm spring day or in midsummer. Drop the top (or at least open the sunroof or roll your windows down). Enjoy the freshness of the earth, the chatter of marsh birds, the sun-dappled wood lots, the sweet breezes.

The simple, unpretentious beauty of rural Wisconsin is a rich gift to soak up and enjoy.

The roads are good and the route has a generous share of easy cruising stretches, some delightful twists and turns, and some great hill country runs.

This drive begins in Neillsville, the site of The Highground—a wonderful tribute to all veterans and those who care for them. It cuts across the rolling hills and fertile farm country where you may encounter Amish or Mennonite people living in accordance with their religious beliefs. They may be using teams of horses to pull their plows or riding along the road in their simple black carriages. You'll find their finely crafted quilts and woodwork for sale in area stores.

Visit Eau Claire and take a drive through a beautiful section of the "coulee country" hills.

If you're really lucky you'll get a big delicious piece of sour cream raisin pie in Osseo. So why wait? Let's hit the trail.

Begin in Neillsville at the junction of Highway 10 and Highway 73/95.

Start the day on a high note at the *WCCN World's Fair Wisconsin Pavilion*, (715) 743-3333. This building was the main entrance to the World's Fair held in Flushing Meadows, New York, in 1964-65. Today it also houses the offices of radio station WCCN and the Pavilion Cheese and Gift Shop. It features posters and memorabilia from that fair as well as the ever-popular Chatty Belle, the giant talking Holstein. Stop to share a thought or two. If you get any wisdom from her just tell your friends "you heard it from the bovine."

The *1897 Jail Museum*, (715) 743-6444, on Fifth St., looks a bit like the local authorities were expecting trouble, with its fortress style and tall turrets. It's operated by the Clark County Historical Society, which offers tours of the former sheriff's residence and the cellblocks. You can see other

exhibits with photos of Neillsville, a military room with authentic uniforms from the Civil War through Desert Storm, antique telephony, and an early jewelry store.

Drive west on Highway 10 about 3 miles. You'll come to the extremely moving memorial *The Highground.* This park honors veterans of all the nation's wars (see article).

Return to 10 and immediately turn north on County G. Drive through this verdant rural countryside and get a look at how beautiful Wisconsin can be. The road stretches out from hill to hill as if it had been painted by an artist working from some ideal country calendar scene. You're likely to see a weathered red barn and big white farmhouse with an old Ford pickup out back; blue denim work shirts and coveralls on the wash line flapping in the breeze; big-eyed Holsteins grazing on a hillside

The Highground

Some people say that Wisconsin has no Grand Canyon, no Williamsburg, no Mount Rushmore. They haven't been to The Highground. This 140-acre memorial stands high on a breezy hill overlooking a half-million acres of gently rolling hills and wetlands, a scene that bears an uncanny resemblance to distant horizons where brave young fighting men left their innocence, blood, and, in some cases, their lives. This park commemorates all veterans who served in American conflicts; and daily, without fail, it moves good people to tears. Specific monuments honor veterans of Vietnam, World War II, and World War I, military nurses, and the Native American veterans of Vietnam, with plans underway for a Korean War memorial and a Persian Gulf War memorial. Don't miss the 100-by-40-foot Earthen Dove Effigy Mound, which serves as a living memorial to past and current prisoners of war. The Gold Star Grove is dedicated to remembering the sacrifices of families who have lost loved ones in our nation's wars. This memorial was built not by government but by people. The purpose is to recognize the human cost of war and to honor courage and sacrifice wherever it has been displayed—without glorifying or denying the pain and suffering of war and life. The Highground was incorporated in 1984 as a nonprofit organization. It is a place for all of us. For information about The Highground or the *Highground Magazine* (quarterly), call (715) 743-4224 or write to P.O. Box 457, Neillsville, 54456-0457.

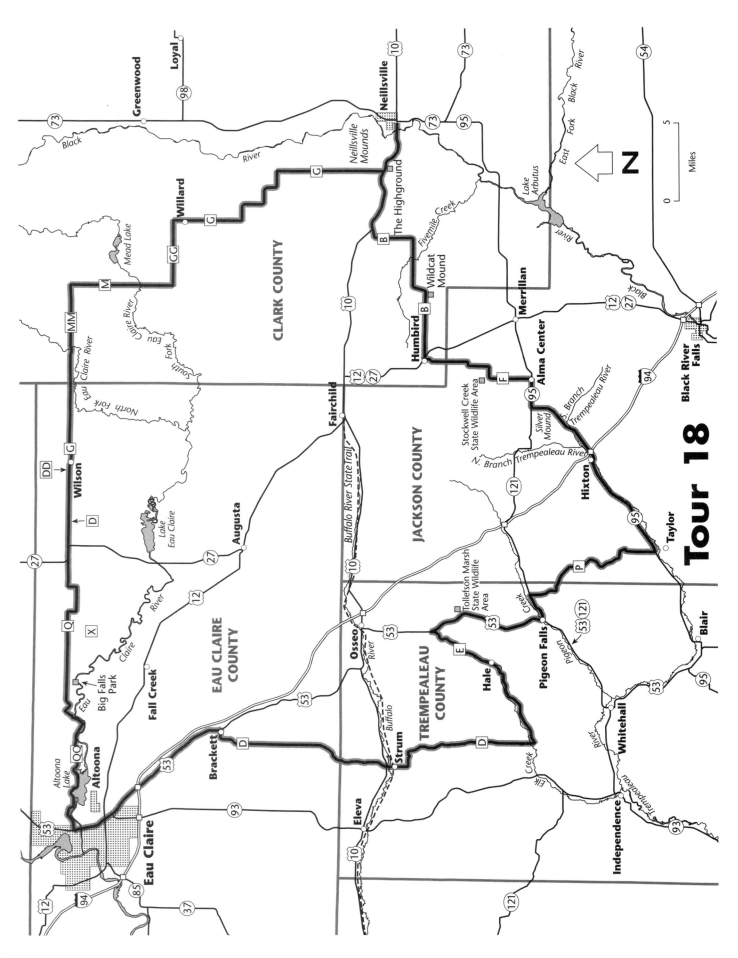

Greenwood
Loyal
98
73
Black
River
Neillsville
10
73
95
54

CLARK COUNTY

Neillsville Mounds
The Highground
G
G
G
Willard
GG
Mead Lake
M
MM
G
Wilson
DD
D
27
27
12

Lake Eau Claire

Augusta
27
12

EAU CLAIRE COUNTY

Fall Creek

Q
X
Big Falls Park
Eau
Claire
River

Altoona
QQ
Altoona Lake
53
12
94
85
37
93

Eau Claire

Brackett
53
D
Eleva
10

Osseo
River
53
Buffalo
Strum
53

TREMPEALEAU COUNTY

Hale
E
D
Pigeon Falls
53 121
53
121
Whitehall
River
Independence
93
121

B
The Highground
Fivemile Creek
Wildcat Mound
Humbird
B
10
12
27
Fairchild

Buffalo River State Trail

JACKSON COUNTY

Merrillan
12
27
Black
River

Alma Center
F
95
Stockwell Creek State Wildlife Area
Silver Mound
S. Branch Trempealeau River
94
Black River Falls

N. Branch Trempealeau River
121
Hixton
95
Taylor
P
Tollefson Marsh State Wildlife Area
Creek
Pigeon
Blair
95
53
Elk Creek
River
Trempealeau

Lake Arbutus
East Fork Black River
River

N
Miles
5
0

Tour 18

and a little tree-lined creek running through a pasture; on a hill, far away, a big green and yellow tractor pulling a plow across the land, turning up huge clods of black fertile soil.

You'll see many of these scenes today, along with pleasant little crossroads communities scattered between. Stop at one of those little country stores and buy some locally made sausage or cheese. Sit on the stoop and drink a Coke. Yes, you can get back, for a few moments, to the simpler days.

Follow G about 13 miles, through Willard, and continue another 0.5 mile to County GG. Turn left (west) on GG, cross a branch of Cameron Creek, and go about 4 miles to County M. Turn right (north) on M, crossing the Claire River, and go about 5 miles to the junction with County MM.

Turn left (west) on MM, crossing North Sterling Creek and, after 5.5 miles, entering Eau Claire County. Stay on MM, crossing Swim Creek and Loper Creek, and go 3 miles to the junction with County G. Continue straight (west) on G and go about 2 miles to Wilson and the junction with County DD.

Proceed west (straight) on DD about 0.5 mile to County D. Stay on D (it will be joined for a short stretch by Highway 27). Go straight on D to the intersection with County X. Turn right (north) on X and go about 0.5 mile to the intersection with County Q.

Turn left (west) on Q and go about 5 miles to scenic *Big Falls Park*. (The short drive from Q is over some gravel roads.)

Go back to Q and continue for another 0.5 mile to the junction with County QQ (Sandusky Drive). Turn left onto QQ and go about 9 miles into Eau Claire, a curvy little drive that follows the Eau Claire River and the north shore of Altoona Lake.

On Birch Street in Eau Claire, go to Highway 53. (For a great variety of Eau Claire–area attractions see Tour 8.)

Turn left (south) on 53 and go for about 9 miles to the town of Brackett and the junction with County D. Turn right on D and drive about 10 miles to the town of Strum. This ride is through lovely rolling hills, and Strum has 200 acres of parkland, a good nine-hole golf course, and camping on Crystal Lake.

Continue through Strum on County D (south) along the Bruce Valley Creek about 9 miles to County E. Turn left (east) on E and go about 4 miles through Pleasantville, then 2 miles to Hale, and another 4.5 miles to the junction with Highway 53.

Quick Trip Option: A 4-mile jaunt north on Highway 53 will take you to Osseo, where the world famous *Norske Nook*, (715) 597-3688, on Seventh St., has been dishing up scrumptious pies for years. *Midwest Living* and *Wisconsin Trails* magazines—among many others—have sent hundreds of pie-hungry readers to this restaurant. The lemon and raspberry varieties are among 16 or so wonderful options, but the real try-it-or-forever-regret-it best is the sour cream raisin pie. (For the adventurous palate, there's often Norwegian lefse at the bakery.)

The Northland Fishing Museum in Osseo, (715) 597-2551, has priceless collections of lures, tackle, mounted lunkers, boats, and motors.

Native American veterans are honored, along with other servicemen and servicewomen, at The Highground near Neillsville. Photo by Gary Knowles.

Turn right (south) on 53 and go about 7 miles into Pigeon Falls and the junction with Highway 121. Pigeon Falls is a Norwegian community settled in 1866. Nestled among the rolling hills and valleys along the Pigeon Creek, the town is named for the once-abundant flocks of the now extinct passenger pigeons that blackened the sky as they passed this way. In town, drive by the Pigeon Creek Evangelical Lutheran Church, built in 1866 on the east edge of the village on Highway 121. If you're looking for something unusual to take home, consider some locally made Norwegian meatball mix. The mix is sold throughout the Midwest and is a staple of the many Norwegian harvest suppers that are consumed each autumn.

Turn left (northeast) on 121 and jog about 0.3 mile to County P. Turn right (south) on P and go about 9 miles to the junction with Highway 95. You'll enjoy this scenic twisting run through the coulee country hills.

Turn left (northeast) on 95 and go about 6 miles through Hixton. This town is named for a man who preferred to stay here rather than go to Minnesota. In the mid-1800s, John Hicks was on a trip to Minnesota to buy land and build a home. The story is that he camped here overnight and by the next day had developed a love for the beautiful surroundings. The town grew up as Hicks Town or, in short, Hixton.

Continue on 95 northwest about 7.5 miles to Alma Center and the junction with County F.

Not every cattle crossing is marked, so be careful as you motor over backcountry roads. Photo by Gary Knowles.

Alma Center is known as the "Strawberry Capital of Wisconsin." If you get here on the right weekend in June for the Strawberry Festival, you can indulge in heaping helpings of the finest strawberry shortcake in the state.

Turn left (north) on F and go about 7 miles to Humbird. This little community is home to *Humbird County Park,* (715) 743-5140, which has a nice picnic facility, a children's play area, and good fishing and swimming.

In Humbird, bear right (east) to County B. Follow B about 9.5 miles to the junction with Highway 10. Turn right (east) on 10 at Snyder

Lake, (715) 743-5140, a great place to fish, camp, picnic, swim, or take a quiet hike.

Stay on 10. In a little more than a mile you'll see an interesting structure built during the Great Depression, the unique *Silver Dome Ballroom,* (715) 743-2743. The building was originally constructed in 1933 as a dance pavilion and is the only one of its kind in the world. The original "floating maple floor" and arching lamella truss design creates a truly romantic dance hall atmosphere.

Continue east on 10 for about 6 miles and return to Neillsville. Along the way, you might want to stop in again at The Highground.

County Forests

Wisconsin's dedication to "the good life" is dramatically evident in its excellent highways, beautiful parks, and vast forestlands. This state effort has been matched on the local level by the huge contribution of many of Wisconsin's counties in setting aside forestlands that help make the state such a scenic place in which to live, work, and play.

All told, 28 counties have set aside 2.3 million acres, almost 3,600 square miles of forestland—an area bigger than the states of Rhode Island and Delaware combined and bigger than the combined size of all the federal and state forestlands in Wisconsin.

The legislation that established county forests had its roots in the vast "wasteland" left by the logging era. In 1928, Langlade County was the first to recognize the importance of reestablishing the forests—because such

action protected land values. Soon, 27 other counties followed suit, and it became evident that not only were land values protected, but also that the forests preserved the land and gave recreational benefits as well.

The county forests legislation stipulated that, with the exception of a very few sensitive areas, these lands are to be open to the camper, the hiker, the hunter, and the bird watcher to use and enjoy. There are more than 1,200 campsites, thousands of miles of hiking, skiing, and snowmobile trails, and access to hundreds of lakes and streams in these county forests.

On this tour you'll pass through many miles of this forested land in Clark, Eau Claire, and Jackson Counties. Be sure to stop at a county park or forest area and enjoy the refreshing fruits of good stewardship.

Tour 19
Where Wisconsin Began

Prairie du Chien—Bridgeport—Wyalusing—Bagley—Cassville—Potosi—Dickeyville—Happy Corners—Sinsinawa—Hazel Green—New Diggings—Shullsburg—Gratiot—Darlington—Belmont—Platteville—Beetown—Bloomington—Patch Grove—Prairie du Chien

Distance: 197 miles

Welcome to the home of the turkey vulture, a bird of prey with a five-foot wingspan and the face only another raptor could love. Welcome to the place that was home to the largest fur-trading community on the upper Mississippi River and that now boasts Wyalusing, the state park with the view that readers of *Wisconsin Trails* magazine voted "the most scenic in Wisconsin." Welcome to the first capital of Wisconsin and the second oldest city. There's so much history here that you can hardly kick a stone without stirring up some historical dust.

Drivers looking for exhilarating backcountry runs will find miles of twisting, climbing, ridge-running elbow-straining, switchbacking, exercise in the hollows and coulees of Grant, Lafayette, Iowa, and Crawford Counties. If that's not enough, wait until you get to "Anti-Gravity Hill," where your car rolls backward, uphill.

This is a tour that you'll want to drive—and then drive again. One lap is definitely just a beginning.

Begin in Prairie du Chien on the Highway 18 bridge over the Mississippi River.

Stop here at the *Wisconsin Travel Information Center* to collect area brochures and state publications and to find out about events in the region. There are good restaurants and lots of antique stores all along this route. The information center can help you find them, as well as good restaurants and lodging in the city.

Prairie du Chien (French for "prairie of the dog") is Wisconsin's second oldest city, after Green Bay, and was a center of trade and commerce long before the American Revolution. Native Americans considered it "neutral territory" for trading, and it was probably named after a Fox chief who was called "Dog"—thus "prairie of the dog."

In 1665 Nicholas Perrot established a trading post here under the flag of France. He called it Fort St. Nicholas. By 1763 the British had assumed control of the territory, and more furs were shipped from here than any other place in the Upper Mississippi Valley. After the Revolutionary War, the area was ceded to the United States. Fort Shelby was built here in 1814. It was captured almost immediately by the British after a loud but minor skirmish

during the latter part of the War of 1812. That was the only "battle" of that war fought in Wisconsin. In 1815 the Treaty of Ghent ended the war and returned the area to U.S. control.

Fort Crawford was built on the same site in 1816 but was abandoned in 1829 because of severe flooding. The second Fort Crawford was built shortly thereafter under the command of Lieutenant Colonel Zachary Taylor and Lieutenant Jefferson Davis (see accompanying article.) *The Fort Crawford and Prairie du Chien Museum,* (608) 326-6960, 717 S. Beaumont Rd., provides many more details about this historic settlement, including the work of Dr. William Beaumont, who pioneered in studying the human digestive system while stationed here.

The settlement's tradition of being a spring and summer rendezvous for trappers, traders, and Native Americans continued for years. The bounty of that era formed the treasure of the Hercules Dousman fortune. His family "house on the mound," *Villa Louis,* (608) 326-2721, Villa Louis Rd., is now one of the premiere sites of the State Historical Society. It is one of the finest Victorian estates on the upper Mississippi and a must-see if you're in the area. You'll also enjoy the *Fur Trade Warehouse Museum,* the *Brisbois House,* and the *Rolette House* on the premises.

The summer *Rendezvous at Prairie du Chien* celebration, (800) 732-1673, still takes place each June and brings in re-enactors from all over the United States and Canada. If you're lucky to be in town on certain days during the summer, enjoy the *Steamboat*

Prairie Du Chien's Presidential Connections

Zachary Taylor and young Jefferson Davis served together at Fort Crawford in Prairie du Chien in 1832. In fact, Davis fell in love with Taylor's daughter, Sarah. Her father disapproved of the relationship because he felt the hardships of the soldier's life made marriage difficult. By 1833 Davis had been transferred to St. Louis; however, he continued to correspond with Sarah and court her. After Davis resigned his commission, he proposed marriage, and the two were wed in Kentucky in 1835, apparently with Zachary Taylor's blessings. Shortly thereafter, they visited Davis's older sister in West Feliciana Parish, Louisiana. Both Davis and his new bride caught either malaria or yellow fever. She died two days after their three-month anniversary.

Zachary Taylor went on to become our 12th president in 1848, serving just over a year before dying in 1850. Jefferson Davis went on to serve in the U.S. Senate until 1861, when Mississippi seceded from the Union and he was named president of the Confederacy.

A marker commemorates Davis at the Fort Crawford Military Cemetery. It is the only such memorial to him north of the Mason-Dixon Line.

CRAWFORD COUNTY

RICHLAND COUNTY

SAUK COUNTY

Wisconsin River

(61)

(14)

(27)

Kickapoo River

Effigy Mounds National Monument

Hazen Corners

(35)

Villa Louis

(18)

Prairie du Chien

Bridgeport

IOWA COUNTY

(23)

Wyalusing State Park

C

(18)

(35)

(18) (133)

Fennimore

Montfort

Dodgeville

(18) (151)

Fennimore Fork

Blue River

C

X

CX

Patch Grove

Wyalusing

(35)

Bagley

A

(133)

GRANT COUNTY

Platte River

Mineral Point Branch

Mineral Point

VV

Bloomington

(35)

Grant River

V

Lancaster

VV

(133)

U

(81)

Beetown

Nelson Dewey State Park

(81)

Cassville

U

(61)

(35)

B

(151)

Belmont

G

G

(23)

Stonefield Village

(133)

Rockville

B

Platteville

G

Darlington

Potosi

(61) (35)

K

Pecatonica River

Mississippi River

(133)

Long Branch Rd.

LAFAYETTE COUNTY

IOWA

W. Banfield Rd.

Dickeyville

HH

H

Indian Creek Rd.

Happy Corners

(11)

Shullsburg

Gratiot

Z

U

N

(11)

W

0   1   2

Hazel Green

New Diggings

Miles

Sinsinawa

ILLINOIS

Dubuque

(20)

Galena River

Apple Canyon Lake

Lake Galena

Galena

Tour 19

Days festival, as the *Delta Queen* and *Mississippi Queen* riverboats make a rare shore stop on their cruises along the Mississippi. Call (800) 732-1673 for current dates.

La Riviere Park on Vineyard Coulee Rd. southeast of the city is an excellent place to hike and enjoy rare prairie plants. *St. Gabriel's Catholic Church*, (608) 326-2404, 502 N. Beaumont Rd., is the oldest existing church in Wisconsin, having been built between 1836 and 1847.

From the information center go east on 18 through Prairie du Chien about 7 miles to Bridgeport and County C. Turn right on C and go about 3.5 miles to County CX. Turn right on CX and go west about 1 mile to County X.

The Prairie du Chien Rendezvous, held every June, continues a celebration of trappers and Native Americans begun in the early days of exploration. Wisconsin Department of Tourism photo by GK.

Quick Trip Option: Turn right on C and go about 2 miles to *Wyalusing State Park*, (608) 996-2261, one of the finest on the Mississippi. This park towers more than 300 feet over the confluence of the Wisconsin and Mississippi Rivers, and there are five spectacular viewing areas where you'll want to have your camera and binoculars at hand. Ancient effigy and burial mounds line the Sentinel Ridge hiking trail while 20 miles of other routes follow old wagon roads and Indian trails. Bird lovers will enjoy spotting scarlet tanagers, wild turkeys, and huge turkey vultures, along with more than one hundred bird species. Camping, swimming, sand cave exploring, and picnicking possibilities abound.

Continue left on County X and go about 3 miles to the town of Wyalusing. This little river burg was laid out by land speculators in 1836 and promoted back East as "Paper City" (existing only on paper as a plan). It didn't sell well and later was renamed Wyalusing which translates roughly as "home of the warrior."

Continue on X another 3 miles to Bagley and the junction with County A. Here you'll run through wooded roads along the Mississippi River bluffs.

Turn left on A, continue south out of Bagley for about 5 miles, and climb the hills to the junction with County VV. Turn right (south) on VV and go about 12 miles, as it travels through the high country and then dives down to the lower river valley. Stop at *Stonefield Village and State Farm Museum*, (608) 725-5210, a Wisconsin Historic Site and home of Wisconsin's first governor, Nelson Dewey. Walk back into an 1890s village and visit the Dewey home. Adjacent is *Nelson Dewey State Park*, (608) 725-5374, an excellent, underused state treasure with effigy mounds, picnic and camping areas, hiking trails, and picturesque views of the river and Stonefield below.

Continue for another mile on VV into Cassville and the junction with Highway 133. Back in 1836 land speculators envisioned Cassville becoming the gateway to the Wisconsin Territory, which included all of what is now Iowa and Minnesota. Many people, including Nelson Dewey, expected that it would become the state capital. Colonel William S. Hamilton, son of Alexander Hamilton, was so enthralled with it that he wrote, "in a word, nature has done all in her power to make it one of the most delightful spots in the far west."

As politics, luck, and commerce would have it, Cassville did not become the capital, but rather has remained a beautiful little river town, now and then discovered by travelers on Wisconsin's Great River Road.

The *Cassville Car Ferry*, (608) 725-5180, operates daily from Memorial Day to Labor Day. It can carry up to nine cars across the river to Turkey River, Iowa.

Two fine bed and breakfast inns welcome guests to Cassville. *The Geiger House,* (800) 725-5439, is an 1855 Greek Revival beauty with three comfortable rooms and offers a full breakfast as well as afternoon tea. The *River View,* (608) 725-5895, was built in 1856 as a boarding house and has four rooms, a Jacuzzi, and great river views.

Cassville is also well known for the hundreds of eagles that gather here in winter to fish near the power plant.

Continue on 133 south out of Cassville for about 19 miles, through Potosi to the junction with Highway 35/61. Potosi is called the "Catfish Capital of Wisconsin," and if you check in the restaurants and bars here you can find some delicious catfish dinners.

The *St. John's Mine*, (608) 763-2121, was operated from 1827 to 1870 and is one of the oldest in Wisconsin. The local natives called it "the snake cave" when they gave explorer Nicholas Perrot a tour in 1690, and the French may have done some early mining here. Today you can see how lead mining was done 160 years ago and hear the story of the lead rush that created boomtowns all over

One of the last original missionary churches in Wisconsin, St. Augustine's, near New Diggings, was built by Father Samuel Mazzuchelli in 1844. Wisconsin Department of Tourism photo by GK.

southwest Wisconsin. The mine is a registered National Historic Site.

Turn right (south) on 35/61 and go about 3 miles to Long Branch Road. Turn right on Long Branch and go about 1.5 miles to West Banfield Road. Bear right on West Banfield for about 1.5 miles and twist onto Indian Creek Road. Follow Indian Creek Road about 3 miles to Highway 35/61 and proceed about 1 mile into Dickeyville and the intersection with Highway 151.

One block west of the intersection you'll find the *Dickeyville Grotto*, (608) 568-3119. This shrine was built in the 1920s by Father Mathias Wernerus, who expressed his deep religious and patriotic beliefs by creating this unusual and provocative structure out of broken glass and concrete. There are beautiful floral gardens to complement this unusual roadside folk-art treasure.

Stay on Highway 35/61/151 right (south) out of Dickeyville and go about 0.5 mile to County HH. Turn left (east) on HH and go about 3 miles to County H. Turn right on H and go about 1 mile to Happy Corners, then continue about 0.6 mile to the junction with County Z. Happy Corners is an old-time favorite gathering spot that took its name from the good time area families shared here.

Continue south (straight) on Z for about 4 miles, through Prairie Corners to Sinsinawa and the junction with Sinsinawa Road (a name that translates as "rattlesnake" in the Algonquian language or "young eagle" in Lakota).

Turn left (south) on Sinsinawa Road and go for about 2.25 miles, then head east and go about 1 mile to Hill Road. Turn left (north) on Hill Road, going 1.5 miles to Highway 11. Turn right (east) on 11, traveling about 3.5 miles into Hazel Green and the junction with County W.

Hazel Green is the place where all of Wisconsin "began"—the place where the land survey that defined the state started in 1831. The *Point of Beginning* is the spot where the fourth principal meridian crosses the Illinois-Wisconsin border, just south of Hazel Green.

To set a reference point, Lucius Lyons, the U.S. Commissioner of the Survey, created a six-foot-tall earthen mound and set an oak timber in the center of it. This timber became the reference point that determined the measurements for every other town, county, city, and lot line in Wisconsin. In the 1970s, state surveyors dug up what was left of the original oak post and replaced it with a modern marker. The historical marker is just south of town on Highway 80. For more information about this State Heritage Area, contact Point of Beginning, P.O. Box 608, Platteville, 53818, (608) 723-4170.

A fight over mining claims in 1820 between James Hardy and Moses Meeker gave this community the name Hard Scrape (after Hardy whose mine was called Hardy's Scrape). Later it became Hard Scrabble until a post office was established and the local folk cleaned up their image by changing the name to Hazel Green.

Quick Trip Option: From here, if you drive south about 10 miles into Illinois on Highway 80 to Highway 84 then Highway 20, you'll arrive in Galena, (888) 777-4099, the home of the Civil War general and later president Ulysses S. Grant. This interesting and historic area shares much history with the early Wisconsin Territory and the lead mining area. It's a beautiful drive, an antique lover's paradise, and a delightful place to visit.

Continue straight (east) on W for about 3 miles to Strawbridge, then for another 2.5 miles to New Diggings. *St. Augustine's Church,*

(608) 744-3438, in New Diggings, was built in 1844 by Father Samuel Mazzuchelli, who built a number of other churches in the area and who is now being considered for sainthood by the Roman Catholic Church. The structure is in the Greek Revival and Italianate style and is the only church of that era still standing. The Masonic Cemetery here was started in 1849 and is the only one in Wisconsin.

Continue heading east on W for about 5 miles to County U. You'll pass over a dry streambed which local historians believe holds a mass burial site of Native Americans who died in a cholera epidemic in the 1840s.

Turn left (north) on U and go about 3.5 miles to Shullsburg. But before you get to Shullsburg, you can experience one of the most fascinating rides in the entire state. It's free and ideal for auto lovers. It's called "Gravity Hill," but I suggest they rename it "Anti-Gravity Hill." As you turn north from County W unto County U (South Judgment St.), you'll pass West Estey St. on your right and the water tower on your left, and then pass Rennick Rd. on your left as County U goes down a fair-sized hill into a valley before climbing up another grade. You'll see a sign for a 25-m.p.h curve. Be sure there's no one behind you, stop on the road just a bit before the sign, facing *downhill,* and put your car in neutral. Slowly it will begin to roll *backwards . . . up* the hill!

Is there some huge lead deposit acting as a magnet pulling your car back?

Probably not. But I won't tell you the secret. Ask around town. After you've taken the ride a few times, drive into Shullsburg and stop at the popular *Brewster Street Cafe and Cheese Store,* (608) 965-3855, where you can buy some locally made cheese, have a strong cup of coffee, and sort it all out!

Shullsburg dates back to the fur trade era and the early 1800s. Jessie Shull traded furs here and discovered that the local Native Americans also had lead to trade. By 1827 word had spread and mining was a booming industry.

The architecture of Shullsburg has been well preserved over the years and a drive through town—especially on *Water Street,* a National Register of Historic Places area—is a visual treat. Self-guided walking tour maps are available, (608) 965-4401. The early town leaders must have been concerned that the rough-and-tumble miners be reminded of their religious beliefs. You'll find streets named Faith, Hope, Charity, and Judgment.

The *Badger Mine and Museum,* (608) 965-4860, offers a tour of a quarter-mile mine 47 feet underground. Exhibits feature mining implements, an early general store, and other area artifacts.

At the junction with Highway 11 in Shullsburg, turn right (east) and travel 11 miles to the junction with County K, in Gratiot. Turn

This building near Belmont marks the site of Wisconsin's first capital, where buffalo robes were leveraged for the votes that made Madison the permanent capital. Wisconsin Department of Tourism photo.

left on K as it winds along the Pecatonica River, crosses Copper Creek, and wanders north and west 10.5 miles to the junction with Highway 23.

Turn right (north) on 23 and go about 2 miles into Darlington. Called the "Pearl of the Pecatonica," Darlington is the county seat of Lafayette County. The *Lafayette County Courthouse,* (608) 776-4820, 626 Main St., has the distinction of being the only courthouse in the nation still in use that was financed by just one person. Matt Murphy, a local miner and administrator of a Civil War fund for orphans and widows, died in 1903 and left money in his will for a new courthouse. Built in 1905-07 at a cost of $130,833.58, Murphy's legacy is this exquisite, cut limestone structure. It has a stained-glass dome, murals, marble walls, brass fixtures, and solid mahogany woodwork. The county had some $716 left over after completing the structure and allocated $200 of that to pay for perpetual care of his grave in Benton. The *Lafayette County Historical Museum,* (608) 776-8340, 525 Main St., has interesting artifacts and documents relating to the history of the area.

Stay on 23 north out of Darlington and go about 6 miles to County G. Turn left (west) on G and drive about 2 miles to Calamine, then about 9.5 miles to Belmont. Continue west through Belmont on G for about 5 miles to *First Capitol State Park.*

Belmont served as the capital of the Wisconsin Territory in 1836, and First Capitol State Park, (608) 987-2122, preserves the Council House and Supreme Court buildings. The 1836 Wisconsin Territorial Legislature was housed in these buildings, with some 120 people sleeping on the floor. One legislator wrote, "The accommodations at Belmont were most miserable, there being but a single boarding house .... Our beds were all full, and the floor well spread with blankets and overcoats for lodging purposes." That legislature enacted 42 laws in a 46-day session and selected Madison as the permanent capital. The next year they met in Burlington, Iowa, and in 1838 moved to Madison.

Continue west on County B for about 4 miles to the intersection with West Mound Road. Here you'll see the world's largest "M," made of 400 tons of limestone set in the hillside. Measuring 214 feet by 241 feet, it's a project of the Mining School at the University of Wisconsin-Platteville that was started in 1936 and first lighted in 1938.

Go about 4 miles on B into downtown Platteville.

Famous today as the summer training home of the Chicago Bears NFL team, Platteville has its roots deep in the lead mining history of southwest Wisconsin. Major John H. Rountree and Major John H. Campbell arrived in 1827 and immediately bought a mine from Emmanuel Metcalf for $3,600. By 1829 there were 150 people living in Platteville, which was named after the long, flat pieces of process lead that came from the gravity-fed smelting furnaces. Thomas Hugill was asked to design the layout of the town and he styled it after his own home in Yorkshire, England. It was planned to create easy access to numerous mineshafts and entrances.

Nelson Dewey, the state's first governor, later came here to become village president in 1860. In 1877, the first long-distance telephone line in the United States was constructed between Platteville and Lancaster by Captain W. H. Beebe.

The UW-Platteville campus is located here and

A Quick Trip to Iowa

Just west across the Mississippi River, in Marquette and McGregor, Iowa, you'll find even more reasons to stay in this area a little longer. Here are a few things to see and do.

Effigy Mounds National Monument, (319) 873-3491, preserves 191 prehistoric Native American effigy mounds and has a visitor's center and museum. Cross the Highway 18 bridge to Iowa and then go north on Highway 76.

The *Miss Marquette Riverboat/Casino,* (800) 4-YOUBET, is docked at Marquette and keeps the spirit of the riverboat gambler alive with 675 slots, blackjack, live poker, craps, roulette, Caribbean stud, let it ride, and more.

Antiquing is a favorite sport in Marquette and McGregor. You'll find a nice collection of shops and emporia in historic buildings and storefronts.

Pikes Peak State Park, (319) 873-2341, at McGregor, is really the first Pikes Peak. It was named for Lt. Zebulon Pike, who surveyed this area in 1805. It's a spectacular viewing spot for watching river traffic and has hiking trails, camping, a waterfall, and a picnic area. It's the Iowa counterpart to Wisconsin's fabulous Wyalusing State Park.

serves as the summer training headquarters for the Chicago Bears. For information about schedules and public viewing, call (608) 348-8888.

The *Bevans Lead and Mining Museum,* (608) 348-3301, 405 E. Main St., traces the development of lead and zinc mining in the area and there's an authentic mine train pulling ore cars that you can ride. The *Rollo Jamison Museum,* in the same building, holds a collection of all sorts of 19th-century odds and ends that Jamison gathered over the years.

The *Mitchell-Rountree Stone Cottage,* (608) 348-8888, at the corner of West Madison St. and Highway 81, was constructed of two-foot-thick dolomite limestone in 1837 for Rev. Samuel Mitchell, who had served as a soldier in the Revolutionary War under General Washington and was present during the surrender of Cornwallis at Yorktown. It was built under the supervision of Major John Rountree, Mitchell's son-in-law and one of Platteville's founders. The interior contains original furnishings of the private residence of the Rountree family. It was kept in its original state until the 1960s when it was turned over to the Grant County Historical Society.

From Platteville, take B west about 14 miles to the junction with Highway 35/61 at Rockville. Along the way, you'll cruise across the Young Branch River, the Wing Branch River, the Platte River, and over too many hills to count.

Turn left (south) on 35/61 and go about 3 miles to the junction with County U. Turn right (southwest) on U and go about 1 mile into Potosi. Stay on U and head northwest out of Potosi for 15 miles to Beetown. This town got its name in 1827 when a miner, Cyrus Alexander, turned over a bee tree looking for honey and instead found a 425-pound nugget of lead. This was jokingly called "bee lead" and the community became Beetown.

Continue through Beetown on U, following the Beetown River, for about 4 miles to the junction with Highway 35. Turn left on 35 and drive about 3 miles to Bloomington. *Taft's Mill Pottery* in downtown Bloomington has an interesting past; the building it occupies was a stone mill built in 1857 that was once considered one of the best mills in the west.

Continue on 35 for about 4 miles to Patch Grove and 1 mile to the junction with Highway 18. Follow Highway 18/35 left (west) about 13 miles to Prairie du Chien, where we began.

For a *Quick Trip Option* when you've finished with Wisconsin, see the article (left) on taking a quick jaunt into Iowa.

Tour 20
On the Wright Roads

Spring Green—Arena—Black Earth—Cross Plains—Middleton—Madison—Pine Bluff—Spring Green

Distance: 148 miles

This tour is all about places and how they can move us emotionally, intellectually, and spiritually. It's about inspired architecture, great driving, and spectacular beauty that will snatch your breath away. It's about twisting highways, paved cow paths, and wandering Native American trails.

It's about Frank Lloyd Wright, who was born near here in Richland Center, took his inspiration from this land, and created art. His works and influence shot out of here and reached around the planet.

You'll see (and maybe visit) buildings that rank with the world's most significant architectural landmarks. You'll see incredible vistas well off the road more traveled. I don't believe you can overdose on scenic beauty, but you may get a severe case of goose bumps.

Those who fancy themselves "driving enthusiasts" will get a day full of everything they hoped for—and more. You might want to lay in an extra set of driving gloves. These roads will firmly fix the bond between you and your automobile—so bring the one you love the best.

I showed much of this route to a small group of persnickety but reasonably sociable auto lovers in the autumn of 1996. With an overlay of fall foliage in brilliant fireworks colors, this route had all jaws agape. Be forewarned and keep your heart medicine in the glove box.

Begin the tour at the *Frank Lloyd Wright Visitor Center* at the junction of Highway 23 and County C just south of Spring Green. This Wright-designed building (that some say reminds them of a Viking ship) has one of the finest views along the Wisconsin River and is the starting point for all Frank Lloyd Wright property tours. It houses an excellent gift shop with truly special items at reasonable prices. Take some home to impress your friends and boss. It also has one of the area's most unique restaurants. Not only is the food good but your small investment can provide great cocktail party openers for years. ("Oh, this reminds me of my lunch at Frank Lloyd Wright's restaurant!") You can sit on real Wright furniture worth more than a Porsche Boxster. Remember, he was short. If you're over five feet, eight inches tall, you may get into some positions they can't duplicate at the

health club! It is the only operating restaurant designed by Wright, and you'll be forever sorry if you don't stop. So stop. Eat. Touch the truly unique.

There is a nice variety of tours available of Wright's Hillside School for architects, Midway Farm, Tan-y-deri House, the Romeo and Juliet Windmill, and Taliesin (his home). Prices vary from moderate to high (but well worth it) and reservations are always recommended. Call ahead, (608) 588-7900, to be sure you can get on the tour you want.

Exit the Visitor Center parking lot, turn right (or was it Wright?) on C, and drive about 4 miles to the junction with Highway 14. Along the way, you'll hug the Wisconsin River and soon come to *Tower Hill State Park*, (608) 588-2116. This is a 77-acre beauty with camping, canoeing, a nature center, bird watching, prairie and woodland flowers, scenic vistas, fishing, and hiking. One walk takes you to a shot tower that produced much of the lead shot used by Union forces in the Civil War.

Pumpkin purveyors prevail in autumn along Highway 14 near Spring Green. Wisconsin Department of Tourism photo by GK.

Turn right (east) on 14 and go 6 miles to Arena. You'll drive past *Peck's Farm Market*, (608) 588-7177, (featuring "Squashaloosa" horses in autumn), a flea market (usually on weekends), and

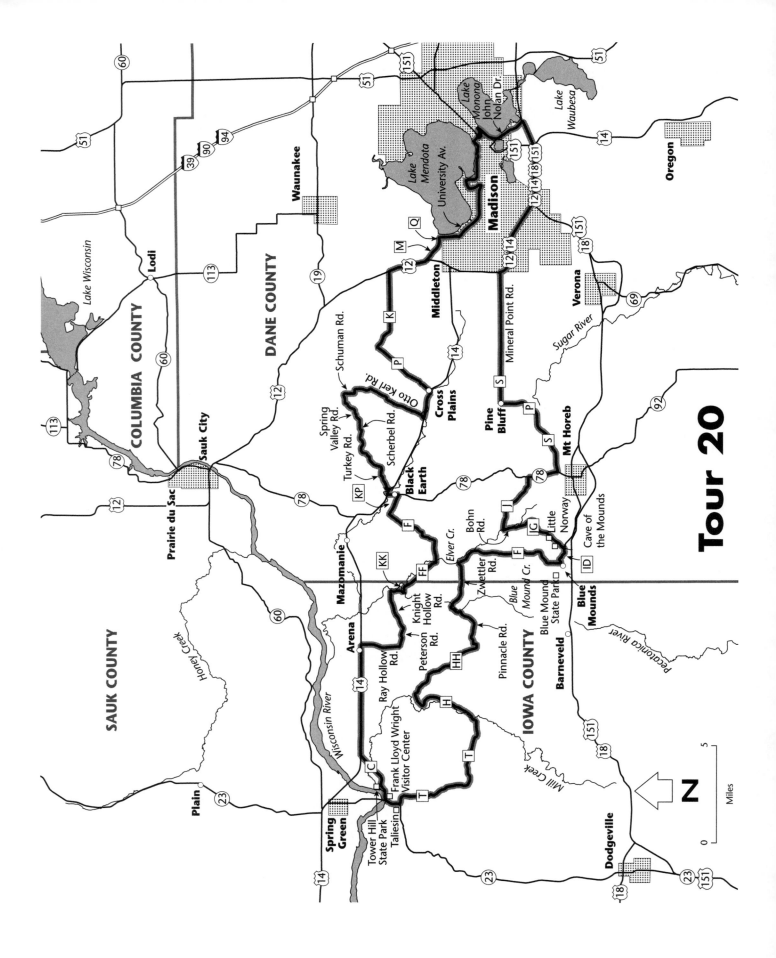

Tour 20

COLUMBIA COUNTY

DANE COUNTY

SAUK COUNTY

IOWA COUNTY

Lake Wisconsin

60

51

113

90
39
94

Waunakee

Lodi

113

19

12

60

78

Sauk City

Prairie du Sac

12

78

Mazomanie

Arena

14

Plain

23

Honey Creek

Wisconsin River

Tower Hill State Park

Spring Green

Taliesin

Frank Lloyd Wright Visitor Center

C

T

T

H

T

Ray Hollow Rd.

Knight Hollow Rd.

Peterson Rd.

HH

Pinnacle Rd.

Mill Creek

Dodgeville

18
151

23

151

18

Barneveld

Blue Mounds

Blue Mound State Park

Cave of the Mounds

ID

Pecatonica River

78

F

Zwettler Rd.

Blue Mound Cr.

KK

FF

Elver Cr.

Bohn Rd.

F

Black Earth

KP

F

Turkey Rd.

Scherbel Rd.

Spring Valley Rd.

Schuman Rd.

Otto Kerl Rd.

P

K

12

M

Q

Middleton

14

Cross Plains

Little Norway

J

G

S

78

S

Mt Horeb

P

Pine Bluff

S

Mineral Point Rd.

12/14

Verona

69

18

151

Sugar River

92

151

Lake Mendota

University Av.

Madison

Lake Monona

John Nolan Dr.

Lake Waubesa

Lake Wingra

12/14/18/151

14

Oregon

51

151

151

51

N

Miles

0   5

a big mouse in Arena beckoning motorists to stop at *Arena Cheese*, (608) 753-2501, where you can buy cheese curds. (But don't buy anything but "today's curds.")

At Ray Hollow Road on the east edge of Arena, turn right and drive 1.9 miles to Petersen Road. As you head into these hollows and run the pretzel roads over these hills, watch for deer, wild turkeys, grouse, pheasant, coyotes, raccoon, possum, and other woodland critters that are truly abundant in these parts.

Turn left on Petersen Road and continue 1 mile to the junction with Knight's Hollow Road. Turn left (east) and go 2 miles through the Knight Valley to County KK. Watch for the red barn.

Turn right onto KK and go 0.7 mile. Turn left, following KK for 2.3 miles along the east branch of Blue Mound Creek to County F. Turn left onto F and drive for 3.9 miles to where it joins County KP. Along the way, you'll pass through the Black Earth Creek State Fishery Area.

Turn right on KP and F and go 1.1 miles to the junction with Highway 78 in Black Earth. Turn left onto 78 and go about 0.5. On the left, you see *The Shoe Box*, (608) 767-3447, a friendly discount shoe store that carries 158 varieties of top quality shoes, is the largest outlet of its kind in the Midwest, and always has great bargains.

On 78, continue to the junction with Highway 14.

Quick Trip Option: If you're looking for a good meal at an unforgettable sports bar, turn left on Highway 14 and drive about 3 miles to *Rookies*, (608) 767-5555, near the junction with Highway 78. Owner Steve Schmitt has an eye-popping collection of authentic autographed baseball and football memorabilia nicely displayed on every wall, in cases, in the restrooms, and behind the bar. Among thousands of autographs, baseball cards, and memorabilia are unusual items, like a 1965 Green Bay Packers NFL Championship ring, a football helmet signed by President Gerald Ford, and a Hula Bowl jersey from 2000 Heisman Trophy winner Ron Dayne. Outside there's a wiffleball field where you can hit plastic baseballs in a scaled-down stadium.

Turn right (east) on 14 and go a couple of blocks to County F. Turn left on F and go about 0.25 mile to Turkey Road. Turn right on Turkey Road and follow it 2.8 miles to Spring Valley Road. This is an exciting run along numerous hillsides and then up and over into the backcountry.

Turn right on Spring Valley Road and go about 1 mile to the junction with Scherbel Road. Turn left and follow Scherbel/Spring Valley Road across the junction with County KP to the junction with Pine Road.

Stay to the right, following Spring Valley Road to Schuman Road, then go up the hill about 1.6 miles to Otto Kerl Road. Turn right (south) and go about 2 miles to Highway 14. Turn left (east) on 14 and go into Cross Plains to the junction with County P. Turn left (north) on P.

Follow P for 4 miles to County K. Turn right on K and go about 3.2 miles to Highway 12. This is a spectacular drive through a beautiful farm valley and the peaceful hamlet of Ashton.

Turn right (south) on 12 and go 2 miles into Middleton to the junction with County M. Turn left on M through Middleton and go about 1 mile to County Q.

Turn right on Q and go about 1.3 miles to the junction with University Avenue. The *Imperial Gardens Restaurant*, (608) 238-6445, on the left at the corner, is a fine Chinese eatery, one of Madi-

Capital Kudos

"Sixty-four square miles surrounded by reality"—that's the way many Wisconsinites, including several governors, have described this politically active, strong university, white-collar community. Ask any Madisonian and they're likely to tell you, "Sure. It's crazy here. We like it like that."

In fact, other people like it too. Wisconsin's capital city has won the praise of dozens of publications and writers. Among them are:

"#1 Best Place to Live in America"—*Money* magazine, July 1998 and July 1996

"One of The Top 10 Cities That Have It All"—*A & E Network*, September 1999

"Best City for Quality of Life"—*Business Development Outlook* magazine, September/October 1999

"#1 Best City for Women"—*Ladies Home Journal*, November 1997

"#1 of America's Most-Wired Cities"—*International Demographics*, March 1998

"2nd Most Kid-Friendly City in America"—*Zero Population Growth*, August 1999

"2nd Best Town for Raising an Outdoor Family"—*Outdoor Explorer* magazine, Summer 1999

"3rd Best City for Business Owners"—*Business Development Outlook* magazine, November/December 1999

"3rd Safest of Nation's 100 Largest Cities"—*Morgan Quinto Press*, January 1996

"4th Best Bicycling City"—*Bicycling* magazine, August 1997 and October 1995

"5th Most Enlightened Town in America—*Utne Reader*, May 1997

"6th Most Mannerly City"—etiquette expert Marjabelle Young Stewart, December 1999

"6th Best Schools in the Nation"—*Expansion Management* magazine, October 1996

"9th Best Place to Live and Work in America"—*Employment Review* magazine, June 1997

"Best Mid-Sized City Travel Getaway"—*Midwest Living* magazine, August 1994

Madison Dining—The World on Your Plate!

If you can't do a world tour this year, you might consider spending a few days foraging in Madison. You can find not only an incredible variety of ethnic and world cuisines to choose from but also food of high quality and reasonably priced. The university, with 40,000 students from 120 countries, and a prosperous professional community with a good deal of disposable income are good patrons with eclectic palates. Bring your appetite. We'll mention a few favorites from among many. Check the *Madison Area Guide* for even more.

Steak: *Delaney's*, (608) 833-7337, 449 Grand Canyon Dr. (also seafood); *Smoky's Club*, (608) 233-2120, 3005 University Ave.; *Mariner's Inn*, (608) 246-3120, 5339 Lighthouse Bay Dr.

Casual: *Dotty Dumplings Dowry*, (608) 255-3175, 116 N. Fairchild St.; *Great Dane Brew Pub*, (608) 284-0000, 123 E. Doty St.; *Nitty Gritty*, (608) 251-2521, 223 N. Frances St.

Chinese: *Hong Kong Cafe*, (608) 259-1668, 2 S. Mills St.; *Imperial Gardens*, (608) 238-6445, 2039 Allen Blvd.

Thai: *Bahn Thai*, (608) 256-0202, 944 Williamson St.

Creole: *Louisianne's*, (608) 831-1929, 7464 Hubbard Ave., Middleton; *Creole Cafe*, (608) 233-6311, 2611 Monroe St.

Pizza: *Paisan's*, (608) 257-3832, 80 University Square.

American Regional: *The Opera House*, (608) 284-8466, 117 Martin Luther King Blvd., with a four-star wine list; *Coyote Capers*, (608) 251-1313, 1201 Williamson St.; *Kennedy Manor*, (608) 256-5556, 1 Langdon St.; *Wilson Street Grill*, (608) 251-3500, 217 S. Hamilton St.; *White Horse Inn*, (608) 255-9933, 202 N. Henry St.; *Quivey's Grove*, (608) 273-4900, 6261 Nesbitt Rd.

Sushi: *Wasabi*, (608) 255-5020, 449 State St.

Italian: *Porta Bella*, (608) 256-3186, 425 Frances St.; *Gino's*, (608) 257-9022, 540 State St.

French-Continental: *L'Etoile*, (608) 251-0500, 25 N. Pinckney St. (with a national reputation).

German: *The Essen Haus*, (608) 255-4674, 514 E. Wilson St.

Seafood: *Captain Bill's Seafood Co.*, (608) 831-7327, 2701 Century Harbor Rd.; *Fyfe's Corner Bistro*, (608) 251-8700, 1344 E. Washington Ave.

Sports Bars: *Babes*, (608) 274-7300, 5614 Schroeder Rd.

Mexican: *Pasqual's*, (608) 238-4419, 2534 Monroe St.; *Laredo's*, (608) 278-0585, 694 S. Whitney Way.

Mediterranean-Persian: *Oceans Brasserie*: (608) 257-3107, 527 State St.; *Dardanelles*, (608) 256-8804, 1851 Monroe St.; *Caspian Cafe*, (608) 259-9009, 17 University Square; *Otto's*, (608) 274-4044, 6405 Mineral Point Rd.

Caribbean: *Jolly Bob's*, (608) 251-3902, 1210 Williamson St.

son's highest rated. (For a few of the city's other top restaurants, see the accompanying article.)

Turn left (east) on University Avenue and enter Madison, driving for about 3 miles to University Bay Drive.

Turn left on University Bay Drive. Very soon on the left, you'll see the *First Unitarian Meeting House*, (608) 233-9774, 900 University Bay Dr. Designed by Frank Lloyd Wright, this famous building was built, in part, by the members of the First Unitarian Society.

Continue to jog, bend, and curve on University Bay Drive for about 1.6 miles until it becomes Observatory Drive. Continue on Observatory Drive into the University of Wisconsin-Madison campus until you come to the stop sign at Park Street. You'll pass the 2.5 acre *Allen Centennial Gardens* (at Babcock Dr. on the left), glide up and down the hills overlooking Lake Mendota, drive past *Washburn Observatory* (on the right, built in 1878), then up Bascom Hill, finally switchbacking down past *Radio Hall*, to Park St., at the base of Bascom Hill.

Quick Trip Option: Head over to *Babcock Hall*, 608) 262-3045, on Linden Dr., which runs parallel to Observatory Dr. Babcock is the source of some of the finest ice cream in Wisconsin. The university has its own dairy and makes superior quality ice cream in some pretty unusual flavors—for example, orange-custard chocolate-chip—that are sold only on the UW campus.

The UW-Madison campus, built on some 900 acres, was founded in 1848 and is considered one of the finest academic institutions and one of the most beautiful campus settings in the nation. Enrollment hovers at about 40,000 students from 120 nations who participate in 4,556 courses in 146 majors. There are 17,000 faculty and staff and 320,000 living alumni. Its faculty and alumni have accounted for 13 Nobel Prizes and 21 Pulitzer Prizes. During its history, the UW-Madison has awarded more doctorate degrees than all but two other institutions in the country. There are 45 libraries with almost six million volumes. The school's budget is about $1.3 billion and state support amounts to $351 million per year.

At Park Street, jog right and then turn left immediately onto Langdon Street. The *UW Memorial Union*, (608) 265-3000, is the Italian Renaissance building (built in 1928) on your left. If you've never seen the Union Terrace on the shore of Lake Mendota (and even if you have), you might want to stop and take a look at one of the favorite places for students to meet friends, solve world problems, hatch a new political party, play chess, or feed the ducks. Be sure to go inside and see the art galleries, exhibits, and Rathskeller.

Follow Langdon Street for about 1 mile until the intersection with Wisconsin Avenue. Langdon is lined with fraternity and sorority houses and other types of student housing.

Turn right on Wisconsin Avenue and continue to the Capitol Building and the Capitol Square. Even though you've been in Madison since driving in on University Ave., you're now in the heart of the city, and it affords a lot of interesting sights. We can touch on only some of them.

Numerous excellent guidebooks have been written about Mad City. If you want to spend some time here, call the *Madison Convention and Visitor Bureau* at (800) 373-6376 and ask for the helpful and free *Madison Area Guide*, which has detailed maps, an events calendar, and information on lodging and restaurants.

Drive around the square one whole lap, then another half lap. Then turn right on Martin Luther King Boulevard and drive one block to Doty Street. Straight ahead, you'll see the Monona Terrace Community and Convention Center, built more than 50 years after it was designed by Frank Lloyd Wright.

Turn left on Doty (it's a one-way street) and go 1.5 blocks to King Street. Turn right on King and drive 1 block to Wilson Street. Turn left on Wilson, go 2 blocks across the railroad tracks, then immediately turn right on Highway 151 (John Nolen Drive). You'll soon be traveling *under* the Monona Terrace Community and Convention Center for a brief stretch.

Stay on John Nolen Drive for about 2.5 miles, crossing Monona Bay and passing the *Dane County Coliseum* and *Alliant Energy Center* on the right.

At the entrance to Highway 12/18 (West Beltline), turn right (west) and stay on it for 8.2 miles to the exit for Mineral Point Road (County S). Turn left (west) at the stoplight and continue on Mineral Point. Along the way, you'll pass a number of shopping centers and malls on Madison's expanding west side, including West Towne at the Gammon Rd. exit, and the Target Shopping Center and the Menards Shopping Center right after you've turned onto Mineral Point Rd.

Drive on S for 6.7 miles to Pine Bluff. At the junction with County P, turn left (south) on County PS. When S splits off to the right, follow it for 5.3 miles to the junction with Highway 78.

The dome of the State Capitol building is one of the largest domes (by volume) in the world. Photo by Gary Knowles.

Turn right (north) on 78 and drive 1.5 miles to County J. This drive to Little Norway and Cave of the Mounds, and over the hills to Spring Green is a real driver's delight. It swings through wooded hills, across and along Elver's Creek,

Turn left on J and go about 1.2 miles to Bohn Road. Turn left (south) on Bohn Road and go about 1.3 miles to the junction with County JG. Bear right on JG and go to the intersection with County ID. While on JG, look for *Little Norway,* (608) 437-8211. This is an award-winning family attraction in a beautiful valley that preserves authentic Norwegian immigrant buildings and artifacts dating back to 1856. Tour guides dressed in traditional Norwegian clothing lead visitors on a trip through time to another age and culture. The beautiful "Stavekirke" is a wooden church building that was constructed in Norway and shipped for display to Chicago's 1893 Columbian Exposition. It is one of the few buildings still remaining from that fair. Little Norway was the recipient of a "GEMmy," an award given by the Midwest Travel Writer's Association for outstanding travel sites.

Turn right on ID (west) and go to the intersection with County F. While on ID, don't miss *Cave of the Mounds,* (608) 437-3038, a registered National Natural Landmark and one of the finest caves in the Midwest. The cave has a great variety of color, shapes, and formations—and a year round temperature of about 50 degrees, so don't forget your sweater!

Quick Trip Option: Drive a few miles farther west on County ID and then turn right on Mounds Park Rd., and you'll be at *Blue Mound State Park,* (608) 437-5711. Climb the observation tower to get a good look at the countryside, swim in the pool, hike, or pitch your tent here.

A Few Things to Do in Madison

There's an incredibly rich variety of things to do in Madison. But since this is a tour, we can touch on just a couple of them.

The city's population is about 203,000 (Dane County is 407,000), and you'll swear that most of them are circling (counterclockwise, please) the Capitol Square on Saturday mornings between April and November. That's because they're shopping at the *Madison Farmer's Market,* one of the finest such produce outlets in the country.

Another great reason to visit the square is the *State Capitol Building,* one of the nation's largest and best structures of its kind. Informative free tours are available, (608) 266-0382.

Stroll along State St. from the Capitol Square to the University Mall. Start at the *Veterans Museum,* (608) 267-1799, on the square and end up at the *Wisconsin State Historical Society Museum,* (608) 264-6555. In between, you'll see the *Children's Museum,* (608) 256-6445, the *Madison Art Center,* (608) 257-0158, great bookstores, art galleries, coffee shops, bars, shops with the usual (and some unusual) gifts, a Lands' End Outlet, and some mighty interesting people.

It took Madison almost 60 years to build Frank Lloyd Wright's *Monona Terrace Community and Convention Center.* It may well be the last of his original works ever brought to completion on the original site for which he designed it. It has five levels and 352,610 square feet of space on 4.4 acres overlooking Lake Monona. Pick up a self-guided tour brochure and treat yourself to a tour of this extraordinary structure. See if you can find the memorial to rhythm and blues singer Otis Redding, who was killed when his airplane crashed in Lake Monona as he was on his way to play a concert here. Ample parking is available. Call (608) 261-4000.

At *Henry Vilas Park Zoo,* (608) 258-1460, you can do the zoo with more than 700 animals in a fine park setting and a great playground on little Lake Wingra. Free admission.

Madison has more bikes than cars, miles of lakeshore bike trails, and plenty of canoes too. To rent a canoe, try *Carl's Paddlin' Canoe and Kayak Center,* (608) 284-0300, 110 N. Thornton Ave. Rent a bicycle at *Budget Bicycle Center,* 1230 Regent St., (608) 251-8413, or *Williamson Bike Works,* (608) 255-5292, 601 Williamson St.

Turn right (north) on F and go about 6.7 miles to Zwettler Road (just across the bridge and past the yellow road sign). Turn left on Zwettler and go 2.5 miles to the stop sign (County K, unmarked). Turn left and go 0.5 mile to Pinnacle Road.

Turn right on Pinnacle Road and go about 2.4 miles to the stop sign (County HH, unmarked). Turn right and drive about 4.1 miles to County H. Turn left on H and go about 3.9 miles to County T. Turn right on T and go 8.2 miles to Highway 23.

You'll drive past *Unity Chapel,* designed in 1886 by J. L. Silsbee. It's said that Frank Lloyd Wright assisted with some of the interior work as one of his very early projects. Wright's former gravesite can also be found along the way (where he was buried from 1959 until 1985, when his wife's will instructed that he be disinterred, cremated, and his ashes scattered in Arizona). A Wright-style grave marker still remains (it's unclear if he designed it); it reads "Love of an idea is the love of God."

From Highway 23 directly ahead, you can look out at the countryside and see some of the fruits of Wright's ideas spread out harmoniously against the horizon. *Midway Farm* is straight ahead. To the left is *Hillside School,* which was first a boarding school run by his aunts that he expanded into a studio and dormitory for his architectural students in the 1930s. On the "brow of the hill" is *Taliesin,* his home and life-long project. The entire 600-acre property is a National Historic Landmark.

Turn right on 23 and go less than a mile back to the start of our tour at the Frank Lloyd Wright Visitor Center.

In the Spring Green area, you will want to walk through town to see the Wright-influenced buildings. A map is included in the *Spring Green Area Traveler Visitor Guide,* which is readily available in the area or in advance by calling (608) 588-2042. The map includes these downtown buildings: M&I Bank Building, the Spring Green Library, the Spring Green Pharmacy, St. John's Catholic Church, Taylor Chiropractic, the Post House Restaurant, and the Spring Green Senior Center.

American Players Theater, (608) 588-2361, just off County C on Tower Hill Rd., is a Tony Award–nominated classical theater company that performs in an outdoor amphitheater and features the work of Shakespeare and other masters. The season runs June through October and each performance is truly a memorable theater experience. Theater dinners are available. (And it's smart to bring your mosquito spray.)

Spring Green is also a great place to shop for art and antiques. Check the local visitor's guide for a list of shops and galleries. *The Round Barn,* (608) 588-2568, houses both a fine restaurant and excellent lodge. If you're lucky, you'll run into

The Frank Lloyd Wright–designed Monona Terrace Community and Convention Center features an enjoyable lakefront pedestrian/bike path. Photo by Gary Knowles.

owners Robert and Derry Graves during your visit. Robert's father worked with Frank Lloyd Wright, and he literally "grew up at Taliesin." Robert, an architect himself, can tell you some good stories about Wright, his work, and the Spring Green area.

House on the Rock Resort (formerly called The Springs) is an 80-unit resort hotel on Tower Hill Rd. just off County C. Designed by Wright-trained architects, including Charles Montooth, it's an incredibly peaceful, relaxed, and comfortable facility, with designer swimming pools, a full fitness center, saunas, whirlpools, steam room, and spa.

The golf course has been rated among the finest in the state. The original 18 holes were designed by Robert Trent Jones Sr., and an additional 9-hole course was laid out in the mid-1990s by two-time U.S. Open Champion, Andy North, of Madison, and Roger Packard. The new layout cuts through the wooded hills and is a perfect complement to the original.

(For more information on one of the area's major attractions, House on the Rock, about 8 miles southwest of Spring Green on Highway 23, see Tour 23.)

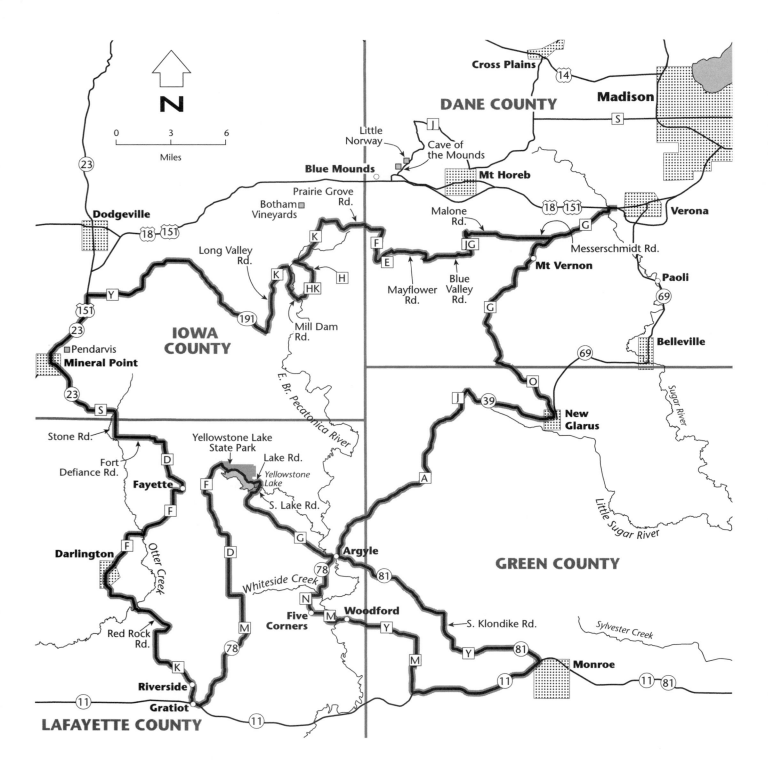

Tour 21

Tour 21
Swiss Cheese and Pasty Dash

Verona—Mount Vernon—New Glarus—Argyle—Monroe—Woodford—Five Corners—Gratiot—
Riverside—Darlington—Fayette—Mineral Point—Verona

Distance: 186 miles

Do you like roller coasters? How about Swiss cheese? Cornish pasties? Limburger cheese? Good. Follow me on this delightful run.

This tour follows some old military trails, Native American paths, and miners routes to uncover a spectacular corner of Wisconsin better known to visitors in 1850 than in 2000. This hilly, mostly unglaciated land in the southwestern part of the state is where the Badger State earned its name and later its reputation as the Cheese Capital of the World.

Today the web of trails and roads is once again drawing visitors, but now it's for the scenery, the great rally roads, the relaxation, and the thrill of rediscovering places long forgotten.

So choose a car that likes corners and twisting roads better than straight ones. Pick a friendly companion who enjoys cheese or who might like to yodel. This is a dash back through history to see a face of Wisconsin that's as captivating today as it was in the 1820s.

Get that motor running—there's fun and a warm welcome ahead.

We'll begin this tour just west of the city of Verona at the intersection of Highway 151/18 and County G. But first, a word or two about Verona. For you bicyclists, the *Military Ridge State Trail* begins on the east side of town and winds west to Dodgeville through some lovely countryside. This 40-mile off-road route follows a path along a high ridge that has been traveled by early Indians, frontier military expeditions, railroads, and now bicyclists. Call (608) 437-7393 for more information.

Verona is the hometown of U.S. Olympic speed skater Casey FitzRandolph, who competed in the 1998 Nagano Winter Olympics and became the first person to skate the 500-meter race in under 36 seconds. If you stop in town you may see him taking a quick break from training to have a shake at the drive-in or to show some kids a few

The Military Ridge State Trail follows a historic route along a gentle incline, making for some 40 miles of outstanding biking. Wisconsin Department of Tourism photo by GK.

Swiss heritage is well preserved at the Swiss Historical Village in New Glarus. Wisconsin Department of Tourism photo.

fine points about soccer. He plans to compete in the 2002 Games in Salt Lake City and is one of the top U.S. skaters with a strong shot at the medal stand.

Quick Trip Option: From Verona you can make a short run 5 miles south on Highway 69 to Paoli, where the old Creamery Building now houses the excellent *Artisan Gallery*. It contains the works of 200 regional artists and the delightful *Creamery Café*, (608) 845-6600, (reservations highly recommended). Nearby is one of Wisconsin's smallest but highest quality cheese emporiums, *The Paoli Cheese Shop*, (608) 845-7031.

From the intersection of Highway 151/18 and County G, turn south on G and go about 5 miles to Mt. Vernon, crossing the Sugar River and cruising through this beautiful hilly and wooded farmland in southwest Dane County.

Stay on G as you join Highway 92 in Mt. Vernon. This town was named after President George Washington's home by settlers who came from Virginia.

Proceed on G and go to the junction with County O. You'll drive near the home site of "Fighting" Bob La Follette, former Wisconsin governor and Progressive leader (off Britt Valley Rd. and La Follette Rd.), then cross Primrose Creek before a climb to Hustad Valley. This tour cuts across miles of picturesque rolling hills, winds along the tops of glacial ridges, and takes you through some of the backroads towns and settlements that sprang up as the frontier moved west and Wisconsin became a state. It's a stunning drive.

Turn left (southeast) on O and go about 8 miles into New Glarus. The route is through rich farmland and past apple orchards (don't miss *Swiss Valley Orchard*, (608) 527-5355, named "Best in Wisconsin" by *Wisconsin Trails* magazine readers), and finally curves into the very Swiss settlement of New Glarus.

This community was settled in an unusual way. Unlike other ethnic communities that grew up as one family after another moved in, New Glarus was a planned group emigration project by people in the Swiss Canton of Glarus. In the 1840s there was a severe economic crisis in Switzerland, and it was obvious that it would be best for some people to move out. The word of the good life, lots of opportunity, and inexpensive land in America reached Glarus. People decided that it would be worth the risk to pack up and start a new life in a new land. A group of scouts was sent to America to look over prospective areas where a new Glarus community might be established. When they got here, they felt the combination of beautiful scenery, good land, and reasonable prices was right.

The advance group bought 1,200 acres of land in the Little Sugar River Valley and began to arrange to bring in the new settlers. On August 15, 1845, 108 of them arrived and began to build "New Glarus." By the 1880s the new residents had begun to build a reputation for their excellent Swiss cheeses. More settlers came to join them. To this day, the ties between local residents and Switzerland remain strong. Look around at the buildings, Swiss flags, the official shields of the Swiss cantons on the light poles, and the displays of Swiss items in the stores. Don't be too surprised to hear Swiss-German conversations in the local taverns (all very friendly places), and if you're in the mood, stop in at *The New Glarus Hotel,* (608) 527-5244, or the *Chalet Landhaus,* (800) 944-1716, and someone will likely be glad to teach you the basics of yodeling.

For Swiss food try these favorite restaurants: *Chalet Landhaus Inn,* (800) 944-1716, which has great rooms too; the *New Glarus Hotel,* (608) 527-5244, where you'll enjoy excellent food prepared under the direction of internationally famous chef Hans Lenzlinger and hear alpine yodeling every weekend; *New Glarus Bakery,* (608) 527-2916, for sweet Swiss treats; *Glarner Stube,* (608) 527-2216, for great Old World dishes; and *Deininger's Restaurant,* (608) 527-2012, featuring fine dining in a splendid Victorian home with big band music.

A good old friendly Swiss-style tavern is *Puempels,* where you can get soup and sandwiches and enjoy some folk art wall murals painted in 1913, 20 years after the place first opened.

One of the newest New Glarus attractions features one of most traditional of European delights, beer. The *New Glarus Brewing Company,* (608) 527-5850, has been hauling home beer festival awards by the barrel ever since it was opened a few years ago. It always has something new to offer, and favorites include Edel-Pils, Uff-Da Bock, and Wisconsin Belgian Red.

The *Swiss Historical Village,* (608) 527-2317, is an affiliate of the State Historical Society; it accurately preserves the unique history of this area in 14 buildings depicting the way of life of those early Swiss settlers.

The *Chalet of the Golden Fleece,* (608) 527-2614, is an interesting, one-of-a-kind treasure museum that displays the eclectic collections of Edwin Barlow. He built the chalet in 1937 and filled three floors with etchings, silver, pewter, quilts, coins, stamps, dolls, woodcarvings, 2,000-year-old Etruscan earrings, and—as they say—much, much more! Don't pass it by.

For a real authentic New Glarus Swiss treat, plan to get to town for the *Heidi Fest* held each June, (800) 527-6838. *Heidi,* the classic Johanna Spyri play, is presented with local actors, including some live goats and kittens. If you hang around town you'll also see flag throwing (a sport), hear yodeling at its best, singing, and alphorn concerts.

In September the town stages an outstanding celebration of Swiss independence, the *Wilhelm Tell Festival.* It's staged outdoors and is accompanied by many other activities.

The Sugar River State Bicycle Trail is a part of the *Ice Age National Trail.* It begins at New Glarus and follows an old railroad grade through the countryside 23.5 miles to Brodhead.

Stay on O to the junction with Highway 39 (Fifth Street) in New Glarus.

Turn right on 39 and follow it north and west out of town 5.6 miles to the junction with County J. Along the way, you might want to take a brief detour on Marty Rd. (Wisconsin Rustic Road 81), a nice little 2.9-mile paved jog through the hills.

As we run through this hilly country, you can begin to get a sense of why the early Swiss settlers—with a little imagination—could look out at the countryside and convince themselves they were still near their Swiss homeland.

Turn left on J and go about 1 mile to the junction with County A. Turn right (west) on A and go 10.3 miles to the junction with Highway 78. Turn left on 78 and go about 1 mile into Argyle and the junction with Highway 81.

Argyle was named for the Duke of Argyle as a tribute to an early Scottish settler, Allen Wright. Bob La Follette spent part of his youth here, living in a home on Milwaukee St. *Partridge Hall,* (608) 543-3960, was built in the 1870s as a furniture store and meeting hall, served as a silent movie theater, and today rents guest rooms and has a fine restaurant. The old movie theater has been nicely restored.

Turn south and east (left) out of Argyle on 81 and go about 8 miles to South Klondike Road. Turn right (south) there and go 2.2 miles through the valley to County Y. Turn left (east) on Y and drive about 4 miles to Highway 81.

Turn right on 81 and go 1.2 miles to the junction with Highway 11 in Monroe. Born in the 1830s, Monroe is another community known for Swiss and Old World tradition, great cheeses, and friendly people. Head downtown to see the century-old (1891) Romanesque *Green County Courthouse,* (608) 328-9430, with its 120-foot clock tower. The square is ringed with historic buildings and interesting shops.

Don't miss *Baumgartner's* restaurant, (608) 325-6157, on the square, a community institution where you can get a local delicacy: Swiss cheese on rye, along with an award-winning local beer, Berghoff, brewed by the J. Huber Brewing Company. A Monroe institution since the 1840s, it is the last of Wisconsin's original small-town, family-owned breweries.

Want cheese? *Alp and Dell,* (800) 257-3355, 657 2nd St., is a great choice for cheese and sandwiches, while *Prairie Hill Cheese,* (608) 325-2918, and *Franklin Cheese Coop,* (608) 325-3725, both offer tours (mornings are best, so call ahead).

Cheese Country

Wisconsin is a state known for it's cheeses, and Green County has long been one of the leading producers. In the 1870s there were more than 200 cheese factories operating here. While you're in the area, taste, taste, taste! Swiss, cheddar, Havarti, Colby, Gruyere, and Butterkase are local specialties, but that's just for starters. Ask the clerk at any cheese counter in the area and he or she will be glad to let you test some great products. You might even build up the courage to ask for some Limburger, an odiferous offering that many in Monroe consider a delicacy. Ask for it at Baumgartners. The last Limburger factory in the country is located outside of Monroe. In fact, it was loud complaints about "smelly Limburger" being hauled to market that eventually resulted in increased exposure for the town. It seems the cheese-makers got tired of hearing the complaints, hauled wagonloads into town, and said, "this will make Green County famous." They've been winning international medals ever since.

But if you want proof that you're in the middle of cheese county, take a short jaunt south on Highway 69 to the *Green County Welcome Center and Historic Cheesemaking Center*, (608) 325-4636, which houses a visitor information center, showcases exhibits on the cheese-making industry, and serves as the starting point for the 47-mile *Cheese Country Recreational Trail* that winds through Green and Lafayette Counties to historic Mineral Point.

One additional Monroe delicacy you should be sure to sample is the European-style chocolate crafted by the Buol family and sold in *Chocolate Temptation*, (608) 328-2462, on the east side of the square. The sweets are hand-dipped and impossible to resist. Buy some as gifts and try to think of reasons not to enjoy them yourself before you get them home!

Monroe has a beautiful old *Art Center*, (608) 325-5700, housed in the old (1869) Methodist Church, which was designed by noted Milwaukee architect E. Townsend Mix. Exhibits are changed regularly and live performances are also scheduled.

Bed and breakfast lovers may want to save a night or two for the grand Victorian *Chenoweth Inn*, (608) 325-5064.

Festivals are a real treat here. In even-numbered years, the "Swiss Cheese Capital of the USA" hosts the huge *Cheese Days* festival, (800) 307-7208, and annually is the host of one of Wisconsin's finest balloon rallies, the *Honda International Pro-balloon Competition*, (608) 325-7648. And railroad fans will want to get to Green County for the annual *Depot Days,* when virtually every community has some railroad event ranging from model railroad displays, to real train rides and the immensely popular "speeder car" rides, (888) 222-9111.

At the junction of 81 and 11 turn right (southwest) on 11 and go 7.4 miles to County M. Turn right (north) on M and drive 3.3 miles to County Y. Turn left on Y and go for about 4.3 miles to County M in the little town of Woodford.

Continue straight (west) on M across the Pecatonica River. Before leaving the area, stop at *Blackhawk Memorial Park*, (608) 465-3390, a 159-acre recreation area with fishing, canoeing, primitive camping, and hiking. Its place in history was set by an 1832 battle in which outnumbered Sauk and Fox warriors, led by Chief Black Hawk, fought frontier militia and regular army troops under the command of Colonel Henry Dodge. A fierce and bloody battle resulted in the death of 17 Native Americans and three of Dodge's soldiers. Black Hawk was chased and finally caught on his flight throughout southwest Wisconsin. His pursuers included three soldiers who would later become presidents, Zachary Taylor, Abraham Lincoln, and Jefferson Davis (of the Confederacy). Two of these, Taylor and Davis, would later be linked by marriage (see the article in Tour 19), and two, Lincoln and Davis, would oppose each other in the Civil War. This park and memorial marker honor the memory of all who died in the historic battle.

Continue on M about 2.2 miles to the junction with Highway 78 at Five Corners. Turn right (north) on 78, crossing Whiteside Creek and cutting through the hills 4.1 miles to the junction with Highway 81 just west of Argyle.

Turn left (west) on 81 and go for 0.4 mile to County G. Turn right (north) on G and go 5.3 miles to South Lake Road. You'll be running along the Mud Branch of the Pecatonica River and arrive just southeast of *Yellowstone Lake State Park*, (608) 523-4427. This 2,600-acre gem has a two-mile-long 455-acre lake, excellent mountain bike trails, great hiking, swimming, canoeing, fishing, and 128 bluff-top campsites.

Turn right (north) on South Lake Road and go 1.4 miles to Lake Road. Turn left on Lake and drive about 3 miles to County F, winding along the scenic north shore of Yellowstone Lake State Park.

At the junction with County F, go 2 miles to County D/G. Turn left on D/G and go 0.3 mile to County D. Turn right on D and cruise an easy and picturesque 7.9 miles to County M.

Go straight on County M/D about 1 mile to Highway 78. Turn left (south) on 78 and drive about 5.3 miles to Highway 11. Turn right on 11 and go about 0.5 mile to County K at Gratiot. This mining community was named after pioneer Henry Gratiot, who first came here in 1825 looking for lead and hoping to live in "free territory." In keeping with that desire, he freed the two slaves he brought with him. As a friend of Chief Black Hawk, he tried to prevent the Black Hawk War, and was instrumental in rescuing two young girls kidnapped by Ho-Chunk warriors.

Turn right (north) on K and travel for 4.5 miles to Red Rock Road. On the way, you'll pass through Riverside, which was once known as "Schultz Ford" and which was quite a bustling little community along the Pecatonica River in 1859. Times, commerce, and the world had pretty much passed it by when a tornado took out the remaining cheese factory and school in 1944.

Go straight on Red Rock Road about 4.2 miles to where it meets with County K.

Continue on K about 1.9 miles to Highway 23. Turn right (north) on 23 and go about 1.7 miles to Darlington and the junction with County F. Darlington was named for Joshua Darling, a New York land speculator who never

In the early 19th century, Cornish lead miners built stone houses in Mineral Point, which now form the State Historical Site of Pendarvis. Photo by Gary Knowles.

made it out west to visit. It was known as "the Pearl of the Pecatonica" because of the freshwater clam shells harvested here that were used to make "pearl" buttons. (For more information on Darlington see Tour 19.)

Go straight (northeast) on F out of Darlington about 9.2 miles to Fayette and the junction with County D. Turn left (north) on D and drive 3.3 miles to the junction with Fort Defiance Road.

Go left (west) on Fort Defiance Road and go 2.8 miles to Stone Road. Go right (north) on Stone Road 1 mile to County S. Turn left (west) on S and drive 1.8 miles to Highway 23. Turn right on 23 and go about 4 miles into Mineral Point and the junction with Highway 151.

Welcome to the place where Wisconsin got its nickname "the Badger State." It was here in the 1820s that prospectors began swarming through the hills in search of lead. In 1829 Iowa County was created, and it included all of southwest Wisconsin. By 1834 a U.S. Land Office was established in the community, and on July 4, 1836, the Territory of Wisconsin was born right here in Mineral Point. Colonel Henry Dodge served as the first territorial governor. As word of the lead boom spread across the country and back to Europe, Cornish, German, and Italian immigrants rushed into the area in hopes of making a life on the new frontier.

Their mark was made, and you'll see it most dramatically here, in the wonderful Cornish stone cottages and buildings—especially at the fascinating State Historic Site of *Pendarvis*, (608) 987-2122. This restored settlement gives you a chance to step into the homes and daily lives of Wisconsin's first citizens. You'll learn that the lead-bearing hill across the road was the site of open mines dug into the earth. *Shake Rag Street* got its name from the practice of women in these little houses along the street waving big pieces of cloth out the window to let the miners across the way know that lunch was ready. Stop at the *Pendarvis Gift Shop* to find a nice variety of local and imported handicrafts, English teas, biscuits, and toffees. (You need not tour Pendarvis to stop at the gift shop.)

The Gundry House, (608) 987-2884, 234 Madison St., operated by the Mineral Point Historical Society, is a mansion whose Victorian-era grandeur has been restored; it's an impressive example of an Italianate-style structure built of finely crafted local sandstone. The house also serves as a museum, with rooms decorated to recall what they looked like during the late 1800s and displaying artifacts from Mineral Point's past.

The most popular dog in town is the zinc statue of a pointer (though he's not pointing) on the Gundry and Grey store building downtown. He's over 100 years old and was put up there to help identify the building. Today he survives as the beloved mascot of Mineral Point.

The *Mineral Point Opera House,* (608) 987-2642, 139 High St., is a 400-seat 1914 gem that once welcomed vaudeville shows. Today it is preserved for cinema, as well as for live performances by the Shake Rag Players, a local theater group, and other live entertainers.

The *Odd Fellows and Rebekah Museum,* (608) 987-3093, at Front and State Sts., is a Federal-style building constructed in 1935 that was the first International Order of Odd Fellows shrine built west of the Alleghenies.

The Badger State

Many visitors to Wisconsin go home disappointed that for all the deer, raccoons, opossum, squirrels, and other wildlife they see on their travels here, they don't see any badgers. This is "the Badger State," isn't it?

Well, yes, Wisconsin does have badgers, but the name came not because there were lots of the animals here but rather from the early lead miners who rushed into the Wisconsin territory. A reporter from back East (some say Horace Greeley) sent back reports of men who came to town, staked out a claim, and started digging in the hillside looking for lead. Many of these miners had no homes other than these holes. Like lots of miners, they were rather snarly and protective of their claims. To the reporter they looked like a hill full of contentious badgers. So the word went out that Wisconsin was "the Badger State." And so it remains.

Mineral Point has become something of an arts and crafts center as well as an antique hunter's dream. Among the many fine shops and galleries you'll want to check out are: *Needlewood Gallery,* (608) 987-2813, 105 Jail Alley, for collectible woodwork by Bert Bohlin; Bruce Howdle's *Ceramic Art Studio,* (608) 987-3590, 225 Commerce St.; *The Johnston Gallery,* (608) 987-3669, for slab-built porcelain and stoneware, 245 High St.; *Mineral Point Toy Museum,* (608) 987-3160, for antique and collectible toys, 215 Commerce St.; *Paper Mountain Books,* (608) 987-2320, selling antiquarian and out-of-print books; *Foundry Books,* (608) 987-4363, which specializes in Wisconsin books and maps; *Old Town Hall,* (608) 987-2835, 220 Commerce St., for Amish quilts, handcrafted dolls, and antiques; and *Jail House Gallery,* (608) 987-2029, for art, pottery jewelry, and antiques, 111 Jail Alley.

Dining favorites include the *Brewery Pub,* (608) 987-3298, a well-regarded local brew pub. For a taste of such miner's delights as the "pasty" pocket sandwich or figgy-hobbin and bread pudding, try the *Red Rooster Café,* (608) 987-9936, 158 High St., or the *Sweet Shoppe,* (608) 987-4881, 60 High St.

As you'd expect, Mineral Point has a number of special bed and breakfast inns. Several good ones include the *Wm. A. Jones House,* (608) 987-2337, a Georgian Revival home built by the U.S. commissioner of indian affairs during the term of President McKinley; the *Brewery Creek Inn,* (608) 987-3298, which is 150 years old; and *The House of the Brau-Meister,* (608) 987-2913, a 1900 Queen Anne–style home with a screened porch and nicely tended gardens. *Red Shutters,* (608) 987-2268, is a home built the year Wisconsin became a state (1848), and it features a fireplace, French breakfast, afternoon tea, and reading library.

Golfers who want to "get the lead out" should try picturesque *Ludden Lake Golf Club,* (608) 987-2888, a good nine-hole layout that golfers of all skill levels can enjoy.

Go northeast out of Mineral Point on Highway 23/151 for 4.1 miles to County Y. Turn right (south) on Y and go to the junction with Highway 191.

You should enjoy these roller-coaster roads that run the tops of the ridges, snake with winding rivers through scenic valleys, and dart across wetlands and woodlots. Drop the top (if you can), open the sunroof (if you have one), roll down the windows (at least!), and see and sense the extraordinary face of backcountry Wisconsin.

Turn left on Highway 191, running southeast along Ley Creek for about 5.1 miles to Long Valley Road. Turn left on Long Valley Road and go about 2.6 miles to County K. Turn left on K and drive about 1.7 miles to Mill Dam Road.

Turn right (south) on Mill Dam Road and travel 2.3 miles to County HK. Turn left on HK and go northeast about 2 miles to County H. Turn left on H and go about 1 mile to County K.

Take a right on K and drive about 2.9 miles along the Pecatonica River to Prairie Grove Road. If you continue north another 0.7 mile to Langberry Rd., then turn left and drive about 0.2 mile, you'll arrive at *Botham Vineyards,* (800) 924-1412, one of Wisconsin's finest wineries.

Turn right (east) on Prairie Grove Road as it winds south about 1.1 miles, jogs east across a little creek at Mound View Road, then goes east another 1.5 miles to County F.

Turn right on F and go to West Blue Mounds Road; turn left and go about 1 mile to County Z. Turn right (south) on Z, crossing Gordon Creek and going about 1.8 miles to County E. Turn left (east) on E and go about 1.1 miles to Mayflower Road.

Go right (east) on Mayflower Road and drive about 3 miles to Highway 78. Turn right (south) on 78 and drive about 0.4 mile to Blue Valley Road. Turn left (east) on Blue Valley Road and follow it about 2.7 miles to County JG.

Turn left (north) on JG and travel about 1.4 miles to Malone Road. Turn right onto Malone Road and go 1.9 miles to Highway 92. Turn right on 92 and go about 1.2 miles to Donald Rock and Messerschmidt Road.

When 92 bends right, continue east on Messerschmidt and go 1.8 miles to County G. Turn left (northeast) on G and go about 3 miles to the junction with Highway 18/151 west of Verona, the starting point of this tour.

Tour 22
Great River, Crooked River, Hidden Valleys

La Crosse—Stoddard—Genoa—Victory—DeSoto—Ferryville—Lynxville—Hazen Corners—
Wauzeka—Steuben—Gays Mills—Rolling Ground—Soldiers Grove—Rising Sun—Fargo—West
Prairie—Newton—Pleasant Ridge—Chaseburg—Pleasant Valley—La Crosse

Distance: 143 miles

Wisconsin has many captivating faces. There's the rugged coastal beauty of Lake Superior and the Apostle Islands, the sparkling glacial lakes and deep forests of the North Woods, and the sun-drenched rolling hills, marshes, and pastures of the Green Lake area. But one profile few people take the time to behold is revealed by this fantastic outing.

You'll first drive south on the lower portion of Wisconsin's Great River Road (a stunning four-star drive in its own right) and then climb some winding roads among the deep "hidden" valleys along the "crookedest river in the world," the Kickapoo. The roads on this route are better known to wild turkeys, pick-up trucks, and horse-and-buggy drivers than to driving enthusiasts.

But why should they have all the fun?

A few stops along the way for apples, cheese, or catfish should please any gourmets in your vehicle. If you have an antiques lover along and you want any rest, I suggest you consider some dark glasses, horse blinders, or chloroform.

So strap on the best car you can find, choose an agreeable navigator, and go take a look at another irresistible side of Wisconsin. You're in for a close encounter with absolute exhilaration.

From the junction of Highway 35 and Highway 14/61 just south of La Crosse, drive south on 35, the Great River Road. (For La Crosse-area information, see Tour 7.) In about 1.5 miles, you'll come to County GI, the entrance to *Goose Island Park*, (608) 788-7018. You may want to make a stop at this 710-acre La Crosse County park along the Mississippi River that has five shelters, 400 campsites, a store, boat and canoe rentals, a bait shop, five boat ramps, fishing, nature trails, swimming, canoeing, and bird watching.

Follow 35 along the river about 5 miles to Stoddard, then 6 more miles to Genoa. Stoddard is a good place to hunt for antiques, while Genoa got its name in the 1860s when settlers of Italian descent decided it resembled Genoa, Italy, enough that they gave it the same name.

Follow the Great River Road along the Mississippi to discover "America's Greatest Undiscovered Drive." Photo by Gary Knowles.

Lock and Dam No. 8 at Genoa has a viewing platform where you can watch river traffic pass through. If you've never seen one of the huge Mississippi River "tows" with barges this is a good place to get a look.

If you're hungry for fish, check out the bars and restaurants in Genoa. They often feature catfish cheeks (yes, cheeks, and they're delicious) and other fish specialties.

Go south on 35 to the *Genoa National Fish Hatchery*. This facility produces two million fish per year in 18 ponds covering 200 acres; self-guided tours are available, (608) 689-2605.

Continue on 35 to the town of Victory, then go another 4 miles to DeSoto. Victory took its name from the battle that ended the Black Hawk War two miles south of here in 1832. DeSoto was named after the Spanish explorer who "discovered" the Mississippi River in the 1540s.

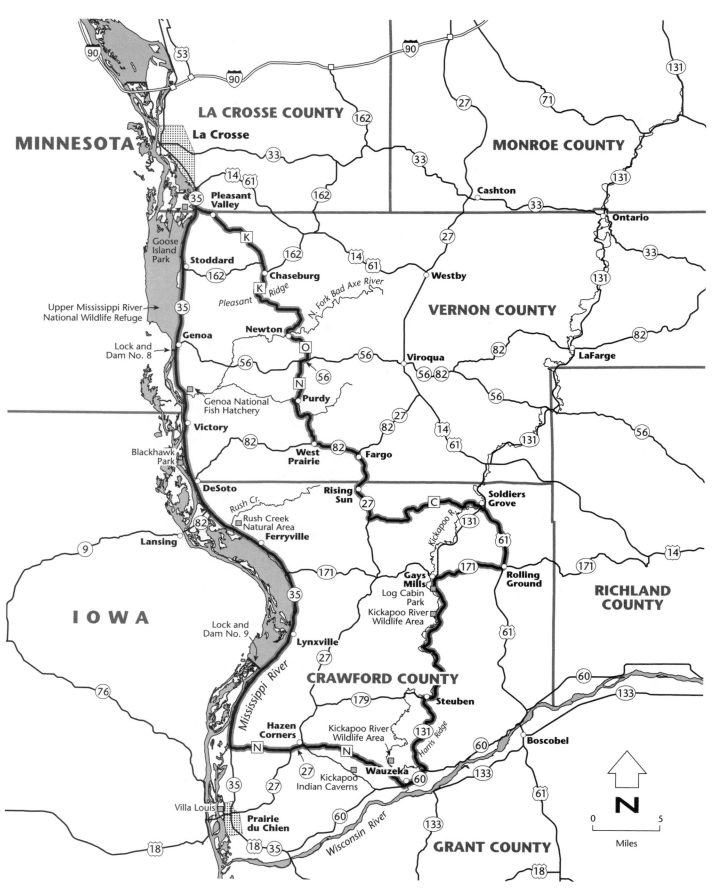

Tour 22

North of DeSoto, you'll find *Blackhawk Park,* an Army Corps of Engineers facility that has great fishing, camping facilities, picnic areas, and historical sites from that battle in 1832.

Follow 35 south another 2 miles to Highway 82. Highway 82 goes west over the mighty Mississippi into Lansing, Iowa, and is the last river crossing until Prairie du Chien about 30 miles farther south.

Stay on 35, past the Rush Creek Natural Area, for another 6 miles to Ferryville. When it was known as Humblebush, the town developed a new sense of civic pride over the advent of the ferry, and the people changed the name to Ferryville. Built along the river and bluffs, it claims the distinction of being the longest "one-street village" in the world. You can stop to enjoy river traffic from the observation deck.

Travel south on 35 for 8 miles to Lynxville. You'll cross several tributaries that flow into the big river, including Sugar Creek, Buck Creek, and Copper Creek. Lynxville took its name from the *Lynx,* a boat that brought in the area's first surveyors in the early 1800s. The river created a deep natural harbor here, and the town became a major stopping point for vessels of all sizes. *Harbor*

House Antiques is a store that has earned a reputation as an excellent stop for local crafts, art, and river country antiques.

Go south on 35 another 3 miles to Lock and Dam No. 9, which forms the largest federally managed pool on the river and which completes some 6,000 openings and closings annually.

Continue south on 35 for 7 miles to the junction with County N. If you go another 5 miles south on Highway 35 you'll be in Wisconsin's second oldest city, Prairie du Chien. For information on things to do there, see Tour 19.

Turn left (east) on N and go about 5 miles to Highway 27. This is a stretch of country road on which you can do some really exciting driving, especially along beautiful Famechon Ridge.

Turn left (north) on 27 and go about 1 mile to Hazen Corners and the continuation of County N. Turn right (east) on N (Dutch Ridge Road) and go about 9 miles to Highway 60 at Wauzeka. The drive is a spectacular one across Wauzeka Ridge. The town of Wauzeka was named after a local Native American who was likely a member of the Ho-Chunk tribe. Legend has

Wisconsin's Great River Road

The Great River Road is a federally designated scenic highway route that runs from Ontario, Canada (the headwaters that feed the Mississippi Basin), through 10 states to the Gulf of Mexico.

In Wisconsin they call the route "America's Greatest Undiscovered Drive" and indeed that may be true. The 250 miles that run with the Mississippi River from Prescott to Dickeyville unfold in one spectacular view after another. Five-hundred-foot bluffs tower over the green valleys below; eagles, heron, Canada geese, trumpeter swans, and huge flocks of migrating birds dot the skies.

Fishing is great up and down the river. Hundreds of fishing boats, pleasure craft, canoes, houseboats, and huge commercial tows with barges travel the water route. Get a good look at them at one of the locks and dams along the way. Most have observation platforms from which you can get a great look or shoot a photo.

This spectacular route is within an easy day's drive of about 80 million people, yet very few ever see it. What's the problem? Well, there are several:

1. The river flows north to south while major highway traffic patterns move east to west. While many people have crossed the Great River Road as they travel from the urban east to the wild west, they only see a quick (but beautiful) segment at La Crosse, Prescott, Prairie du Chien, or Dubuque. The Great River Road, for most travelers, isn't a route to where they're going. It's a point on their route that they cross.

2. The Great River Road isn't a four-lane expressway (in most places) and the route isn't a straight line. *(Well Hallelujah!)* So it takes some time to wind around those curving roads. You slow down a bit driving through towns like Alma and Ferryville, which are built on one long street that follows the river.

3. The multistate organization that's in charge of the entire Great River Road, the Mississippi River Parkway Commission, was established to oversee creation of a multistate highway route. Populated with road builders and local politicians, the commission did a great job of overcoming regional biases to get the job done. But their forte was never promotion—and anyway, driving the whole route requires more time and planning than most modern families have. Some state units (especially in Wisconsin and Minnesota) have had good state-level assistance and enthusiastic committees, but even they have been under-funded to adequately reach and maintain a significant level of promotional visibility.

So with a route that goes the wrong direction and is too slow for a fast crowd and underpromoted in an increasingly competitive marketplace, the Great River Road—spectacular, friendly, relaxing, and hospitable as it may be—lies awaiting discovery and appreciation.

However, for the driving enthusiast, it's an oyster on the half shell. *Bon appetit.*

For a free driving guide to the Great River Road, call (800) 432-8747.

Apples!

The Gays Mills area is one of the world's most concentrated apple-growing regions. It all started in 1905 when two local men, John Hayes and Ben Twining, collected some of the fine local apples to show at the Wisconsin State Fair. They won first place and were so enthused they entered Gays Mills apples in a New York apple show. They won another first. The State Horticultural Society was excited by the recognition and urged the establishment of trial orchards all over the state in hopes of building commercial production. The society planted five acres on High Ridge with five varieties thought to be especially well suited to the climate. By 1911 things were growing nicely and Gays Mills growers organized to promote apple sales. Today there are some 1,500 acres of apple orchards in Crawford County. Growers produce hundreds of varieties, including unusual specialties like Kickapoo Spice, Jonamac, Honey Crisp, and Orange Winter. All are available at *Kickapoo Orchard*, (608) 735-4637, about 3.5 miles east of Gays Mills on Highway 171. The best times to visit the orchards are spring, when the blossoms are in full bloom, and fall, for the colorful and delicious harvest.

it that he either broke away from his tribe or was exiled. He set up a permanent camp here at the mouth of the Kickapoo River.

Quick Trip Option: The *Kickapoo Indian Caverns*, (608) 875-7723, are the largest underground caves in Wisconsin. These fascinating chambers contain evidence of habitation by humans for hundreds of years. Tours are available. From Wauzeka, take Highway 60 west about 2 miles to Dutch Hollow Rd. Turn right and drive another 2 miles.

Turn left (east) on 60 through Wauzeka and go about 2 miles to Highway 131. Turn left (north) on 131 and go about 7 miles to Steuben, running through picturesque hills along Harris Ridge. The name of this town honors the

What's in Those Barges, Anyway?

You've climbed the observation tower to see those long Mississippi River towboats pushing barges, but what the heck is in them?

The most common items moved on the river are petroleum products: gasoline, fuel oil, kerosene, and lubricating oil from the refineries in Texas and Louisiana headed north. There is also much coal going upstream from Illinois and Kentucky.

The downriver shipments include corn, wheat, oats, barley, and rye headed for New Orleans, where they will be reloaded onto ocean-going freighters and sold abroad. Other shipments include scrap iron, iron, steel, fertilizers, sulfur, cement, aluminum, sugar, and dehydrated molasses.

Towboats regularly push 15 to 20 barges with a combined weight of 20,000 tons. The tows are diesel powered.

German General Baron von Steuben, who fought on the colonist side in the Revolutionary War.

Continue north on 131 for 4 miles to Barnum, another 7 miles to Bell Center, and then 2 miles to Gays Mills and the junction with Highway 171.

The road parallels the Kickapoo River on the left, with all its twists and turns and meanderings. Throw in all the hills and valleys on this route, and you've got quite a ride.

Gays Mills was named for James B. Gay, who came to Crawford County in 1847, the year before Wisconsin became a state. He built a dam and sawmill, and people started to move into the area. He persuaded his brothers John and Thomas to follow. John built a flour mill in 1865, and the town was named to honor the pioneering work of the Gay brothers.

This area is world famous as a center of apple orchards, and you'll probably want to plan a trip this way in autumn so you can taste the fruit freshly picked (See article).

Just south of Gays Mills on Highway 131 is *Log Cabin Park*, (608) 735-4341, a Crawford County Historical Society project that illustrates the construction techniques of pioneers and has exhibits of early pioneer life.

Turn right (east) on 171 and go about 6 miles to Rolling Ground and the junction with Highway 61, a rollicking ride over High Ridge and hills packed with apple orchards.

Turn left (north) on 61 and drive about 6 miles to Soldiers Grove and the junction with County C. Soldiers Grove, on the bank of the Kickapoo River, probably earned its name when the soldiers chasing Black Hawk across these hills in 1832 camped here. Prior to that time it was called Pine Grove.

The village is known today for the fact that the community chose to move its business district to avoid periodic destructive floods rather than trying to "tame nature." Also noteworthy is the town's decision to build a new community using the best of modern technology. In keeping with an enlightened level of energy conservation, the new business district uses primarily solar power for 50 percent of its heat. Soldiers Grove has thus come to be known as "the Solar Village." Call (608) 624-5209 for more information.

At the south edge of town is *Beauford T. Anderson Memorial Park*, which honors Crawford County's Medal of Honor winner. The wayside also lists 637 Medal of Honor recipients from 11 Midwestern states and has a wall listing 1,200 area residents who served their country in conflicts from the Civil War to Desert Storm.

Canoeists flock to the Kickapoo River to enjoy the twists and turns of "the crookedest river in the world."
Photo by Gary Knowles.

Turn left (northwest) on C and drive about 10 miles to Highway 27. Turn right (north) on 27 and go about 3 miles to Rising Sun. They say this town was named by T. H. Wilder, an early settler who was dismayed by two weeks of rain. When the sun came out, he knew exactly what he'd name the town.

Continue north on 27 about 3 miles to Fargo and the junction with Highway 82. Turn left (west) on 82 and go about 3 miles to West Prairie and the junction with County N. Turn right (north) on N and go 4.5 miles to Purdy, through the Purdy Valley, then about 3 miles to Highway 56.

Turn right (east) on 56 and go 0.6 mile to County O. Turn left (north) on O and go about 2.8 miles to Newton on the North Fork of the Bad Axe River. Continue on O north, then west to the junction with County K at Pleasant Ridge. There are many Amish people living in this area so please drive carefully and be alert for horse-drawn buggies. You may find some fine Amish crafts, woodwork, and quilts in area stores.

Turn right (north) on K and drive about 10 miles to the junction with Highway 35. Along the way, you'll go through Chaseburg and Pleasant Valley, follow South Chipmunk Coulee, and experience enough hills and dales, ridges and valleys to last nearly a lifetime.

Turn right (north) on 35 and go about 1.5 miles back to the Highway 14/61 junction, our starting point just south of La Crosse.

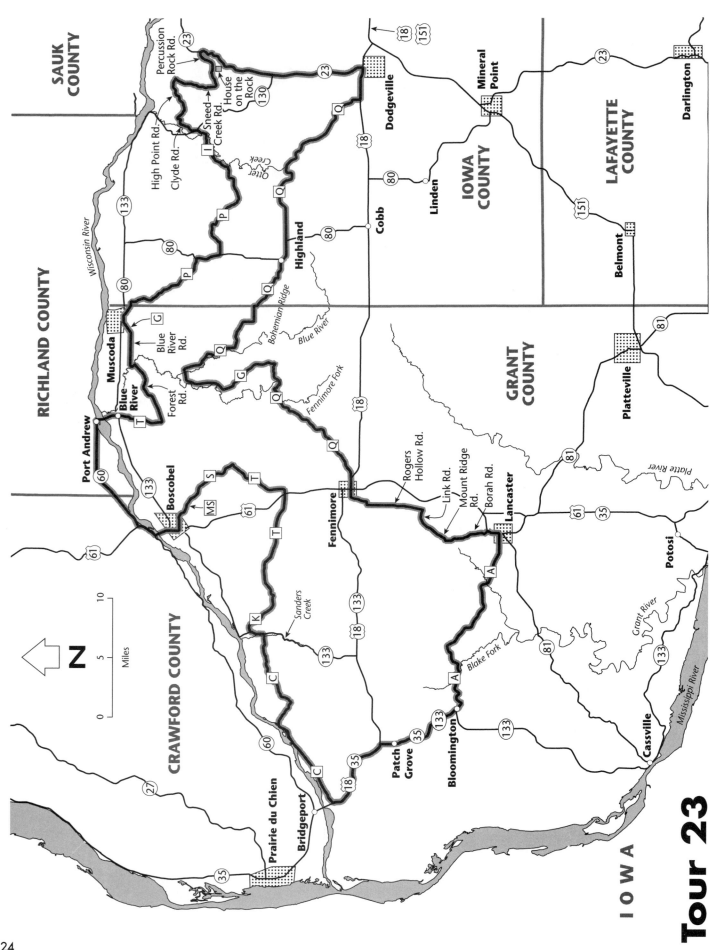

SAUK COUNTY

Percussion Rock Rd.
House on the Rock
Sneed Creek Rd.
High Point Rd.
Clyde Rd.
Otter Creek

23
130
23
23
18 151
18
151
Mineral Point
Darlington

RICHLAND COUNTY

Wisconsin River
133
80
80
P
P
G
Blue River Rd.
Muscoda
Blue River
T
Port Andrew
60
133
Boscobel
S
MS
61
T
T
K

LAFAYETTE COUNTY

Q
Q
Q
Q
Q
G
Forest Rd.
Bohemian Ridge
Blue River
Fennimore Fork

Dodgeville
Q
18
Cobb
80
80
Linden

IOWA COUNTY

Highland

GRANT COUNTY

18
18
Rogers Hollow Rd.
Link Rd.
Mount Ridge Rd.
Borah Rd.
Lancaster
A
A
Platteville
81
151
Belmont

Fennimore
133
18
133
Sanders Creek
C
60
C
18
35
Patch Grove
35
133
Bloomington
Blake Fork
133
81
81
133
Grant River
Cassville
Potosi
61
35
61
Mississippi River

CRAWFORD COUNTY

Prairie du Chien
Bridgeport
27
35

N
Miles
10
5
0

IOWA

Tour 23

124

Tour 23
You Can Barely Get There from Here

Dodgeville—Muscoda—Blue River—Port Andrew—Boscobel—Bridgeport—Patch Grove—Bloomington—Lancaster—Fennimore—Highland—Dodgeville

Distance: 174 miles

Hey, driving enthusiasts: as Woody Guthrie wrote, "this land was made for you and me!" Indeed.

Southwestern Wisconsin's Driftless Region has everything we love: switchback roads that chase their tails along the sides of steep forested hills, long stretches of roller-coaster highway stretching way off over the horizon, places where you have to downshift going uphill, scenic pullouts that take your breath away, drives along river roads through tunnels of trees, friendly communities with little cafes that still serve home cooking.

This is the real-life equivalent to the idyllic places you see in those car commercials. Even the ad guys don't believe they really exist anywhere. That's just Hollywood, Madison Avenue, and some clever work by a computer wizard. But hey—don't tell them. They're wrong. And the places that do exist are even better than the enhanced video version. And this tour has plenty of these enchanted spots. So give them a try, including a diner for a cup of country coffee and apple pie.

Begin in Dodgeville at the junction of Highway 18/23.

Colonel Henry Dodge left St. Genevieve, Missouri, and brought his family to this area in 1827, hoping to make a fortune in the lead-mining boom. He led the successful chase and capture of Chief Black Hawk in 1832, was a popular leader among the miners, and was said to enjoy wearing his buckskins and horse pistols around town. President Jackson appointed him the first governor of the Wisconsin Territory. This city and the state park just north of town honor his memory today.

The foundation for the *Iowa County Courthouse,* (608) 935-0399, downtown was laid in 1859, making this the oldest continuously active courthouse in the state.

More recently, Dodgeville has become home to the corporate headquarters for the *Lands' End* clothing company. An outlet store is located downtown, (608) 935-6207. Another outlet, *Walnut Hollow Woodcraft,* (800) 950-5101, is also a popular stop. Dodgeville is the home of this company, the nation's largest manufacturer of woodcraft products. You can buy seconds and overruns here for up to 70 percent off retail.

Shopping in the historic downtown is double the fun—you get to see great old buildings and enjoy unusual shops. *Carousel Collectibles and Antiques,* (608) 935-5196, has lots of glassware, pottery, and furniture, but its real specialty is restoring carousel animals. *Linens and Accents* is a great Victorian gift shop, (608) 935-5659, while *Metropolitan Art,* (608) 935-7011, is an art studio, gallery, and educational center in an old auto dealership building.

To get a taste of the local culinary favorite, a Cornish pasty, stop at the *Quality Bakery,* (608) 935-3812. At *Thistle Hill,* (608) 935-9123, a home store, you might want to buy a personally autographed copy of owner Carla Lind's book on Frank Lloyd Wright.

There are lots of good rooms available in Dodgeville, making it a good place to use as the base for this tour. Some examples: *The New Concord Inn,* (800) 348-9310, has an indoor pool and whirlpool, the *Best Western Quiet House and Suites,* (800) 528-1234, has a pool and fitness center, while *The House on the Rock Inn,* (888) 935-3960, also has an indoor pool.

To experience one of the best bike trails anywhere, get on the *Military Ridge State Trail,* (608) 437-7393. It extends east from here for 40 miles on an off-highway rail grade (2-5 percent incline) to Verona. Along the route you'll see beautiful rolling hills, farms, wetlands, forests, and lots of sky.

The Museum of Minerals and Crystals, (608) 935-5205, on Highway 23 just north of the city, has a surprisingly large and eclectic collection of rocks, minerals, crystals, and fluorescents from around the world.

The Driftless Region

As a travel destination, Wisconsin has built a solid reputation on its 15,000 lakes and beautiful forests. Most of the state was sculpted by glacial action over tens of thousands of years.

But there is a huge area in southwest Wisconsin that was never covered by the last ice age—or any other. This area is called the Driftless Region and this tour runs through it.

This region is strikingly different from the wet and gravelly glacial landscapes of the north and east. It stands as dry upland in southwestern Wisconsin. Much of this region is a rolling plain, with no glacial sediment. It has been shaped and formed by streams that cut deep ravines and left steep hillsides and a maze of narrow, twisting ridges and valleys.

There are very few natural lakes, bogs, or marshes in this part of the state. Blue Mound in eastern Iowa County was a landmark for Native Americans and early settlers. It stands as an erosion remnant rising high over the surrounding plain. This driftless landscape is the result of many thousands of years of erosion. By contrast, the Kettle Moraine area (see Tour 6) is relatively young by geological standards—about 12,000-15,000 years old or younger.

For driving enthusiasts, the Driftless Region is an extraordinary natural theme park of winding roads, steep hills, and roller-coaster switchback drives set in a landscape of spectacular beauty. Enjoy the ride.

Southwest Wisconsin has some of the finest country roads in the Midwest. Photo by Gary Knowles.

Drive north out of Dodgeville on 23 about 10.6 miles to Percussion Rock Road.

Along the way you'll pass a couple of quirky attractions, starting with the *Don Q. Inn*, (608) 935-2312, famous for its bizarrely themed guestrooms and a rare Boeing C-97 Stratocruiser sitting out front.

Not nearly as wild is *Governor Dodge State Park*, 608) 935-2315, which, at 5,000 acres, is Wisconsin's second largest park. Steep hills and scenic bluffs, two lakes, and deep valleys make this a popular spot for hiking, camping, and picnics. Horse fanciers will enjoy the bridal trails and equestrian campground.

Farther along on 23, you'll come to what has been described as "the Grand Canyon of roadside attractions," *House on the Rock*, (608) 935-3639. It's Wisconsin's most popular privately owned tourist attraction, drawing some 500,000 visitors per year. The legendary Alex Jordan built the house as a weekend retreat, not a tourist attraction. He started charging a small fee after word began to spread that he had built an interesting house on a chimney rock. He spent the money to collect things he was interested in, like music machines, maritime artifacts, and Tiffany-style lamps—and to build things as his fantasy dictated, like a four-story-tall sea monster, a dark-side "organ room," and a full-sized "playing" circus orchestra. It has been called "a monument to creativity and imagination," "a work of genius," and " the most unusual three-mile walk in the world." The world's largest carousel, the gun collection, the Infinity Room, and the Heritage of the Sea exhibits are just a few examples of the most popular features.

(If you follow Highway 23 another 8 miles north, you'll arrive at the Spring Green area. See Tour 20 for details.)

Turn left (west) on Percussion Rock Road and go a twisting, rolling, hilly 3 miles to the junction with Snead Creek Road. Turn right on Snead Creek Road and dash 2.4 miles to the junction with High Point Road. Turn left on High Point Road and go 3 miles to the junction with Clyde Road. These are all great runs through wonderful tunnels of trees and along twisting paths.

Turn left on Clyde Road and go south 1.7 miles to Clyde and the junction with Highway 130 and County I. Cross 130 and go straight on I southwest for 6.1 miles. You'll cross Otter Creek twice, pass County N, be joined by County P, and pass County PP.

Stay on P as it turns right (northwest) off I and follow it north and then west for about 5 miles to the junction with Highway 80. Jog right (north) on 80 and go 1.4 miles to County P west. Turn left (west) on P and go for 6 miles to the junction with Highway 80/133 in Muscoda. Welcome to the "Morel Mushroom Capital of the World." Every spring these hills are invaded by devotees of the delicious morel mushroom. A huge festival is held in spring to celebrate and eat these wonders of the fungus world.

Turn left on 80/133 and go a short distance to County G. Go straight on G about 1 mile to Blue River Road. Turn right on Blue River Road and go 2 miles to Forest Road.

Turn left on Forest Road and follow its twists along Oak Ridge 4.6 miles to County T. Turn right on T and go about 2.7 miles to the town of Blue River. Continue another 1.6 miles across the Wisconsin River to the junction with Highway 60 at Port Andrew.

Quick Trip Option: Turn right (east) on Highway 60 and go for about 2.5 miles to Eagle Cave Rd.; turn left and drive to *Eagle Cave*, (608) 537-2988, Wisconsin's only known onyx cave.

Turn left (west) on 60 and go about 8 miles to the junction with Highway 61. Along the way, you'll pass the communities of Sand Prairie and Westport before entering the Knapp Creek Unit of the Lower Wisconsin River State Wildlife Area.

Follow Highway 60/61, then stay south on 61 and cross the Wisconsin River. On the south side of the bridge you'll find a pleasant park area where you can picnic, fish, or just sit and watch the river flow by.

Continue into Boscobel to Mary Street (County MS). This friendly community is known as the birthplace of the Gideon Bible. In the heart of downtown Boscobel you'll find the *Boscobel Hotel*, (608) 375-4714, where in 1898 two Christian traveling salesmen shared a room and conceived the idea of a Christian's traveler's' association. Their dream became reality in the formation of the world famous Gideon Society, which has since placed millions of Gideon Bibles in lodging facilities throughout the world. The hotel was built in 1863 and originally known as the Central House. It is made of native limestone and listed on the State and National Registers of Historic Places.

Turn left (east) onto Mary Street (County MS) and in 2 miles bear right (southeast) on County S. Continue on S for 4 miles along Sanders Creek to the junction with County T. This is a great ride through spectacular rolling hills and farm country.

Turn right (southwest) on T and cruise about 3 miles along a scenic ridge. Then turn west, crossing Highway 61, and go about 8 miles to County K.

Turn right on K and go for 3 miles, following the Big Green River and then meeting Highway 133. Turn left on 133 and drive for about 1 mile to County C. Turn right on C.

After you cross the Little Green River, you'll begin a "full-attention-please" drive that's as exciting as any in this book. The road zigs, zags, dips, curves, darts, and dashes through the heavily wooded Woodman-Millville Unit of the Lower Wisconsin River State Wildlife Area. There are stretches of road on which you'll be running like a deer darting through the hills. And about halfway through the ride, you'll be following the Wisconsin River along its south bank below Campbell Ridge.

Stay on C for about 12.6 miles to the junction with Highway18/35 southeast of Bridgeport. Turn left on 18/35 and go 5.3 miles southeast to Highway 133. (If you turn right on Highway 18/35, you'd be headed to Prairie du Chien. See Tour 19.)

Turn right (south) on Highway 35/133 and go 6.4 miles through Patch Grove and Bloomington (see Tour 19) to County A. Turn left on A as it curves along the Blake Fork of the Grant River and heads through farm country for 14.2 miles to Lancaster .

In Lancaster, turn left (north) on Highway 61 and go through town to County K. Turn left on K and go 0.5 mile to Borah Road. Turn right on Borah and drive about 2.5 miles to Mountain Ridge Road. Bear right and go about 2 miles to Link Road. Go straight on Link Road 0.5 mile to Rogers Hollow Road.

Turn left (north) and follow Rogers Hollow Road about 4.5 miles into Fennimore to 12th Street. They say that the town was named after John Fennimore, who settled near the old military road leading to Prairie du Chien. During the Black Hawk War he mysteriously disappeared and local settlers chose to remember him by calling the community Fennimore Center. In 1881 the name was shortened to Fennimore.

The *Fennimore Doll and Toy Museum*, (608)

Fennimore's "Dinky" is a narrow-gauge train that rail buffs, kids, and just about everyone else will enjoy riding. Wisconsin Department of Tourism photo by Don Davenport.

822-4100, has everything children living in simpler times adored: dolls, trains, trucks, cars, tractors, and even circus toys.

The *Fennimore Historical Railroad Museum*, (608) 822-6144, has exhibits relating to the community's rail history. There's the famous "Dinky" narrow-gauge train, which operated from 1878 to 1926, and a Davenport 1907 2-6-0–gauge steam locomotive with a water tank. Children will enjoy riding the 15-inch gauge train.

To sample some delicious area cheese, stop at the *Fennimore Cheese Store*, (608) 822-6416, 1675 Lincoln Ave. Ask for cheese curds that were made today—not only for the better taste but also for the better squeak. *And eat them right away.* Tomorrow, they'll be just cheese.

Turn right on 12th Street and go 0.5 mile to Highway 18. Go straight (east) on 18 for 0.6 mile to County Q. Turn left on Q and run 9.8 miles past Castle Rock to the junction with County G.

Turn left (north) on G, swinging along Bohemian Ridge, then going north and west 6.9 miles to the junction with County Q. Turn right (southeast) on Q and go 10.3 miles into Highland and the junction with Highway 80, crossing the Blue River and running along Red Oak Ridge along the way.

Follow County Q/Highway 80 right, then left through Highland for 1.7 miles. Stay on Q as 80 turns right. Follow Q about 12.3 miles to Highway 18.

Turn left (east) on 18 and drive about 1.6 miles back into Dodgeville where we started.

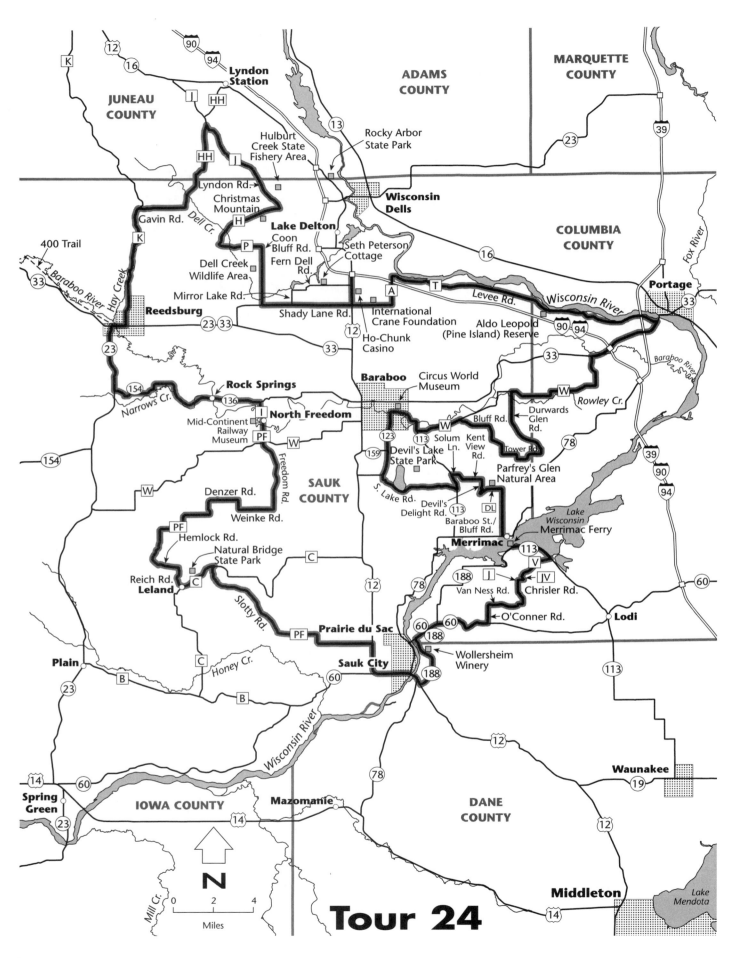

Tour 24
Dells Road Show—The Baraboo Range

Wisconsin Dells—Reedsburg—Rock Springs—North Freedom—Leland—Sauk City/Prairie du Sac—Merrimac—Baraboo—Portage—Wisconsin Dells

Distance: 154 miles

They're loads of fun for today's Dells visitors, but the Ducks have a proud history as amphibious troop carriers in World War II. Wisconsin Department of Tourism photo by GK.

Stop anyone on the street in New York City, Los Angeles, or Sydney, Australia. Ask them what they know about Wisconsin. Chances are good that even before you hear the word *cheese* they will say something about the Wisconsin Dells.

Such is the power of two of the world's greatest promoters, Civil War-era photographer H. H. Bennett and the Dells' greatest booster of the last half of the 20th century, Tommy Bartlett.

Bennett's photos and stereographs of the fantastic Dells scenery were the MTV of the 1880s home. Most everybody back then had seen his most famous photo, of a man doing a death-defying leap at Stand Rock. Bartlett's pioneering work in radio and showmanship—not to mention his bumper stickers—made "Mom, Dad, Let's go to the Dells!" the number-one cry of the Baby Boomer generation in the Midwest.

And the thing to remember is that even with all this promotion and razzle-dazzle, it wouldn't have worked if you had a bad experience when you got there. The truth is, the Dells is a beautiful, fun, exciting, and relatively satisfying family vacation place.

And yet there's one great "ride" that many have missed—the ride you can take in your car out of the Dells through the beautiful, rugged, ancient handiwork of Mother Nature, the Baraboo Hills.

That's what this tour is for—to give Dells-area visitors an incredible option. To enjoy the Dells—for sure—but then to take another day and get out to see the rest of the spectacle the glacier and millions of years of natural events have left behind.

Oh, and by the way, those roads in these hills and gorges are not only pretty to behold but are absolutely as packed with thrills and excitement as if Tommy Bartlett himself had drawn up the routes.

So ride the Ducks, slip through river narrows, pass through Fat Man's Misery, and don't miss the dancing waters; but whatever else you do, plan to hit the road. Don't miss the back roads portion of the Dells thrill show.

Start at the junction of I-90/94 and Highway 12 just south of Wisconsin Dells. Head south on 12 for about 1.5 miles to Shady Lane Road. As you drive, watch for *Ho-Chunk Casino,* (800) 746-2486, open 24 hours a day with 48 blackjack tables, 1,700 slot machines, high stakes bingo, the great Stand Rock buffet, a gift shop, smoke shop, and lots of special events. A beautiful new hotel, with 320 rooms and an excellent gourmet restaurant (the Copper Oak) opened in the summer of 2000.

Turn right (west) on Shady Lane and go 4.5 miles to Coon Bluff Road. Before you get to this road, you might want to detour a bit and turn north on Mirror Lake Rd, follow Fern Dell Rd., and view Frank Lloyd Wright's famous *Seth Petersen*

Cottage, the only one of his buildings operated as a one-unit bed and breakfast cottage; and it's usually booked solid for 12 to 18 months in advance! (608) 254-6551.

Turn right (north) on Coon Bluff Road and go 2.9 miles through the Dell Creek Wildlife Area to County P. Turn left on P for 2.1 miles to County H. Turn right on H and go 3.8 miles to Lyndon Road, passing *Christmas Mountain Village and Golf Club,* (608) 254-3971, on the way. This is an excellent 18-hole course.

Turn left (northwest) on Lyndon Road and go 2.4 miles through the *Hulbert Creek State Fishery Area* to County J. Turn left on J and

The Essential Dells

The Wisconsin Dells has been entertaining visitors for almost 150 years and it's a great place to use as a base for this tour. After a full day of driving through the Baraboo Range, you'll be ready to soak in a whirlpool, check out the thrill show, or dine at a great restaurant. The Dells has just what you're looking for—and then some. *The Wisconsin Dells Visitor and Convention Bureau,* (800) 223-3557, publishes an excellent guide to the area. It's about the size of a phone book and makes interesting reading. Get one (free) before you visit, because there's so much new to do that even the locals can barely keep up.

But like going to Ireland and not kissing the Blarney Stone or going to Australia and not seeing a kangaroo, there are some essential Dells experiences that are so "Dells" that you would feel cheated if you got home and hadn't done them. So plan to:

1. Take the *Upper Dells Boat Tour,* (608) 254-8555, the wonderful three-hour one that visits 15 miles of rocky river sites like Stand Rock and Fat Man's Misery that H. H. Bennett helped make famous.

2. Ride the *Original Wisconsin Ducks,* (608) 254-8751, the amphibious vehicles rescued from World War II that take you on a one-hour, 8.5-mile ride through the Lake Delton Area. The drivers crack corny jokes that are so silly you'll laugh like crazy. And the scenery is outstanding.

3. See the *Tommy Bartlett Thrill Show,* (608) 254-2525, with its comfortable outdoor amphitheater seating, dancing waters, exciting water-skiers, pole climbers, wheel walkers, and whatever new acts they've added this year. Pay a little extra and sit up front, closer to the action—it's worth every penny.

4. See *Tommy Bartlett's Robot World and Exploratory,* which includes a display of the Russian Mir Space Station. This is an authentic piece of history that's worth a visit. The Robot World exhibits are fine, but the MIR is what makes it all worthwhile.

5. See the *H. H. Bennett Photo Studio Historic Site,* (608) 253-3523. Bennett was a Civil War-era photographer whose images of Wisconsin logging and the Dells rank

with the best of the 19th-century photo pioneers. If you can think of an early Dells image, it's probably one of his. His photos enticed generations of visitors to come here—and they still do! Bennett's studio has always been an excellent choice for a visit, and now that it's an official State Historic Site you can bet the exhibits will be great.

6. Walk the strip (Broadway from the bridge to the stoplights in Wisconsin Dells). Buy some fudge and eat it all before you get back to your hotel.

7. Play mini-golf at *Pirates Cove,* (608) 254-7500, or *Shipwreck Lagoon,* (608) 253-7772. Okay, so it's a silly game. But I bet I can beat you!

8. Go to a water park. This is a relatively new Dells phenomenon, but it's essential and definitely one that has earned a spot on the must-do list. You can buy a day pass at a place like *Noah's Ark,* (608) 254-6351, or *Riverview Park* and *Waterworld.*

9. Stay at a luxurious water park hotel. A fairly recent trend has resulted in facilities that have everything under one roof, and has made the Dells a bustling place all year long. Try the *Wilderness Hotel and Golf Resort,* (800) 867-9453, with its huge indoor-outdoor water park, top-class amenities, a challenging new golf layout, and new Fields at the Wilderness restaurant operated by the award-winning Field brothers. Or consider *Great Wolf Lodge,* (800) 559-9653, a luxurious hotel (formerly called Black Wolf Lodge) with many special suites, a large water park, and fitness facilities in a beautiful North Woods-style log lodge.

10. Ride some go-carts. Along with fudge, they're a good, quick shot of fun.

11. Eat. For four outstanding dining options try sea food, steaks, and wines at *Jimmy's Famous Del-Bar,* (608) 253-1861; coconut shrimp in the Valentino Room at *Wally's House of Embers,* (608) 253-6411; or prime rib and a bottle of red wine at either the new *Fields at the Wilderness,* (800) 867-9453, or the original *Field's Steak & Stein,* (608) 254-4841.

travel 3.4 miles to County HH. Turn left (south) on HH and go 4.6 miles to Gavin Road.

Turn right (west) on Gavin Road and drive 2.3 miles to County K. Turn left on K, winding along Hay Creek 3.4 miles to County F. Turn left (south) on County FK and go 2.8 miles to Highway 33/23 in Reedsburg.

Reedsburg, named after D. C. Reed, who came to the area in the 1840s to buy an iron mine, has some notable attractions that are very much worth experiencing. *Pioneer Log Village and Museum,* (608) 524-3419, located 2 miles east of Reedsburg on Highways 23 and 33, features seven preserved log buildings complete with antique furnishings. The pioneer settlement displays 1890s log homes, a church, blacksmith shop, and school.

The *Museum of Norman Rockwell Art,* (608) 524-2123, 227 S. Park St., is said to house the world's largest collection of endearing Rockwell art—4,000 pieces.

The "400" Trail, (608) 524-2850, is a bike and hiking trail named for the Chicago & North Western passenger train that ran along here. The train traveled 400 miles between Chicago and Minneapolis-St. Paul in 400 minutes. Wetlands, songbirds, sandstone bluffs, wildlife, rolling croplands, and country pastures add to the fun of "doing the 400." The trail runs 22 miles from Reedsburg to Elroy, where you could connect with the famous Elroy-Sparta State Trail or the Omaha Trail.

In Reedsburg, go less than 1 mile west on Highway 33/23, turn left on Highway 23, and go for 3.4 miles to Highway 154. Turn left (east) on 154, driving across the Baraboo North Range along Narrows Creek through Rock Springs.

Continue on 154 for 6.1 miles to the junction with Highway 136 in Rock Springs. Follow 136 east for 2.3 miles to County I. Turn right on I and go 1 mile to North Freedom. Stop in North Freedom at the *Mid-Continent Railway Museum,* (800) 930-1385, for a chance to slip back to the days of the steam engine, visit an 1894 Chicago & North Western depot, and ride a real steam train puffing through the hills. On special occasions there are first-class accommodations and meals served. Call for reservations and a schedule. This is a great place to shoot photos too!

Continue south from North Freedom on County PF 1 mile to Freedom Road. Go straight on Freedom Road and wind through the woods for 3.6 miles to Weinke Road. Turn right on Weinke Road and go 1.8 miles to the Y junction with Denzer Road.

Turn right (north) on Denzer Road and drive 1.4 miles to where County PF turns left (south). Follow PF for 6.4 twisting and turning miles to Hemlock Road. Turn left (east) on Hemlock Road and go 1 mile to Reich Road.

Turn right on Reich Road and drive 1.2 miles to County C in Leland. Turn left (northwest) on C and go 2 miles to *Natural Bridge State Park.*

The glaciers didn't get to this ancient gem hidden in the woods—and neither do many visitors. The main feature is a natural sandstone arch 25 feet high by 35 feet wide, similar to the kind you see in Arches National Park in Utah. Radiocarbon dating has determined that this site was used for shelter by Native Americans as long as 10,000-12,000 years ago. Some scientists suggest that it has likely been used continuously for shelter, lodging, and as a scenic rest stop for some 500 generations—only six by non-natives. The park totals 530 acres, including a 60-acre scientific area. A self-guiding nature trail winds through part of the scientific area and describes the uses of forest plants by Native Americans. A hiking trail, two miles long, is located in the woods on the other side of the highway. Wildflowers dot the trail in summer, pileated woodpeckers flit from tree to tree, and now and then a turkey vulture glides by. Call (608) 356-8301 for more information.

Continue on C to Slotty Road (Rustic Road 21).

Quick Trip Option: Continue east on County C past Slotty Road for about 7 miles to the junction with Highway 12. Turn left (north) on 12 and drive 0.5 mile, watching for *Dr. Evermor's Sculpture Park* on the left. (If you see Delaney's scrap yard or

The Golfer in The Dells

H. H. Bennett put the Wisconsin Dells on the tourist map back in the 1800s, but it was Madison's two-time U.S. Open winner Andy North, with golf course architect Roger Packard, who put the championship golf course, *Trapper's Turn,* (608) 253-7000, in between the waterslides and thrill shows. In 2000 he added another new 9 (The Arbor) to the highly regarded layout to make 27 excellent holes. Now the course has lots of good company. *Coldwater Canyon,* (608) 254-8489, got 9 new holes as a 77th-birthday present. Now an 18-hole gem, this picturesque course gives you an eyeful of some beautiful parts of the Dells. *Christmas Mountain,* (608) 254-3971, is an excellent challenge with lots of elevation changes and hungry flora to grab wayward shots. *The Wilderness,* (608) 253-4653, is a dramatic resort course that does justice to the Dells woods and water.

In the Baraboo area, *Baraboo Country Club,* (800) 657-4981, is probably one of the finest undiscovered, unpretentious, and picturesque courses you'll find in the area. The Baraboo Bluffs set the backdrop for elevated tees, undulating (fast!) greens, and lots of water to attract your Titleists. *Devil's Head,* (800) 472-6670, is a real challenge that just might have been the work of Old Salt! The course runs along some 6,725 yards of finely manicured resort grass. There's plenty of fairway, but you'll probably stray into the woods, find the prairie grass, or run right into a stone wall (yes, that's right) if you're not careful. Enjoy the views.

Bluffview, you've gone too far north.) Turn left and enter an attraction that is considered by some to be one of America's 10 most interesting sites. This museum-menagerie, which you can walk or drive through, is a fanciful collection of metal sculpture created from all manner of scrap iron. The creations range in size from a shoebox to a tilt-a-whirl. The park is free and open all year.

Turn right on Slotty Road, going 5.3 miles to County PF. Turn left (east) on PF and go 5.3 miles to Highway 12.

The Wollersheim Winery

The Wollersheim Winery produces award-winning wines and you'll want to try them. But it is also an important living link in the history of the development of the California wine industry, which today produces some of the world's finest wines.

Go back to the 1840s. The Wisconsin lead boom was peaking and immigrants were starting to establish other businesses in Wisconsin. Just across from Prairie du Sac, on a scenic hillside overlooking the Wisconsin River, a young Hungarian count, Agoston Haraszthy, established what he expected would be a productive vineyard. He had high hopes but the severe Wisconsin weather was just too much. After several disappointing vintages with major winter damage to his vines, he set out for California to look for gold. But the story doesn't end there. Haraszthy's activities are well documented, as he eventually became known as the founder of the California wine industry.

The vineyard Haraszthy started on the banks of the Wisconsin River was taken over by Peter Kehl, who made wine with various American grape varieties and Riesling. After he died, his son took over the business, and he began making fortified spirits, which he sold as far away as Maine. When he died in 1899, the vineyard was turned into more traditional cropland for a time and then was left nearly abandoned. In 1972 Bob and JoAnn Wollersheim bought it in hopes of restoring the vineyard and operating a winery.

Today the Wollersheim Winery is the finest, most productive, and most award-winning in the Midwest. Working with their son-in-law, winemaker Philippe Coquard, who is originally from the Beaujolais region of France, Bob and JoAnn produce some 96,000 gallons of fine wine per year. Most of the acreage is devoted to winter-hardy French-American hybrids and some experimental *vitis viniferas*. Their main grape is called Marechal Foch, a very reliable and versatile variety. Wollersheim makes five different wines: Prairie Blush and Prairie Red from the young, flat vineyards, Ruby Nouveau and Domaine du Sac from the medium-aged and medium-slope vineyards, and Domaine Reserve from the oldest and steepest vineyard. These wines carry the appellation "Lake Wisconsin Viticultural Area." The Wollersheims also buy grapes especially grown for them by vineyards in Oregon, Michigan, and New York.

Wollersheim wines are sold primarily in Wisconsin. In addition to this facility, the couple has purchased the Cedar Creek Winery in Cedarburg (near Milwaukee) and now operate it as well.

You can take tours here, sample many varieties, and sit back to watch eagles soar over the river. Or if you get here in autumn they'll even let you stomp grapes in a vat. It's a great place to stop and turn your accelerator foot purple. Bob is also a car lover and enjoys driving his Miata through the Baraboo Range.

Turn right on Highway 12 and drive about 3 miles to Sauk City and Prairie du Sac. These side-by-side towns are a center for eagle watching. In winter, the great birds feed at the open water of the Wisconsin River near the power plant; however you can see them all year long. There's an eagle viewing station along the river in downtown Prairie du Sac. Mornings tend to be good times to watch them feeding. You can recognize them by their white heads and dark-brown body coloring. They have wingspans of up to eight feet. They mate for life and can live 20 to 30 years.

The Sac Prairie area, as the region is sometimes known, was home to August Derleth, Wisconsin's most prolific author. No other writer has matched his output of stories about the Badger state. Environmentalists count him as one of their own. In fact, he was "earth-aware" long before a deep concern for nature had a fancy name. The lower part of the Sauk City Library has the Derleth Room, and *Leystra's Venture Restaurant*, (608) 643-2004, on Phillips Blvd. in Sauk City has Augies Room. The Sauk Prairie *Chamber of Commerce*, (608) 643-4168, has developed a brochure, "Walking Tour of Historic Prairie du Sac," that includes many spots his readers will recall from his works. If you want to buy any of his books, better check used bookstores because most are out of print. *The August Derleth Society* at P.O. Box 481, Sauk City, 53583, strives to maintain his legacy and keep his works before the public.

Stay on 12 south for 1.5 miles, crossing the Wisconsin River, to the junction with Highway 188. Most of the roads from this point on probably have more twists, turns, curves, steep climbs, and downhill runs per mile than any other tour in this book. The great high bluffs, shoreline runs, tunnels of trees, and glacially sculpted surroundings make this an incredible drive, with a "wow factor" that goes way into the red zone and bends the needle. I predict you're going to love it.

Turn left (east) on 188 and go about 4 miles to the junction with Highway 60. Before you get there, however, be sure to stop at the *Wollersheim Winery*, (800) 847-9463, about halfway down the road. Even if you're not a wine lover, this winery should definitely be on your list of places to visit. You can sip, swirl, and spit if you like or just savor the surroundings. (See article).

Turn right on Highway 60/188; after 1.2, miles 188 turns to the left. Continue another 3 miles on 60 to O'Conner Road. Turn left (north) on O'Conner and go 1 mile to the Y intersection with Van Ness Road.

Bear right (east) on Van Ness and drive about 2 miles to Chrisler Road. Turn left (north) on Chrisler, which is joined by County J after 1 mile; continue for another 0.5 mile to County JV. Turn left on JV and go to County V.

Turn right (northeast) on V and go 1.7 miles to Highway 113. Turn left on 113, winding 2.1 miles to the *Merrimac Ferry*. There has been a ferry here across the Wisconsin River since 1848, when Chester Mattson started the service as part of a contract to build a road linking Baraboo and Madison. He charged $.05 per person, $.25 per horse, or $.40 for a team of oxen. The state assumed operations in 1933 with the boat *Colsac I*. It was replaced in 1963 with the *Colsac II* (the name comes from the counties, Columbia and Sauk, that it links). It operates *free* 24 hours a day, seven days a week until it suspends operation when the river freezes over. Carrying about 200,000 vehicles per year, it is the last free ferry in the nation. It is on the National Register of Historic Places.

Some people living in the Merrimac area have asked the state to build a bridge to make it more convenient for them to cross the river. However, in January 2000, Governor Tommy G. Thompson announced that a study had shown overwhelming public support to continue the ferry service. He said a new larger ferry will be commissioned that will probably begin service in 2002.

Leave the ferry and follow Highway 113/78 to Baraboo Street in Merrimac. Turn right on Baraboo Street/Bluff Road and go 2.5 miles to County DL. *Devil's Head Ski and Golf Resort* is straight ahead.

Turn left (west) on DL and go 0.3 mile to *Parfrey's Glen Natural Area* on your right.

Hikers and nature lovers, take note: this quarter-mile hike through a rocky gorge is one of the finest nature walks in the area. The walls of the glen are sandstone, with embedded pebbles and boulders of quartzite. They reach a height of up to 100 feet. The glen stays cool because so little sunlight gets in. Plants that line the route include yellow birch, mountain maple, red elder, clintonia, and mountain club moss. Birders will want to watch for the winter wren, Louisiana water thrush, black-and-white warbler, and the Canada warbler. The environment is quite sensitive, so please stay on the trail.

Continue about 1 mile to Devil's Delight Road. This aptly named little circuit is a fun ascent up the steep bluff, through the woods, and back down the other side.

Turn right on Devil's Delight, going about 1 mile to Kent View Drive. Turn left on Kent View and go 1.2 miles to Solum Lane. Turn left (west) on Solum Lane and go 0.3 mile to Highway 113.

Turn left (south) on 113 and drive about 1 mile to South Lake Road. Turn right on South Lake Road, going 4.5 miles through a tunnel of trees to Ski Hi Road/South Shore Road and Devil's Lake.

Ride the *Colsac II* across the Wisconsin River at Merrimac; it's the last free ferry in the country. **Photo by Gary Knowles.**

Devil's Lake State Park, (608) 356-8301, is the most popular park (by number of visitors) in the Wisconsin park system. It is located between glacially carved terminal moraines and is one of the nine units of The Ice Age National Scientific Reserve. There are about 105 species of birds that nest in the park, including the winter wren, the Canada warbler, the Acadian flycatcher, and the red-bellied woodpecker. There are 10 kinds of snakes, including a few timber rattlesnakes, several species of turtles, amphibians, fish, approximately 40 kinds of mammals, and lots of invertebrates.

The spring-fed lake varies in depth to 50 feet, with surrounding bluffs rising 500 feet above the lake. The hills here are quartzite rock, which consists of grains of sand tightly bonded together. The sand was left as glacial rivers flowed into shallow seas that covered this area a billion years ago. Over the ages, the sand accumulated and became sandstone (a porous rock) and eventually quartzite (a non-porous rock).

Devils Lake State Park is the most popular park in the Wisconsin state system, which was 100 years old in 2000. Photo by Gary Knowles.

After thousands of years passed, the seas shrunk and the quartzite buckled up and formed what is now referred to as the North Range and the South Range. The trough between them filled with softer rocks. The area dried out and stayed that way for thousands of years. The Baraboo Valley was carved by natural forces of erosion and running water during this era.

Another influx of seas covered the region and deposited sediments on the area we call the Baraboo Hills today, on the sides of the quartzite ranges, and in the gorges. Eventually the region was covered over by this sand. Again the seas withdrew and an ancient river washed away most of the sediments from the Baraboo Hills and the surrounding area. The quartzite bluffs were exposed again, and the rivers likely created the Lower Narrows Gap and the Devil's Lake Gap.

It was then up to the Wisconsin glacier to finish the project. Some 15,000 years ago the ice sheet scraped over the area. The glacier enveloped the eastern half of the Baraboo Hills but missed the western part. It changed the course of that ancient river and left huge rock dams at the two open ends of the Devil's Lake Gap. So we can thank the glacier for leaving this wonderful landscape for us to enjoy—at least until nature decides to redo it all again.

For an extraordinary way to see these hills and understand what you're looking at, join the narrated *Time Travel Geologic Tours,* with geologist Paul Herr, (800) 328-0995. He spins amazing and true stories of the geological development of the area.

Continue on South Lake Road, then turn right on South Shore Road, going 1.1 miles to Highway 123. Bear left on 123 and go 1.6 miles into downtown Baraboo, to Walnut Street.

Baraboo got its name from a French trader who had a trading post at the mouth of what we now call the Baraboo River, but it got its fame from the Ringling Brothers, who started their circus business here. They brought their circuses back to town to spend the winters from 1884 to 1918 on the bank of the Baraboo River.

Today their rich legacy and that of other great circuses are preserved as the *Circus World Museum,* (608) 356-8341, 550 Water St. This is no stuffy barn full of dust bunnies. Here real circus performers thrill big-top audiences daily, real animals are on hand, a genuine carousel ride carries kids of all ages to fantasyland, and there is a huge display of the world's greatest collection of antique circus wagons.

The Sauk County Historical Museum, (608) 356-1001, 531 Fourth Ave., has fine exhibits of quilts, military equipment, tools, and furniture in 14 rooms of a 1903 mansion.

Downtown you'll find the fabulous *Al. Ringling Theater,* (608) 356-8864, 136 Fourth Ave. This gem was built in 1915 and was said to be inspired by the Grand Opera House of the Palace of Versailles near Paris. It has been hailed as the earliest example of what can accurately be called a movie palace by the Theatre Historical Society of America.

On the square downtown, you'll find an interesting assortment of gift shops, art galleries, latte bars, and craft stores. You better allow some time to browse and buy. For dining, try the *Little Village Café,* (608) 356-0507, 406 Fourth Ave., serving an eclectic menu of creative dishes, or the *Sand County Café,* (608) 356-5880, 138 First St., which serves delicious "upscale casual" nouvelle cuisine.

The *Ochsner Park Zoo,* (608) 355-2760, corner of Highway 33 and Park St., is the 27-acre home to a fine exhibit of native Wisconsin animals, as well as some others from around the world. There are shelters and picnic areas available too.

In Baraboo turn right on Walnut Street and go 0.4 mile to Water Street. Turn left on Water (Highway 113) and go southeast 2 miles to County W. You'll be heading back out into the Baraboo Hills for some sensational roads. You'll climb some bluffs, switch back down some ravines, drive through tunnels of trees, maybe scare up some wildlife, and enjoy a feast of great scenery.

Turn left on W (east), going 2.3 miles to Bluff Road. Turn right on Bluff and drive 2.8 miles to O'Neil Road at the Y intersection. Bear right on Bluff and go 0.5 mile to Tower Road.

Turn left (east) on Tower and go 2.5 miles (down some steep hills) to Durwards Glen Road. Turn left on Durwards Glen, going 3.7 miles to County W.

Turn right (east) on W and wind 6.1 miles along Rowley Creek to Highway 33. Turn right (east) on 33, crossing the Baraboo River and going under I-90/94 and Highway 78, and drive to the junction with Blackhawk Road (Rustic Road 49) just south of Portage.

Portage has a long history as the place where Native Americans, explorers, and other river travelers would carry their canoes from the Fox to the Wisconsin Rivers. A few miles east of town, along Highway 33, is the site of Fort Winnebago, and the *Surgeon's Quarters* have been preserved from that 1828 fort, (608) 742-2949. Closer to Portage, just off Highway 33, stands the *Old Indian Agency*

House, (608) 742-6362, built as a home in 1832 for Indian agent John Kinzie. He wrote *Wau-Bun,* a book that is considered one of the finest depictions of life at the edge of the Wisconsin frontier. Portage was also the home of suffragette, activist, and writer Zona Gale, who won a Pulitzer Prize in 1921 for her stage comedy *Miss Lulu Bett.* Tour the *Zona Gale House,* (608) 742-7744, 506 W. Edgewater St., to get a closer look at her life.

Turn left on Rustic Road 49 (which also becomes Levee Road) and drive for about 11 miles to County T. This is a fabulous run through the Aldo Leopold Reserve (Pine Island Reserve), along the levee that follows the Wisconsin River through wetland marshes, native prairie grasses, cropland, and wooded lots.

Bear right on T and go for 2.8 miles to County A. Turn left (south) on A and go for 1.4 miles to Shady Lane Road. Turn right on Shady Lane and go 0.5 mile to the *International Crane Foundation,* which is well worth a stop. Here you can see how an international effort has helped save some of the endangered species of cranes. Naturalists from this facility have done pioneering work with their counterparts in Russia, India, Afghanistan, China, Australia, and other parts of the world to save the cranes. Take a tour and you'll have the rare opportunity to watch young cranes exercise with their human "chick parents." You'll see that each crane has its own personality and style! Call (608) 356-9462 for more information.

Continue west on Shady Lane about 1.6 miles to the junction with Highway 12. Turn right and follow 12 back to the Dells area.

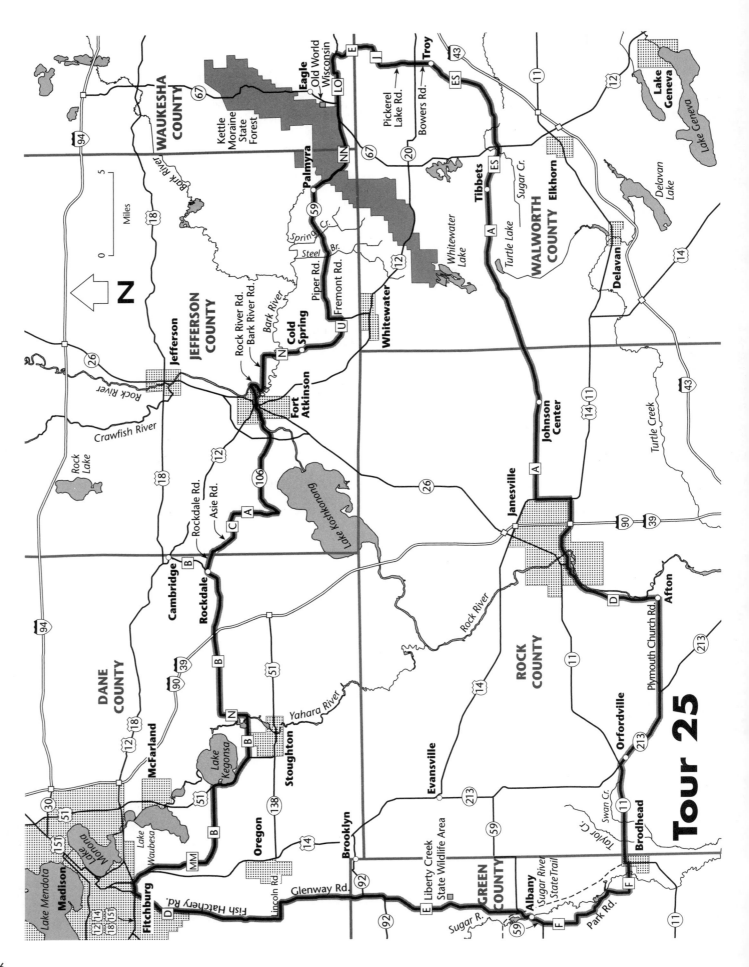

WAUKESHA COUNTY

67

Kettle Moraine State Forest

Eagle
Old World Wisconsin
E
LO
NN
Palmyra
67
59

Spring Cr.
Steel Br.
Piper Rd.
Fremont Rd.
U

Rock River Rd.
Bark River Rd.
Bark River
N
Cold Spring

JEFFERSON COUNTY

Jefferson
26

Rock River

Crawfish River

Fort Atkinson

12

106

A

Rockdale Rd.
Asie Rd.
C

Rock Lake

Lake Koshkonong

26

Cambridge
B
Rockdale

39
90

B

51

DANE COUNTY

McFarland
12 18

N
B
Stoughton

Yahara River

Lake Kegonsa

51

Oregon
138

B

MM

Lake Waubesa

Lincoln Rd.

Glenway Rd.
92

Fish Hatchery Rd.
D
Fitchburg
12 14
18 15

Lake Monona
Lake Mendota
Madison
151

30
51

14
Brooklyn
92

Troy
43
ES
Pickerel Lake Rd.
Bowers Rd.
20
67

11

Lake Geneva
Lake Geneva
12

Tibbets
ES
A

Sugar Cr.
Turtle Lake

WALWORTH COUNTY
Elkhorn

Delavan Lake
Delavan

14

Whitewater Lake
Whitewater
12

43

Johnson Center
A
14 11

Janesville
A
90 39

11

ROCK COUNTY
Rock River

14

D
Afton

Plymouth Church Rd.
Orfordville
213

Turtle Creek
213

11

Evansville
213

Liberty Creek State Wildlife Area

59

Swan Cr.
Taylor Cr.

Brodhead
11

Albany
Sugar River State Trail
F
F
Park Rd.
11

GREEN COUNTY

E
92

Sugar R.
59

Tour 25

136

Tour 25
Hill and Prairie Run

Madison—Fitchburg—Albany—Brodhead—Orfordville—Afton—Janesville—Johnson Center—
Millard—Tibbets—Troy—Palmyra—Whitewater—Cold Spring—Fort Atkinson—Rockdale—
Cambridge—Stoughton—Madison

Distance: 164 miles

One of Abraham Lincoln's visits to Wisconsin included an overnight stay at the Lincoln-Tallman House in Janesville. Photo by Gary Knowles.

To the south and east of Madison is an area filled with gently rolling hills, fertile farmland, Midwestern prairie, glacial lakes, rivers, marshland, and orchards. The beauty of this route builds mile by mile in a subtle accumulation of impressions and nuances. You'll see a picturesque panorama of farm county, drive across a bright prairie, turn down a rustic country lane, and watch a family of wild turkeys strut across the road. For off-road diversions and entertainment, there's Wisconsin's capital city, Broadway theater in the country, historic sites, antiques, boutiques, and craft stores galore.

This is a route that's as enjoyable in your Roadmaster or Miata as it is in a classic T-Bird or Model-T. You can enjoy it on a Goldwing, a Sportster, or a classic BSA. No matter what you ride, it's a great loop cruise that covers a lot of scenic roadway not on the usual tourist map.

Start in Madison at the Beltline (Highway 12/14/18/151) and Fish Hatchery Road (County D). (For things to do in Madison, see Tour 20.)

Drive south on County D out of Madison, passing through Fitchburg and going 8.5 miles to the T intersection at Lincoln Road. Turn left (east) on Lincoln and go 1 mile to Glenway Road. Turn right (south) on Glenway and drive for 6 miles. Follow it as it's joined by Highway 92 for 1 mile. The trip will transport you from Dane County's mix of urban congestion, suburban sprawl, new homes, old farms, wooded lots, and newly cleared building sites into rural Green County.

At the junction with County E, turn left on E and go 8.1 miles into Albany and the junction with Highway 59. Along the way, you'll pass through the Liberty Creek State Wildlife Area and cross the Sugar River.

In Albany, the *Albany Historical Museum,* (608) 862-3423, 17 N. Water St., is a good place to get a feeling for the people and culture of the area. There are several good bed and breakfast inns here. Two are the *Albany House,* (608) 862-3636, which has a master bedroom with a fireplace, and

137

Oak Hill Manor bed and breakfast, (608) 862-1400, 401 E. Main St., a 1906 home with corner bedrooms that sparkle in the sun, candlelit breakfasts, a gazebo, and even bicycles for guests.

Turn right (west) on 59 and go 1.6 miles to County F. Turn left on F, go about 2 miles to Park Road (Rustic Road 27), and turn left. This is a splendid 4.3-mile dash through a wooded marsh area. Watch for deer, migratory birds, and wild turkeys.

At the junction with County F, turn left and go for 1.7 miles to Brodhead and the junction with Highway 11.

Brodhead is the south terminus of the 22-mile *Sugar River State Bicycle Trail,* (608) 527-2334, that runs across Green County to New Glarus. The *Brodhead Historical Museum,* (608) 897-4150, housed in a restored railroad depot, has features and exhibits illuminating local history. Then, spend some time on a walking tour of the post–Civil War–era *Exchange Square Historic District,* with its Italianate and Queen Anne–style architecture. A brochure of the walk is available at the museum.

Turn left (east) on 11, crossing the Rock County line, then Taylor Creek and Swan Creek and going about 6 miles to Orfordville and the junction with Highway 213. Turn right (south) on 213 and go 5 miles to Plymouth Church Road.

Turn left on Plymouth Church and go 5.6 up-and-down miles to Afton and the junction with County D (Afton Road). Turn left (north) on D, following the Rock River for 6 miles into Janesville to Highway 11 East/Business 14.

Janesville traces its name and settlement back to 1836 when Henry Janes traveled to this area following the end of the Black Hawk War in 1832. Today it's a town filled with historic buildings and gardens.

The most noteworthy site may be the *Lincoln-Tallman House,* (608) 752-4519, 440 N. Jackson St. This Italianate home had Abe Lincoln as an overnight guest in 1859 when bad weather prevented his return to Illinois. The bed in which he slept, as well as other original family furnishings, are preserved in this interesting 26-room mansion that has many modern touches for a house of that era.

The Rock County Historical Society's *Helen Jeffris Wood Museum Center,* (608) 752-4519, 426 N. Jackson St., is housed in the recently renovated 1910 Prairie-style home of Stanley Tallman. It has changing exhibits related to the area and southern Wisconsin.

Rotary Gardens, (608) 752-3885, 1455 Palmer Dr., sits on 15 acres and features the sculpture *Dialogue: World Peace through Freedom* and 11 internationally themed gardens, including English Cottage, French, Italian, Japanese, Sunken, and Perennial. There is a wildlife sanctuary and access to the Ice Age Trail.

If you need some motorized racing adventure, try *Amazon Station,* (608) 757-2FUN, where go-carts are available; also there's mini-golf, video games, target shooting, indoor flag football, soccer, and refreshments.

Tour lovers will enjoy Janesville. Manufacturers that give tours include the *Wisconsin Wagon Company,* (608) 754-0026, makers of hand-crafted wooden toys and the Janesville Coaster Wagon; *Country Furniture by Schuler's,* (608) 754-4052, with furniture made from old pine boards; *Gray's Brewery,* (608) 752-3552, a family-owned beverage company since 1856 offering fine beers; and *General Motors Truck and Bus Plant,* (608) 756-7681, a 3.5-million-square-foot complex with cutting-edge robotics technology. You also can visit *MacFarlane's Pheasant Farm,* (800) 345-8348, 2821 S. Highway 51, to see hatching pheasant chicks or buy some pheasant products.

A truly unique Janesville stop is the *Heider Farm,* (608) 752-2224, 2739 S. River Rd., featuring the world famous Miracle, the white buffalo whose birth in 1994 was seen as an important spiritual event signifying both fulfillment of a Lakota prophecy and a return of peace and harmony by many Native Americans.

Turn right on Highway 11 East/Business 14 and travel through Janesville about 4 miles to Highway 14. Turn left (north) on 14 and go 2 miles to County A.

Turn right on A and cruise for about 20 miles to the junction with County ES. You'll cross some rich farmland and pass through Johnson Center and Johnstown, cross into Walworth County, and run north of Turtle Lake, through Millard and Tibbets.

Turn right on ES and go about 8 miles to Bowers Road at Troy. Along the way, you'll cross Highway 67 at Abells Corners, cross Sugar Creek, and swing north through Troy.

Turn left on Bowers Road and go north about a mile to Highway 20. Cross 20 as it becomes Pickerel Lake Road and go about 2 miles to County J. Turn right (east) on J and go for 1.2 miles to County E.

Turn left on E and go 2.4 miles to County LO. Turn left on County LO and go 3.1 miles to Highway 67. After turning left on 67, go about 1 mile to County NN.

Turn right (west) on NN (Little Prairie Road) and go 3 miles to County H in Palmyra. You'll drive through the *Kettle Moraine State Forest,* an area very popular with off-road, fat-tire, rough-terrain bicyclists who love to ride the Emma Carlin and John Muir glacial bike trails.

Palmyra was named after an oasis city in the Syrian desert. This quiet little community has an interesting downtown area. In summer and autumn, watch for farmers with produce at roadside stands. The *Carlin House and Turner Museum*, (262) 495-2412, 112 N. Third St., has changing exhibits, a children's dress-up room, and a gift shop.

Follow H about 1 block to Highway 59. Turn left (west) on 59 and go 3.2 miles to Piper Road. Turn right on Piper Road and drive about 5 miles, crossing Spring Creek and Steel Brook, to Fremont Road. Turn left on Fremont and go less than 1 mile to County U.

If you stay on Fremont Rd. for another mile, you'll arrive in the city of Whitewater, which was first settled in 1836. Today it's a vibrant community of 13,500, including 10,500 students at the University of Wisconsin–Whitewater, which keeps the local cultural and arts scenes pulsating with exhibits, events, and entertainment. The campus, on W. Main St., was established in 1868. It has art gallery exhibits, lectures, musicals, theater productions, concerts, and historical markers, including the *Historical Log Cabin* located behind Hyer Hall. It was the first house built in Whitewater, in 1836.

Stop and shop at antique stores or grab a latte at a coffee shop. Or take a walking tour that includes a visit to Indian mounds dating back to 200 A.D. The *Whitewater Historical Museum*, (262) 473-2966, 301 W. Whitewater St., is housed in a refurbished 1850 railroad station.

The Ice Age Bicycle Trail segment starts at the Whitewater Lake ranger station southeast of town and continues through Johnson Center to Evansville (48.7 miles).

Turn right (west) on U and continue about 1 mile to County N. Turn right (north) on N and drive 4.7 miles, crossing Galloway Creek, passing through Cold Spring, and crossing the Bark River.

At the junction of Bark River Road (Wisconsin Rustic Road 84), turn left (west) and go 2.1 miles to Rock River Road. Enjoy this trip through wooded farmland. Watch for the sign to the artesian drinking fountain that is supplied with water from deep below the ground. You may see cranes, heron, wild turkeys, deer, owls, muskrats, and raccoons.

Turn right (north) on Rock River Road and go 0.7 mile to Highway 106 at the edge of Fort Atkinson.

Recently named "one of America's hottest little boomtowns" by *Money* magazine, Fort Atkinson was first established as a fort during the Black Hawk War in 1832 by Brigadier General Henry Atkinson. Originally called Fort Coscong, it had some 4,500 troops stationed here. Later settlers decided to honor Atkinson by naming the community after him.

The *Hoard Historical Museum and Dairy Shrine*, (920) 563-7769, 407 Merchants Ave., is named after former Wisconsin governor W. D. Hoard, who is considered the "father of Wisconsin's dairy industry." His Civil War–era mansion and home now holds an outstanding collection of information on the Black Hawk War, Native American artifacts, Civil War historical items, pioneer history, quilts, and settlers' items. On display is a restoration of the first frame house built in Fort Atkinson, the Dwight Foster House, in 1841. The Dairy Shrine preserves the rich heritage of the dairy industry in Wisconsin, with everything from milk stools, cow blankets, butter molds, and photos of champion cows to a dog-powered butter churn.

The Fireside Dinner Theater provides popular Broadway musicals in a venue set among the cornfields, along with outstanding dining and five gift shops (see accompanying article).

Turn left on 106, following it 8.7 miles as it winds through Fort Atkinson, runs north of Lake Koshkonong, and reaches the junction

Broadway Is Alive and Well in a Cornfield

Even after more than 20 successful years, it's still a surprise to some people that there's professional, Broadway-caliber theater out on the prairie in between the cornfields near Fort Atkinson, Wisconsin.

The *Fireside Dinner Theater*, (800) 477-9505, south of Fort Atkinson on Highway 26, is one of the Midwest's finest dinner theaters and Wisconsin's number-one year-round motor-coach attraction. The Fireside serves and entertains more than 450,000 guests each year.

The dinner theater is different from most in that it has a top-quality restaurant that can serve 1,000 guests and a separate but connected professional 652-seat theater. This arrangement avoids the common dinner theater problem of clinking dishes and wait staff interfering with the presentation of the play, and the less-than-ideal situation of having dessert in the dark. The Fireside menus are varied to complement the theme of each show.

The Fireside was built by the Klopcic family and is now operated by the second generation, who believe that a warm personal greeting, a great product and friendly, attentive service are the secret to success.

David Wolfran, the chef at the Fireside, was trained by the famous Culinary Institute of America; and the artistic director, Ed Flesch, has been in professional theater and has directed professional actors for over 20 years. Actors are auditioned and hired from the same pool of talent that feeds theaters in New York, Chicago, and Minneapolis.

The Fireside stages four plays that each run six to eight weeks, including a special annual Christmas show so popular that it runs from mid-October to Christmas.

The Fireside also operates several gift shops that feature fine collectibles, unusual imports, and specialty items that relate to the theme of the plays. The shops are open to the public, including those visitors not going to the current production.

In January 2000 the Fireside received the prestigious GEMmy Award from the Midwest Travel Writers Association. The award recognizes "outstanding travel destinations, attractions and experiences that exemplify the joy of discovery that travel holds and special experiences that make travel such a positive experience and rewarding adventure."

Barns, especially older ones, are disappearing from the Wisconsin countryside, but this tour will take you past some fine survivors. Photo by Gary Knowles.

central Wisconsin the largest Norwegian colony in the United States.

The strong ethnic influence continues today with the huge *Syttende Mai* (17th of May) annual festival celebrating Norway's independence.

Downtown Stoughton is a pleasant stretch of shops and old tobacco warehouses. There are excellent antique stores, gift shops, craft stores, coffee shops, and art galleries.

There are four historic districts in Stoughton with a fascinating array of architectural styles, and many buildings are on the National Register of Historic Places. Be sure to see the *Stoughton City Hall*, (608) 873-6677, 381 E. Main St., a Romanesque Revival beauty with a great clock tower and a second-floor opera house. The *Stoughton Historical Museum*, (608) 873-4797, 324 S. Page St., built in 1858 as a Universalist Church, holds historical artifacts from the area. The *Chamber of Commerce* office, (608) 873-7912, 532 E. Main St., is in a 1913 railroad depot.

At the end of Main St., the *Home Savings and Loan Building* contains rosemaling by Stoughton resident Ethel Kvalheim, who was honored by the King of Norway with the St. Olav Medal for her excellent work.

This area produces tobacco (used mostly for cigar wrappers); at one time Dunkirk Township produced more tobacco than any other township in the country.

with County A. Turn right (north) on A and go for 2.6 miles to County C. Turn left on C and travel for 1.5 miles to Asie Road.

Turn right on Asie and go for 1.3 miles to Rockdale Road. Turn right on Rockdale Road and drive about 1.5 miles to County B in Rockdale, the smallest incorporated town in Wisconsin with a population of 235.

Quick Trip Option: If you take County B north about 3 miles, you'll come to Cambridge, "the Salt-Glazed Pottery Capital of the World" and a favorite with artists and shoppers. Among the best of many shops are the famous *Rowe Pottery Works,* (608) 423-3935, 217 W. Main St.; *The Pantry,* selling gourmet and specialty foods; and *Reflections of Culture,* (608) 423-3223, with wonderful Native American work. There are numerous antique and craft stores as well, many of them assembled under one roof in the *Cambridge Antique Mall,* across the street from Rowe Pottery.

From Rockdale, follow B south and then west for about 13 miles, crossing Highway 73 and I-90 and joining Highway 51 just north of Stoughton. The friendly community of Stoughton was settled in the 1840s when a major wave of Norwegian immigration made this part of south-

Turn right on Highway 51/B and drive for 3 miles to where B turns left (west). You'll be skirting the southwest shore of Lake Kegonsa (an Indian word meaning "lake of fishes").

Turn on B and go for 7.6 miles to the junction with County MM. Turn right (north) on MM and continue straight about 4.1 miles to the intersection with Highway 14. Follow 14 to the Beltline (Highway 12/18/151) in Madison, turn west on the Beltline, and follow it about 0.6 mile to Fish Hatchery Road, where we started.

Tour 26
Rustic Run on Wisconsin's Riviera

Lake Geneva—via Wisconsin Rustic Roads—Lake Geneva

Distance: 59 miles

The beautiful Lake Geneva area has been a favorite getaway for Chicagoland people for generations. They say that back at the turn of the century the wealthy estate owners would catch a train out of Chicago after work on Friday, ride up to the end of the lake where their steam-powered yachts were waiting, and race across the lake to their mansions.

Today there are lots of fine accommodations, great restaurants, championship golf courses, and more fun than ever.

The one drawback to this area—at least for the purpose of this book—is that there has been a lot of development in the rural areas, along the lakes and rivers. That makes it pretty difficult to put together a big "back roads" tour.

But, thanks to the Wisconsin Rustic Roads System, it is possible to put together a wonderful loop tour that's got some excellent rural runs—and then will still give you time in Lake Geneva for shopping, eating, playing golf, or just relaxing. Whatever suits your pleasure. Have some fun! There are lots of jogs and turns on this route. If you get off course, just jog back and enjoy even more rustic running!

We'll start just west of the heart of Lake Geneva, at the intersection of Highway 50 and Rustic Road 29 (Snake Road).

The Oneota and Hopewell people were the first to live here 3,000 years ago; then, more recently, the Potawatomi lived beside this "clear water" they called "kish-way-kee-tow." They left, reluctantly, following the 1832 Black Hawk War—but not until 1836 when they were forced out and the new immigrants started moving in.

By 1837 the town of Lake Geneva was platted and land was selling for about $1.25 per acre. By 1840 the town was growing and even had two hotels. Following the Civil War, the lake became a resort favorite with wealthy Chicago families, and visitors included Mary Todd Lincoln, General Sherman, and General Sheridan. President Calvin Coolidge favored the area for his "summer White House." The coming of the railroad increased tourism and development of the area, and in winter ice cut from Lake Geneva was sent back to Chicago

One of the most unusual boat trips in the country is the "mail run" offered by the Geneva Lakes Cruise Line. Wisconsin Department of Tourism photo by GK.

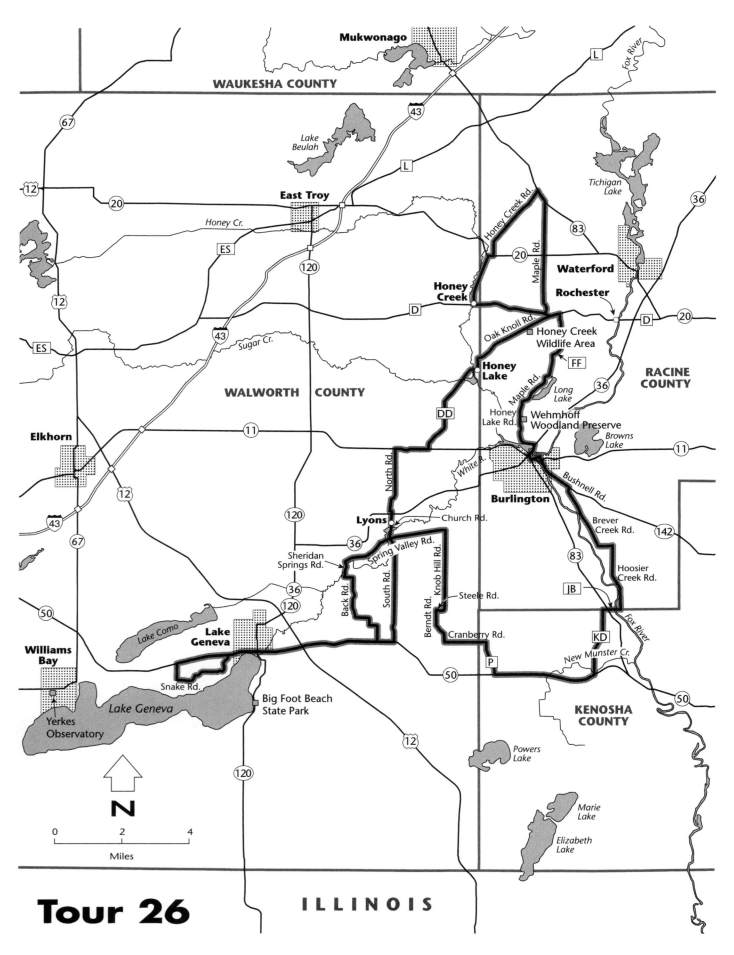

Mukwonago

WAUKESHA COUNTY

67

Lake Beulah

43

Tichigan Lake

36

12

20

20

L

L

East Troy

Honey Cr.

ES

120

Fox River

Honey Creek Rd.

Maple Rd.

20

83

Waterford

Rochester

Honey Creek

D

D

20

Oak Knoll Rd.

☐ Honey Creek Wildlife Area

FF

36

RACINE COUNTY

43

Sugar Cr.

ES

WALWORTH COUNTY

Honey Lake

Maple Rd.

Long Lake

DD

Honey Lake Rd.

Wehmhoff Woodland Preserve

Browns Lake

Elkhorn

11

11

White R.

Burlington

Bushnell Rd.

12

North Rd.

Church Rd.

Lyons

36

Spring Valley Rd.

Brever Creek Rd.

142

Sheridan Springs Rd.

83

Hoosier Creek Rd.

67

36

120

South Rd.

Back Rd.

Berndt Rd.

Knob Hill Rd.

Steele Rd.

JB

50

Lake Como

Lake Geneva

Cranberry Rd.

KD

Fox River

Williams Bay

Snake Rd.

50

P

50

New Munster Cr.

☐ **Big Foot Beach State Park**

12

KENOSHA COUNTY

50

☐ **Yerkes Observatory**

Lake Geneva

Powers Lake

↑

N

Marie Lake

120

Elizabeth Lake

0   2   4

Miles

Tour 26

I L L I N O I S

Horses, barns, and other vestiges of life in simpler times line the rustic roads near Lake Geneva. Photo by Gary Knowles.

for the city dwellers' "iceboxes." Today the town reflects its heritage in the great architecture, fine old homes, lake estates, and the residents' continuing appreciation of the good life on the "clear water."

Lake Geneva is Wisconsin's second deepest at 135 feet. It has 5,262 acres of water and is 7.6 miles long by 2.1 miles wide. A beautiful 26-mile walking trail, using old Indian paths, circles the entire lake. You can get a map to it from the *Chamber of Commerce,* (800) 345-1020, 201 Wrigley Dr.

Here are some of the many attractions in the area.

The *Geneva Lake Cruise Line,* (800) 558-5911, at the Riviera Docks in downtown Lake Geneva, offers narrated lake tours, Dixieland cruises—and the famous "mail run," where a fast-stepping U.S. Postal Service carrier delivers mail by cruise boat from mid-June to mid-September. The docks are in the *Riviera,* a beautiful 1933 structure, where big bands led by Tommy Dorsey and Louis Armstrong once played.

Big Foot Beach State Park, (262) 248-2528, has camping, hiking, and swimming facilities.

The *Geneva Area Museum of History,* (262) 248-6060, features fine exhibits of local historical items, while at *Yerkes Observatory,* (262) 245-5555, in Williams Bay, you can see the world's largest refracting telescope. There are many fine lodging options, but favorites include the *Grand Geneva Resort and Spa,* (800) 558-3417 or (262) 248-8811; *The Cove of Lake Geneva,* (800) 221-0031, an all-suite hotel; the *Geneva Inn,* (800) 441-5881, an elegant resort-inn; *Harbor Shores Best Western,* (888) 746-7371, with deluxe rooms; *Case's Turn of the Century,* (262) 248-4989, a bed and breakfast with a great porch and gardens; *Oaks*

Inn, (262) 248-9711, a bed and breakfast in a private lakeside mansion; the *T. C. Smith Inn,* (800) 423-0233, a B & B in an 1845 downtown mansion; and *The Watersedge of Lake Geneva,* (262) 245-9845, the place Chicago gangster Bugs Moran escaped to in the 1930s.

Great food in the area comes in all styles. Here are a few of many good restaurants: *The Cactus Club,* (262) 248-1999, is the place for southwestern cuisine; at the Abbey resort, (262) 275-6811, the *Monaco Dining Room* has continental cuisine, and *La Tour de Bois* specializes in French cooking. *Popeye's,* (262) 248-4381, is a great casual place for barbeque, chicken, burgers, and apple pie. The Grand Geneva resort features the *Ristorante Brissago* for authentic Italian cuisine and the *Newport Grill* for excellent steaks and seafood. The *Red Geranium,* (262) 248-3637, is a wonderful intimate dining experience.

Antique hunting and shopping are a true delight here, with one hundred shops in the downtown area alone. And golfers will need every club in the bag. The area has some of the finest courses in the state (see article).

Get a free guide to all the things going on in the area by calling (800) 345-1020.

At the intersection of 50 and Rustic Road 29 (Snake Road),

Golfing on Wisconsin's Riviera

The pleasingly posh *Grand Geneva Resort* offers two challenging golf courses. The Brute, at almost 7,000 yards, has long been a favorite of "Big Bertha" hitters, while the Highlands is a challenging Scottish re-do of that lovable old iconoclast, Briarpatch. At *Geneva National Golf Club,* (262) 245-7000, you can choose from three 18-hole championship courses designed by and named for living legends: the Palmer, Trevino, and Player. Each course is a beauty that will require your whole set of clubs. *The Hillmoor Golf Club,* (262) 248-4570, has been testing resort-goers since 1924. Nearby in Fontana you can play the spectacular *Abbey Springs,* (414) 275-6113, a well-manicured layout at The Abbey resort overlooking Lake Geneva.

just west of Lake Geneva, turn left onto Rustic Road 29 and drive for 3.6 miles back to 50, all the while "snaking" south toward the lake, then winding west through some country beauty (great in autumn!).

Turn right (east) on 50 and go about 2.4 miles to cross Highway 120, another 1.4 miles to pass under Highway 12, and then 2.2 miles to Rustic Road 12 (Back Road). Enjoy this great drive along "Wisconsin's Riviera."

Wisconsin's Rustic Roads

Recognizing that much of the rural beauty of the state was disappearing as suburbs grew into the countryside, the Wisconsin State Legislature established Wisconsin's Rustic Roads System in 1973 to preserve some of the essence of our rural heritage.

To qualify as a Rustic Road, a roadway must have outstanding natural features, like rugged terrain, natural prairie, wild lakeshore, or outstanding vistas that make the road unique. The roads must be lightly traveled and thus are almost never "great shortcuts" or fast alternate routes to anywhere. By their nature, these roads are out of the way and quiet paths that recall a less hectic time. Most Rustic Roads are at least 2 miles long and have a speed limit of 45 mph. Some are gravel but many are paved (all of those we take in this book are paved).

The Wisconsin Department of Transportation works closely with local units of government to mark the roads with a distinctive brown and yellow rectangular sign that says "Rustic Road" and has the road number.

You can get a free guide to all 84 Rustic Roads (as of April 2000) by calling the Department of Tourism at (800) 432-8747. As Governor Tommy G. Thompson says in his introduction to the booklet, "Shed the hustle and bustle of other places and surround yourself in the serenity of very special places."

Turn left (north) on Rustic Road 12 and follow it along Back Road, Jones Road, Sheridan Springs Road, Buckby Road, and Spring Valley Road for about 4.7 miles to the junction with Church Road on your left. (Church Road is Rustic Road 12 for another 0.7 mile).

Continue straight (east) on Spring Valley Road, which becomes Rustic Road 11, for about 1.5 miles to the junction with Knob Road. Turn right on Knob Road and go about 2.7 miles to Steel Road and then to Berndt Road (Rustic Road 36). Turn left on Berndt and go for about 1 mile to Cranberry Road (also Rustic Road 36).

Turn left on Cranberry Road, going about 1.3 miles into Kenosha County and the junction with Dyer Lake Road (County P). Turn right (south) on Dyer Lake Road and travel about 1.1 miles to Highway 50.

Turn left (east) on 50 and drive for about 3 miles to the junction with County KD.

Turn left (north) on KD, crossing New Muenster Creek and traveling about 2 miles to County JB.

Turn right (east) on JB across Highway 80, going about 0.4 mile to Hoosier Creek Road (Rustic Road 42). Turn left (north) on Hoosier Creek Road, traveling 2 miles to Brever Creek Road (still Rustic Road 42) and continuing northwest for 4.4 miles to the junction with Highway 142 (Bushnell Road).

Turn left on 142 and go northwest for about 1.1 miles into Burlington and the junction with Highway 11. Jog north and west a few blocks on 11 to Highway 83 (right) then about a block to Grove Street to the junction with Highway 36 North.

Turn right on 36 North and go about 0.4 mile over the railroad tracks, past Echo Lake Park, and turn left (watch for the green and white street sign "To Honey Lake Road"). Continue north on Honey Lake Road (Rustic Road 2), following the small brown Rustic Road signs and traveling through a canopy of trees past marshes and the Wehmhoff Woodland Preserve.

Follow the Rustic Road signs as the road curves right (about 1.6 miles from its start) and becomes Maple Road. Continue for 1.9 miles to Academy Road. Turn right on Academy and go for 0.5 mile following the Rustic Road 2 signs left onto Heritage Road. Continue for 1 mile to County D, which is Washington Avenue. Turn left on D and jog 0.4 mile to Maple Road. Turn right on Maple, going 2.2 miles to Highway 20, another 1 mile to Hill Valley Road, and another 0.7 mile to Highway 83, the end of Rustic Road 2.

Turn left (northwest) on 83 and go about 0.4 mile to Honey Creek Road. Turn left (southwest) on Honey Creek Road, going about 2.5 miles to Highway 20.

Jog right (west) on 20 for about 0.1 mile, then jog left on Honey Creek Road for about 1.5 miles to the community of Honey Creek and the junction with County D. Turn left on D and go 2.3 miles to Oak Knoll Road (Rustic Road 25).

Turn right (southeast) on Oak Knoll Road and go for 2.5 miles through the Honey Creek Wildlife Area to County DD. Turn left on DD for about 3.2 miles to Highway 11

Turn right (west) on 11 and go for about 1 mile to the junction with North Road. Turn left (south) on North Road and drive 2 miles into Lyons.

Continue straight (south) on Church Street (Rustic Road 12) for about 0.8 mile, jog left on Spring Valley Road to South Road (Rustic Road 11), and continue south about 3.2 miles to Highway 50, cruising through country woods and farmland.

Turn right (west) on 50 and drive about 4.5 miles back about into Lake Geneva.

Tour 27
Black River Ramble

Black River Falls—Hatfield—Millston—Cataract—Sparta—Four Corners—Melrose—Hegg—Whitehall—Taylor—Black River Falls

Distance: 162 miles

Gently rolling hills dotted by farms is a scene repeated hundreds of times throughout Wisconsin. Wisconsin Department of Tourism photo by GK.

If you enjoy spectacular scenery, Native American history, astronauts, biking, folk art, and like to stop at excellent out-of-the-way historic sites . . . well, grab your camera, binoculars, and antiques guide. We've got a tour for you.

We'll do a good deal of running up, down, and across coulees, bluffs, hills, marshes, and places you've never seen before. Bring plenty of film. And some cash. Watch for garage sales, flea markets, and farm markets where you may find some treasure—or just a great apple.

This tour demonstrates that there's a lot of Wisconsin still waiting for its much-deserved moment in the spotlight. Your advantage is to get there before the rest of the world finds out.

So what are you waiting for? Go. Go!

Start in downtown Black River Falls at the junction of Highways 27/12 and 54.

Black River Falls is the gateway to the 65,000-acre *Black River State Forest,* (715) 284-1400. The town was first settled by trappers and traders about 1819 and before that by the Ho-Chunk people. Today their descendants operate the *Majestic Pines Bingo and Casino,* (800) 657-4621, with 400 slot machines and an excellent buffet; it's about 4 miles east of town on Highway 54. For a free guide to the area, call (800) 404-4008.

Head north from town on 27/12 for about 3 miles to the junction with County E. Turn right (northeast) on E and drive to the junction with County K in Hatfield. Here you can enjoy the eclectic collections at the *Thunderbird Museum and Shops,* (715) 333-5841. You'll find 21 rooms filled with art, Native American artifacts, antique weapons, dolls, local minerals, and other collections.

Turn right (south) on K and follow it to the junction with Highway 54, crossing the Black River just south of beautiful Lake Arbutus along the way.

Turn left (east) on 54, go about 6.5 miles to North Settlement Road (Rustic Road 54), and turn right (south). Enjoy this 12.5-mile drive through the Black River Forest and pine-scented air. At the *Dike 17 Lookout Tower* you can get a view of the surrounding marshland. Watch for sandhill cranes, migratory birds, bald eagles, and deer.

Continue on North Settlement Road (still Rustic Road 54) for about 11 miles to County O and then the town of Millston. Continue on O to the junction with Highway 27, crossing, along the way, Clear Creek, Stony Creek, and Shamrock Creek and driving through the town of Shamrock.

Turn left (south) on 27 and go to the junction with County II/B in the town of Cataract. As you pass through it, you'll notice Dustin Creek, which was the site for the early settlers' gristmill and sawmill. The swiftly flowing water inspired the town's name.

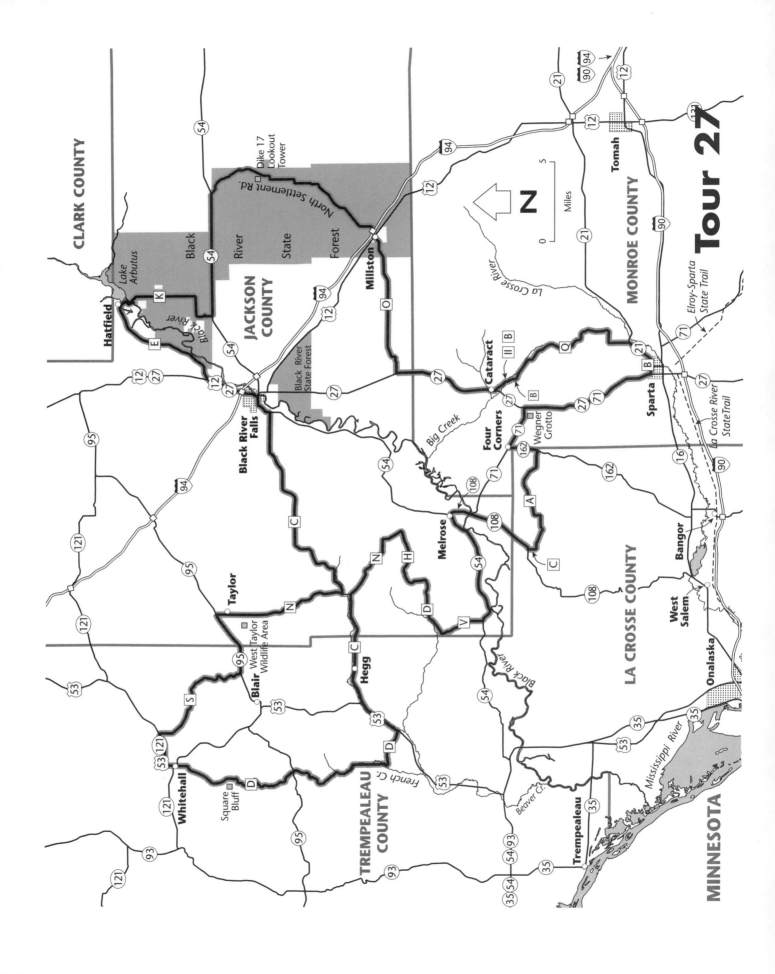

Tour 27

N

0 5 Miles

CLARK COUNTY

JACKSON COUNTY

MONROE COUNTY

LA CROSSE COUNTY

TREMPEALEAU COUNTY

MINNESOTA

Lake Arbutus

Black River State Forest

Dike 17 Lookout Tower

North Settlement Rd.

Hatfield

Black River

Black River Falls

Millston

Taylor

West Taylor Wildlife Area

Blair

Hegg

Whitehall

Square Bluff

Melrose

Four Corners

Cataract

Wegner Grotto

Big Creek

Black River

French Cr.

Beaver Cr.

La Crosse River

Elroy-Sparta State Trail

La Crosse River State Trail

Sparta

Tomah

Bangor

West Salem

Onalaska

Trempealeau

Mississippi River

Turn left onto II/B and go about 1 mile to where the road splits into County II and County B. *The Little Falls Railroad and Doll Museum*, (608) 272-3266, is located just east of Cataract on County II. Housed in two separate buildings, the museum showcases dolls from the 1800s to the present. The railroad museum has rolling stock, magazines, railroad memorabilia, a telegrapher's station, a 1,000-book library, and a Milwaukee Bay Railroad caboose.

Follow B about 0.9 mile to the intersection with County Q. Turn right (south) on Q and follow it to the junction with Highway 21. Turn right and follow 21 into Sparta.

Sparta was first settled in 1849 and thought to have been named to honor "the Spartan courage of the pioneers" who were the first to establish roots here. Today it is best known as "the Bicycling Capital of America," with access to the famous *Elroy-Sparta State Bicycle Trail* (34 miles and three tunnels) and the *La Crosse River State Trail* (21 miles). Some 60,000 trips are made each year on the Elroy-Sparta Trail alone, (608) 462-2410.

The *Deke Slayton Memorial Space and Bicycle Museum*, (608) 269-0033, features the memorabilia of Sparta's native-son astronaut, along with interactive displays, original artwork, and several space suits. Slayton flew in the Mercury and Apollo programs and NASA has generously helped make this exhibit a real winner. The adjoining bike museum is also an enjoyable stop.

The *Monroe County Museum*, (608) 269-8680, located in the former Masonic Temple, houses local history displays and is an excellent source of genealogical information.

The *Ben Biken Statue* is a huge fiberglass statue of a bike that was made in Sparta and is a favorite local photo spot, at the intersection of South Water St. and Highway 16.

At the junction with County B in Sparta, continue straight (west) on B and go about 0.5 mile to Highway 27/71. Turn right (north) and proceed out of Sparta for about 7.5 miles to where 71 splits off from 27 and turns west.

Soon after the split on Highway 71, look for the *Wegner Grotto*, (608) 269-8680, a beautiful piece of 1930s folk art sculpture built by Paul and Matilda Wegner, German immigrants who wanted to create a memorial to their American patriotism and religious beliefs. You'll find about 30 pieces of art built with concrete and glass. There's a 12-foot replica of the *Bremen*, the ocean liner that carried them to America, their 50th anniversary wedding cake, a peace monument, wishing well, church, an American flag—and an art fence around it all. The work has been purchased and preserved by the Kohler Foundation.

Follow 71 for about 2.4 miles to Four Corners and the junction with Highway 162. Turn left (south) on 162 and go to County A. Turn right

(west) on A (True Road) and follow it to the junction with County C, crossing Sand Creek along the way.

Turn right (north) on C and go for about 1 mile to the junction with Highway 108. Turn right on 108, driving into Jackson County to the junction with Highway 54 at Melrose.

Turn left (west) on 54 and go to the junction with County V, cruising through the Red School Valley and the town of North Bend.

Turn right (north) on V and proceed to the junction with County D at South Beaver Creek. Turn right (east) on D and go to the junction with County H. Turn left (north) on H and drive to the junction with County N.

Turn left (northwest) on N and go to the junction with County C. Turn left (west) on C and

How Cows and Rail Barons Made Wisconsin Good for Sports Cars, Motorcycles, and Bicycles

She's cute and cuddly (pun intended) and has been called "the foster mother of the human race," but you probably didn't know that in addition to giving us cheese, ice cream, and milk mustaches, it was the dairy cow that teamed up with rail barons to make Wisconsin such a great state in which to accelerate a Porsche, hug a curve on a Harley, or pedal a Trek.

You see, the cow likes to be milked twice every day (some three times!) and when farmers get that milk it's relatively perishable. They have to get it to market—quickly and reliably. In Wisconsin's early days that meant getting it to a cheese factory nearby, usually by horse and buggy and in milk cans. And that meant good roads. Well, farmers were pretty much in political control so they decided that a good road system stretching well into the hills and coulees was an absolute necessity. Their strong support for improved (and, ultimately, *paved*) roads connecting every farm in every valley has resulted in Wisconsin having one of the finest primary, secondary, and tertiary highway systems in the world. It's these "milk roads" that are also sensational for backcountry cruising in your roadster, on a motorcycle, or on a bicycle.

So, tip your hat to the next cow you pass. And, while you bicyclists are at it, be sure to thank those rail barons too. It's the rights of way that they used, abandoned, and then turned over to the state that have made Wisconsin a world leader in the development of off-highway biking. The granddaddy of them all, the famous Elroy-Sparta Trail, passes through three tunnels and has camping and services along the route. There are 14 other trails covering some 800 miles of abandoned rail right of way. Get a free *Wisconsin Biking Guide* listing all of them by calling the Department of Tourism at (800) 432-TRIP.

So if you ride a bicycle, raise a toast to those old rail moguls whose "highways" now give you access to some beautiful backcountry scenery. And you there, on your Sportster or in your Mustang—how about a little "toot" for ol' bossy and the pack of heifers as you come over the hill!

Head down any beautiful country road in this tour and very soon you'll spot a herd of Holsteins. Wisconsin Department of Tourism photo by GK.

proceed to the junction with Highway 53. Along the way, you'll pass through the community of Hegg, named after Colonel Hans Christian Heg, Wisconsin's famous Civil War veteran and commander of the 15th Wisconsin Norwegian Regiment, Colonel Hegg,.

This is Trempealeau County, originally Lakota territory. The name means "mountain that stands in water" and refers to the bluffs that extend right to the edge of the Mississippi River. It is known as one of Wisconsin's leading dairy and agriculture areas. There are some 38,000 milk cows, mostly Holstein, and about 10 million chickens in the county. It ranks 54th out of the top 100 dairy counties in the U.S. It is also one of the most scenic. Its elevations vary, from marshy stream bottoms and wetlands to limestone bluffs reaching 1,396 feet in some places. Watch for wildlife—white-tailed deer, songbirds, game birds, and wild turkeys—as you roll by.

Turn left (southwest) on 53 and proceed to the junction with County D. Turn right (west) on D and follow it as it swings north, near French Creek Church, then crosses French Creek. Keep your camera handy. This whole spectacular route begs to be photographed.

Continue going north on D into Whitehall, crossing Lakes Coulee Creek and Highway 95, passing west of Peterson Coulee, and running along Irvin Creek.

Whitehall was settled in the 1850s but it was agriculture and the Green Bay and Western Railroad that spurred its growth. The village was organized in 1873. It is thought that the name refers to Whitehall, England, since many of the settlers were English. Today this area is favored by many Amish people, and their traditional lifestyle is evident throughout the region.

In Whitehall, pick up Highway 53/121 and proceed northeast about 2 miles to the junction with County S at Coral City. Turn right (south) on S and go to Highway 95. Turn left (east) on 95, crossing back into Jackson County and continuing to the junction with County P and County N.

Turn right (south) on N, passing Taylor on the left and continuing to the junction with County C, crossing French Creek and Skutley Creek along the way.

Turn left (east) on C and continue to the junction with Highway 54 just south of Black River Falls. Turn left (north) on 54 and return to the junction with Highway 27/12 in Black River Falls.

148

Tour 28
Winging It Around Horicon

Sun Prairie—Keyeser—Columbus—Fall River—Beaver Dam—Leipsig—Oak Grove—Waupun—Kekoskee—Mayville—Hustisford—Watertown—Richwood—Hubbleton—Waterloo—Marshall—Sun Prairie

Distance: 145 miles

A critical habitat for thousands of migrating birds, the Horicon Marsh has been designated as a "Wetland of International Importance." Wisconsin Department of Tourism photo by GK.

The spectacle of the Canada geese migration through the Horicon Marsh National Wildlife Refuge is a natural wonder that you just have to see to believe. Hundreds of thousands of geese fill the sky and their honking is as loud as a Manhattan traffic jam. When a field of them takes off all at once, a huge *whooosh* fills the air.

To get to the marsh you can take the same old highways (pretty good ones, really, but we've seen them too many times before), or you can wander in, taking some wonderful trails, old roads, and hilly little runs that add zest and a bit of discovery to the run.

With the same wild spirit that drives the geese, I feel the lure of the narrower road, the tug of the woods and marshes, the compelling call of the route that meanders along every elbow of the river. This is the way to see the wild. Leave those four-lane roads to the long-haul truckers with a delivery to make. I'll see you out on the old milk run, cutting through the cattails and poking around the pussy willows.

Start in Sun Prairie at the junction of County C (Hoepker Road) and Highway 151.

Sun Prairie is the town where the most famous of American women painters, Georgia O'Keefe, was born in 1887. She lived in this area and left as a teenager, never in her 98 years to return—or even to look back fondly, as near as anyone can tell. Too bad. She went first to New York and then to the desert and red rock area of Arizona, where she created exotic paintings of rocks, flowers, and bleached cattle bones; she also had buzzards and scorpions for company. Just think of what greater works she might have left if she had instead drawn her inspiration from her own backyard, applied her awesome talents to the Canada goose, the Horicon Marsh, and the natural beauty of Wisconsin!

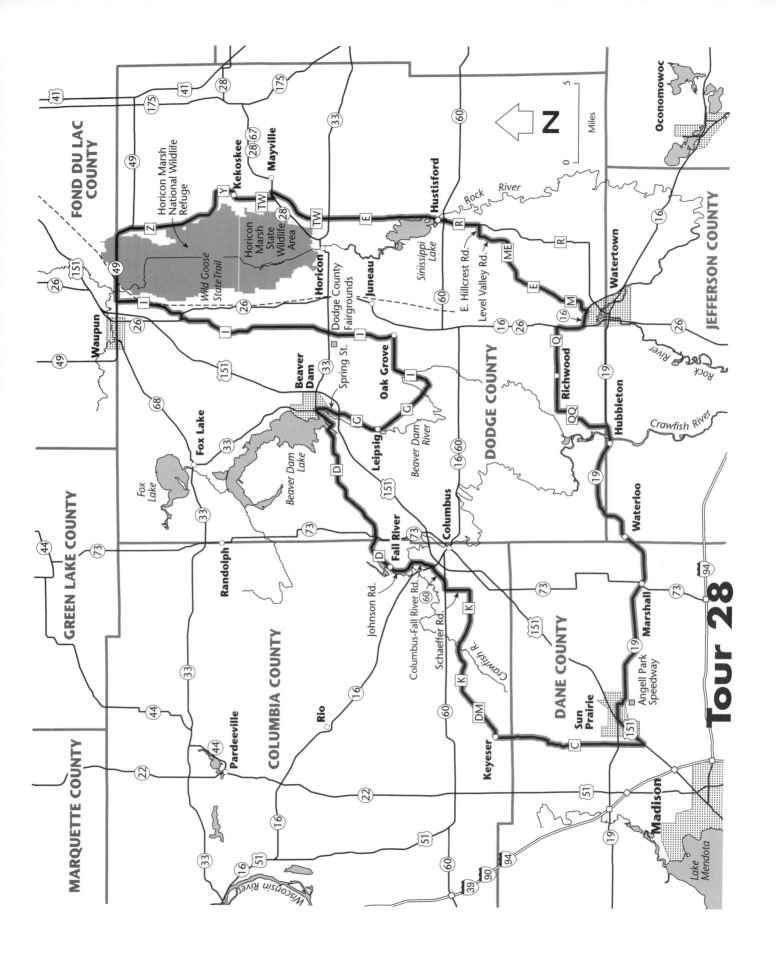

MARQUETTE COUNTY

GREEN LAKE COUNTY

FOND DU LAC COUNTY

COLUMBIA COUNTY

DODGE COUNTY

JEFFERSON COUNTY

DANE COUNTY

Horicon Marsh National Wildlife Refuge

Horicon Marsh State Wildlife Area

Wild Goose State Trail

Dodge County Fairgrounds

Kekoskee

Mayville

Hustisford

Horicon

Juneau

Watertown

Oconomowoc

Waupun

Fox Lake

Beaver Dam

Oak Grove

Leipsig

Fall River

Columbus

Richwood

Hubbleton

Waterloo

Marshall

Sun Prairie

Keyeser

Randolph

Rio

Pardeeville

Madison

Spring St.

Johnson Rd.

Columbus-Fall River Rd.

Schaeffer Rd.

E. Hillcrest Rd.

Level Valley Rd.

Sinissippi Lake

Rock River

Rock River

Crawfish River

Crawfish R.

Beaver Dam Lake

Beaver Dam River

Fox Lake

Wisconsin River

Lake Mendota

Angell Park Speedway

Miles

N

Tour 28

Go north on C for 9.3 miles to County DM at Keyeser. We'll be driving across lots of farm country and plenty of wetlands today, so you'll see Canada geese, cranes, ducks, and other migratory birds all along the way. Also, watch for the beautiful, gnarly, twisted burr oak trees that look like they belong in a story about the Headless Horseman and Sleepy Hollow!

Turn right on DM and go for 2 miles to the junction with County K. Go straight (northeast) on K for 8.3 miles across the Crawfish River and Robbins Creek to Schaeffer Road.

Turn left on Schaeffer and go 1.4 miles to Highway 60. Turn right (east) on 60 and drive for 1.8 miles to Highway 16 and Columbus-Fall River Road.

Quick Trip Option: Turn right on 16 and visit the town of Columbus, known for its huge (150 dealers) *Antique Mall,* (920) 623-2669, 239 Whitney St., and (in the same building) the *Christopher Columbus Museum,* (920) 623-1992, with more than 2,000 souvenirs of the 1893 Chicago Columbian Exposition. Downtown, don't miss the Louis Sullivan–designed *Farmers and Merchants Bank* building, (920) 623-4000, 129 W. James St., or the *Columbus City Hall,* (920) 623-5900, built in 1892 to honor the 400th anniversary of the discovery of America.

Jog left on 16 for 0.1 mile, then turn right on Columbus-Fall River Road. Follow it 2 miles to Johnson Road. Turn right on Johnson and go 0.6 mile through Fall River to County D.

Bear right on D and go for 11.1 miles to the junction with County G.

Turn right (south) on County D/G and go 0.4 mile to D; turn left and go 1.3 miles to County G (Spring Street) in Beaver Dam.

Beaver Dam, with a population of 14,000 people, is the largest community in Dodge County and is the center of an area with many parks and recreation areas. The city is on Beaver Dam Lake, which stretches 14 miles to Fox Lake and has 41 miles of shoreline. The *Dodge County Museum,* (920) 887-1266, 105 Park Ave., in the Williams Free Library Building, houses the first automobile delivered in the county, Native American artifacts, and displays showing pioneer life in Wisconsin. Sewing fans will want to stop at *Nancy's Notions* (home of the *Sewing with Nancy* Wisconsin Public Television program), 333 Beichl St., (920) 887-0391.

Turn right on G and go about 8 miles to the junction with County I, traveling across Highway 151, following Beaver Dam Creek past the German settlement of Leipsig, and driving across Shaw Brook.

Turn left (northeast) on I and go about 4.8 miles to Oak Grove and the junction with County A. A little less than halfway through this

The Horicon Marsh

The Horicon Marsh National Wildlife Refuge (22,287 acres) is what remains of an ancient lake bed formed by the Green Bay lobe of the Wisconsin glacier about 10,000 years ago.

Many Native Americans lived and hunted along the marsh, including Paleo-Indians (nomadic hunters), Hopewellian Indians (mound builders), and Woodland Indians (Potawatomi and Ho-Chunk). In 1846 a dam and lumber mill were built on the south end, creating the world's largest man-made lake. The dam was removed in 1869 and the area reverted to marshland.

The state portion of the refuge (southern third), called the *Horicon Marsh Wildlife Area,* (920) 387-7860, was established in 1927, and the federal refuge (northern two thirds) was established in 1941. The area was designated a "Wetland of International Importance" by the Ramsar Convention and a "Globally Important Bird Area" by the American Bird Conservancy. It is one of the world's most important wild areas for migratory birds. Administered by the federal Fish and Wildlife Administration, it is the world's largest freshwater (and cattail) marsh at 32,000 acres.

The area hosts from 100,000 to 300,000 Canada geese every year and you'll see them in wetlands and fields all along this tour route. The Canada geese you see here weigh from 7 to 10 pounds and have a wingspread of up to six feet. They fly from 100 to 1,000 feet above the ground while on feeding flights and as high as 9,000 feet when migrating. They normally fly about 40 mph but can reach up to 70 mph with the right tailwind. At the end of April they migrate north to Canada's Hudson Bay area where they raise families. They return to Horicon in late September to mid-October. Their life span is about five years in the wild, 30 in captivity.

The marsh also provides habitat for 268 species of birds, including ducks, cranes, herons, and shorebirds. It's a popular place to visit, and estimates place the number of travelers through the area at 400,000 per year.

The Wild Goose Bicycle Trail, (920) 386-3700, skirts the west side of the marsh and runs for 34 miles from Juneau to Fond du Lac. The annual *Horicon Bird Festival,* (920) 387-2685, takes place each May, with activities for every bird lover and outdoor enthusiast. Early morning field trips offer opportunities to see a great variety of birds; there are workshops teaching bird identification, bird-banding demonstrations, a wildlife art show, and a wildflower identification program.

stretch, you'll pass through the area known as Pumpkin Center, which really lives up to its name in the fall; try to visit it then.

Turn left (north) on I (it is joined by County A for about 5 miles) and drive about 14 miles to Highway 26. Along the way, you pass the Dodge County Fairgrounds, cross Highway 33, drive through Rolling Prairie and Burnett Corners, and cross Mill Creek.

Turn right (east) where 26 briefly merges with County I, then follow I left (north) for 4.5 miles to Highway 49 just east of Waupun. You'll run along the western border of the Horicon Marsh National Wildlife Refuge (HMNWR), (920) 387-2658, then cross Plum Creek. (See article.)

Quick Trip Option: Waupun, home to the state prison, also has seven outstanding pieces of historic sculpture. The most famous may be Earl Fraser's *End of the Trail.* Fraser used Chief John Big Tree as a model, whom you may recognize, since his face was used as the model for the face on the buffalo nickel and the old Pontiac automobile emblem. For a guide to city sculpture call (920) 324-3491. *The Waupun Heritage Museum,* (920) 324-3491, is located in the Carnegie Library, 22 S. Madison St., which was built in 1907 using $11,653 donated by industrialist Andrew Carnegie. Also Waupun becomes "Truck City USA" the second weekend of August every year, as it welcomes anyone with a truck (about 500 on average) to join in the parade and fun.

Turn right (east) on 49 and go 5.2 miles to County Z. Along the way, you'll cross into the northern end of the HMNWR, where the *Horicon Auto Trail* pull-off is located.

Turn right (south) on Z and drive 7.5 miles to County Y. You'll be skirting the east side of the HMNWR. About halfway along, you'll come to the road for the Visitor's Center (well worth a stop to pick up helpful materials, meet the rangers, and see exhibits).

Turn right (south) on Y and go 1 mile to County TW and Kekoskee, the site of a former Ho-Chunk village; the name means "friendly village."

Turn right on TW and go west, then south, 2.8 miles to Highway 28/TW. Stay on TW, jogging left 0.2 mile on 28, then turn right (south) on TW and drive 6.2 miles to County E.

Quick Trip Options: Going east on Highway 28 for a short distance will take you into Mayville, known as "the Historic Gateway to the Horicon Marsh." Don't miss the *White Limestone School* building, (920) 387-3474, on North Main St. It was used as a public school for 125 years, from 1857 to 1981. During part of that tenure (1880-1897), the

school housed children from kindergarten through high school. The Hugo Fenske Animal Room is full of mounted animals Mr. Fenske shot on safaris and some trophy fish. The Edgar Mueller photo gallery displays his work focusing on natural and rural Wisconsin. A superb collection of arrowheads, baseball history, and Boy Scout items are also in the museum.

The Hollenstein Wagon and Carriage Factory Museum, (920) 387-5530, 55 N. German St., is operated by the Mayville Historical Society and includes vehicles built here in the 19th century.

Be sure to drive through the historic downtown and stop (maybe spend a night) at the beautiful and famous *Audubon Inn,* (920) 387-5858, which was built in 1896. The inn also serves delicious food and is ranked among the top restaurants in Wisconsin. Antiques shoppers will like *The Treasure Trove,* (920) 387-5777, and the *Carriage Haus,* (800) 665-1375 or (920) 387-4099.

Going west on Highway 28 for about 4 miles will bring you into Horicon, which was once a huge Ho-Chunk village. The name is based on a Mohican word meaning "clear water." For a map that will guide you on a historical walking tour, contact the Horicon *Chamber of Commerce,* (920) 485-3200. *The Horicon Historical Society,* (920) 485-3200, is located in the Georgian-style *Saterlee Clark House* (built in 1860) at 322 Winter St. This is a good stop for history lovers and those who like Native American artifacts. *Horicon Ledge Park,* (920) 387-5450, east of town off Highway 28 and Raasch's Hill Rd., is an 82-acre recreational area with camping and picnic areas. It's at the edge of the Niagara Escarpment and offers interesting hikes, unusual rock formations, and lots of scenic views. Check here with *Blue Heron Tours* for guided adventures into "the Everglades of the North," (920) 485-4663. One of the more interesting places to eat in the area is the *Pyramid Restaurant,* (920) 885-6611, on Highway 33 between Horicon and Beaver Dam.

Travel straight on County E 4.6 miles to the junction with County R in Hustisford. The town was named for John Hustis, who built his home here in 1851. You can tour the *Hustis Home,* (920) 349-3501, and enjoy historical artifacts dating back to the founding of the town.

Follow R south 2.7 miles to East Hillcrest Road. Turn right on East Hillcrest and go 0.7 mile to Level Valley Road. Turn left (south) on Level Valley, going 1.8 miles to County ME.

Turn right on ME and go about 1 mile to County E. Go straight (southwest) on E for 4.6 miles to County M. Turn left (south) on M and travel 2 miles to Highway 16 just northeast of Watertown. Watertown is the home of the historic *Octagon House,* (920) 261-2796, 919 Charles St. This large pre-Civil War house has 57 rooms and five floors connected by a spiral stair-

Don't miss the marvelous spiral staircase at Watertown's Octagon House. Wisconsin Department of Tourism photo.

case. Also on the grounds is the building that housed the first kindergarten in the United States in 1856.

Turn right on Highway 16, heading northwest, then north, for about 3.4 miles to County Q. Turn left (west) on Q, going for 6.2 miles through Richwood to County QQ.

Turn right (west) on QQ and travel 2.7 miles to Highway 19. Turn right on 19 and go for 20 miles into downtown Sun Prairie. You'll drive through the communities of Hubbleton, Portland, Waterloo, and Marshall, where you can ride the Mad Mouse roller coaster and two others, as well as miniature trains at family-friendly *Merrick's Little A-Merrick-A Amusement Park*, (608) 655-3181. You know you'll be getting close to Sun Prairie when you see the Angell Park Speedway.

Continue straight ahead on 19 for another 2 miles to Highway 151. Turn left on 151 and go south for about 1 mile back to County C where we started.

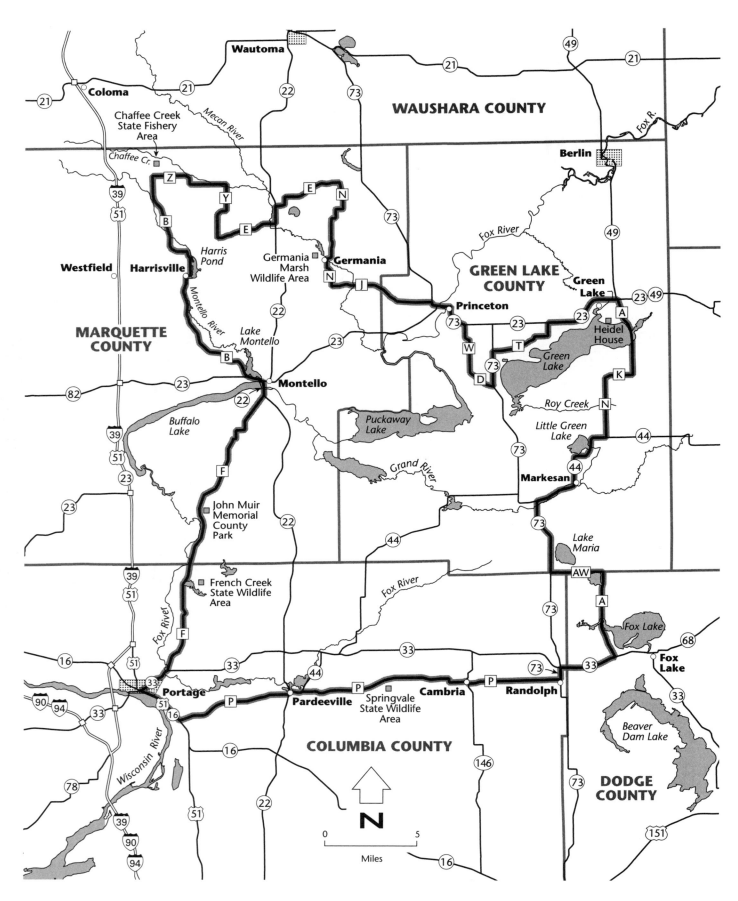

Tour 29

Tour 29
Green Lake and John Muir Country

Green Lake—Markesan—Fox Lake—Randolph—Cambria—Pardeeville—Portage—Montello—Harrisville—Princeton—Green Lake

Distance: 137 miles

The magnificent beauty of Wisconsin's glacial lakes, forests, marshes, and wetlands has been widely acknowledged, but many people don't realize what a major role these areas played in inspiring the man who is called "the father of the National Park System." John Muir grew up about 10 miles north of Portage at Fountain Lake Farm. It was here that he developed a love of nature and a respect for all living things that so profoundly informed the rest of his life and work.

Indeed, this area of wild Wisconsin can be a source of inspiration even to us today. Drive along these marshes and watch the squadrons of Canada geese flying in. Cruise through the woods and smell the fresh air. Sit by the shore of a glacial lake and watch the clouds sail by.

This route is also designed to give you a chance to see Wisconsin's historic resort country around Green Lake. This, the deepest of Wisconsin's inland lakes, has been a preferred family destination for more than a century. An Old World tradition of warm welcomes and gracious hospitality has earned this area top marks as a place where one can relax and enjoy the best of lake living. The panorama of natural beauty just adds to the fun of driving these less-traveled roads and enhances the joy of discovering these unpretentious little towns.

Get behind the wheel and let the road carry you off to an extraordinary place.

Start this tour just outside of Green Lake, at the junction of Highway 23 and County A.

The problem with starting this tour in Green Lake is that you may not go very far. There's good reason—many good reasons—to merely arrive and stay, just as visitors have been doing for generations.

The Green Lake area scores high marks in virtually all vacation activity categories: superior accommodations, critically acclaimed dining, spectacular surroundings, big-game and pan fishing, lots of open water to sail, nationally ranked championship golf courses, abundant wildlife, specialty shops and boutiques, fine arts and folk craft, super antiquing, well-preserved historical sites, great bicycle trails, excellent hiking trails, narrated boat tours, beautiful beaches and pools, and warm Wisconsin hospitality. Here are just a few of the special places and attractions.

Named "Wisconsin's Best Resort" by *Wisconsin Trails* magazine readers in 1999, the *Heidel House Resort and Conference Center,* (800) 444-2812, 643 Illinois Ave., is the place you remember when you recall your most insouciant summer vacation days. The resort's original manor began as a private residence in 1890 and has been serving up lake country living since it opened to the public on New Year's Eve, 1945. The Heidel House delivers the ideal mix of traditional resort ambiance with premiere-level guest services.

There are three restaurants on the resort grounds: the Boat House, the Sun Room, and the critically acclaimed *Gray Rock Mansion,* (920) 294-3344, featuring seasonal gourmet cuisine. Golf packages include hassle-free tee times at the local top courses. The Heidel House offers boat tours of Green Lake aboard the *Escapade,* a 60-foot, two-deck yacht that provides totally relaxing sightseeing, brunch, and cocktail cruises. Seasoned area fishing guides are available to help you sort out the panfish from the lake trout from the muskies—and catch them! A full program of children's activities is offered at "Camp Heidel." If you just want to stretch out and soak up some warm rays, this is the place. The resort is also known as a great spot for conferences, seminars, and retreats.

Thrasher's Opera House, (920) 294-6403, 506 Mill St., was built in 1910 and is now fully renovated. It is used for plays, films, and performances; but whatever is happening when you're in town, be sure to get a look at it.

The area is a shopper's delight. A few of the shops to discover include *Wisconsin Gold and*

You can get a great tour of Green Lake aboard the *Escapade,* a 60-foot tour boat based at the Heidel House Resort. Photo by Gary Knowles.

The Green Lake area, with top courses like Lawsonia Links and Woodlands, is considered one of Wisconsin's finest golf getaways. Photo by Gary Knowles.

Green Lake Golf Legends

Resorts and the honorable sport of golf grew up together in the Green Lake area. The state's oldest course, *Tuscumbia,* (920) 294-3240, was started in 1896 and is still a worthy 18-hole (6,301 yards, par 71) challenge today. It's located right in the town of Green Lake

The development of the Lawsonia course in the 1930s put the world on notice that Wisconsin was serious about great golf. The Scottish-style open course (6,764 yards, par 72) rambles over hills and prairie carpeted with ball-devouring grasses and strategically placed bunkers waiting to test the mettle of duffers who wander by. In the early 1930s the golfing trinity of Ben Hogan, Sam Snead, and Byron Nelson played in the Little Lawsonia Open. Time has done nothing but add to the luster. The elevated greens (one built on top of a railroad car!) could drive even a teetotaler to drink on this "dry" American Baptist Assembly property. But that's not all. The relatively new (1991) 18-hole Woodlands course (6,618 yards, par 72) is a perfect counterpoint to the Links. Carefully carved out of virgin timber, it offers beautifully distracting views of Wisconsin's deepest lake and stands as the perfect modern complement to the traditional course. On all counts, course design, course mainte-nance, and hospitality, the *Golf Courses of Lawsonia* (as it is now officially called) is a champion. Call (800) 529-4453.

A short drive away, off Highway 49 just south of Berlin, is *Mascoutin Country Club,* (920) 361-2360, an excellent, well-manicured 27-hole course (6,821 yards, par 72) designed by Edward Lawrence Packard. Century-old trees, undulating greens, sand traps, and water challenge golfers of all skill levels.

Scharenberg's Golf Resort, (608) 297-2278, at White Lake, takes full advantage of the scenery with an 18-hole Western-style layout of 6,359 yards that plays to a par 72.

More good courses, like *Thal Acres Golf Club,* (608) 296-2850, near Westfield, and *Waushara Country Club,* (920) 787-4649, north of Green Lake on Highway 21, offer additional options for a Green Lake-based golf outing.

Gem Company, (920) 294-3955, 507 Mill St., for fine gold and silver jewelry; *Sadie Hawk Antiques,* (920) 294-6575, W1969 S. Lawson Dr., which seems to always have a good selection of furniture and collectibles; *Wallengang's,* (920) 294-3386, a cheese haus, gift shop, antique shop, and ice-cream parlor well worth a visit; the *Nordic Village Shops,* (920) 294-0266, on Highway 23, which has a nice variety of toys, antiques, and gift items; and *Mill Street Junction,* (920) 294-6338, 493 Hill St., which offers gourmet food specialties, a wide variety of gift items, and home accessories. *Hamilton's at the Heidel House,* (920) 294-0229, a shop known for extraordinary taste, specializes in sophisticated clothing for women.

Want to put a little high-flying adventure in your life? *Wisconsin Majestic Balloons,* (920) 748-3464, offers hot-air balloon flights over this beauti-ful lake country.

The Green Lake Conference Center, (800) 558-8898, is a 1,000-acre gem that had its begin-nings in the 1880s when Green Lake–area vaca-tioners Victor and Jessie Lawson bought the land. It was purchased by the Chicago Stone Company in 1925; a few years later the Lawsonia Golf Course was built, along with an 81-unit hotel. The resort operated as a gambling casino until the Great Depression forced foreclosure. It was purchased by the American Baptist Assembly in 1943 and is now used for various conferences year around. The grounds are open to view, so drive past the gates and see the two Lawsonia courses and other sites amid a wonderfully serene setting. (For more on area courses, see the accompanying article.)

At the junction of 23 and A, turn right (south) on A and go 3.5 miles to the junction with

County K. Along the way, you'll pass Indian Point, drive over the Green Lake Inlet, and pass Forest Glen Beach.

Continue straight on County A/K for 1 mile, then turn right (west) on K and go 1.5 miles to County N. Turn left (south) on N, cruising 3.3 miles over Roy Creek to Highway 44.

Turn right on 44 and travel west, then south, for about 4 miles to the junction with Highway 73 in Markesan, passing, along the way, Little Green Lake (at 465 acres one of Wisconsin's most productive muskie lakes).

Markesan is said to get its name from its friendly people, who are as friendly as the people in the Marquesas Islands in the Pacific Ocean.

The Grand River Valley Museum, (920) 398-3031, 214 E. John St., has over 5,000 square feet of artifacts depicting some harrowing events in the Grand River Valley during the 1800s, including the Mackford Murder, counterfeiting, a payroll wagon raid, granite mining, and a dynamite explosion.

Turn right (west) on Highway 44/77, go about 2 miles, then turn left (south) on Highway 73, going 4.2 miles to County AW. Turn left on AW and travel 2.6 miles to County A.

Turn right (south) on A, watching for wildlife, and go about 5 miles to Highway 33 just west of the town of Fox Lake.

You may want to take a quick run to Fox Lake, which is home to some intriguing attractions. The *Depot Museum,* operated by the Fox Lake Historical Society, is housed in an 1800s vintage depot building, with exhibits of Native American culture, Civil War memorabilia, and many other historical artifacts. For more information, call the *Fox Lake Chamber of Commerce,* (800) 858-4904 or (920) 928-3777. Fox Lake was a recruiting center during the Civil War, and of about 100 recruits who went into battle, only 10 returned. The local cemetery has many Civil War–era graves.

This community has a strong link to jazz history as the place where Grammy Award-winning musician Bunny Berigan grew up. A historical marker at the entrance to town honors his work. He is buried here and the community holds a music festival in his honor on the third Sunday each May.

Antique hunters will want to check out *Meta's Antiques,* (920) 928-6494, in downtown Fox Lake. A nice variety of resorts and cottages is available for rent on Fox Lake. Call the Chamber of Commerce for a booklet with current listings.

Turn right (west) on 33 and travel about 3 miles to Highway 73 in Randolph. Turn left on 73 and go about 0.5 mile to County P. Turn right (west) on P and cruise 15 miles to the junction with Highway 22 in Pardeeville. On the way, you'll go through Cambria and the *Spring-*

vale State Wildlife Area (watch for Canada geese, cranes, blue heron, ducks, songbirds, and white-tailed deer).

The *Myrtle Lintner Spear Museum,* (608) 429-2250, in Pardeeville features artifacts relating to Columbia County farm and home history.

Just south of town on Highway 22 is the unusual *LaReau's World of Miniature Buildings,* (608) 429-2848, which houses many scale models, including those of a German castle, the Washington Monument, Mt. Rushmore, the White House, and the Statue of Liberty.

Turn left (south) on 22 and drive about 3 blocks to County P. Turn right on P and go about 6 miles to Highway 51/16. Turn right (north) on 51/16 and travel about 3 miles to Highway 33 in Portage. (For information about Portage see Tour 24.)

See many of the world's most famous buildings—in miniature—at LaReau's near Pardeeville. Wisconsin Department of Tourism photo by Jim Bach.

Wisconsin honey, maple syrup, and preserves are sweet bargains at shops and country markets throughout the state. Photo by Gary Knowles.

Follow 33 east 2 miles to the junction with County F. Turn left (north) on F and cruise about 18 miles to Highway 22. This is a great drive along the famous Fox River, through the *French Creek State Wildlife Area* (loaded with birds and animals) and past *John Muir Memorial County Park.* There's a marker here about the famous Wisconsin-born naturalist who first learned to love nature at his boyhood home in this area and who went on to become the father of the National Park System. He helped plant the lilacs and maple trees on this land.

Turn left (northwest) on 22 and go about 2 miles to the junction with County B in Montello. Downtown, you'll see the *Montello Waterfall,* on the site of a former quarry (1879-1976) that produced world-famous Montello Red Granite—the hardest granite in the world and used in the famous tomb of Ulysses S. Grant. Wisconsin's largest tree, a cottonwood 23.2 feet in circumference and 132 feet tall, stands at the intersection of Highway 23 and Park St.

For fine Wisconsin cheese, sausage, maple syrup, honey, and other Wisconsin specialty products, stop at *Underwood Market Specialty Cheese and Gifts,* (608) 297-2799, 567 Underwood Ave. Montello is also a great place to do some antique hunting.

Turn right (northwest) on B and cruise about 16 miles to the junction with County Z. You'll thread your way between Lake Montello, Kirby Lake, Birch Lake, Peters Lake, and Clearwater Lake, then run along the Montello River to Harrisville, past Harris Pond, across Westfield Creek and Tagatz Creek, ending up near the *Chaffee Creek Wildlife Area.*

Turn right (east) on Z and drive 4.5 miles to the junction with County Y. Turn right (south) on Y and go about 3.1 miles to the junction with County E. Turn left (east) on County E/Y, go for about 0.7 mile, and then follow County E straight (east) as Y turns to the south.

Stay on E about 8.2 miles to County N. Turn right (south) on N and go for about 7 miles to County J, traveling through the *Germania Marsh Wildlife Area* and the town of Germania.

Turn left (east) on J, going about 6.2 miles to Highway 73. Turn right (south) on 73 and proceed into downtown Princeton.

Princeton is known throughout the Midwest for its many antique stores and Saturday flea markets that feature almost 200 vendors with antiques and collectibles and draw thousands of people to Princeton City Park from May through October.

Visit *Caron Orchard,* (920) 295-6730, W3649 County J, where you can pick your own cherries and buy apples, plums, and pears, as well as jams and jellies; there's also a petting zoo.

Want to get out on a river? Try the *Mecan River Outfitters,* (920) 295-3439, 3 miles west of town on Highway 23. They'll help organize your trip on the Mecan River, set up pheasant hunts, or arrange horse-drawn sleigh rides in winter.

From Princeton, go east on Highway 23 for about 2 miles to the junction with County W. Turn right (south) on W, going about 1.8 miles to County D. Turn left (southeast) on D and drive about 1.5 miles to Highway 73.

Turn left (north) on 73 and go about 2 miles to County T. Turn right (east) on T and drive for 4.6 miles to Highway 23, passing the Green Lake Conference Center and the Golf Courses of Lawsonia.

Turn right (east) on 23 and drive about 4.3 miles back to County A where we started.

Tour 30
The Best Roads Wiggle

Sparta—Wilton—Ontario—Bartons Corners—White City—La Farge—Avalanche—Bloomingdale—Middle Ridge—Rockland—Sparta

Distance: 114 miles

If you're looking for a drive that has more twists and turns per mile than any other in this book (and, remember, I look for those roads on every route), you've found it! This run through the Driftless Region of Wisconsin will take you up some steep hills and ridges, and around twisting corners. This route is a corkscrew, not a knife.

These are Wisconsin's Zen roads. They move with the rhythm of the hills, up, up, and over. They curve and bend and twist with the mood of the land. Like water sliding down a hillside, they flow with the contour, taking their direction from the form. The rarest things here are straight lines and right angles. This is the land of the wrinkle, the ripple, the wave, the undulation. Follow the road and you will lose your sense of following the road. You drive, but you do not drive. You are tracing the form of these hills, feeling them, listening to them by running your car over their curves. First you become the highway, then you become the hills.

Bring your camera, the one that shoots those panoramic views. The scenic vistas run the full horizon and spill off at both sides of your windshield. There's a round barn, old windmill, beautiful river, or a cow mailbox around every corner.

Bring your binoculars too. You'll want to look off in the distance to see into another coulee or maybe get a closer view of a heron or a rare bird. And yes, you can stop for ice cream, cheese curds, or apples along the way. Garage sales, antique stores, craft shops, and artist galleries abound throughout this region.

Sparta is the biggest settlement you'll encounter, but there are great shops, restaurants, and country stores to discover in these great little towns. Breeze by too quickly and you'll miss an important reason for this tour.

But enough of the talk. Life is doing. See you on the road.

Start at the junction of Highway 16 and Highway 71, just southeast of Sparta. Before setting out into the countryside, take a little time to explore Sparta, known as "the Bicycling Capital of America," with about 55 miles of bike trails close by. (See Tour 27 for a list of these and other major attractions in the Sparta area.)

Turn south on 71 and go 3.5 miles to the junction with County AA. Turn left on AA and go 8.5 miles to the junction with County A, crossing Farmers Valley Creek and running east, then north, on a zigzag course through the hills.

Turn right (east) on A, going about 8.3 miles through the Coles Valley to the junction with County M. Follow County A/M about 0.4 mile east to where County M turns south.

Turn right (south) on M and go 5.5 miles along Sleighton Creek to the junction with Highway 131 and into the town of Wilton. The town was settled in the 1840s when Esau Johnson came up the Kickapoo River and decided to stay. Stop in the *Visitor Center,* (608) 435-6666, located in a caboose right next to the Elroy-Sparta Trail in town. The center offers brochures for area attractions and accommodations and a photo display of village and railroad history.

Turn right on 131 and go about 9 miles to Ontario and the junction with Highway 33,

Visitors are never in doubt that Wisconsin is, first and foremost, an agricultural state. Wisconsin Department of Tourism photo by GK.

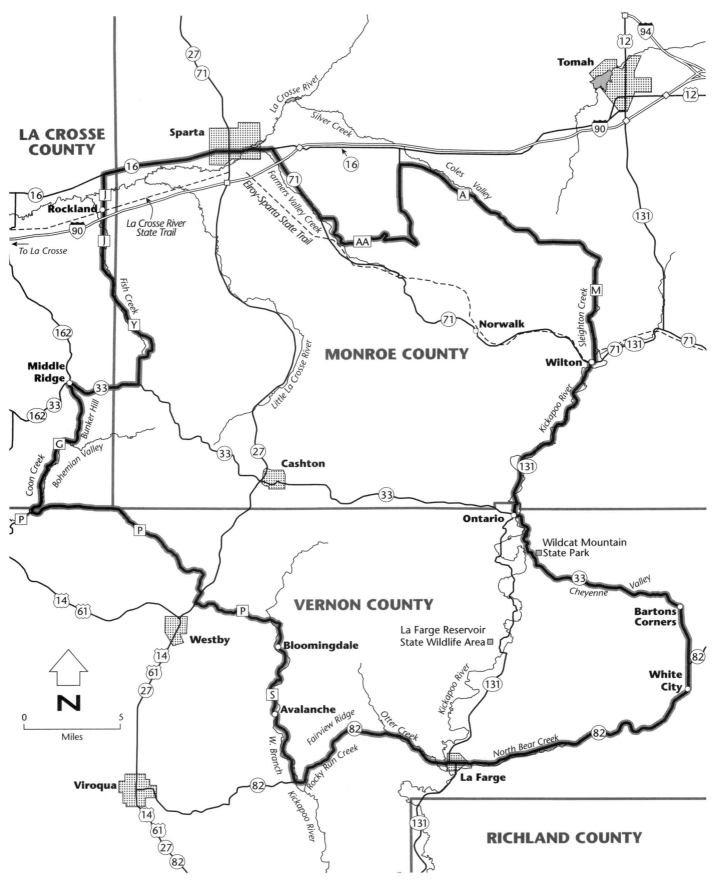

Tour 30

twisting and turning south along the Kickapoo River (the "Crookedest River in the World").

Ontario, (608) 337-4381, is the "Gateway to the Kickapoo River." Many canoeists start their trips down the river here. The full river trip—from Wilton to Wauzeka—is about 70 winding miles and takes about three days. The scenery is spectacular, with towering bluffs, deep woods, rock formations, and country farm scenes along the route.

There are liveries and outfitters in both communities. In Ontario, the *Kickapoo Paddle Inn* (800) 947-3603, rents canoes, provides shuttles, and sells burgers at the drive-in, while *Mr. Duck Canoe Rental*, (608) 337-4711 and *Drifty's Canoe Rental*, (608) 337-4288, also offer a shuttle service.

Turn left on 33 and head south about 1.5 miles to *Wildcat Mountain State Park*. This 3,600-acre beauty, (608) 337-4775, is one of two in the state that offers facilities designed for horseback camping as well as regular camping. There are spectacular views, with high bluffs, picnic areas, and outstanding hiking trails.

Continue to snake and switchback your way on 33 through the hills of Cheyenne Valley about 7.5 miles to Bartons Corners and the junction with County V. Turn right (south) on V for about 2.4 miles to the junction with Highway 82.

Follow Highway 82/County V south about a mile to White City, where 82 swings to the west. Stay on 82 west, following North Bear Creek about 10 miles to La Farge. Antique and craft hunters will want to check out the town's shops for treasures and discoveries.

Continue on 82 west out of La Farge and go about 8 miles to the junction with County S. Along the way, you'll follow Otter Creek, climb to Fairview Ridge, run along Rocky Run Creek, and cross the West Fork of the Kickapoo River.

Quick Trip Option: Here's an afternoon diversion well worth the trip. From La Farge, take Highway 82 west for an enjoyably twisting 16 miles to the town of Viroqua. It's favored by travelers for its great antiques stores, a well-preserved downtown, and great dairy stops (like the *Viroqua Dairy*, (608) 637-3529, known for huge ice cream cones). You can also get Amish baskets, birdhouses, and quilts at modest prices from the back of black wagons on Saturday mornings. Two excellent bed and breakfast inns are the *Viroqua Heritage Inn*, (608) 637-3306, and the *Eckhart House*, (608) 637-8644. Lucy Stone, a local resident, was an antislavery leader and an early defender of women's rights who delivered a rousing 4th of July speech here in 1856. Jeremiah Rusk, elected governor in 1881 and appointed as the first U.S. secretary of agriculture by President Benjamin Harrison in 1889, was a prominent local citizen. For a free guide, call Viroqua Partners at (608) 637-2575.

Turn right (north) on S and slither your way for 3.5 miles along the West Fork through hills known as the Ocooch Mountains to the town of Avalanche. The town was named for the area just east of town whose terrain looks as if it had been the scene of an avalanche.

The Kickapoo River Valley

The profound beauty of the Kickapoo River Valley on a sunny spring morning obscures the fact that this area has seen severe flooding on many occasions, as well as having an equally unpleasant experience as a victim of government improvement programs. The river, whose name comes from the Algonquin word meaning "goes this way, then that," has had quite a half century.

Beginning in the 1930s various government proposals called for a dam to be built to control the flow of the river, avoid flood damage, and spur economic development. These plans called for the purchase of homestead and farm property and the displacement of families that in some cases traced their local roots back for generations.

In 1962 the U. S. Congress approved the plan, and seven years later the purchase of some 140 farms had begun, often from very reluctant property owners who were persuaded that the economic and flood control benefits to the community would be worth their sacrifice.

Construction of the dam at La Farge started in 1970 but it was beset with problems. The Environmental Protection Act had just been passed and the project was one of the first to be required to file an environmental impact statement. Studies showed that endangered plants grew in the valley and that the dam might hurt water quality. After modifications were made to the plans, construction was resumed, and by 1975 the dam was about 50 percent complete. Wisconsin Senator William Proxmire asked for a cost-benefit study. It came back negative, and the project was stopped with some $18 million having been spent.

Controversy ensued for the next 20 years. Various proposals to build a smaller dam, give the land back to the people, and pursue other development options all failed to win approval. The first real progress came in 1992 with the formation of a broad-based group, the Citizens' Advisory Committee to the Kickapoo Valley Project. This group focused on the future of the valley, established priorities, and ultimately saw legislation passed in 1996 to return 1,200 acres of the purchased land to the Ho-Chunk (Winnebago) nation and 7,300 acres to the state of Wisconsin. The lands will be preserved in a natural state and only developed to enhance outdoor education and recreation opportunities. In addition, some roads are to be improved and some restoration work will be done to wells and farm sites.

Today the spectacular views, the rock outcroppings, and the crooked river are here for all to see and appreciate. But as deep and twisted as the Kickapoo River is (this way, then that), so are the feelings of those who gave up homesteads, saw farms torn down, and moved children out of school districts for a program that never happened and for economic gain that was never realized.

For a helpful map/brochure to the Kickapoo Valley call the Kickapoo Valley Association at 608-872-2504.

Amish and Mennonite families have lived in these peaceful valleys for many years, so please respect their right to the road. Photo by Gary Knowles.

Jog through town on S and continue north about 3.5 miles through Bloomingdale and another 1 mile to the junction with County P. (If you're in Bloomingdale in the spring, the flowers and blossoms will show you why the Norwegian settlers gave this community its name.)

Turn left (west) on P and go 3 miles to join Highway 27 and then follow P another 13.1 miles to the junction with County G, an exhila-

Up Close and Personal in Amish Country

These roads through the Kickapoo River Valley pass near some thriving Amish communities. The Amish way of life is based on the belief in humility, strong families, and hard work.

You may see traditional black horse-drawn buggies as you enjoy these backcountry roads. Some farms offer homemade products, such as quilts, leather goods, wooden toys, bentwood furniture, baked goods, or candy for sale. Watch for signs along the road or check some of the small town shops.

If you'd like a personal introduction to the Wisconsin Amish community, you might want to contact *Down a Country Road,* a gift shop and guided tour service operated by Chuck and Kathy Kuderer. Although the Kuderers, along with their children, Jenny, Jason, Jeremy, and Janessa, are a non-Amish farm family, they provide a service that will ensure your respectful introduction to Amish ways.

Down a Country Road is located on Highway 33, 2 miles east of Cashton and 8 miles west of Ontario. Make reservations by calling (608) 654-5318. Tours are scheduled on Thursdays, Fridays, and Saturdays.

rating extended sprint through the hills and valleys of coulee country.

Quick Trip Options: Want to get a look at the lives of early settlers in the Kickapoo Valley? Visit *Norskedalen,* "Norwegian Valley," (608) 452-3424, where you can see a restored pioneer homestead. The Thurne Visitors Center has nature museums, a gift shop, and library. The whole complex is on County PI, about 1.5 miles past the junction of County P and County G.

Another option is the community of Coon Valley, about 2.5 miles farther along to the southwest on County P. *The Stockman's Inn,* (608) 452-3181, features homemade desserts and has a back bar dating from the 1920s.

Turn right (north) on G and drive about 7 miles to the junction with Highway 33, following Coon Creek up the Bohemian Valley, then running along Bunker Hill to Middle Ridge.

Turn right (east) on 33 and drive 3 miles to the junction with County Y. Turn left (north) and go about 10 miles (County Y becomes County J) to the junction with Highway 16, following Fish Creek through the farmlands and bluffs, across I-90, and through the town of Rockland.

Turn right (east) on 16 and drive about 5 miles back to the junction with Highway 71 southeast of Sparta.

More Great Titles from Trails Books

Activity Guides
Wisconsin Underground: A Guide to Caves, Mines, and Tunnels in and around the Badger State, Doris Green
Paddling Illinois: 64 Great Trips by Canoe and Kayak, Mike Svob
Paddling Northern Wisconsin: 82 Great Trips by Canoe and Kayak, Mike Svob
Great Minnesota Walks: 49 Strolls, Rambles, Hikes, and Treks, Wm. Chad McGrath
Great Wisconsin Walks: 45 Strolls, Rambles, Hikes, and Treks, Wm. Chad McGrath
Best Wisconsin Bike Trips, Phil Van Valkenberg

Travel Guides
Wisconsin Family Weekends: 20 Fun Trips for You and the Kids, Susan Lampert Smith
County Parks of Wisconsin, Revised Edition, Jeannette and Chet Bell
Up North Wisconsin: A Region for All Seasons, Sharyn Alden
The Spirit of Door County: A Photographic Essay, Darryl R. Beers
Great Wisconsin Taverns: 101 Distinctive Badger Bars, Dennis Boyer
Great Wisconsin Restaurants, Dennis Getto
Great Weekend Adventures, the Editors of Wisconsin Trails
The Wisconsin Traveler's Companion: A Guide to Country Sights, Jerry Apps and Julie Sutter-Blair

Home and Garden
Creating a Perennial Garden in the Midwest, Joan Severa
Bountiful Wisconsin: 110 Favorite Recipes, Terese Allen
Foods That Made Wisconsin Famous, Richard J. Baumann

Historical Guides
Walking Tours of Wisconsin's Historic Towns, Lucy Rhodes, Elizabeth McBride, and Anita Matcha
Wisconsin: The Story of the Badger State, Norman K. Risjord
Barns of Wisconsin, Jerry Apps
Portrait of the Past: A Photographic Journey Through Wisconsin, 1865–1920, Howard Mead, Jill Dean, and Susan Smith

For Young People
Wisconsin Portraits: 55 People Who Made a Difference, Martin Hintz
ABCs of Wisconsin, Dori Hillestad Butler and Alison Relyea
W Is for Wisconsin, Dori Hillestad Butler and Eileen Dawson

Other Titles of Interest
The I-Files: True Reports of Unexplained Phenomena in Illinois, Jay Rath
The W-Files: True Reports of Wisconsin's Unexplained Phenomena, Jay Rath
The M-Files: True Reports of Minnesota's Unexplained Phenomena, Jay Rath

For a free catalog, phone, write, or e-mail us.

Trails Books
P.O. Box 317 • Black Earth, WI 53515
(800) 236-8088 • e-mail: info@wistrails.com
www.trailsbooks.com